MARKETING AND MANAGEMENT IN THE HIGH-TECHNOLOGY SECTOR

MARKETING AND MANAGEMENT IN THE HIGH-TECHNOLOGY SECTOR

Strategies and Tactics in the Commercial Airplane Industry

DOMENICO FERRERI

Foreword by Giorgio Zappa

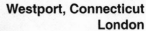

Westport, Connecticut
London

Library of Congress Cataloging-in-Publication Data

Ferreri, Domenico, 1946–

  Marketing and management in the high-technology sector : strategies and tactics in the commercial airplane industry / Domenico Ferreri ; foreword by Giorgio Zappa.

    p. cm.

  Includes bibliographical references and index.

  ISBN 1–56720–524–0 (alk. paper)

  1. Airplanes—Marketing. 2. Jet planes—Marketing. 3. Aerospace planes—Marketing. 4. Aircraft industry—Management. 5. Aerospace industries—Management. 6. Aeronautics, Commercial—Forecasting. I. Title.

HD9711.A2 F47   2003

629.133'34'0688—dc21   2002067915

British Library Cataloguing in Publication Data is available.

Library of Congress Catalog Card Number: 2002067915
ISBN: 1–56720–524–0

First published in 2003

Praeger Publishers, 88 Post Road West, Westport, CT 06881
An imprint of Greenwood Publishing Group, Inc.
www.praeger.com

Printed in the United States of America

The paper used in this book complies with the
Permanent Paper Standard issued by the National
Information Standards Organization (Z39.48–1984).

10 9 8 7 6 5 4 3 2 1

Copyright Acknowledgments

The author and publisher gratefully acknowledge permission to use illustrative material from both Boening Business Services Company and aviationX as cited within source notes.

CONTENTS

ILLUSTRATIONS

FIGURES

Chapter 2

Chapter 4

TABLES

Chapter 2

FOREWORD

The industrial scenario defined hereafter links the possibility of a commercial airplane manufacturer to stay in the market and improve its position directly with its ability to interface with the external environment. In fact, business management, particularly in the aeronautical field, is the outcome of a complex process that considers the enterprise at the center of different interests that often must be taken into account, together with the company's goals and objectives.

COMPANY STRATEGIES

The aeronautical industry has been considered by governments as important and particularly critical for several reasons, which together define the economical and technological value of this sector. Such relevance is witnessed in the care that the most advanced countries put into directing and supporting the national aeronautical industries (both public and private).

In an industrial sector characterized by such enormous interest and by products with a very high technological content requiring huge investments, the aeronautical companies have developed, since the 1960s, an articulated network of horizontal and vertical collaborations (both opportunistic and structural). Therefore, for the companies operating in the aeronautical field, the exploitation of international alliances as a strategic option assumes great significance in business management. Moreover, companies now need a clear strategy with precise applicability to their own distinctive characteristics in order to gain a long-lasting and stable competitive advantage that will persist beyond the success of a single program.

Notwithstanding these considerations about the existence of acknowledged company strategies, the sector has been characterized by a distortion. The managers of most companies of the aerospace (and defense) sector (often public companies) on the one hand were urged to pursue more general objectives beyond those of profit, but on the other hand, they would be exempted from responsibility if the economic results fell below expectations.

At a glance it would appear that the "standard" approaches to marketing and management of the enterprises, applicable to most industrial sectors, have not been largely applied in the civil aeronautical field. This may be because the sector has been protected for many years, and because the firms have been charged with objectives and goals beyond their own responsibilities. However, before reaching such a conclusion, a deeper analysis would be necessary.

The book deals with these aspects in trying to find analogies and differences between the commercial airplane business and other industrial sectors, and in determining basic competitive strategies and possible specific competitive advantages.

CHANGES IN THE OFFER SCENARIO

At the end of the cold war, and because of the contemporary crisis of air transportation in the early 1990s (although momentary), those firms working in the aerospace sector that have focused exclusively on effectiveness have incurred great difficulties, and sometimes they have been forced to cease operation altogether. To the contrary, those that had maintained a proper balance between spent resources and obtained results have been forced into some degree of restructuring but have survived.

The offer scenario in the commercial airplane sector is now quite different from what it was just a few years ago; and some additional changes can be foreseen for the competitive strategies of the two residual players (Boeing and Airbus)—particularly for the long-range market segment. In fact, it seems that the two companies have rather conflicting views about the future of long-distance air transportation. Airbus's theory is that future market challenges will need a traditional solution, satisfying the large traffic demand at the congested hubs (particularly in the Far East region) with the very large A-380 aircraft, able to transport many passengers on one trip. On the other side, Boeing believes that the answer for the future is a more innovative solution—the ability to carry passengers "from where they are, to where they want to be" by means of smaller and faster aircraft. Thus, Boeing pursued the Sonic Cruiser project although it abandoned it for the more realistic *Super Efficient Airplane*.

The impact of this innovative concept on the industry seems very significant, because it will introduce a new challenge into aeronautics, and will try to restore the company's traditional market dominance severely eroded by Airbus in the last years.

THE REGIONAL AIRPLANE INDUSTRY EVOLUTION

In the regional aircraft sector, the changes that have occurred in the competitive scenario in the last 10 years have been even greater, at least in terms of new entrants and exits. In fact, in addition to the above-mentioned factors, this sector has been strongly influenced by the progressive extension of the applications of jet propulsion technology to a business aircraft (30 to 70 seats) segment, until recently traditionally dominated by turboprop engines.

The first entrants, thanks to the wider market acceptance of the regional jet airplanes, have been able to develop and launch other members, positioning themselves in a very solid market condition. Turboprop sales have fallen, and thus the less efficient producers have exited from this market.

CHANGES IN THE AEROSPACE AND DEFENSE INDUSTRY

The above-mentioned events in the civil aeronautical sector are part of a wider crisis that has affected the aerospace and defense sectors over the last few years. The implications go well beyond the international collaborations experienced up to this point. Reference is made particularly to the recent and continuous evolution of the offer scenario in the aerospace and defense sectors in the United States—which is going through acquisitions, disposals, and mergers—and to the response of the European companies operating in the same fields.

The European industrial restructuring process is proceeding, if compared with the United States, more gradually and following some additional intermediate steps because of the different national conditions and peculiarities. In these last years, we have seen the privatization of some state-owned companies (CASA in Spain, Aerospatiale in France, Finmeccanica in Italy), the consolidation of national firms (BAe/Marconi merger in the UK, Aerospatiale/Matra in France), and the first transnational multibusiness company in Europe, with the creation of EADS in 1999.

The ongoing consolidation of European activities in aerospace and defense on a continental basis does not mean to deny transcontinental cooperation. The future integrated European companies should not be built upon the concept of a "Fortress Europe" against a "Fortress USA," but instead, Europeans must be open to transatlantic and intercontinental cooperation. In this context, collaborations with the U.S. manufacturers in some product areas are welcome when specific business opportunities can be exploited.

The European aerospace and defense industry, after these last years of intense consolidation, is now in a stage in which there are two main actors, EADS and BAE SYSTEMS (the former integrating horizontally the "national champions" of three European nations—France, Germany and Spain—and the latter vertically integrated and more focused in the field of defense). There is also a third player, Finmeccanica.

This articulated structure reflects the fact that the number of problems increases with the complexity of the activities to be merged. Single-sector companies have a certain number of advantages, such as the focus on product, incisiveness, directness, and the ability to react quickly to market needs. Despite these possibilities, there are also evidences (related to synergy among the sectors, possible economies of scale, transfer of technologies, pooling of resources) that may suggest a clustering of some industry sectors in multisector companies to obtain the same competitiveness as the multisector U.S.

companies.

For example, this approach permits counterbalancing the typical cyclical slowdown of the civil sector with the more stable (to a certain extent) defense sector, as is the case of the scenario resulting after the tragic events of September 11, 2001. The effects of the commercial aviation crisis are expected to be partially compensated by the current increase in defense expenditures.

In this context, Europe seems to have chosen an intermediate solution with the creation of a number of operating sector joint ventures owned essentially by these three actors, in which all (or nearly all) of the European capabilities are grouped, and capable of being "primes" in the global market. Of course, this brings many problems, such as those related to ownership structure, the balanced locations of offices and factories, and the possibility of transatlantic collaborations that may be indispensable in some specific product areas.

In Europe, the near future will probably focus on industrial rationalization. The biggest challenge will be to integrate the companies' activities, cultures, employees, and organizations, which are presently still fragmented and have product overlaps and duplications. Probably we will watch other events until a new and, we hope, more advanced and stable equilibrium will be reached. Maybe then another book on the subject will be appropriate.

Giorgio Zappa
President of Alenia Aeronautica S.p.A. and Alenia Spazio S.p.A.

PREFACE

This preface should be a window through which the reader may understand the landscape of the book before reading it. From that window, I invite my readers to explore further. In this direction, the preface will deal with the book's target market and the issues and subjects treated in it.

This book is written primarily for executives, strategic marketers, and decision makers who are or will be responsible for marketing management and competitive strategies in the civil aeronautical field. It will also be useful to a wider range of readers from related industries such as air transportation and airport operations. It is also intended for others who want to understand the aeronautical business, particularly for students of business management schools.

Quite a few authors of marketing management or competitive strategy books have considered it necessary to include some examples of company case studies in their texts.

But management and strategic marketing discussions specifically addressed to the aerospace industry are few. This lack of scholarly exploration is surprising, since aerospace (especially on the private/civilian side) is a field where the strategic factors are meaningfully dominant in the definition of distinctive advantage and the competitive strategies.

The aerospace business has many characteristics typical of the industrial goods and high-tech sectors, but it is also has some unique features: an extremely high financial burden (and risk for the private sector investors), and a high unit cost, two conditions that are not typical of the other two industrial sectors. Therefore, the first step in this book is to analyze the aerospace (and defense) industry and its evolution due to the change of strategic and political scenarios in the United States and Europe, and to understand the new market structure and the aerospace companies' struggle for survival.

While a common goal of the companies inside the aerospace (and defense) sector appears to be the search for *critical mass*, the patterns followed to achieve consolidation appear to be different for different individual business segments. Therefore, to avoid ambiguity and vagueness, this book focuses on one specific business area. The analyses then concentrate on the civil aeronautical business, from the small regional aircraft to the giant wide-body airplane, dealing with questions such as:

- Are traditional interpretation methods of the company behaviors still valid, or is the peculiarity of the aeronautical sector such that the established schemes are not applicable?

- What are the elements that must be analyzed in defining strategy?

- How are the marketing elements, in this specific case, specialized?

- What are the rules of the "sporty game"? [NEWHOUSE 1988]

- What makes for success in marketing jetliners?

This work attempts to answer these questions by analyzing how aeronautical companies implement their activities in the management of their businesses.

It is interesting to see whether a company behaves as expected in a specific situation, to identify the strategies it uses, and to see what is predictable according to the "doctrine" of management theory.

The goal here is not to describe the methodological aspects of different techniques, which are well illustrated in individual subject manuscripts; but rather to explore the decision-making process used in specific cases of the civil aeronautical field. This exploration will fill a void in current management and marketing literature.

The structure of the book addresses two levels:

1. The *strategic level* (Chapter 2) aims to determine whether or not the aerospace companies' behaviors (particularly in the civil aeronautical sector) correspond to the most modern competitive strategies of marketing and management.

2. The *tactical level* (Chapters 3 through 6) deals with the marketing mix management by civil aeronautical companies in order to reach their objectives. That is the right blending of the four *Ps*: product, price, place and promotion, the controllable variables of the marketing theory.

Chapter 1 is an introduction to basic marketing concepts and their evolution. It is aimed at understanding the subsequent application to the aerospace and civil aerospace industry that is the major topic of the book.

Chapter 2 first provides a broad view of the recent evolution of the aerospace (and defense) industry and tries to predict short-term developments in the field for both Europe and the United States. In fact this part deals with the two main challenges of the industry: the consolidation of the United States aerospace and defense sectors that has taken place by means of mergers and acquisitions during the years 1990s; Europe's response to that consolidation as it faces the challenge through integration of its military and civil aerospace and defense industries. From there, the chapter focuses on the aeronautical sector and attempts to understand the airliner's business in terms of strategic marketing. For this purpose the author highlights the general characteristics of this industry and then identifies strategic groups, competitive forces, critical success factors, and firms' objectives.

The next chapter (Chapter 3) provides a definition, evaluation, and comparison of the aeronautical product: the airplane. The first section presents some of the techniques of marketing investigation which, in the aeronautical sector, assume a high degree of sophistication. Some very simple correlations are introduced that show the relationships between weight, performance, and general characteristics of an airplane used in the early stages of airplane design. With this very simple analytical approach, it is possible to draft a general layout of the airplane at a very low cost, easily adaptable to changing market requirements before the final configuration is "frozen."

Chapter 4 is dedicated to the economics of the commercial airplane program, including costs and price. Private commercial companies and many nonprofit organizations face the difficult task of setting a price on their products or services, but the challenge of pricing an airplane in the transport aircraft market is an even more complex problem. Price is the only element in the marketing mix that produces revenue; the other elements represent costs. This chapter explores the various factors a firm must consider in order to identify its own price policy (and variation) during the product life cycle.

Chapter 5 refers to airplane commercialization, which consists of the identification and targeting of marketing facilities, the selection and use of marketing channels, and the methods of offering the product to customers. It is useful for this purpose to refer to the "augmented product" concept that is most important in understanding the peculiarity of "place" meaning in the aeronautical industry.

Chapter 6 is dedicated to the promotion and sale of the commercial airplane. The purchasing process is long and complex. The buyer reaches a decision after the analyses of a wide range of alternatives and at the end of a decisional process that can last for years. The different analyses made by the technical departments of seller and buyer are commonly called the "airline analysis" and will be the major focus of this chapter. Some of the most important commercial airplane sales of the last 30 years are examined in order to determine the main factors that influence the final decision to buy an aircraft and thus to understand the relevant elements of winning proposals.

ACKNOWLEDGEMENTS

This book represents to a certain extent the synthesis of my professional experience, up to now, which began in the 1970s when, as a young aeronautical engineer, I was sent by my company (Aeritalia, currently Alenia Aeronautica) to the United States to participate in a joint-venture program between the major Italian aeronautical firm and the Boeing company for development of a new airplane, the 7X7, that became later the Boeing 767. That period was particularly stimulating, as I had to juggle two different cultural approaches to the way the aeronautical industry was seen. The first, typical of a European university education, was an approach in which both theoretical aspects and the value of synthesis were paramount. The second, typical of the U.S. business world and of Boeing in particular, was an approach in which pragmatism and practical problem solving techniques were the norm. This book should reflect the synthesis of these two approaches.

I would like to begin by thanking both Aeritalia/Alenia Aeronautica, which gave me the opportunity to start my professional career across the Atlantic, and Boeing, whose superb technicians and managers shaped my overall professional skill.

Let me think of this book as more than a summary of my own experience, but rather as a compendium of knowledge acquired by the many Italian technicians who worked (like me) in Seattle at Boeing in the early '70s. That group of engineers continued their professional life by participating through the years in many international aeronautical programs, making Alenia one of the most technologically advanced aeronautical companies.

The writing of this book took a long time, as many original analyses and data elaboration were performed during weekends, vacations, and the limited time I could spare from the demanding schedule of my daily activities. A first draft was written many years ago during my stay in Naples as a marketing analyst within Alenia's commercial division. There, knowledge of all aspects of aeronautics was deep and widespread. In such a fertile environment, it was relatively easy to define the basic concepts of the book.

In this respect I am indebted to Filippo Caronia and Maria Ludovica Schneider for their suggestions on the selection of relevant material and to Giuseppina Ciotola for her valuable help in putting together a overall draft. The completion and enhancement of the book were more difficult and time consuming. These were accomplished in Rome while I worked at Alenia's headquarters. A major effort was required in order to add an original contribution to the existing literature. To this end, I am grateful to Marco Lupo, Angelo Pansini, and Domenico Libertucci for their contributions and suggestions that helped to significantly improve the content of the previous draft.

Mr. Lupo has contributed to the elaboration of the product chapter, particularly the conceptual design and the airplane sizing paragraphs. In addition, he reviewed and continuously updated the second chapter (related to aeronautical industry characteristics), keeping track of the industry's continuing evolution.

Mr. Pansini helped me very much in adopting a strategic approach to Chapter 2, which deals with the civil aeronautical industry in the last decades. He also contributed by drafting part of the chapter on price and has given significant suggestions on several subjects.

Mr. Libertucci took on the burden of transforming the draft into something ready for publication according to the rules given by the publisher. That was not an easy task, considering the need to deliver a work not only intellectually sound, but also well organized and consistent.

I must also thank some friends who polished and transformed my poor English: First, thanks are due to Franco Bernazzani, who shared with me the experiences in Seattle in the early '70s, Allison Annette Foster, and Riccardo Sarti for all the long hours spent in this process.

Even though there is no book on the market about the same overall subject, nevertheless this book takes advantage of the many papers and works on similar topics that are recalled in the bibliography. I also took advantage of the comments and suggestions given by the first readers of the unpublished draft. While I am grateful to all of them. I remain the only responsible for any errors or omissions should be contained in the book.

Finally, this book would not have been possible without the patience of my wife Mina and my two children, Florinda and Egidio. In fact, it has been written mostly at home during many hours that would otherwise have been devoted to my family. Therefore, gratefully, I dedicate this book to them.

1

MARKETING CONCEPTS

1.1 EVOLUTION OF MARKETING SCOPE

1.1.1 Customer-Oriented Marketing

Marketing was born as a means of carrying out a specialized function, supporting two management activities: determining market objectives and checking sales. According to a limited vision, marketing has a static competence, as a tool for gathering, providing, and updating data. According to a wider vision, marketing has also the scope of assessing products, analyzing the competition, examining the adopted distribution channel efficiency, and studying the promotional advertising initiatives that support the sales.

1.1.2 Competitor-Oriented Marketing

The above considerations stress the marketing concern with meeting the customers' needs. However, "The true nature of marketing today involves the conflict between corporations, not the satisfying of human needs and wants. If human needs and wants get satisfied in the process of business competition, then it is in the public interest to let the competition continue. But let us not forget the essential nature of what marketing is all about." [RIES AND TROUT 1986: p.7]

"To be successful today, a company must become competitor-oriented. It must look for weak points in the positions of its competitors and then launch marketing attacks against those weak points." [RIES AND TROUT 1986: p.4-5]

1.1.3 Strategic Marketing

The concept of marketing can be enlarged by connecting its responsibility to the whole life of the firm. In this context, marketing becomes a strategic function in defining and achieving the firm's long-term objectives. In other words, marketing is used as a tool to give the company some distinct competitive advantages over other firms operating in the same sector, assuring a long period of survival.

From the firm's perspective, the above definition requires the ability to select the most important elements of a winning strategy. The first is a correct business definition that identifies the arena in which the company will compete. The width of the arena is defined along the following dimensions [DAY 1991]:

- Functions carried out by product

- Technology incorporated in the products

- User groups

- Stage of the value-added chain

The relative importance of these dimensions may vary with the type of business and the adopted strategy.

The second element is exactly the definition of the strategy, in order to give an indication of the way to search and obtain the competitive advantage. Strategic marketing seems to have taken most words and expressions from the military field, such as *war, flank, attack, guerilla, weak points,* and so on. The marketing manager in business definition and assessment makes an evaluation of the external world and of the competitive environment just as a general makes his evaluation before going into battle. But the similarities stop there.

"Especially in the high-tech sectors, firms have to think in terms of creating new markets rather than of fighting only to share the existing one. This implies the challenge to stimulate potential customers on creating new needs and wants but also to be sure to fully understand the solutions that are proposed." [SEBASTIANI 1995: p.9](translated from the original Italian by author).

1.1.4   Social Marketing

In today's world, where some natural resources are approaching their limits and the environment is rapidly deteriorating, an increased awareness of social responsibility is required–especially from the major companies. In the long term, the economic success a company may achieve by operating without concern for the ecological disasters it may provoke will have repercussions affecting the total framework of the economic and social system and, therefore, the firm itself.

Social marketing represents ways of thinking about the firm's future in society. Forecasts will then include some qualitative considerations, concerns, and boundaries as well as traditional and quantitative variables, in order for the firm to develop its future according to the perceived needs of the society's quality of life. Such an evolution depends on the ability of the firm and its management to enlarge the horizon of the company's goals beyond the narrow limits of its short-term sales purpose.

1.2 INVESTMENT GOODS MARKETS IN THE HIGH-TECH SECTORS: THE SPECIAL CASE OF THE AEROSPACE INDUSTRY

1.2.1 Investment Goods Market Characteristics

The distinctive feature of industrial goods market essentially resides on reduced numbers of customers and therefore on the crucial importance of each of them.

1.2.1.1 Sales Concentration

Given the limited number of major customers in industrial goods markets, each customer represents a significant part of the total sellers' share. In addition, each client often manifests needs and behaviors different from those of other customers, but none may be neglected, even though this means additional supplier efforts. The seller is forced to follow and manage each customer separately.

1.2.1.2 Structure and Distribution of Power in the Market

Because of the relevance of each single customer in terms of a single seller's share of its total sales, each client's contractual power is high; sellers may try to diminish such power by creating the conditions for an "obliged fidelity" from the customer side.

1.2.1.3 Complexity of the Purchase Process

Marketing and sales activities in the industrial goods sectors take a long period of time; business perpetuation (maintaining the same customers) plays a fundamental role and is probably the most important factor of success in the business. The seller is therefore keenly interested in building strong and lasting relationships with customers, even when there is not a particular sale under way.

1.2.1.4 Derived Demand

The particular nature of the industrial goods sectors' demand increases the importance of a profound knowledge of the customers' needs. In fact, each producer's decision must be based not only on market characteristics and competitors' behaviors, but also on the customer's market knowledge; that is, the final customer's needs. This, in the end, will determine a product's success or failure, and the manufacturer cannot completely rely on the other's interpretation of their wants and needs.

1.2.2   High-Tech Sectors Characteristics

In R.T. MORIARTY's and T.J. KOSNIK's opinion, while it is well known that high-tech product (or service) marketing is far different from other sector marketing, there is still a certain confusion about what the differences are. We may define technology the sum of techniques that must be used to develop a new product or to offer a new service. Technology may belong to persons, materials, processes, facilities, or tools.

According to common sense, it seems logical to speak about high tech when a company uses a large number of highly qualified technicians or when it spends a large amount of money in research and development (R & D) activities, well above average for the industry. Associated with this definition is the assumption that in a high-tech sector, the products have a high content of technology and (because technologies evolve quickly) will become obsolete in a short time. Without opposing this rather traditional definition, it seems important to emphasize more modern and comprehensive definitions, where the technology content is a factor but not the one that characterizes the sector.

According to R.T. Moriarty and T.J. Kosnik, the main problem of the high-tech market is its uncertainty. High-tech companies, according to these authors, are confronted each day with certain unknowns: market uncertainty (doubts about what the market will require in terms of new technology) and technological uncertainty (the risk associated with whether or not the company will be able to fulfill the market expectations). [MORIARTY AND KOSNIK 1995]

For RENATO FIOCCA and IVAN SNEHOTA in their "Marketing and High Tech", the relationship between seller and buyer, already relevant in industrial goods markets, becomes critical in high-tech sectors. In fact, the extreme complexity of high-tech products makes it of paramount importance that the customer properly and fully uses the product potential. Therefore, what differentiates high-tech products is not primarily the content of the advanced technologies, but rather the experience that will be necessary for the customer to fully understand how to use them. [FIOCCA AND SNEHOTA 1995]

JOHN F. CADY takes a similar position; for him, the customer capability to fully understand and use the product is the key factor in determining strategies to penetrate the market in the high-tech sectors. For Cady, therefore, the most important element needed to compete successfully is the manufacturer's ability to help the buyer to "metabolize" the product. This factor, rather than the capability for developing the technologies, constitutes the basis on which the operators should work to identify, develop, and keep the competitive advantage. [CADY 1995]

SERGIO DE VIO, in an essay entitled "Marketing Activity and Product Potentiality," introduces the concept that the high-tech market is characterized by "not-completed" and "not-finished" products, or also by potential for expansion, which corresponds only to latent and potential consumers' needs.

Promotion and marketing activities become very similar to those made by consultants, and linkages between sellers and buyers are based completely on credibility, trust, professionalism. [DE VIO 1995]

While the above theories and opinions are different, it nevertheless seems possible to find some common elements:

- The relevance of uncertainty and risk

- The emphasis on product potentiality that must be explained well to the customer

- The very close relationship between seller and buyer that derives from the above elements

- The possibility of creating new markets through the identification of new uses of the same product rather than solely through penetration of the existing market

1.2.3 The Special Case of the Aerospace Industry

The aerospace product is a mix of high tech, but these are not all developed on purpose for being applied on it. Seldom does a new product launch represent a technological breakthrough, other than with a new generation of aircraft, such as the jet vs. the piston airplane. Rather, a new airplane always represents the cutting edge of the state of the art in the technologies involved.

The unitary cost of products is so high that purchasing often involves a nation as a whole and its government. The total number of aircraft produced by model and manufacturer is limited to hundreds and seldom more than one thousand. The development cost of a new project has increased so much that, in the case of failure, a company's life itself is jeopardized.

This may occur because, when the decision to proceed with production is made, the number of acquired orders is far below the foreseen break-even point. In addition, referring to the civil side of the business, the following consideration may be made: Each customer and each sale is important because it helps the next one, allowing the reduction of the selling price. In fact, each subsequent airplane may be produced at a lower cost due to the significant learning effect in this business.

The initial purchase of an aircraft type by an airline is its most important and vital investment because, once the decision is made, the airline commits itself to use that specific type of equipment for a long period ahead. Airplane demand is determined by the airline's level of activity, which in turn is linked to air traffic trends. This latter factor is connected to the health of the economy, because the disposable income of travelers depends on that. This complex interaction of variables is the reason why airplane demand is cyclical, depending on the general status of the economy, which typically experiences stagnation and recovery periods.

Another general characteristic of the sector is demand instability, because several years may elapse between the initial stage of placing an order and the final airplane delivery. During this period of time (usually from 1 to 3 years), something may change. The operator may find that the ordered aircraft type no longer complies with the changed operating environment and its present needs.

Thus, the civil aeronautical business has the typical characteristics of the industrial goods market (essentially a small quantity produced and derived demand) in addition to the characteristics of high-tech sectors. The civil aeronautical industry is also characterized by extremely high financial risk and unit cost not generally seen in the other two industrial sectors.

2

CHARACTERISTICS OF THE CIVIL AERONAUTICAL INDUSTRY

2.1 EVOLUTION OF THE AEROSPACE (AND DEFENSE) INDUSTRY

The events covered in this section describe the evolution of the civil aeronautical industry and highlight the major changes faced by the aerospace and defense sectors in the last few years. These changes challenge companies in their future collaborative efforts, well beyond the pure opportunistic alliances based on a particular product or program. Reference is made to the present evolution in the U.S. aerospace and defense sectors, with many mergers and acquisitions, and the envisioned response of European companies operating in the same sector. A few elements relative to changes in the political, social, and macroeconomic scenarios that may have caused or helped such events to happen are outlined in the present chapter, together with some consideration of the possible future U.S. and European aerospace and defense industry structure.

2.1.1 The Evolution of Defense Industry

Profound changes in strategic and political scenarios have drastically and dramatically rescaled the threat of global and catastrophic conflict. At the same time, many more hidden and unforeseeable risks have emerged, originating from political, social, and economic instability in many areas of the world. Peace dividends are accompanied by newly emerging threatening trends.

The demand for defense products is undergoing an extensive redefinition. Major changes heavily impacting defense industries can be summarized as follows:

- Military budget constraints that have characterized the sector from the fall of the Berlin Wall to the tragic events of September 11, 2001, creating reduction with a resultant production volume dilution[1].

- Defense research and development (R & D) costs and the developmental cycle currently far exceeding the capability of assessing entrepreneurs' ability to anticipate unexpected risks.

- Increased uncertainties and threats due to economical and political instability, exacerbated by potential ethnic disputes and terrorist threats.

- An increasing need for mobility and flexibility in defensive weapon systems, as well as a high rate of demand for accuracy and lethality in smaller weapon stocks (defense forces need all systems to be linked by modern command, control, communication, and intelligence systems).

2.1.2   Evolution of Aerospace Industry

During the early 1990s, the aerospace industry experienced its worst economic crisis since World War II. This brutal recession, which combined a sharp decrease in both military and civil activities and was the consequence of two factors:

1. Drastic cuts in defense spending by NATO countries due to the end of the Cold War.

2. Shrinking demand for new aircraft by airline companies, which were only sluggishly recovering from the severe slump that had begun in 1990.

Between 1991 and 1994, the production of aerospace equipment decreased sharply. Despite some positive signs such as increasing air traffic, growth prospects remained uncertain for the aerospace industry over the next few years. The reasons were the still-fragile state of the airline industry and the ongoing depressed conditions affecting the military sector.

The demands of future aerospace and defense systems are leading to products with highly increased complexity. Development of such products requires broad-based research, elaborate design offices, and costly engineering efforts. This situation is exacerbated when completely different products are substituted for product lines due to fundamental changes in technology or innovative approaches to requirements. To recover these investments, a much broader market base is required. [AECMA 1997]

Major changes are also occurring in the production pyramid that characterizes business in these sectors. Third-tier (and maybe second-tier) manufacturers that produce structural parts and/or components are under strong pressure to meet lower prices, higher quality, and shorter delivery times. Therefore, the number of players is diminishing, but this process is slowed by government support that continues to help national industries for security and other reasons.

2.1.3 Facing the Challenge: the Industry Response

To face challenge of the new political and strategic scenario most companies inside the aerospace and defense sectors are searching a new critical mass through consolidation, although the pattern followed to reach the goal appears to be different among them.

2.1.3.1 Restructuring and Consolidation

During the '80s and '90s, the industry was characterized by many mergers and acquisitions of major U.S. and European companies. In order to become more competitive and global, these companies bought smaller companies or single businesses from others, or even merged with competitive firms of similar size and business activities. The availability of financial backing from the banking system during this period also facilitated the process.

Many players' motivations in pursuing such a policy, a practice that reached its height in the second half of the 1990s, may be considered of two types:

• Acting on the belief that "bigger is better"; that is, any size increase, even in areas different from the company's core business, would bring benefits.

• Acting with the main goal of increasing the core business, either because the company was fighting to survive or because the company was trying to improve its position in order to maintain its lead in the sector.

The U.S. defense and aerospace industry is dominated today by four large companies: Boeing – Mc Donnell Douglas, Lockheed – Martin, Northrop – Grumman[2] and Raytheon. Historically, the United States has viewed the defense and aerospace industries as national industries, mainly for reasons of security but also for the extraordinary significance that these industries have in the development of the whole country. Timing of this consolidation process is shown in Fig. 2.1.

An analogous process of mergers and acquisitions has occurred in Europe (Fig. 2.2). Until the recent creation of EADS (European Aeronautic Defense and Space Company), such processes have usually taken place between companies from the same nation, creating the "national champions." Thus, the internalization of industrial defense activities in Europe has been carried out mostly through opportunistic alliances for development of specific products (joint ventures or consortia such as Tornado, Airbus, Eurofighter).

2.1.3.2 The Search for a Critical Mass

The degree of consolidation of a business segment is often measured on the basis of two factors:

1. The ratio between the number of firms actually present in a segment and the maximum number of players the business segment is able to bear, where this maximum number is given by

$$N_{max} = \frac{\text{Segment demand}}{\text{Critical mass}}$$

In turn, to obtain the critical mass, that is the value of minimum turnover for a company to survive in its competitive arena, four independent variables must be investigated:

a.   The rough order of magnitude (ROM) of companies' turnover.

b.   The ranking of the major competitors and their aggregate turnover.

c.   The economic situation of most companies.

d.   The status of alliances in the business segment.

2.   The intensity of external factors toward globalization; for example, the business internalization, the R & D expenses level and (inversely) the demand growth rate.

Following is an example showing how further consolidation of the European and U.S. aerospace and defense industries can be predicted, starting from today's situation. The most significant data needed to perform such an analysis are illustrated in the following pages separately for the European and U.S. industries. Figure 2.3 and Table 2.1 show, respectively, the companies' turnover, the number of military programs in production or under development, and the domestic markets' magnitude. It is evident that the structure of the U.S. industry is already more consolidated and rationalized. This is true not only because the number of residual players in each U.S. business segment is generally lower, but also because the number of programs (both in production and under development) is smaller, while the captive demand is more than twice that in Europe ($86 billion versus $37 billion for Europe).

As to the number of programs under development (Table 2.1), there is an exception in the segment of combat airplanes where the United States has initiated the Joint Strike Fighter (JSF) development that is becoming an intercontinental collaboration between the United States and Europe, with BAE Systems (BAES), and other European countries, joining the program.

As to the number of players, from the comparison between Figure 2.4 and Figure 2.5, it is possible to note that the only business segments in which the difference between the United States and Europe is higher are military aircraft (five in Europe versus three in the U.S.). Consequently, a further restructuring of the industrial structure in the U.S. will likely be limited to the disappearance of only one player in some business, with the exception maybe in the satellite business (Figure 2.4).

The evaluation of the European aerospace and defense industry evolution, instead, appears to be quite different after the creation of EADS: A wide restructuring is foreseen in all business areas with one or two large residual manufacturers (perhaps three in the electronic sector for defense) in each business segment (Figure 2.5).

Figure 2.1
U.S. Defense and Aerospace Industry Consolidation

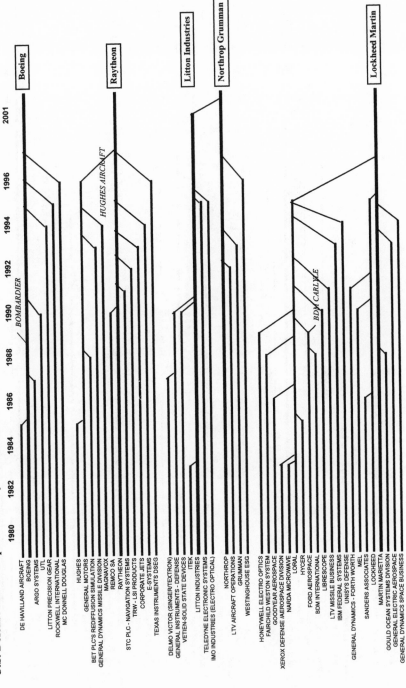

Figure 2.2
European Defense and Aerospace Industry Consolidation

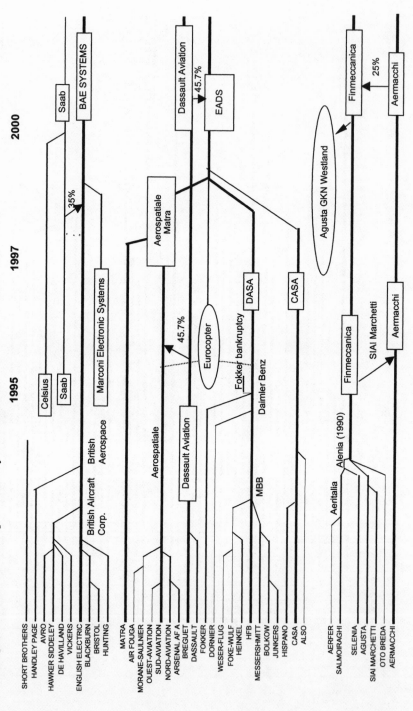

Figure 2.3
U.S. and European Companies Comparison — 2001 Sales (Bil $) — Only Aerospace and Defense Related Activities (Excluding Engines Manufacturers)

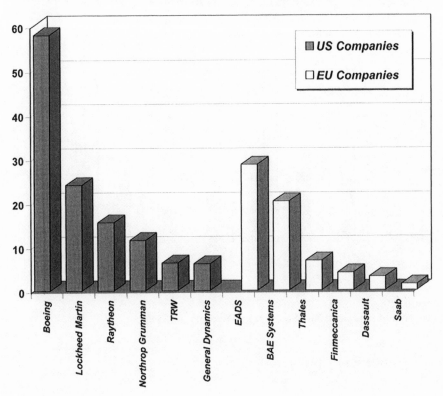

Table 2.1
Military Programs in USA and Europe

	USA		EUROPE	
	PRODUCTION	DEVELOPMENT	PRODUCTION	DEVELOPMENT
COMBAT AIRCRAFT	4	1	6	0
MILITARY TRANSPORT	2	0	4	1
HELICOPTERS	5	1	7	2
S/A MISSILES	5	2	11	3
ANTITANK MISSILES	2	1	2	2
ANTISHIP MISSILES	1	0	5	1
TANKS	1	0	4	0
ARMOURED VEHICLES	2	1	4	2
DOMESTIC MARKET (VAL '99)	52 B$ + 34 B$ R&D		28 B$ + 9 B$ R&D	

Figure 2.4
Present and Estimated Number of Manufacturers in USA

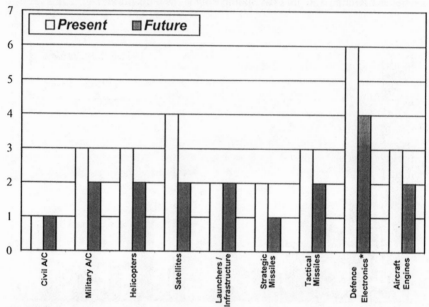

Figure 2.5
Present and Estimated Number of Manufacturers in Europe

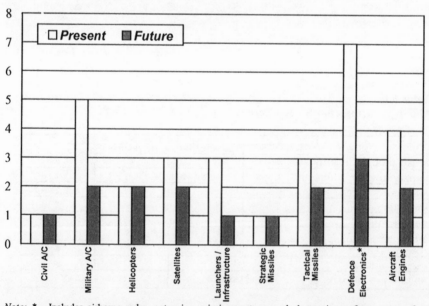

Note: * - Includes airborne radar, optronics, mission systems and electronic warfare systems for military aircraft

Only through this kind of consolidation will it be possible to reach a critical mass (in engineering, production, R & D, and so on) needed because of the reduced military demand and the competitive pressure brought on the market by increasingly efficient U.S. players.

2.1.3.3   Consolidation Patterns: Sector Versus Multisector Companies

On the other side, there are strong arguments supporting the clustering of specific industry sectors into multisector companies in the United States. These arguments are related to synergy, technological cross-fertilization, diversity, innovation potential, economies of scale, financial strength, and risk balancing.

Transnational restructuring began with joint ventures for individual sectors of business, such as helicopters, satellites, undercarriages, and sonar. Problems of mergers increase with the complexity of the merged business. Single-sector companies feature a number of benefits, such as product-customer focus, the leanness of the organization, and both the flexibility and the agility to react to market changes. [AECMA 1997]

2.1.4   Differences Between U.S. and European Industry Response.

2.1.4.1   U.S. and European Industry Comparison

Let's consider the status on both sides of the Atlantic. The European data will refer to the 15-nation members of today's European Union (Figure 2.6). The U.S. defense budget between 1990 and 1999 has decreased 22% in real terms (from $360 billion to $280 billion in 1997 dollars), and is, on average, about 50% higher than the sum of the 15 European nations' budgets. It is also significant that the combined defense budget of the of the 15 European Nations experienced smaller decrease; since 1990 it has decreased about 10% in real terms.

Research and development (R & D) is a field that is of paramount importance in an advanced industry such as aerospace and defense. U.S. expenditures are almost three times those of Europe. Between 1994 and 1997, the U.S. R & D defense expenditures amounted to about $38 billion yearly, while in Europe the value was around $12 billion.

Although the turnover may not be the best and most significant parameter in comparing the companies' capabilities and results, it gives an idea of the companies' sizes and possible economies of scale that they can achieve. The dimensions of an integrated European industry are not small. One can imagine consolidating the results of the major European players on the basis of the 1999 data, putting together, for this example, Aerospatiale, Alenia, BAES (BAE SYSTEMS), CASA (Costrucciones Aeronauticas SA), DASA (Deutsche Aerospace AG), and Saab; the turnover is about $35 billion, which is comparable to that of the biggest U.S. players (Figure 2.3).

Figure 2.6
Europe / USA Comparison — Gross Domestic Product and Defense Expenditures
(as Percent of GDP)

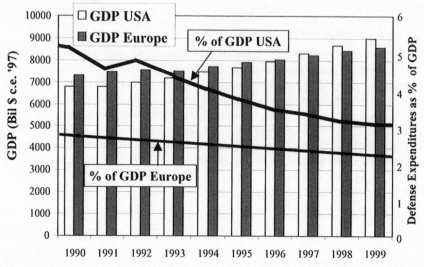

2.1.4.2   U.S. Industry Strategy

By far the largest competitor in the world aerospace market is the U.S. industry, with up to 58% of the world aerospace business (in terms of consolidated turnover), while the EU stands at 29% (2000). The end of the Cold War has changed the frame of reference, and the U.S. industrial system has immediately reacted, modifying its strategy in terms of both defense policy and industrial objectives. The U.S. government has favored the merger process by lessening the antitrust rules in the early 1990s.

In 1993 Martin Marietta has acquired the Aerospace Division of General Dynamics and in the March of the following year failed to buy Grumman for $1.9 billion, that was acquired by Northrop a few week later.

Understanding that it was not possible to grow up and be the leader through continue acquisition Martin Marietta accepted to merge with Lockheed a few month later, creating the Lockheed-Martin giant.

Lockheed Martin has then acquired the Defense activities of Loral for $9.1 billion. Later Northrop bought the Aerospace division of Westinghouse for $3 billion fighting against Loral. Also Raytheon, one of the biggest firms of the Defense sector, bought part of the Chrysler activities in the aerospace business for $455 million.

To all these operations the Antitrust Authority of justice Ministry has given green light including the Rockwell and Mc Donnell Douglas acquisition by Boeing. Further acquisitions include the purchase by Raytheon of the defense activities of Hughes Electronics, controlled by General Motors; total Raytheon turnover after this move reached $21 billion. A few months earlier Raytheon bought the defense activities of Texas Instruments for $3.5 billion in cash.

This consolidation process has been facilitated by U.S. government's stated policy to maintain the superiority of U.S. aerospace and ensure that federal investments are focused and effective to promote continued U.S. leadership in aerospace and aviation.

It has been very helpful for the U.S. Aerospace companies the establishment of the Advocacy Center within the Department of Commerce. The Center is very important for the U.S. export strategy and works in co-ordination with the 19 federal agencies of the Trade Promotion Co-ordinating Committee (which include the Department of State, the Export Import bank, and the Department of Defense).

By means of such changes, mergers, and acquisitions, the U.S. aerospace and defense market has the following characteristics:

- It is dominated by one purchaser, the Department of Defense (DoD).

- It has a dimension about twice that of the whole of Europe.

- It is composed of larger companies, whose number is constantly decreasing.

- It is strongly interested in a dual use of technology because some firms operate in both fields.

- It is inclined to export more than in the past, to compensate for federal budget cuts.

2.1.4.3 European Industry Strategy

The very beginning of the European aerospace and defense industry consolidation process can be traced to two fundamental political events that occurred between the end of 1997 and the first months of 1998. The first was a Trilateral Statement issued by the French, German, and British governments on December 9, 1997, that invited industry—and particularly Aerospatiale, British Aerospace, and DASA—to elaborate and present by March 31, 1998 a plan for the integration of the "national champions."

After the response to this invitation made by the firm partners of Airbus in a common document dated March 27, 1998, in which was shown the will to begin the reshaping and integration among industries, a certain number of questions arose from the still existing individual defense policies of the nations.

On April 21, 1998, the defense ministers of the United Kingdom, France, Germany, Spain, and Italy met in Paris and examined the companies' response, identifying actions on some key areas in order to help the restructuring process.

The second event was a letter of intent, which was later signed (July 6, 1998) by the defense ministers of six nations (the former five plus Sweden), aimed at harmonizing existing national regulations, which were still particularly complex in Europe and lacking homogeneity, for historical and cultural reasons.

The integration process, started in 1997 and continuing with the letter of intent, led to many attempts to create a sizable company to compete against the U.S. competitors. The talks (aimed at merging DASA and BAES) collapsed, and finally the British company bought (in December 1998) Marconi Electronic Systems from GEC Marconi, later to become BAE SYSTEMS and to attain a U.S.-like dimension. In the same year, BAES acquired 35% of the Saab military aircraft to reach a more competitive positioning in the fighter aircraft business.

DASA, together with Aerospatiale Matra (the merger of Aerospatiale with Matra Haute Technologies—the defense unit of France Lagardere), on October 14, 1999, signed an agreement for the creation of the new company, EADS, marking a critical step in the consolidation of the European aerospace and defense industries. Shortly afterwards, CASA joined the team. The company was officially formed on July 20, 2000. EADS represents the first example of a true transnational multibusiness company. This company ranks as the world's third largest in aerospace and defense, behind Boeing and Lockheed Martin in the United States. In 2000, EADS was first in the production of helicopters, second in production of civil airliners and missiles, and third in producing satellites. It is Europe's leading fighter aircraft constructor, with a 43% stake in Eurofighter and a 45.75% holding in France's Dassault Aviation, which makes Rafale fighter aircraft.

The creation of BAe-Marconi and EADS allowed Europe to have two multibusiness companies with total revenues of the same order of magnitude as those of the main U.S. players (Boeing excluded). However, it was not enough to achieve the necessary critical mass and to eliminate duplications of R & D efforts, production, and commercial activities. Therefore, negotiations began among the primary players (BAE SYSTEMS, EADS, Finmeccanica, and GKN Westland) to set up their own strategic single business alliances with the aim of transforming their operation into a global player.

The following joint ventures (JVs) were established:

- AMS (Alenia Marconi Systems, comprised of 50% Finmeccanica and 50% BAE SYSTEMS) operating in the field of defense electronics.

- Astrium (75% EADS and 25% BAE SYSTEMS).

- MBDA (Matra BAE Dynamics Alenia - 37.5 % EADS, 37.5% BAE SYSTEMS, and 25% Finmeccanica) in the missile systems sector.

- Agusta-Westland (50% Finmeccanica and 50% GKN) in the helicopter sector.

The two new macro areas of aggregation (EADS and BAE SYSTEMS) have been created with a different concept of optimization and different characteristics, but both aimed at improving performance and gathering all of the possible advantages for the markets and shareholders. EADS is born from the horizontal integration of the French, German, and Spanish "national champions," while BAE SYSTEMS preferred to follow the concept of vertical integration, merging the military aircraft business with strong competencies in the areas of defense electronics and systems integration.

In the European context, the third player is Finmeccanica, grouping the main Italian industrial activities in aerospace and defense. In order to maintain full visibility and control of its business, Finmeccanica is pursuing a strategy of alliances based on establishing parenthetical sector JVs with the other main players to reach a business dimension able to compete in the international arena. GKN is present in one JV only, the helicopter sector. In the future, other single-business JVs appear possible, notably in the fields of avionics and underwater systems and equipment and maybe military aircraft.

The increased competitiveness of the new integrated industry, to be reached not only through industrial rationalization but also through a better choice of product lines, will also have beneficial effects on the export market. This rationalization of product lines can be achieved only with the support or a new system of establishing requirements at the European level no more as a sum of multiple national requirements.

The reduction in the number of programs shall also free resources for increased R&D activities, that are urgently in need of more attention. But maybe as important as the industrial integration is the creation of the integrated European Defense market. It will be no more possible to have three or four almost contemporary fighter programs such as Eurofighter, Rafale, Gripen, or multiple missile or multifunction radar programs.

The achievement of a sufficient critical mass in terms of industrial dimension and internal market size is mandatory to compete effectively with the U.S. industry.

2.2 STRUCTURAL ANALYSIS OF THE AERONAUTICAL INDUSTRY

The product cycle through which an aircraft is realized involves a high number of companies, organized in a complex and hierarchy-structured system, leading to the integration, in the airplane, of parts, components and finished products, realized in the airframe, propulsion system and equipment-avionics sub-sectors.

The competitive scenario presents strategic groups of companies according to their interest in similar products and their following similar strategies. The outside world may influence the company's targets and strategies directly or indirectly.

The macroenvironment is formed by (or may be shown through) the variables that normally cannot be controlled or affected by the company (that is of political and economical nature), but are to be taken seriously into account for its business development.

Great direct impact is given to the company by the consumers' preferences, emerging technologies, competition structure, existing rules, replacement products etc., representing the company micronvironment that the company can and must influence and control.

2.2.1   Aeronautical Industry Sectors

The aeronautical industry includes four sectors: the airframers, the engines, the systems, and the avionics suppliers.

The *airframe area* deals with companies devoted to design and production of wings, fuselage, tail, nacelles, and thrust reversers, but few are also capable of dealing with the whole aircraft architecture and design, and the systems integration. These prime companies are the main actors in this segment, even if their role, from a manufacturing point of view, may consist only of the assembly of various parts coming from subcontractor companies. The primes playing this role are not great in number due to the high level of know-how needed to accomplish the tasks.

The *engines area* includes companies that design and produce, in whole or in part, aeronautic engines of any type (turbojet, turbofan, propeller driven—turboprop or pistons) and all necessary devices for interfacing the airframe and onboard systems. In this segment too there is not a great number of companies because of the high level of technology and knowledge required.

The *avionics area* deals with the design and production of all onboard electronic instruments that are necessary to manage the aircraft with full efficiency and safety (flight instruments, navigation, communications, weapon systems). Avionics is a very specialized area in which companies try to focus their efforts toward applied technology in sensor or device production.

The *systems area* refers to all remaining nonelectronic systems (such as landing gear, hydraulic systems, electrical systems, and fuel systems) that are on board the aircraft. Although this segment of the business is highly specialized, the concentration in the industry is lower, allowing numerous, relatively small companies to compete.

In the sphere of each of these areas then, it is possible to distinguish between the military production and that destined to the civil market. The following analysis will be focused on the area of the airframers, relative only to fixed-wing aircraft and to the civil production, and in particular to the firms that complete the final integration of the aircraft. It is undeniable that the aeronautical subsector dealing with airplanes has hinged on the activities of the integrators, which, beyond the design of the general architecture of the aircraft, also prepare the installation of the power plant groups and all other equipment and systems produced elsewhere but delivered to the integrator for final assembly. The integrator has the responsibility of not only the technical and production aspects of a program (planning, development, production and testing), but also the managerial/organizational aspects (coordination of suppliers, flow of materials, and timing), the commercial aspects, and after-sale support to customers. [VICARI 1991]

Since the production activities and the competitive strategies of the prime manufacturers are characterized by a strong interaction with the firms engaged in the other industrial segments that feed the production flow leading to integration of the aircraft (component and systems suppliers), the analysis will be widened to the study of the collateral and inferior levels of the network of firms that participate in the development of aeronautical programs.

2.2.2   The Macroenvironment

Among the forces of the macroenvironment that predominantly affect the characteristics of the sector are those of a political nature. All of the advanced countries have an interest in developing strong aeronautical industries for the purpose of assuring a certain degree of technological and production autonomy in a sphere that has significant implications for the security of a nation, as well as its industrial and economic development.

Also the international political picture influences the structural characteristics of the sector, since it determines the budget parameters for defense and for investments in R & D. Such influences have direct consequence on the aeronautical military industry and indirect consequences on the civil industry, if we take into account the spillover that comes to the second from the activities of the first.[3].

In addition, the political/public sector employs barriers and boundaries to protect a nation's industrial interests (such as protectionist measures, direct support to national firms, political guiding of demand, assistance for sales to foreign countries, and so on), which strongly affect the strategies and competitive conditions in the international aeronautical industries of the different states.

Also, the technological factor plays an important role in defining the structural characteristics of the sector, since the innovations of product and of process represent a crucial competitive weapon for the aeronautical firms. This statement is based on the following considerations:

- The aeronautical sector constitutes one of the major areas of technological progress in our century and is characterized by high-intensity technological innovation.

- The aeronautical product originates from the convergence of technologies involving different sectors of activity and evolving according to different trajectories of development. The aeronautical product is then a concentration of high technologies with consequences for many other sectors (electronics, mechanics, science of the materials, chemistry, propulsion, installation, and so on).

- The aeronautical sector is characterized by strong direct or indirect government involvement, beginning with research activities, with the objective of assuring the adequate technological base necessary for the satisfaction of national defense requirements and of assuring the creation of a solid industrial tissue.

From these considerations, it is understood that very often the sources of technology are external to the firm and are located in centers of research (public or private), government agencies (civil or military), university institutes, bodies for certification and control, and so on. Thus, in order for the firm to achieve the competitive advantage that comes from innovation, it is necessary to have the ability to acquire, manage, and adapt its own strategic needs to technologies mostly developed externally.

There is then the influence of the forces of economic nature—the cyclic phases of international conjuncture, like the conditions of an energy crisis or of a stagnation of the world economy—that have often affected the aeronautical industry. There is a strong correlation (although with some delay) between the level of aircraft sales and the demand for air transport, in turn clearly connected with the level of the economic activity of the nation, measurable via the gross domestic product or GDP (Figure 2.7).

Other special forces can interfere with the aeronautical industry. First, there are movements of opinion, which have influenced and will condition the aeronautical industry to an increasing extent. The environmentalists' groups contributed (together with considerations of economic viability) to the U.S. abandonment of the development of the civil supersonic of the first generation and affected heavily the Concorde's commercial success, with regard to initial prohibitions of U.S. flyovers.

Finally, the modification of behaviors (such as the economic, social, or demographic evolution of some social layer or of some geographical areas) influence the demand for air trips and, as a consequence, the industries producing aircraft.

Such factors change the relative ratio among the various users of air commercial transport (tourist traffic, business, occasional, scheduled, charter, and so on) and alter the types of connections (length of routes, load factor), affecting the technical characteristics of the aircraft.

Figure 2.7
Air Travel Demand, Economic Activity Level and Commercial Aircraft Orders

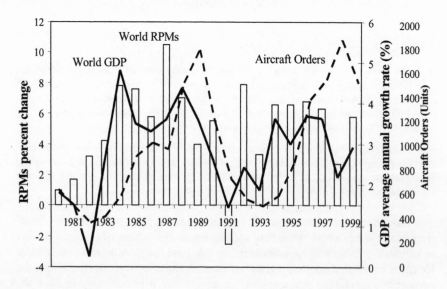

2.2.3 The Microenvironment

This analysis of the microenvironment aims to identify and appraise the typical characteristics of the sector under examination through the following steps:

- Identification and evaluation of the structural characteristics of the sector.

- Identification of the perimeter of the competitive arena and segmentation of the business.

- Definition of the joint characteristics of the offer.

- Identification and evaluation of the relevant characteristics of the demand. [ABELL 1986]

The whole of the observations and reflections drawn from these first analyses will proceed in evaluation of the sector, focusing on the analysis of the competition.

The last one will be articulated in three successive steps: identification of the *competitive relevant forces,* the *competitive basic strategies,* and the *behaviors and performance of market leaders.* [PORTER 1985]

2.2.3.1 Structural Characteristics of the Aeronautical Sector

The aeronautical industry constitutes the specific type of international sector commonly known as the global aggregate sector. The international sectors have two distinct peculiarities:

1. They represent the industrial sectors whose perimeters go beyond those geographically defined in terms of domestic demand.

2. They constitute those sectors in which the competitive advantages could increase with the extension of production and commercial activities beyond the national border. In this case, the strategic path of the opponent firms and the relative competitive positioning has meaning only on a worldwide basis.[PORTER 1986]

The specific characteristics of the international sectors depend on the characteristics of the markets and of the products. The market may be geographically homogeneous or heterogeneous; the product may be standardized or diversified. The characteristics of the markets and the products determine incentives for internationalization of activities. In Figure 2.8, the different international sectors are situated on the basis of the criterion of product/market just introduced.

In the upper left area are the sectors with high costs of globalization, because they are characterized by the need for high differentiation of the product, brought about by national differences in customers' wants or by regulation from the local government. In this case, firms can widen their own activities to an international level, but to the cost of an outstanding effort to second the needs of the different local markets.

Figure 2.8
Types of International Industrial Sectors

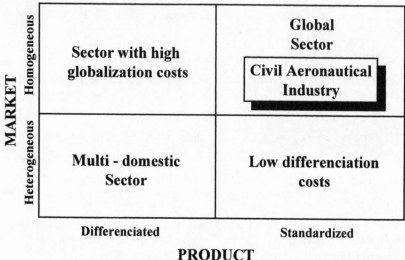

MARKET Homogeneous	Sector with high globalization costs	**Global Sector** Civil Aeronautical Industry
Heterogeneous	Multi - domestic Sector	Low differenciation costs
	Differenciated	Standardized

PRODUCT

Source: Elaboration on T. Leavitt. "The Globalization of the Markets." *Harvard Business Review*, May - June, 1983

The implication is that this type of business can be undertaken only by firms with outstanding technological, financial, and marketing capabilities, and sometimes only by those with preferential access to the political channels of a country.

The lower right area defines a sector in which, by means of few and small modifications, a product standardized to the local requirements can be obtained. The different characteristics of the domestic markets (in this case, by definition, heterogeneous) render convenient the decentralization of activities associated with commercialization of the product. Nevertheless, this may happen with costs relatively contained, given the elevated uniformity or insufficient differentiation of the product.

In the lower left area are those industrial sectors in which the competition in each country is essentially independent of that in other nations. In these sectors, competition is determined by local factors. The firms can still achieve a competitive advantage with internationalization of activities, but they will pay a price for the necessary modification and adaptation of products in order to meet specific local needs and for the maximum transfer of activities to each of the individual markets.

In the upper right area are the so-called aggregate sectors, which are those characterized by a standardized product and by a geographically homogenous market. The margin of choice as to whether or not to compete internationally, in this case, is much reduced because the opportunity exists to widen the market significantly and/or to achieve economies of scale in extending the activities on a global basis. [LEAVITT 1983]

The aeronautical industry is positioned inside this area: The market is in fact made of international and national operators (primarily airlines) that have very similar standards—the first because of direct competition, and the second because local norms relative to comfort and to security are very similar to those of other countries (being very often governed by international bodies).

The product presents then standard characteristics, being practically the same model sold throughout the world, except for some irrelevant modifications requested by a particular user that are usually satisfied by changes in the internal configuration of the aircraft or by means of adopting different equipment and engines[4]. The aeronautical industry is an industrial sector where the internationalization of activities has become indispensable. In fact, the sector is characterized by a high intensity of financial investments made possible only by extending the boundaries beyond domestic markets.

The factors that induce aeronautical firms to compete on a worldwide scale are related to costs, which are always higher for the development of a new program. In addition, there are associated advantages to externalization and/or to sharing the activities of aircraft production and development with other firms. These phases of an aeronautical program tend to present an increasing degree of internationalization, with the prime being willing not only to externalize or share quotas with other firms, but also to involve partners or suppliers more deeply in the program and to share technological, financial, and commercial risks with them. It is not only the technological complexity of the design and production process that induce aeronautical firms to extend their activities worldwide, but also the vastness of the potential market and the complexity of the sale process.

The acquisition of an aircraft (civil or military) by a nation is still promoted by participation of local industries in the program. The associated burdens of commercialization and after-sale assistance have achieved such magnitude that retrieval results are very difficult without extending the area of commercialization of the product to a global level, taking advantage of volume economies in the costs of marketing and other support activities. This naturally imposes the constitution of a sale team and of a network for technical assistance to the airlines worldwide. The efficiency in managing such activities represents a main condition for competing with success in the business.

These economic motivations for an aggregate strategy, in addition to other motivations more specifically industrial that will be analyzed later (such as economy of scale and the effect of experience) have notably increased the degree of concentration in the sector that was already high because of the technological content of products, the level of costs, and the barriers to entry and exit.

After the merger between Boeing and McDonnell Douglas in 1997, there are two remaining players in the large commercial jet arena: the Airbus consortium and the Boeing giant in the United States. Also, the number of competitors in the regional aircraft segment has decreased, first through the creation by individual nations of the national champions and later by means of international accords and/or acquisitions and/or exits that constitute the most significant phenomenon of the sector in the last few years.

2.2.3.2   Business Segmentation in the Civil Aeronautical Sector

The civil aeronautical sector includes both commercial, regional, and general aviation businesses. The first is the sphere of activity of firms that practice commercial transport, with public flights on request (charter) or with scheduled flights. The second differs in its focus on smaller equipment and shorter stage length. The third, general aviation, includes business aviation (private transport for business), various forms of aerial work (such as air taxi, aerial photography, publicity, light cargo, aerial motion shooting, and aerial agriculture), and public activities such as teaching, pleasure trips, and tourism.

The great variety of uses of the airplane, together with the extensive area of potential end-users and an ample range of technological solutions to satisfy the demand, lets us understand that one of the most important and sensitive phases in the analysis of the aeronautical sector is the correct identification of the different areas of business. The multidimensional approach seems applicable for defining each area with precision. The goal is to identify the groups of users, the use destination, the applied technologies, and the degree of verticalization of the activities of the manufacturer; in substance, who uses the aeronautical products, for which use, through which technological modality, and, finally, in which part of the chain of value generation are located the different firms of the sector. [ABELL 1986]

A possible segmentation of the business under examination by means of this approach uses the type of propulsion (the technology) as a significant variable, the offered service (the use destination expressed by range and seating) and the final customers (groups of users). A graphic representation of the segmentation of the business through the multidimensional approach is indicated in Figures 2.9 and 2.10. Figure 2.9 refers to the complete production of the civil aeronautical industry. A representation of this kind, that examines the aeronautical industry as a whole, could be used for a comparison with an industrial sector whose products are finalized to an alternative modality for the transport of goods and persons. Figure 2.10 is an example of the application of multidimensional identification to the business of general aviation.

The AHEFLBCD parallelepiped refers to aircraft destined for flight schools (groups of users) for training (use destination). The figure shows that propulsion (technology) can be of different types, because it can be designed for basic flight schools (whose business is then defined from the BCDLHGMI cube) or for advanced schools that use more sophisticated aircraft, fast turboprop or jet.

The opportunity to use the previously considered variables (propulsion, autonomy, size, groups of users, and so on) in the sphere of civil transport airplane production comes both from the ability to define the boundaries of the business with precision and from the ability to obtain a common segmentation for aircraft manufacturers and users (airlines), with evident advantages of generality and transparency.

Figure 2.9
The Civil Aeronautical Industry Market Segmentation through the Multidimensional Approach

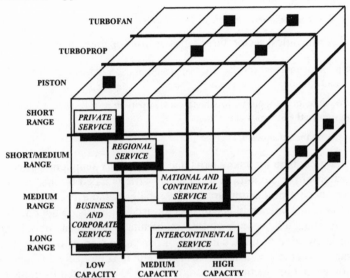

Source: Elaboration on D.F. Abell. *Business e Scelte Aziendali*. Milan: Italian Edition, IPSOA, 1986

Figure 2.10
General Aviation Business Identification through the Multidimensional Approach

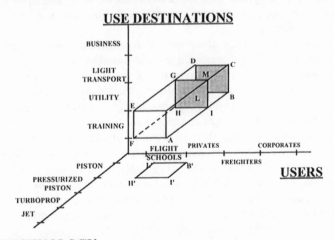

The figure refers to companies acting in the same value chain phase

Source: Elaboration on D.F. Abell. *Business e Scelte Aziendali*. Milan: Italian Edition, IPSOA, 1986

Following the analysis, the segments relative to general aviation aircraft will be excluded, and attention will be focused only on products destined for commercial and regional transportation.

2.2.3.3. Joint Characteristics of the Offer

In the aeronautical sector, three types of firms operate, including:

- The prime manufacturers that are responsible for the finished product and provide for its integration.

- The equipment's suppliers, in whose context particular relevance assume the firms that produce the avionics apparatuses.

- The engine manufacturers.

In addition, there are many parts and components suppliers that coordinate in production of the aircraft. Such firms are differentiated by the technological content in specific production areas. "Essentially without exception, the prime manufacturers that operate in one of the industrial segments do not operate in the other three. Though it becomes almost impossible to design an aircraft without a profound knowledge of the technology of the propulsion or of the electronics, the airframer, engine, and avionics firms operate in completely different spheres of technology and production." [VICARI 1991: p.33](translated from the original Italian by the author)

From the above, it is clear that the "production cycle, by means of which one creates an aircraft, is organized into a complex and hierarchical system, through which the final assembly of parts, components and finished products are realized and then integrated into the subsystems of the airframe, of the power plant and of the equipment." [VICARI 1991: p.34](translated from the original Italian by the author)

Such a system has been effectively represented through a pyramid, inside which are shown all firms that participate in the production of an aircraft (Figure 2.11). The pyramid representation furnishes a picture of the different types of all firms belonging to each sector, and it depicts the different hierarchical levels of companies that participate in the programs (in terms of technological, economic, and production efforts) as primes or suppliers.

It is interesting to note that the number of the prime manufacturers of fighter aircraft, (and missiles and helicopters) is still higher than that of manufacturers of commercial aircraft. That large number is tied to the fact that many nations without particularly advanced aeronautical industries (such as Argentina, Taiwan, South Africa, and China) have, however, developed autonomous capabilities to produce some fighter airplanes in order to maintain industrial freedom in the sensitive sphere of defense.

Located at the top of the pyramid (first level) is the firm leader, which designs, develops, and organizes the complete program. The firm leader is responsible not only for the activities of planning and final assembly, but also for those of marketing and product support. In addition, the firm leader carries out the role of collecting the flow of parts (in the form of components or finished products) coming from the lower levels. The firm leader makes agreements with other smaller companies creating therefore an ample range of diversified settlements that go from the accords for subassemblies supply to the minority risk-sharing role.

To the top of the pyramid belong those few firms that enjoy the technological and financial resources and market control that allow them to manage and carry out the development of a program in all phases. [ESPOSITO, RAFFA, AND ZOLLO 1989]

The exacerbation of the main selection criteria (competitiveness in the level of costs, punctuality in delivery time, and high qualitative standards), the adoption of additional factors of choice, and the transfer of roles and responsibility from the firm leader to the intermediary levels of the production pyramid are bringing a profound modification of the traditional supply chain of the aeronautical sector (Figure 2.12a).

Figure 2.11
The Productive Pyramid in the Civil Aeronautical Industry

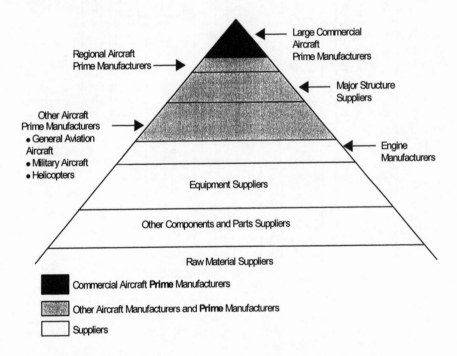

Source: Elaboration on T.J. Bacher, *International Collaboration on Commercial Airplane Programmes*. Conference Sponsored by Society of Japanese Aerospace Company. Tokyo: 1983

Figure 2.12
Supply Chain

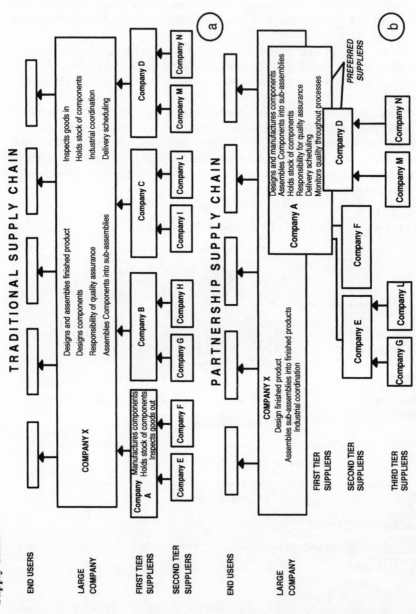

Source: Elaboration on EC *DG III*, 1994 (Bristol Polytechnic)

In the near future, these changes will bring about optimization of the connections between prime and suppliers (Figure 2.12b). That modification will lead to an evolution of the role of some suppliers from the traditional subcontractor role to a conditional partnership role with the integrator, and it will also result in the creation of a first-level supply constituted by preferred suppliers.

The preferred supplier will collaborate with the final integrator in planning the components, quality management, and delivery logistics. The preferred supplier will furnish the equipped subsystems that will be directly incorporated in the final product. In reality, some preferred supplier will assume the function of smaller prime firms that are at the top of a production pyramid.

Conventional suppliers firms will represent the second-tier of the sector. The third level will be made of niche firms with a high level of specialization, or firms whose products are characterized by a small systemic and technological content. This approach will be surely followed in the design and production of next-generation airplanes such as the Boeing Sonic Cruiser.

The fragmentation of the offer, deriving from the technological, production, and market diversification of the sector of the suppliers, determines the firms' ability to pursue different competitive strategies and different operating modalities (Table 2.2):

- Strategies of cost leadership, which requires cost-related capability and emphasis on production tools.

- Strategies of differentiation or focusing, which requires quality or performance-related capabilities and emphasis on the processes and/or the products.

Table 2.2
Issue and Strategic Options for Business Participants

COMPETITIVE STRATEGIES	CAPABILITIES	FEATURES	OPERATING OPTIONS				
			MOVE OPERATIONS TO LOWER COST REGIONS	IMPROVE UTILIZATION VIA CONSOLIDATION	INVEST IN WORLD CLASS MANUFACTURING FACILITIES	CENTRALIZE ACTIVITIES FOR IMPROVED FOCUS (CENTERS OF EXCELLENCE)	INVEST IN PROPRIETARY PROCESSES
COST LEADERSHIP	COST RELATED	ADVANCED TOOLS	☑	☑	☑		
DIFFERENTIATION	QUALITY RELATED	IMPROVED PROCESSES			☑	☑	
FOCALIZATION	PERFORMANCE RELATED	EXOTIC MATERIALS					☑

2.2.3.3.1 Strategic Groupings of Aircraft Manufacturers in the Civil Transport Airplane Sector

ESPOSITO, RAFFA, AND ZOLLO [1989] show that the manufacturers of civil aircraft can be aggregated on the basis of competitive relevant factors substantially related to the modalities of presence in the competitive arena, such as the technological level of the products, and the segments of covered market and width of the production range. A close correlation exists between the characteristics of the products expressed by the first indicator and those of the manufacturers expressed by an index of the second type.

The technological level of an aircraft can be represented by the combination of its technical and economic characteristics. More precisely, it can be supposed that such a level is in relation to its cruise speed (as far as technical characteristics are concerned) and its operating costs (affecting economic performance).

It is important to note that the economic performance of an aircraft is antithetical to its technical performance (a turboprop plane has lower operating costs but also lower speed when compared with a jet airplane of the same size), and therefore the whole technological content derives from a trade-off between these two characteristics.

Taking the approach of ESPOSITO, RAFFA, AND ZOLLO [1989] and dividing the aircraft on the basis of segment of market presence (defined by the number of seats) and technological level, in 2001 three main categories result (Figure 2.13):

- The first (AT3) is characterized by a technologically low level, which includes almost exclusively the pistons and the turboprop aircraft for feeder and commuter services.

- The second (AT2) includes jet aircraft distinguished by an intermediate technological level with respect to two extreme layers. The number of programs in this segment are limited at present, but a great many projects are under study or development.

- The third category (AT1) represents more technologically advanced products.

The first significant dividing point is the demarcation between turboprop aircraft belonging exclusively to the first category and those with turbofan propulsion.

Only recently, this clean separation has been blurred by the development of small jets such as the EMB-145/135, the CRJ-100/20, and the 328 Jet. All three derived from already existing platforms (biz-jet or turboprop) with some adaptations for new utilization (CRJ-100) or for new motorization (EMB-145 and 328 Jet).

The highest number of products is in the turboprop and small jet market. In many cases these products are made by firms that are not in countries that enjoy high industrial and technological levels.

Figure 2.13
Products Positioning in the Technology /Market Segment Matrix (Year 2001)

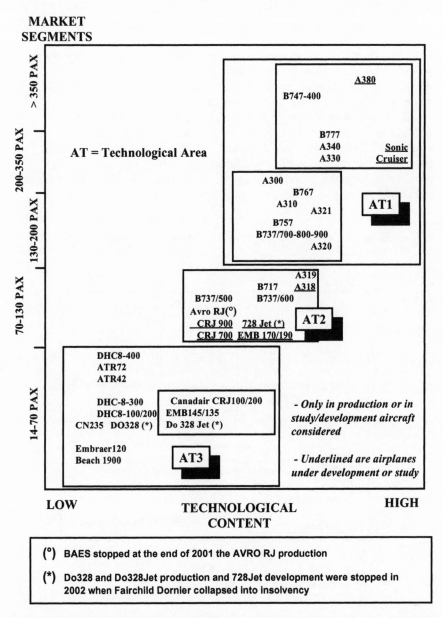

Source: Elaboration on E. Esposito, M. Raffa, and G. Zollo. *Tre Livelli di Impresa nello Sviluppo di un Prodotto High-Tech: Evidenze Empiriche a Supporto della Rete di Imprese e dell'Impresa Rete,* 1989

The lower part of the AT2 area also includes airplanes whose technological content is similar to that of the small jet segment. Until a few years ago, before the regional jets boom, the situation was quite different; the number of firms able to overcome the entry barriers to such a specific market segment was more limited.

The aircraft of the technologically more advanced area (AT1) are those produced by the market leaders. Their technological complexity, from which derive the huge costs of development, limits the number of firms capable of managing production programs for these aircraft.

Beginning with Figure 2.13, replacing the specific products with the firms and taking into account the presence of the firms in one or more technological areas with one or more products in each of them, it is possible to classify the firms in terms of width of production range. From this classification, it is possible to map the strategic groupings from which to begin analyzing the competitive strategies of the firms engaged in that sector (Figure 2.14).

Figure 2.14
Manufacturers' Strategic Grouping in the Civil Aeronautical Industry (Year 2001)

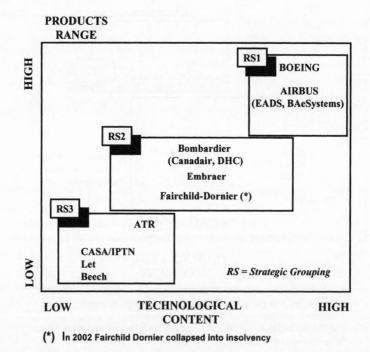

(*) In 2002 Fairchild Dornier collapsed into insolvency

Source: Elaboration on E. Esposito, M. Raffa, and G. Zollo. *Tre Livelli di Impresa nello Sviluppo di un Prodotto High-Tech: Evidenze Empiriche a Supporto della Rete di Imprese e dell'Impresa Rete,* 1989

The following observations can be made:

- In the aeronautical sector, the competitive arena presents the strategic groupings, which are the groups of firms recognizable by the quantity and quality of the products (in terms of the factors previously introduced).

- A close correspondence exists between the similarity of the firms in terms of these two elements and their similarity in terms of size, technological ability, and financial capability (comparable modalities of competitive strategies).

- None of the main competitors competes in all segments of offer (from commuters to wide-bodies/long range). The great variety in the civil transport airplane business would seem to offer aeronautical companies ample opportunities for diversification. In reality, the outstanding differences among the products and the markets have induced firms to serve a number (however limited) of business areas in which they can develop some specific segments and a number (however small) of types of aircraft. The firms widen their offerings in this way due to the necessarily high investment needed to satisfy an extremely sophisticated and fragmented demand.

- Product diversification increases with the technological level of a company.

DASA (now part of EADS) is an unusual case in that, after a strategy of acquisition and diversification (induced also by a goal of unifying all of the German aerospace industry into a single entity), it eventually concentrated its own industrial presence in the production of the great commercial jet (Airbus). This concentration occurred after a process of disposal that began with the abandonment of the Fokker (regional aircraft) and the sale of the Dornier (commuter aircraft) to Fairchild.

2.2.3.4 The Demand for Aircraft

As with all investment goods, the demand for civil aircraft is a derived demand, and therefore it depends on the level of activity of the air transportation companies.

As has been emphasized previously, the demand for air transport is extremely sensitive to the condition of the world economy, to which is connected the available income of the traveling population. From this series of mutually dependent influences derives the variability of cycles and the mobility of the demand for civil aircraft.

2.2.3.4.1 Air Transportation Development: Mergers and Alliances of Major Airlines

2.2.3.4.1.1 Liberalization in air transportation

The deregulation of 1978 also meant a new approach in airline business outside the United States: European, Latin American, Asian, and CIS (Community of Independent States) airlines experienced a freer market. The need to restructure the national airlines has led some to struggle for survival, while others have improved their economics and gained a wider international presence. As Europe has removed regulations, there are now more frequent flights, better services, lower fares, and greater use of smaller aircraft in many markets. [ROLLS ROYCE PLC 2000]

The airline industry is different from most other industries in that, after a period of many entries at the beginning, there is a period of stability and then the consolidation process with the consequent reduction of the actors. As usual, the degree of consolidation depends on the competitive structure of the market, but it is limited to some extent by regulation. Deregulation in 1978 in the United States made possible the birth of new airlines, but the number of failures has also increased; the net effect has been a more concentrated industry. Europe experienced a similar situation. [TARRY 1999]

2.2.3.4.1.2   Developments in air transportation

"The air transport system has already expanded to accommodate a 170% increase in air traffic over the last twenty years. . . . It is a matter of debate as to how the system will accommodate a further doubling of passengers traffic by 2020." [ROLLS ROYCE PLC 2000: p.24]

Many activities are improving the management of air transport infrastructure and, although in the near term problems will persist, these improvements could reach their goal in the long term, accommodating the increasing demand. In fact, in the last 10 years there has been a growth in passenger travel by 7% yearly, despite the presence of many congested areas. At the same time it is expected, due to the presence of well developed markets, that the growth of the world travel for the most congested areas will be lower than the foreseen 5% yearly (in the next 20 years). [ROLLS ROYCE PLC 2000]

Primarily in Europe, North America, and Asia, the "global measures to alleviate en-route congestion include the Future Air Navigation System (FANS) and reduced vertical separation minima (RVSM). RVSM reduces vertical separation from 2,000 ft (600 m) to 1,000 ft (300 m) in airspace above 28,000 ft (8,500 m)." [ROLLS ROYCE PLC 2000: p.24]

2.2.3.4.1.3   Airline alliances

"The primary attraction of alliances is instant access to new markets. They provide the opportunity to capitalise on rather than compete with other airlines' hubs. Revenues enhancements is sought through capturing premium-fare passengers with improved, coordinated products, and better service on connecting flights. Cost reduction opportunity increases as alliances mature. Early measures include capacity sharing and elimination of duplicated flights. Longer term cost benefits come through greater purchasing power and shared resource management." [ROLLS ROYCE PLC 2000: p.27]

The development of alliances in the early 1990s did not provide the expected benefits because of the downturn in the industry, but in a stable condition benefits would be seen, and the related cost savings could outweigh the direct earning benefits (See Table 2.3). [TARRY 1999]

Table 2.3
Airline Alliances

	Code Share	Alliance	Joint Venture / Merger
Characteristics	Impression of wider network	Broader & Deeper Linkage	Two into one
Benefits	Additional Traffic	Wider traffic reach, opportunities to save costs	Network, Yield Maximization, Co-ordination
Necessary Conditions	* Coincidence of Objectives * Regulations	* Coincidence of Objectives * Regulations	* Coincidence of Objectives * Regulations
Areas of Conflicts	None	Overlap	* Basis for benefit * Domicile * Labour * Management * Strategy * Overlap * Valuation
Degree of Integration	Negligible	Some	Total
Examples	Qualiflyer (11 airlines, 3,6% market share)	* Star (15 Airlines, 21.1% market share) * Oneworld (8 airlines, 15.9% market share) * Wings (3 airlines, 9.6% market share) * Skyteam (6 airlines, 12.1% market share)	

Source: Elaboration on C. Tarry. *Airline Economic – Results & Prospects*. IATA, September 1999

2.2.3.4.1.4   U.S. airline industry consolidation

The dominance of a few airlines in the U.S. market has been a fact for 70 years. After the separation of airlines from aircraft manufacturers imposed by the U.S. government in 1934, domestic carriers evolved into the "Big Four" (TWA, Eastern, American, and United), plus PanAm for international flights. After deregulation Eastern and PanAm have disappeared, but the concentration remains. [AVMARK AVIATION ECONOMIST 2001]

Table 2.4 shows some relevant data for the major U.S. airlines. In order to appreciate the degree of industry concentration, several different parameters could be taken into account; here the cumulative percent of RPM (revenue per passenger mile) as a function of the number of airlines has been selected because it was considered the most significant. ASM (Available Seat Mile) are also included.

Data show that the airline industry in the United States is very heavily concentrated. In fact, the first three airlines listed carried out a traffic amount in excess of half (52.1%) of the total U.S. figure. The first 10 airlines shown are responsible for 91.4% of total U.S. traffic, leaving only 8.6% for all remaining passenger airlines (national and regional). These last airlines are still relatively unconcentrated because, out of 120 (83 regional and 37 national), only 10 account for about 53% of their own total traffic (Table 2.5).

In March 2001 American Airlines received approval from a federal bankruptcy court to purchase TWA. But the trend toward concentration has ceased due to the presence of antitrust laws that have reduced the possibilities for mergers between companies. The latest examples of these laws in action were the Justice Department's block of the United/US Airways merger in July 2001 and the Airline Merger Moratorium Act of 2001[5].

Table 2.4
Top 10 Major U.S. Airlines — Year 2000

	RPM	ASM	Revenues	Net earnings or (loss)	A/C	RPM % cum
	(millions)	(millions)	(000)	(000)		on US Total
American/TWA	129,767	179,237	23,287,000	547,000	903	18.7
United	125,374	173,409	19,532,000	50,000	604	36.8
Delta	106,500	145,293	16,741,000	826,000	605	52.1
Northwest	78,157	102,032	11,415,000	256,000	429	63.4
Continental	63,373	85,065	9,899,000	342,000	372	72.5
US Airways	46,487	66,127	9,248,000	(142,000)	418	79.2
Southwest	41,697	59,144	5,649,000	625,000	344	85.2
America West	18,878	26,778	2,290,000	2,072	164	88.0
Alaska	11,839	19,998	1,749,000	(64000)	95	89.7
American Trans Air	11,672	16,189	1,291,000	(15,000)	58	91.4
US Major Total	**633,745**					
US National/Regional Total	60,009					
US TOTAL	**693,754**					

Source: Elaboration on data from ATW's. *World Airline Report*. 2000.

Table 2.5
Top 10 U.S. National / Regional Airlines — Year 2000

	RPM	ASM	Revenues	Net earnings or (loss)	A/C	RPM % cum
	(millions)	(millions)	(000)	(000)		on US Nat / Reg Total
Hawaiian	5,589	7,156	607,000	(18,000)	29	9.3
Air Tran	4,066	5,792	824,000	47,000	54	16.1
Sun Country	3,239	4,556	281,000	(41,000)	15	21.5
Spirit	3,044	4,269	312,000	(6,000)	28	26.6
Continental Micronesia	3,028	3,858	512,000	33,000	22	31.6
Continental Express	2,912	4,674	844,000	11,000	166	36.5
American Eagle	2,675	4,321	1,452,000	-	261	40.9
Frontier	2,565	3,989	472,000	54,000	25	45.2
National	2,540	3,932	268,000	(35,000)	16	49.4
North American	2,205	2,777	78,000	1,000	5	53.1
Total	**31,862**					
US National/Regional Total	**60,009**					

Source: Elaboration on data from ATW's. *World Airline Report*. 2000.

2.2.3.4.1.5   Changing the airline industry structure in Europe

In the European market, the following air transport trends seem likely to continue:

- The liberalization of the global air transport market.

- The privatization of airlines and airports.

- The harmonization of competition and environmental policy within the European Union (EU).

- Concentration within the global air transport market, for the time being in the form of alliances between airlines from different continents.

- As a result of the previous four developments, increased international competitive pressure on airlines and airports in Europe.

- A blurring of the national identity of airlines and airports. Future investments of airlines and airports will be where expectations of profit are the greatest.

- A shortage of capacity at the major European hub airports and the risk of continuing inefficient use of European airspace. . . .

- A rise in the number of direct connections, to some extent avoiding the hubs, which will be operated by smaller, independent airlines or semi-independent subsidiaries of the major airlines. [NETELENBOS 2000]

Regarding the concentration in the airline industry in Europe, about 55% of the traffic is carried by the top 10 airlines, as shown in Table 2.6.

Table 2.6
Top 10 European Major Airlines — Year 2000

	RPM (millions)	ASM (millions)	Revenues (000)	Net earnings or (loss) (000)	A/C	RPM % cum on Total EU
British Airways	72,983	102,649	13,230,000	213,000	288	12.2
Air France	56,354	72,249	10,750,000*	369,000	231	21.6
Lufthansa	54,393	72,331	8,634,000	594,000	243	30.7
KLM	37,033	46,524	6,115,000	67,000	98	36.9
Alitalia	25,435	35,277	5,146,000*	(241,000)	148	41.2
Iberia	24,585	33,313	3,793,000	157,000	159	45.3
Swissair	21,023	28,525	10,076,000*	(1,791,000)*	75	48.8
SAS	14,072	20,940	5,054,000*	(295,000)*	155	51.1
Sabena	12,069	17,880	1,969,000	(278,000)	78	53.2
Turkish	10,679	15,963	1,539,000	(111,000)	73	54.9
Total	328,626					
EU TOTAL**	598,105					

* Group
** CIS and ex WPC countries included (RPM value is about 24,600 millions, 4% share on EU total)

Source: Elaboration on data from ATW's. *World Airline Report*. 2000.

This value, if CIS and former WPC (Warsaw Pact Countries) countries considered in the analysis are excluded, would increase up to about 57%; thus, the western countries still show a moderate level of concentration. In the regional sector (Table 2.7), the cumulative share of the top 10 (out of 80) in regional traffic is at 76%, representing a high level of concentration. The United Kingdom (three airlines) and Germany (two airlines) are the leaders of the segment.

2.2.3.4.1.6   The airline industry in the rest of the world

The rest of the world, of course, is not a homogeneous area; major airlines exist in the Asian Pacific, which is in a phase of strong reorganization and consolidation. Although Asia's airlines still have a relatively good local market, many of them are now seeking to become major players on the world stage. But the combined force of the major players in the world market could represent a serious threat to Asian airline expansion. Some Asian airlines do aspire to be global actors and would be natural partners for U.S. and European carriers, but they must first develop a better understanding of how the game is played.

In the Asian Pacific area, the cumulative traffic share of the top 10 airlines (out of 76) sits at 69.1%, showing a big degree of concentration. Japan, with two airlines, takes leadership of the segment (Table 2.8). To underline the growing importance of the Asian airline industry, if the total Asian RPM value (about 448,000 million) is compared with the total figure of about 665,000 million for the rest of the world (all non-U.S. and non-European airlines, including those of Asia itself), it is possible to note that the Asian market takes 67% of the rest of the world's traffic. Furthermore, the Asian top 10 (total RPM value of about 309,000 million) represent almost 47% of the rest of the world's traffic.

Table 2.7
Top 10 European Regional Airlines — Year 2000

	RPM (millions)	ASM (millions)	Revenues (000)	Net earnings or (loss) (000)	A/C	RPM % cum on Total EU
Olympic	5,439	8,380	-	-	32	25.3
Lufthansa CityLine	2,180	3,646	909,000	50	59	35.4
Meridiana	1,469	2,858	-	-	21	42.3
KLM uk	1,371	2,270	-	-	26	48.7
Eurowings	1,322	-	-	-	42	54.8
Crossair	1,230	-	791,000*	(15,000)	84	60.5
Brit Air	1,058	1,636	273,000	7,000	37	65.4
KLM Cityhopper	825	1,179	-	-	26	69.3
British European	740	1,330	-	-	31	72.7
Air Nostrum	713	1,013	263,000	-	31	76.0
Total	**16,347**					
Regional EU Total**	**21,497**					

* Group
** Based on ERA Airlines - Regular & Affiliate 1st Members list

Source: Elaboration on data from ATW's. *World Airline Report*. 2000.

Table 2.8
Top 10 Asia Pacific Major Airlines — Year 2000

	RPM (millions)	ASM (millions)	Revenues (000)	Net earnings or (loss) (000)	A/C	RPM % cum on Total Asia
Japan Airlines	54,634	74,739	13,487,000*	324,000	171	12.2
Singapore Airlines	43,459	-	5,113,000	742,000	96	21.9
Qantas	41,428	-	5,486,000	312,000	107	31.1
All Nippon	38,424	57,434	10,125,000*	318,000*	140	39.7
Cathay Pacific	28,946	-	4,426,000	541,000	68	46.2
Thai Int'l	26,025	-	2,869,000	113,000	80	52.0
Korean Air	24,882	34,225	3,089,000	(357,000)	111	57.5
Malaysia Airlines	23,290	30,325	2,350,000	(350,000)	92	62.7
China Airlines	15,558	20,525	2,181,000	89,000	52	66.2
Air New Zealand	12,878	20,525	-	-	84	69.1

Total	309,523

Asia Pacific TOTAL**	448,004

* Group
** The Rest of the World RPM Total amounts to about 665,000 millions (Asia Pacific included)

Source: Elaboration on data from ATW's. *World Airline Report*. 2000.

2.2.3.4.1.7   The airline industry as a whole

As far as major airlines are concerned, the highest degree of concentration belongs to the U.S. airline industry, followed by those of Asia and Europe. In the regional airline business, the European industry is more concentrated than that of the United States. Antitrust laws have reduced the possibilities of mergers between companies, halting the increase in concentration. For this reason, although the aerospace industry is now trying to achieve international mergers in the move toward globalization, airlines are instead setting their hopes on alliances.

2.2.3.4.2   The Demand for Commercial Aircraft

2.2.3.4.2.1   Historical data

Figure 2.15 furnishes historical data on the distribution of the demand for commercial aircraft, in the form of the different categories of classification. The more significant notations are probably relative to the seating and to the geographical distribution of the aircraft.

North America represents the most significant base of users, with more than a third of all of the fleet world. Europe and the United States together achieve around two thirds as the two principal markets for commercial aviation. These two regions have achieved a phase of maturity that will translate into stabilization of the growth rate of demand, while the rest of the user bases will grow, especially in the Far East. Still relevant is the number of turboprop aircraft used for commercial transport (around 20% of the total), much less than in the past (in 1993 this figure was 33%).

Figure 2.15
Some Business Segmentation Modalities

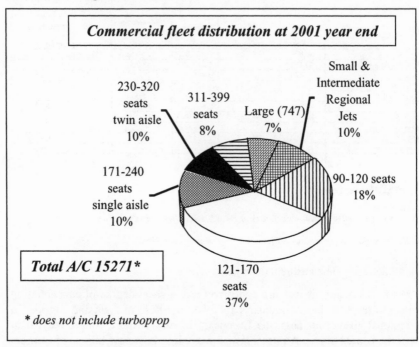

Commercial fleet distribution at 2001 year end

- 230-320 seats twin aisle 10%
- 311-399 seats 8%
- Large (747) 7%
- Small & Intermediate Regional Jets 10%
- 90-120 seats 18%
- 121-170 seats 37%
- 171-240 seats single aisle 10%

Total A/C 15271*

* does not include turboprop

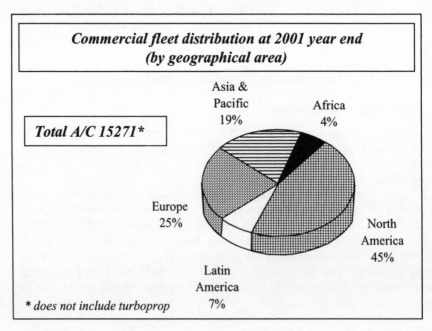

Commercial fleet distribution at 2001 year end (by geographical area)

Total A/C 15271*

- Asia & Pacific 19%
- Africa 4%
- North America 45%
- Latin America 7%
- Europe 25%

* does not include turboprop

In addition, this number would be higher if it included airplanes smaller than 19 seats, whose use nevertheless has been decreasing, to the advantage of bigger aircraft.

2.2.3.4.2.2 The differing views of Boeing and Airbus on forecasting traffic growth

Two main manufacturers (Airbus and Boeing) have differing views on how the future growth of demand will be accommodated (notwithstanding a substantial agreement about the world passenger growth rate—around 4.8% to 4.9% over the next 20 years[6]). Boeing predicts that traffic growth will be met with increased point-to-point flights and additional frequencies, while Airbus forecasts a new trend in larger airplanes, mainly due to traffic congestion and slot limitations at main airports. This disagreement leads to considerable differences in the prediction of future average seats per departure figures. Starting from a value of about 180 in 2001, Boeing foresees a slight increase (190 average seats) until 2017, while Airbus predicts a higher value of about 215 average seats in 2017.

As far as the growth of single segments is concerned (although the data of Figure 2.16a and 2.16b are not directly comparable), the two manufacturers substantially agree on the growth of the small and intermediate jets segment (up to 90 seats), predicting a doubling of the share and a decrease of the share of subsequent segments (up to 170 seats).

Alternatively, their visions are quite different for the wide-body market. Airbus forecasts a sharp increase of the "large" segment (less than 400 seats) share, while Boeing predicts that the demand will shift progressively from the large segment to the intermediate (B-777 and A-340) segment, which will therefore experience a share increase.

2.3 COMPETITIVE FORCES

It is now possible to depict the significant competitive forces, those critical factors that characterize the intensity and nature of the competition in the sector. The competitive relevant forces determine the attractiveness of different areas of business and the competitive positions of firms that compete in them.

PORTER [1986] recognizes the following forces, the presence and degree of which determine the likelihood of success in a given sector:

- The threat of newcomers (whose degree of risk is directly correlated to the height of entry barriers that protect the firms already operating in the sector).

- The negotiating power of buyers.

- The negotiating power of suppliers.

- The intensity of competition.

- The threat of substitute products.

- The influence of certification and control bodies.

- The influence of antitrust authorities.

- The influence of environmental issues.

2.3.1   The Threat of Newcomers: Entry Barriers

Many authors have explored a possible correlation of the entry barrier with specific factors that characterize it. In this analysis, reference will be made to two types of barriers. The first consists of those wider sectorial barriers relative to the general technological, economic, and industrial levels of the nations to which the manufacturers belong. The second type includes competitive barriers unique to the high-technology markets and closely related to firms operating in them.

2.3.1.1   Sectorial Entry Barriers

The technological complexity of an aeronautical program and the necessity of finding financial resources mean that adequate economic and industrial size are necessary for entry to this sector. These size requirements apply not only to the firms themselves, but also to the nations to which they belong.

It is possible to define some indexes to measure the level of a nation with respect to that of the market

$$\text{Technology level} = \frac{(\text{R \& D Expenses / GNP}) \, \text{Country}_i}{(\text{R \& D Expenses / GNP}) \, \text{Leader Country}}$$

$$\text{Economic level} = \frac{(\text{GDP}) \, \text{Country}_i}{(\text{GDP}) \, \text{Leader Country}}$$

$$\text{Industrial Index} = \frac{[(\text{Ind. Prod. Turn.} + \text{Serv. Prod. Turn})/\text{GDP}] \text{Country}_i}{[(\text{Ind. Prod. Turn.} + \text{Serv. Prod. Turn})/\text{GDP}] \, \text{Lead. Country}}$$

It is also possible to represent the combination of these three indexes graphically, as shown in Figure 2.17. The dashed lines from point B1 to point B6 show the combination of technological levels necessary to produce aircraft in to the classes formerly identified. The B1 line corresponds to the position of the market leaders, which manufacture the greatest and most sophisticated aircraft.

Each solid line represents the position of a particular nation during 2 different years. In the case under examination, during the period from 1984 to 2000, the nation represented by line B3 has acquired the technological capability and almost the necessary economic size for making turboprop aircraft with more than 20 seats.

Figure 2.16
Fleet Distribution at Year End

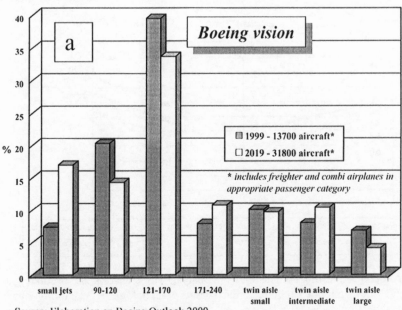

Source: Elaboration on Boeing Outlook 2000

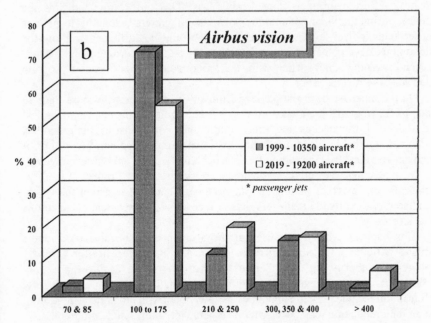

Source: Elaboration on Airbus, Global Market Forecast 2000-2019

Figure 2.17
Commercial Aircraft Industry Entry Barriers

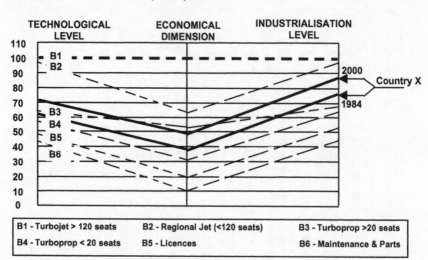

B1 - Turbojet > 120 seats	B2 - Regional Jet (<120 seats)	B3 - Turboprop >20 seats
B4 - Turboprop < 20 seats	B5 - Licences	B6 - Maintenance & Parts

Another interesting conclusion from analysis of the chart is that producing a regional jet aircraft requires the same technological capability and industrialization necessary for the production of a commercial jet, but the economic effort required is considerably less. This observation explains the recourse to international collaborations by manufacturers belonging to nations whose technological level and industrial size would be sufficient to allow the autonomous development of a medium-large jet aircraft program, but whose financial potential is not sufficient for the economic demands of such a program (such as in the Airbus case).

On the other hand, in the passage from B3 (turboprops with more than 20 seats) to B2 (regional jets), economic size is not a relevant factor; technological and industrial dimensions are more important. For firms in such nations, graduation to the level of producing regional aircraft requires an effort of technical and industrial upgrading that has been undertaken only in recent years.

In managing the civil aeronautical business, the "Product Liability" represents an aspect of paramount importance. That is the responsibility the manufacturer (and its top managers) has to face should an accident occur to one of its airplanes.

This happens when the causes of the accident may be attributed to the airplane malfunctioning, although it has obtained a regular certification given by the proper authority. In fact, before the reasons of the accident are fully explored, if the manufacturer is not properly assisted and backed by top level political and technical establishment of its own country, a quick deterioration of the product reputation may occur with heavy impact on the whole program.

The above constitute a real "barrier to entry" in the business for actors that do not feel strong enough to face alone this risk, although they may have enough technical, industrial and financial strength. This is an additional reason for the international collaborations spreading.

2.3.1.2   Competitive Entry Barriers

The main competitive entry barriers in the aeronautical sector include the following factors:

- The acquisition, protection, and development of technological knowledge.

- The size of the necessary investments to operate in the sector.

- The high degree of financial, technological, and market risk.

- The need to attain a competitive level in costs.

- The conversion costs of the buyer. [VICARI 1991]

2.3.1.2.1   Acquisition, Protection, and Development of Technological Knowledge

Technological knowledge constitutes the whole of intangible resources owned by a firm already working in the sector. These resources may be internal, representing the patrimony of scientific, technical, production, financial, managerial and marketing knowledge; or they may be external, constituting the credibility that the firm enjoys among its shareholders, customers, and suppliers. A great many technologies specific to the aeronautical industry do not constitute an insurmountable entry barrier, but this does not mean that aeronautical technology is easily available. It should be emphasized that the world leader positions are still occupied by those firms that hold the more advanced technologies, capable of developing the more complex and expensive programs for the production of jet aircraft.

In addition, the necessary knowledge is characterized by the experience of learning by doing. Technology can be acquired, but the experience and applicability to the production organizational process that allow correct technological development are less easily transferable.

The nature of the entry barrier is seen clearly in the case of Airbus, which was able to take an order from a U.S. airline (Eastern) only a few years after its first delivery was made in Europe. This elapsed time (7 years) was necessary for Airbus to gain the confidence and trust of U.S. operators and to create an image equivalent to that of the American colossuses (Boeing and MDD). The order consisted of 23 A-300s.

2.3.1.2.2   Size of the Financial Investment Necessary to Operate in the Sector

One of the most significant entry barriers in the aeronautical sector is the necessary level of investment. In 1999 dollars, the nonrecurring costs for the design, development, industrialization, and certification of a new regional jet aircraft amounted to about $1.5 to $2.0 billion. For the production of a new aircraft of the class and technological level of the B-747, it has been calculated that costs would amount to about $7 billion, while for a larger and more advanced airplane, still with conventional architecture, the cost would be approximately $10 to $12 billion (see Figure 2.18, although the airplanes considered are of different size).

The analysis of the total costs of a program (costs sustained not only for the design and development of an aircraft, but also for its production—in a hypothetical case where 600 are produced—management and acquisition of materials, power plant, and equipment) allows the following observations (Figure 2.19):

- Approximately 50% of the total cost is attributed to the manufacturing of elements and the structural subassembly (both within the competence of the prime manufacturer or the subcontractors).

- About 30% to 35% of the total costs concerns the acquisition of raw materials for the equipment and the engines.

- Development and engineering absorb about 15% of the total costs.

- Program management (the responsibility of the prime) consumes about 5% of the total costs of the program [EUROMART STUDY REPORT 1988]. However, such activity is critical with regard to needed capabilities, for joint ventures between firms. In fact, program management requires systemic capabilities that only the sector leaders have, and it represents an activity of high value.

Figure 2.18
Commercial Airplanes Development Costs Escalation

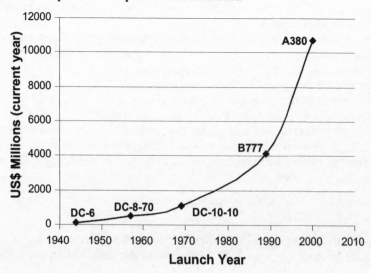

Figure 2.19
Typical Cost Distribution — Commercial Transport Aircraft Program: First 600 Units

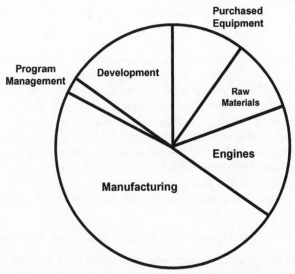

Source: Elaboration on Boeing. *The Economics of Civil Aircraft Industry*. Seattle, WA: 1981.

The activities that absorb the most substantial portion of program time and cost before airplane delivery are those of design and development. Once the development phase is complete, the aircraft must be put on the market as soon as possible, since timeliness represents one of the conditions of competitive advantage and thus of the commercial success of the program. That projection implies that design capabilities must also include the ability to manage quick passage from design to series production.

There are at least two other causes that determine such endlessly increasing costs, relative to the launch of new programs. First, there is the substantial increase in the complexity of aeronautical products. This has consequently induced more complexity in the production process of a new aircraft. The second reason comes from progressive divergence of the technological paths followed by the aeronautical civil industry when compared to those followed by the military industry.

In the past, the development of civil aircraft often derived directly from programs originating in the military sphere. The actual supremacy of the aeronautical industry in the United States draws from its military program, matured in the 1960s. The first jet aircraft to have a large commercial success, the B-707, derived from the KC-135, an aircraft used for personnel transport and in-flight refueling, was initially acquired in 800 units by the U.S. Department of Defense. The B-747, from which came most of Boeing's enormous profits, originated from the specifications for an aircraft for military transport. Boeing lost the competition (won by the Lockheed C-5 Galaxy), but it had accumulated so much knowledge (completely paid for by the DoD) that it was able to create a strong program.

The actual operating needs of military aircraft, on the other hand, set the emphasis on requirements ever more distant from the needs of commercial aviation.

Consider, for instance, the stealth technologies, which clearly have no application in the civil sphere; the studies relative to flight with high angles of incidence; or those regarding advanced performances of takeoff and landing, which also have little direct fallout on the commercial aircraft.

Probably the areas of propulsion and of avionics will allow for the future crossover of technologies with beneficial fallouts in civil applications.

Monitoring the market before development of a new program and after-sale support constitute the two critical factors for success. The high fixed costs of an ample, sophisticated marketing organization and a large, efficient net of commercialization and product support represent another important barrier to entry.

2.3.1.2.3   High Degree of Financial, Technological, and Market Risk

The financial risks of an aeronautical program are associated with the fact that in the face of high initial investments, there is a notably long payback period, which is seldom shorter than 10 to 12 years. The rate of return on the initial investment, historically, has rarely been positive. The competitiveness of the sector, in fact, limits reliance on increases in sales price, while the proliferation of competing products lowers the sales volume of a given model. All that, in a situation of continuous and huge increases in launch cost, move the break-even point (the point at which the program begins to make profits) farther ahead. The already long payback period could be additionally increased by devaluation of the dollar (the currency always adopted for aircraft marketing), increasing the financial risk, already high due to the amount of the initial investment.

The potential negative effects of this last risks obviously bear on the non-U.S. manufacturers, and it would be only partially offset by the lower costs of the raw materials (also valued in dollars). The aeronautical industry is, in fact, characterized by a significant added value and by a relevant entity of labor costs. Additional problems are created by the length of the development cycle of an aircraft, due to continual technological innovation and from the entry on the market of new products.

Further, market risks are associated with the length of time elapsing between the launch date of the program and the first deliveries. During the years that pass between these two dates, demand preferences and the available funds for acquisition can drastically change (due to sometimes unforeseeable events), forcing the manufacturer to alter a project, to review the company's forecasted market share, and to change production-site size.

2.3.1.2.4   Level of Production Costs

The average cost of a product is influenced by the consistency of sales achieved during its life cycle. Cost containment goals are then relevant to economies of scale and the effect of experience, which both depend directly on the level of sales.

2.3.1.2.4.1   Economies of scale

We will follow VICARI in the illustration of this subject. The notion of economies of scale includes at least two types of phenomena:

- Reductions in cost resulting from carrying out the same activity in more efficient ways in the face of greater quantities (economies of size).

- Reductions in cost deriving from division (via a higher sales volume) of the costs of activities that produce intangible output, such as R & D or marketing (economies of volume).

Economies of size are of a technological nature and are associated primarily with production processes, in terms of such factors as size and capacity of production sites, their degree of mechanization and automation, and so on. The processes in turn correlate to product characteristics and to the quantity produced within a given period of time.

The characteristics of aeronautical production have not, in the past, allowed extensive use of the mass production techniques on which economies of size are based. In fact, the use of highly specialized production machinery has been limited by the complexity of the product (requiring a highly labor-intensive process), the continual innovations and modifications required by aeronautical products (necessitating flexibility in production), and the reduced number of total units of a given model. Only a few aircraft cross the threshold of 500 to 600 units sold. Very few have reached and passed the level of 1,000 deliveries. Moreover, the rigidity of specialized factories cannot be reconciled easily with the quantitative and temporal uncertainty and the demand that characterizes the sector.

The recent introduction of planning and production systems managed by computers represents a turning point for the aeronautical industry, allowing it to achieve two previously incompatible objectives: flexibility and efficiency. The Computer Aided Designing / Engineering / Manufacturing (CAD/CAE/CAM) systems have allowed diversification and a numerically significant mix of different models. Without these systems, diversification would require cost increases for new tooling. But even these changes (which make it possible to take full advantage, even in the aeronautical sector, of economies of size), have been limited by an increasingly important phenomenon: the trend toward externalization, promoted by the possibility to break up the production process into basic components and by the primes' desire to give external suppliers the production of parts with reduced added value.

While the importance of economies of size is limited, the role of economies of volume is increasing, particularly in the areas of design and development, marketing and sales, and promotion. The costs of design, development, marketing, and sales show a continual tendency toward growth. These are mostly fixed costs whose relative magnitude decreases with the number of aircraft over which they are spread.

The economies derived from an increase in sales volume are due to the following:

- The costs of marketing can be divided among all models of an offered range, with a level of sales obviously higher than that of an individual model.

- The costs of R & D for a single model or family of airplanes renders the expected sales level critical. The tendency to develop various models from a basic version answers the airlines' need for product lines of aircraft with a high commonality and responds to the manufacturers' need to spread design and development costs across several versions of the basic model.

One of the ways firms currently maximize economies of volume is the creation of alliances, which allow both distribution of intangible output costs (R & D, promotion, marketing, and so on) among the partners and widening of the base market. This recourse to cooperation is now so frequent that it has become one of the primary competitive options peculiar to the sector, as will be discussed later. [VICARI 1991]

2.3.1.2.4.2   The learning effect

The learning effect results in a decrease in the hours necessary to produce each aircraft, as the quantity of aircraft increases. This phenomenon is represented by the learning curves shown in Figure 2.20.

Here the importance of the sale of the first units of a total of some hundreds of sold airplanes. The relevance of the experience effect finds its motivation in the skilled, labor intensive nature of the aeronautical industry. Continual innovations in production and processes, the systemic complexity of an aircraft, and the need to maintain qualitative standards of absolute excellence limit the possibility of adopting mass production techniques.

The reduction in the amount of work required to manufacture each airplane with the increase of the already completed production is tied not only to increases in manpower skills, but also to the increased knowledge of the engineers and technicians (that constitute a considerable percent of the work force) and, more generally, to a growth of learning at the organizational level. Therefore the marginal costs of production decrease while the volumes of output increase. [GOLASZEWSKI AND KLEIN 1998]

2.3.1.2.5   The Buyer's Conversion Costs

The cost savings that can be obtained from fleet commonality (such as spares inventory—including engines—and flight crew cross-qualification) are one of the most important variable for an airline in determining aircraft type.

Figure 2.20
Learning Curve Phenomenon

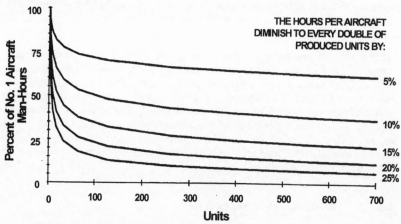

This main factor may lead to the acquisition of an airplane type already present in the fleet (or of a different airplane, but one made by the same manufacturer) instead of a dissimilar model, even if the price of the former is higher. [GOLASZEWSKI AND KLEIN 1998]

An additional entry barrier that may be considered, therefore, is the cost of conversion for the buyer, which is represented in those burdens that the airline would incur if it should decide to adopt a different supplier for a given product. The high costs of conversion have even translated into an important strategic option form the manufacturer's viewpoint. The manufacturer may choose to cover an ample range of offer with a family of aircraft characterized by a high degree of commonality. In this way, the buyer's resistance to changing the composition of its current fleet is increased (according to the effect of obliged fidelity), rendering the entry of new competitors more difficult.

2.3.2 The Influence of Buyers

The high costs of conversion facing an airline that changes suppliers would seem to put the manufacturers in a condition of contractual advantage over their customers. In reality, the buyers' contractual power remains very strong for the following reasons:

- In many cases, the aggregate sales volume of a particular model to an individual airline result in a very high percentage of the total sales of that model. This aspect is becoming more relevant now that a process of consolidation and concentration in the air transport sector is underway, with the creation of airlines that manage fleets of considerable size.

- There has evolved a tendency to involve the airlines in some of the major technical choices in the development phase of a new program. On the one hand, this practice favors the manufacturer because it reduces technological, financial, and market risk, since it results in the production of a final product that is a better fit with the demand. On the other hand, the customer benefits (particularly when a major airline is concerned) because it can influence some important decisions of the manufacturer.

- Frequently, a manufacturer's customer is not an airline but a leasing company. About 18% of the orders for commercial airplanes commissioned in the period from 1991 to 2000 have involved a form of leasing[7]. This contractual model offers the airline more freedom of acquisition, because the contract's duration is shorter with respect to the operating life of the aircraft. The introduction of leasing contracts has elevated the structural flexibility of the airlines, allowing them to modify their strategy and pursue the evolution of the competitive situation. However, leasing contracts have also increased the buyers' contractual power, given the consistency of orders from leasing companies.

2.3.3   The Influence of Suppliers

As far as production activities are concerned, first-level firms enjoy the technological, financial, and market capabilities to manage and execute the development of an aeronautical program in all its phases, capabilities that protect them from technological dependence on second-level firms. Because the industry is so cyclical and demand for airplanes so mobile (with production facilities alternating periods of working under and over capacity), the leading firms have sharpened their ability to change their own make/buy ratio accordingly.

These considerations do not apply to the manufacture of propulsion systems and avionics. While most of the components for airframe assembly and small systems may be produced by a considerable number of firms, avionics systems and engines are two important exceptions, as only a few manufacturers are able to produce them. This exception is clearly linked to the level and intensity of the exclusive knowledge necessary to produce these two specific classes of products. Although the prime requires a profound technical knowledge of propulsion and electronics and has the ability to produce most parts of the airframe in-house, it cannot do the same for the supply of engines and electronic systems. So, in the case of propulsion systems and electronic equipment, the prime is technologically dependent upon its supplier firms.

In the area of turbofan engine production, only three industrial colossuses exist today: Rolls Royce, General Electric, and Pratt & Whitney; plus two international consortia—CFM International and IAE, International Aero Engine, (the first made from Snecma and General Electric, and the second from Rolls Royce, Pratt & Whitney (P&W), the Japanese Aero Engine, MTU, and Fiat). Other firms in the field of small turbofan production for regional jets and business aviation aircraft and in the field of power plants for turboprop aircraft are Allison (now a subsidiary of Rolls Royce), AlliedSignal, BMW/Rolls Royce, and P&W Canada. This concentration has developed in the last decade due to the long cycle of realization of this specific product (the time needed to develop an aircraft is shorter than the time span from design to commercialization of a big turbofan), the soaring costs of development, the relevant technological barriers, and the need to secure a worldwide market.

Historically, the relationship between engine and airframe manufacturers has been an uneven one. At any given point, one of the two has exercised a kind of contractual power over the others. Sometimes this has been due to the technological superiority of the engine manufacturer (in the case of some important innovations like the pure jet or high bypass ratio fans). In other cases the airframer, because it offered the advantage of more options (sometimes also due to political considerations), has imposed its own contractual power.

One should take into account that, until the end of the 1960s, each new aircraft was designed for a specific engine model, and only for that one. The B-747 was the first aircraft characterized by interchangeability. This aircraft was designed to receive two different types of propulsion systems. Beginning with this innovation, the relationship between airframe and engine manufacturer has changed over time, becoming more balanced by the needs of the airlines. Now the prime manufacturers must respond to the choices of airlines, which may request specific engine models. One aircraft is designed for the use of an ample range of alternative engines. For almost every aircraft operating today, there are at least two available options offered by the most important aeronautical engine manufacturers. They supply the power plant not only for the basic models, but also for the derivative versions of the aircraft.

A similar concept applies to avionics systems. For the integrated instrumentation systems destined for commercial jets, the choice is limited to two suppliers, Rockwell-Collins and Honeywell, whereas the Bendix-King is specialized primarily in the production of systems designed for general aviation. Also, in this case, the industrial consolidation is tied to the high technological and financial barriers (additionally higher with the introduction of digital integrated systems) and to the globalization of the market approach.

The strong ties between the avionics users and manufacturers and between these manufacturers and airframers are evident if one considers that, beginning with the basic apparatus that constitutes the standard of a given aircraft, the airlines require customized modifications, including not only the number and composition of instruments, but also customized graphics, display colors, the system instructions, and so on.

One model of aircraft, then, is usually designed to house different configurations of avionics systems and products from different suppliers. This capability doesn't stretch to all of the avionics systems: the demand can be divided into two categories. The first is "aircraft specific" (supplier furnished equipment) and includes systems made by one avionics supplier and provided by the aircraft manufacturers. It includes guidance and control systems, flight management systems, internal platforms, displays, central processors, and other systems whose characteristics depend on the type of aircraft to which they belong. The second is independent of the type of aircraft and is oriented to satisfy the airlines' required specifications (buyer-furnished equipment). It includes navigation and communication systems, satellite warning systems such as TCAS (Traffic Collision Avoidance System) or GPWS (Ground Proximity Warning System), and satellite systems such as GPS (Global Positioning System) or SATCOM (Satellite Communication). [INTERAVIA AEROSPACE REVIEW 1995]

Given the unique aspects of each aircraft model's systems, sometimes an avionics manufacturer rather than being a mere subcontractor supplying specific equipment and/or systems participates in the risk of the program for the entire activity and related development costs of its own responsibility. Examples of this type of risk participation are represented by Honeywell's development of MD-11 avionics at its own expense, and Sextant Avionique, which is a risk partner in the DHC-8-400 program under the SFE (Supplier Furnished Equipment) name.

2.3.4   The Intensity of the Competition

The interdependence that characterizes the sector makes the rivalry between firms extremely intense. This intensity is heightened by five main structural factors:

1. *The enormous costs and recurrent excesses of production capacity.* The high fixed costs, which give little flexibility in the industrial structure and push all firms in the sector to maximum use of their own production capacities, create a greater vulnerability to the eventual cyclic decline of demand and the resultant necessity of making any concessions required by the customer.

2. *The height of the exit barriers.* This is tied to different factors, particularly the high cost of reconversion associated with the high degree of specialization: in facilities, production modes, professional techniques, and commercial abilities. Political and social obstacles that may be equally important in preventing the exit from the sector such as the keeping of the occupational levels and the safeguard of an important activity from the technological and strategic point of view.

3. *Government support for the aeronautical industry.* Due to the strategic character of the industry, government support contributes to the maintenance of an excess of production capacity in some firms that otherwise would be condemned to disappear from the market.

4. *Differences in the competitors' strategies, countries of origins, cultural and political values, and managerial approach*—These elements enhance the mutability of the competitive market, contributing to diversification of the rules of the game.

5. *Strong dependence of the aeronautical sector on macroeconomic variables (particularly the price of oil, general economic conditions, and fluctuation of the exchange rates).* These factors introduce elements of instability that could result in an imbalance between demand and offer.

The above partially explain the absence of collusive accords in the sector. Other reasons must be identified in the fact that the reduction of the intensity of competition that such agreements provide (through the increase in the concentration, price controls, controls of the channels of distribution, and the accords in the areas of sales and so on) do not represent a very significant competitive lever in this case. Critical factors for success, in fact, are the quality, performance, reliability, degree of innovation of the aircraft, delivery time, after-sale support, and most recently sales financing. All of these factors represent elements of intense competitiveness, antithetical to the possibility of the leading firms' creating latent accords to control the market.

The technological excellence of products naturally affects the price of the aircraft, which remains anyway depending on the market. Thus, the margins of maneuverability are limited for competing firms, rendering price a strategic variable only in cases where the superiority of operating performance or product differentiation is such that it can be easily appreciated by the market

In commercial aviation, instead, the airlines put the emphasis on other discriminating factors, such as the perfect fitting of the aircraft to the needs of the network, the vanguard of the technological solutions, the level of comfort, the reliability and the price is only one of the main determinants. In the case of less sophisticated turboprop and jets in the regional aviation, the price remains the main strategic determinant.

2.3.5   The Threat of Substitute Products

The advantage of the aircraft in terms of speed (and, consequently, time savings) over other means of transportation limits the presence of substitute products at present and in the immediate future. The recent introduction of high-speed trains, for example, could represent a threat only for turboprop aircraft used for commuter and feeder services, because commuter trains provide options for short to medium routes at a lower price/performance ratio with similar door-to-door travel time. It is projected that speedy trains will cause a 70% loss of short-haul routes of regional aircraft.

In the last few years an increasing threat to the commercial aviation sector has come from fractional ownership programs, whose basic concept is to sell customers a certain number of hours per year to be flown on business jets of various sizes.

These initiatives, launched initially in the United States and now also being introduced in Europe and Asia, are showing some success not only with wealthy private clients but also as an alternative means of transportation for companies' top management.

It is expected that after the terrorist attacks of September 11, 2001, this mode of travel will increase due to its intrinsic higher security and shorter embarking and disembarking time.

Another threat to the air transport market is the increasing use of videoconferencing, which may substantially reduce the number of business trips in the future, because it allows outstanding savings of time and money. For example, business travelers presumably represent a major part of the customer base for future supersonic air travel, and they could instead choose videoconferencing as a legitimate alternative to a trip. The effect on conventional aircraft is limited by the fact that business trips constitute only a part, although not small, of the total.

2.3.6   The Influence of Certification and Control Bodies

The presence and activities of the public certification and control authorities in the aeronautical business benefit the industry in several ways. They contribute to the definition of norms and requirements that constitute a reference point for manufacturers, by offering valuable guides in the area of design and development, eliminating indecision. Technological progress of the sector is also improved by their relationships and collaborations with main manufacturers resulting in continuous improvement in the reliability and security of the aircraft.

There are also aspects of certification and control activities that have indirect consequences on the intensity of competition. The need to adapt to tight and continually evolving requirements, the complexity of the aircraft, and other changing needs (such as environmental concerns) make it essential to possess relevant financial and technological resources to adopt and maintain the basic norms and align with new ones. These aspects can represent a significant entry barrier, particularly for firms entering the sector for the first time and/or going into new and more binding segments of the market.

Product control methods represent a sensitive aspect of the development of new aircraft, in which firms combining experience and longstanding relationships with the certification and control authorities enjoy relevant advantages.

2.3.7   The Influence of Antitrust Authorities

The strategic, technological, and economic importance of aeronautical production has, in the past, subjected the sector to significant scrutiny from government authorities, which keep close check on compliance with laws regulating industrial competition. In effect, state intervention in the form of financing for R & D activities, production support and sales support, has always been very important. This government involvement, in some cases, constitutes not only a competition factor among firms, but also a competition factor among political, industrial, and production systems, which negatively affects the free market.

Two concurrent factors are changing this situation:

1.   The creation of industrial homogenous aggregates of different nations from large areas such as the CEE (European Economic Community), NAFTA (North American Free Trade Agreement), or the NICs (New Industrialized Countries) of the Far East. In each region, rules have been introduced in an effort to create a fair competitive climate, which will allow balanced development of all firms in the region.

2.   A general heightened awareness of the scarcity of available resources and the need to orient the firms toward new managerial criteria that favor operational efficiency, profitability, and business competency.

The decrease of government support will contribute to these more favorable conditions because it induces firms to more quickly optimize of the use of their own production factors. The actions of such antitrust authorities today significantly affects the strategic choices of firms, especially with respect to their external development—in other words, the strategies put in place to improve their position via product/market alliances, mergers, or acquisitions.

In the European community, for example, a committee appraises the feasibility with respect to antitrust norms of each kind of accord among firms: those accords that create joint control of the business (joint ventures) and those that create a position of dominance in the market for one entity participating in a merger or acquisition. A practice has been introduced that is expressed through criteria, by now generally adopted, that provide guidance on the nature of the accords (determining cases and specific guidelines) and on their compatibility with the rules of free competition.

Particular attention is given by antitrust authorities to joint accords (joint ventures), as these, more than others, can conceal threats to free competition through opportunistic behaviors by the participant firms. The committee distinguishes between two types of alliances (subject to different groups of rules) in identifying the nature of a joint accord between firms: joint ventures of a cooperative type, and joint ventures of a concentrative nature. The main difference between these two types of agreements are their reversibility and their duration in time.

Cooperative accords are temporary and reversible, with participating firms remaining independent of each another. An example of cooperative accords is a program alliance. Joint ventures of the cooperative type are subject to less limiting rules, from the point of view of their compatibility with free competition. Nevertheless, since the simple coordination of competitive behaviors could constitute a threat to free competition (as in cases involving syndicates), cooperative accords are appraised for their effects on the competition and their commercial exchanges between nations. When a coordination of competitive behaviors creates organizational and structural changes in the firms that participate in an accord, therefore creating a new entity that carries out the functions of an autonomous firm, then it becomes a concentrative accord.

Both cooperative and concentrative joint ventures must satisfy the rules of compatibility with free competition, which consider variables such as the percentage of the resulting market, the range of joint products, and the contractual power of the customers, so that dominant positions are not created. If this occurs, it must be foreseeable that such positions will be quickly eroded by other competitors' entry into the market, and that the potential reduction of costs that will follow the accord (and that will likely be passed on to customers) is not negligible.

More precisely, a joint venture of either the cooperative or concentrative type is determined incompatible with the conditions of free competition when the following conditions are met:

- It increases the participants' combined market percentage to such an extent that they enjoy conditions of quasi-monopolistic extra profits, deriving particularly from more freedom in determining sales prices.

- It raises irreversibly (not temporarily) the entry barriers in a manner that prevents the access of new actors.

- It reduces the contractual power of customers, limiting their choices to an unacceptable extent and introducing conditions of obliged fidelity.

- It allows the new entity to act independently from its competitors, weakening their position to such an extent as to create negative conditions for market development and satisfaction of demand.

- It seems to be an accord of a predominantly commercial nature, oriented to elevating the percentage of market and extending the range of the product offer; increasing, at the same time, the economic dependence of the clientele and widening the margins of price maneuverability, without making a real contribution to the technical and economic progress of the sector as a whole or without adding a precise advantage for the final consumers, or without producing significant benefits in terms of increasing the partners' efficiency (reduction of costs). [IL FORO 1992]

A concentrative accord, creating a higher level of integration among the partners, must comply with the more stringent requirements because, with a higher level of integration, the firms create serious threats to the integrity of free competition and to the satisfaction of the needs of the final product consumer. In practice, the accords benefit only the partners in joint ventures, and not the complete sector.

On the other hand, a concentrative accord can also bring maximum benefit to a sector in terms of streamlining the offer, efficiency of production, enhancement of R & D, and product innovation. The firms bear responsibility for demonstrating that the act of concentration, beyond protecting the competition according to the criteria previously listed, has additionally contributed to a remodeling of the sector, with positive effects on growth perspectives that go beyond the simple coordination of competitive behaviors. In order to demonstrate the concentrative nature of the accord, the following prerequisites must be satisfied:

- The joint venture must fall under the joint control of all potential partners (a prevailing position may not appear). Otherwise, it will belong to a different classification (that of cooperative behavior, or of a merger or acquisition), subject to different rules.

- The joint venture must be structural, meaning that it is to have an enduring and autonomous presence on the market, carrying on all functions of an independent entity not linked with those of the parent companies. (This translates into operating terms as a need to have a separate business plan for the new entity.)

- The joint venture must not be a tool to coordinate strategies of the individual parent companies in activities that are not included in the objectives and business sector of the alliance. When the potential partners use the accord to disguise behaviors that result in coordination of their operations in other sectors in which they both compete, the accord is not approved by the relevant authorities. [EUROPEAN COMMISSION COUNCIL REGULATION 1990]

In the field of civil aviation the Commission of European Communities decided to intervene in two major occasions: the tentative made by the ATR consortium in 1991 to acquire the Canadian De Havilland firm and the intention of Boeing to acquire MDD in 1997. A paragraph of this chapter is dedicated to this last event.

2.3.8 The Influence of Environmental Issues

The stringent rules issued by certification authorities to limit aircraft noise and emission pollution [8], are a very important issue affecting the international aviation community with several implications from the political, economical, industrial, and technological points of view. Since the early days of commercial aviation, the development of air transport services flying over already congested and polluted cities, and the airports' proximity to population centers, have raised the question of environmental measures.

The main international body active in this field is the International Civil Aviation Organization (ICAO) and its Committee on Aviation Environmental Protection (CAEP). The ICAO initiated work on environmental issues related to aviation as early as 1968 and has issued a number of Standards and Recommended Practices (SARPs) for noise and aircraft engine emissions[9]. The ICAO's standards and recommendations are collected in Annex 16 to the Convention on International Civil Aviation, Volume I (Aircraft Noise) and Volume II (Aircraft Engine Emissions).

Designers and technicians, when designing an aircraft or an engine, must take into account these standards, understanding all possible implications on detailed component design of existing and/or future rules about noise generation and gas emissions.

2.3.8.1 Noise Regulations

Annex 16, Volume I, sets noise certification standards for the production of new as well as existing types of subsonic aircraft and helicopters, and certification guidelines for future supersonic aircraft. In the United States, a separate section of the Federal Aviation Regulations (identified as FAR Part 36) has been created to ensure compliance with Annex 16.

Noise levels for subsonic jets are specified in Chapters 2 and 3 of Annex 16; the current maximum levels of noise are shown in Figure 2.21 as a function of maximum takeoff weight and number of engines[10]. Chapter 2 noise limits apply to aircraft produced with an airworthiness certificate before October 6, 1977 (for instance, B-727, B-737-200, DC-9), and Chapter 3 noise limits apply to more recent aircraft.

To limit the noise generation of older (Stage 1 and Stage 2) aircraft[11] still in use, several restrictions have been imposed on their operation[12]. Consequently, many aircraft have been retired or recertified to Stage 3 via "hushkits," reducing allowable gross weight (to achieve better climb-outs) and /or using reduced power settings.

All aircraft in current production easily satisfy the maximum noise levels (for instance, the B-777 and the A-340 are about 20 dB below the Chapter 3 level). The progress in this field is enormous: A B-777 can make less than one-tenth the noise on departure as a B-727-200, even though it carries more than twice as many passengers.

But this progress does not appear to be sufficient because, under pressure from international environmental groups, international bodies are debating the phaseout of the noisiest Stage 3 aircraft, a problem primarily affecting the large elderly fleet in the United States, but also those in Latin America, Russia, and Africa. At the beginning of 2001, the ICAO recommended a new stricter noise standard (10 dB lower, on a cumulative basis, than the current Chapter 3 standards) for new aircraft design, effective January 1, 2006, and procedures for recertification of existing aircraft meeting the new standard.

2.3.8.2   Emission Regulations

Most human activity is having a negative effect on our climate. The international community during the United Nations Climate Change Convention (CCC) agreed to prevent the harmful effects of climate change, and in 1997 the Kyoto Protocol established targets for reductions in levels of gas emissions in industrialized countries[13].

How this is going to affect the aviation community is as yet uncertain, but airlines and airports are concentrated sources of emissions, and aircraft are perceived as energy-inefficient for short-haul operations (compared with other ground transportation modes).

The ICAO engine emissions standards were first established in 1980 in Annex 16, and they have been progressively revised to take into account the increasing international concern over global problems such as climate change and ozone layer depletion.

In 1999, new emission standards were established (representing a further reduction by an average 16% with respect to the 1993 standards) that will be applicable to new engine designs after 2003.

The aircraft gas turbine exhaust emissions limits recommended by the ICAO[14] are:

Pollutant

Smoke	(Number)	The lower of $83.6 \, \text{Foo}^{-0.274}$ or 50	
Hydrocarbons, as CH_4	(Dp/Foo)	19.6	
Carbon Monoxide	(Dp/Foo)	118.0	
Oxides of Nitrogen, as NO_2	(Dp/Foo)	ICAO '86	40+2 poo
		CAEP 2	32+1.6 poo
		CAEP 4*	19+1.6 poo if OPR<30
			7+2 poo if OPR >30

* applicable in 2004

Aviation emissions presently account for just 3.5% of the human contribution to global warming from fossil fuel use; this figure, according to projections by some experts in this field could grow to 15% (most probably 5–6%) by 2050 due to the fact that the effects of the increasing traffic, with an annual growth rate of around 5.3%, will produce a worsening of total emissions anyway[15].

According to some experts, a combination of actions are expected to compensate, although not completely, for traffic growth in an effort to comply with the Kyoto Protocol target for CO_2 emissions:

1. Fleet renewal and scrapping of old aircraft—thanks to the progress achieved by engine makers in the past 20 years in reducing fuel consumption (per pax-kilometer flown) and thus CO_2 emissions by some 40%—will improve average fleet fuel consumption per Revenue Passenger Kilometer (RPK) by about 1.5% per year, with a cumulative reduction of around 25% by 2012.

2. Increased aircraft average seating capacity, longer sector lengths, and higher load factors should bring further fuel burn gains of about 15% in the period.

3. Air Traffic Control (ATC) optimization could mean a fuel reduction of around 12%.

4. A fuel charge (or a tax mechanism) and the emissions trading [16] proposed in the Kyoto Protocol package could have a further beneficial impact. [INTERAVIA AEROSPACE REVIEW 2000]

The sector is under considerable pressure to meet environmental concerns, and the main engine manufacturers [17] are already working to develop solutions for future low-emissions technologies.

2.4 BASIC OBJECTIVES AND STRATEGIES OF FIRMS IN THE AERONAUTICAL SECTOR

The internal and external firm's objectives together with possible strategic alternatives generally pursued are observed and discussed in this paragraph.

The targets of an aeronautical company, being it a state company or a private one (that in any case represents the national champion), are generally so important that go beyond the goals of good economic results and of profit. This is the consequence of the strategic character assigned to the aeronautical industry, since it is considered as a high technologies concentration and a driver of innovation, and as such as an incentive for the whole national industry.

Figure 2.21
Certification Standard (ICAO Annex 16) — Maximum Levels

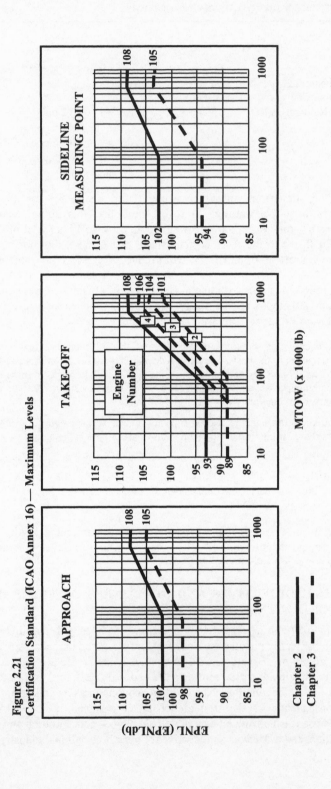

2.4.1 External Objectives (Nonprofit Goals)

The strategic value of the sector determines the external objectives of the aeronautical firms; that is, development guidelines not directly related to the strategies and objectives of individual firms (internal objectives) but related instead to objectives of the whole industry, decided by the national governments in exchange of the financing and support assured, especially in case of difficulties experienced by the national firms. The interest manifested by the public operator for the sector under examination is due historically to the importance that it assumes for internal defense. A national aeronautical industry is decisive in assuring autonomy in the main field of the procurement and maintenance of aerial weapons for defense, contributing to technological freedom and liberation from external interference.

The technological significance and the role of catalyst that the aerospace industry is able to carry out for the goals of complete industrial tissue of a nation constitute two additional motives for the strategic value of the sector under examination. Table 2.9 highlights where the application of aeronautical technologies produces technological spin-offs in industrial spheres sometimes very far remote.

Table 2.9
Some Examples of How Advances in Aeronautical Technology Provide Benefit in Other Industries

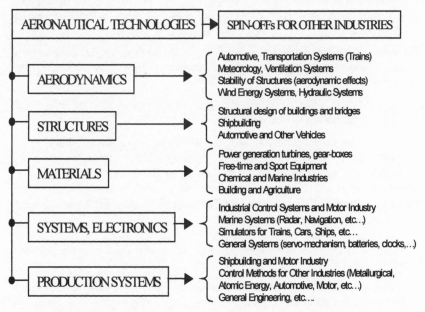

A last significant aspect regarding aeronautical production concerns the outstanding economic and social benefits that it contributes to a nation. It can offer a positive contribution to exports and, as a consequence, to the equilibrium of the commercial trade because it can produce an intense inflow of money due to the high unit value of the product. It also creates a significant human resource base with high knowledge intensity.

It contributes a positive national image, constituting an important bridge for the products of other industrial sectors on foreign markets.

Government intervention into the affairs of a privately held firm is limited to research support and the general support of the products of national firms.

In the firms under public (government) control, on the other hand, nonprofit objectives have traditionally been privileged giving strong support to the companies' strategies.

In any case, the governmental bodies employ a series of tools for protecting the national aeronautical industry and its strategic role. According to VICARI [1991] they are:

- Protective measures (when not against subscribed international agreements):

  - imposition of customs duties on imports.

  - introduction of technical guidelines to disadvantage foreign products, limiting imports.

- Interventions of direct support to national industries: facilitated loans and/or grants to finance R & D activities or to acquire capital goods to favor production investments.

- Politics of demand—concession of credits to the airlines for the acquisition of aircraft produced by the domestic industry and political pressure on the flag company for influencing the acquisition choices.

2.4.2   Internal Objectives

As in many other industrial sectors, the strategic objectives pursued by individual firms in the aeronautical industry derive from a necessary compromise across different aims. According to VALDANI [1986], the most relevant in terms of necessary strategies and possible consequences on the internal organizational structure and on the strategic positioning with respect to the other competitors are the following:

- Widening of the profit margins or increasing the market share in the context of a growth strategy.

- Protecting the business segments in which the firm is already present and/or developing new segments.

- Remaining in or abandoning the less profitable market segments.

2.4.2.1 Widening of the Profit Margins or Increasing the Market Share in the Context of a Growth Strategy

Market share and profitability do not constitute two antithetical objectives. It is even evident that the firms with dominant quotas in their markets are those that enjoy the most substantial margins of profit on their investments, with respect to the smaller competitors. The firms are able to achieve both objectives due to the fact that increasing market share:

- They achieve relevant advantages in economies of scale and on the learning curve in almost all functional areas of a firm.

- They acquire market power, in the sense that they possess a greater ability to affect the levers of the marketing mix and the benefit of an image of higher prestige and reliability in the eyes of the customers.

Particularly, the firms characterized by a high market share enjoy ample margins of price maneuverability because possible reductions affect total revenue to a smaller extent. Therefore, they can try this means of weakening smaller firms. Additionally, they can discourage potential newcomers or maximize short-term profits by increasing the product price with a limited loss of market share, because their demand curve is less elastic than that of the smaller competitors (as will be demonstrated later in the discussion on economics of an aeronautical program).

Nevertheless, in the short term, the acquisition of market share rarely translates into profits. The objective of market share can not be achieved quickly, in the short term, with a substantial profit margin. It takes significant financial investment and very strong organizational support to develop the production and commercial activities necessary to achieve this objective. Reference is made particularly to the launch of new models (and/or of derivatives) or to particularly aggressive and expensive promotional campaigns.

The following notes summarize the subject of profit versus market share in aeronautics:

- It has been previously emphasized that the relevance of cost of the program limits the profit margins.

- It has also been emphasized that the payback extension postpones the start of profit generation in the life cycle of a program.

- It has been stated that the firm must assure the considerable financial margins necessary for investment in new cash-absorbing models, for continual innovation of the product line and to support a global and coordinated commercial network.

- It has been noted that it is difficult to increase sales income by increasing price per unit, unless such a price-per-unit increase is justified by evident product features (technological features or performance superiority).

- Finally, it has been indicated the outstanding importance of factors such as economies of scale and the learning effect and their dependence on the production volume.

The structural characteristics of the aeronautical sector let us conclude that the competitive strategies of the leader firms are generally aimed at gaining a stable and lasting competitive position (a strategy for the defense and consolidation of the position) rather than at realizing high profit margins in the short term.

2.4.2.2   Protecting Present Business Segments and/or Developing New Market Segments

The goal of sales volume and profit margin increases can also be achieved through a strategy of selective growth based on the defense and consolidation of the current segment position in which the firm is traditionally present, or on penetration into new segments of business with high growth potential. Often the firm needs to widen its frontiers through access to markets not previously entered, through the development of completely new products. Otherwise, the firm risks exiting the business or being perceived as a niche manufacturer, in comparison with competitors working on a wider offer. Or it cannot succeed in developing a product in a large enough volume to fulfill its own capacity or to obtain profits from the program.

In doing so, the firm has to face two additional risks (other than those tied simply to technological and financial uncertainties):

- The firm must obtain strong knowledge of the new market and must gain a good standing with potential customers. The business strategy can cause additional commercial costs (that may pull customers away from their previous aircraft suppliers), in addition to those necessary to adapt current products or to develop new ones for the new segment.

- The reaction of threatened firms, as direct action toward those firms working already in a specific market segment is often a less desirable approach because it may induce a reprisal that could negate the anticipated advantages and cause an erosion of profit margins. A smoother approach, such as a joint venture, may be more appropriate.

MDD has pursued a strategy of concentration in two market niches: short-range narrow-bodied aircraft and long-range wide-bodied aircraft. For each segment, MDD has protected its own position through the development of models belonging to the same product family, with savings and commonality as success factors. This strategy could be advisable in a phase of market deceleration and crisis of demand.

As soon as the demand had risen again, due to the airlines' ability to invest money in more advanced and valued aircraft, MDD faced the problem of renewing and/or widening its own product line. The large size of necessary investment along with its minor position on the market prohibited Douglas from solving the problems alone, so it had to merge with Boeing.

An exemplary case is Airbus, which entered the jet market with the A-300, with competitors such as MDD (McDonnell Douglas) and Boeing offering 100- to 400-seat model (particularly Boeing). Airbus was forced to develop the A-320 and its derivatives: A-321, A-319, and A-318. In addition, it had to develop the A-330/A-340 families, and more recently to launch the A-380 family to compete in all segments of the business.

2.4.2.3 Remaining in or Exiting from Market Segments with Low Profit Margins

Disinvestment and *harvesting* are possible strategies in the case of a mature or declining market, or in business areas with a high competitive intensity that influences profitability and the level of risk. In the aeronautical industry the dilution of activities and in the long term exiting, are the strategies pursued by firms that have exploited the low market segments to assure access to the business, abandoning them when they have attained the technological and commercial skill necessary to move toward the upper areas.

The passage from one market segment to another depends, in each case, not only on the competitive capability of the firm, but also on the height of the barriers to mobility from one strategic grouping to another. This means that the upper layer of the civil aviation market (that of the commercial jet) will probably remain characterized by the presence of the two global competitors.

The move toward more sophisticated product segments often coincides with standstill market cycles and/or with phases characterized by an intensification of competitive pressure, since this situation makes the business less profitable for firms with relevant skills and structures. These features mean fixed costs that could be rewarded only by entry into markets characterized by high unit value products, high profit margins, and high volumes.

This is what DASA did with the Dornier's sale to American Fairchild of 80% of Dornier with the aim to be able to relaunch the Dornier brand in the regional segment, renewing completely the products range through the development of the 328 Jet and the 728 Jet families. Unfortunately, this strategy failed and Fairchild Dornier collapsed into insolvency in 2002. Instead, DASA, after having disengaged from the turboprop segment, decided to invest outstanding financial and industrial resources in other activities with higher technological content and greater market values, aiming to circumvent the leadership of Aerospatiale in the Airbus consortium.

Also, BAES gradually reduced its activity in the turboprop aircraft business with the disposal of ATP and Jetstream production lines and lately also in the regional jet segment, ending the production of the AVRO family in 2001, after trying to exploit all of the residual business opportunities with small product improvements that did not need large investments[18]. BAES remains, instead, heavily involved in Airbus, with wing design and production for all aircraft.

The ATR (Avion de Transport Regional) consortium, beginning with its turboprop products, has tried to pursue a strategy of diversification toward the segment of jets with less than 100 seats, with the goal of increasing profitability and entering a market with greater growth rates. (Later in the book, the reasons why this initiative was unsuccessful will be discussed.) In the recent history of the regional aircraft sector, other unsuccessful cases may be noted, such as those of CASA and IPTN (Industri Pesawat Terbang Nusantara), which, in the early 1990s, worked on two new and advanced fast turboprop projects—the CASA-3000 and the N-250. With these, they tried to enter into the business.

2.4.3   Critical Factors for Success

Once the competitive significant forces and the external and internal objectives shaping the aeronautical industry have been identified and described, it is possible to estimate how much they determine and influence competition between firms in the sector. This approach leads to identification of the critical factors for success (CFS), those competencies essential for a firm to satisfy market needs and to achieve its own objectives.

Determination of the CFS, based on the hypothesis that success is due to excellence in only a few critical areas corresponding to specific activities of the firm, also agrees with modern theories on the unicity of basic competitive strategy.

Tables 2.10 through 2.13 show the CFS specific to the aerospace industry that apply also to the aeronautical industry. They point out those elements that are considered essential for the development and preservation of a strong and durable presence in the aerospace industry:

- Government support.
- Effective management of human resources and production processes.
- Exploitation of technology.
- Effective implementation of marketing and sales activities.

Table 2.10 highlights the essential role of government support in all phases of a strong national aeronautical industry—its birth, development, and maintenance. In the first two stages, direct government support is often necessary, especially in areas such as R & D, industrial investments, and defining policies for the evolution of the sector.

The search for primary investment sources is one of the cornerstones of strategic planning for high-tech firms in the aeronautical industry. Government support can assume different forms, depending on how and to what extent the government is, or wants to be, involved in the industry. Throughout the stages of birth and development of a strong aeronautical industry, government support can be essential, also, to international alliances, through a precise industrial policy and a clear vision of the evolution of the specific sector. The government can facilitate the realization of international partnerships aimed at technological innovation, development of new programs, or helping the national industry gain high-value activities.

Table 2.10
Key Success Factors — Government Support

> **Government support and implementation of key-actions is vital to ensure a sustained, effective and competitive Aerospace Industry**

Government support

Direct

Step 1: *Establish base for industry development*

Set and communicate a clear vision for industry development
Set appropriate direction for R&D establishments, Companies and Industry bodies
Stimulate and protect domestic demand/programs
 - Domestic and global market analisys
Promote industry structure
 - Tax incentives
Aerospace R&D support
 - Direct subsidy of pre-competitive R&D

All industry participants receive benefits of major technological advances with limited exposure risk

Step 2: *Build capability in value added activities*

Stimulate technology advance through R&D cooperative
 - Collaborative research incentives
Set industry quality standard
 - Promote the action of regulatory and technical bodies (eg FAA)
Promote international industry partnership
 - Free access to international collaborative programs
Avoid wasting resources on non competitive projects
 - Maximize utilization of available resources
Stimulate a focus to compete in world market
 - *"Commercial"* focus to develope products that can be sold worldwide
 - Be prepared to change vision to reflect changes in mark

International cooperation produces access to technologies developed overseas

LACK OF DIRECTION

Step 3: *Build sustainable competitive industry*

Investment in infrastructures and human resources
 - Education and training programs
 - Facilities modernisation
Industry incentives and indirect support
 - R&D founds available to whole industry

Non-financial support to assist development of infrastructure and human resources enhances whole industry-base and its global competitiveness

Indirect

Low National Industry Capability **High**

Source: Elaboration on Bain & Co., *World Aerospace Overview*, 1993

Only in the third phase can the financial support be reduced and replaced with other indirect forms of support, to R & D programs and development of human resources.

Table 2.11 highlights the peculiarities of the aeronautical industry in the field of organization, human resources, and production process management. It shows how to manage the highly specialized human resource pool typical of the aerospace sector, which represents an enormous amount of knowledge and specific experience that is difficult to replace because of the accumulated years of learning by doing that it represents. The table emphasizes the uniqueness of an industry that must produce high-quality products at a lower production cost to improve the profitability of its programs. This CFS also impacts the design and organization of the production process, which must consider relevant areas inside the firm (benefits from the volume and experience effect) and outside the firm (suppliers and customers).

Table 2.12 highlights the skills necessary to identify and select the critical technologies that will protect and improve the competitive position. The recent evolution of the sector has made some of these skills fundamental—for example, identifying a firm's distinctive competencies. The ability to develop and master the technologies associated with aeronautical products is required by the internal complexity of aircraft (particularly considering the convergence of the different technological areas). This ability is also needed to exploit technological variables as a major factor in increasing the competitiveness of products and enlarging the elements for the differentiation of the own offer. Often the sources of knowledge are outside the firm and located in research centers, universities, or other firms. The firm must acquire the ability to dialog with these entities, choosing the best approach to facilitate the transfer of knowledge from each.

Table 2.13 depicts the last of the CFS in the aeronautical industry: the ability to create a marketing structure capable of effectively carrying out all of the main functions required for a successful interaction with the market:

- Market analyses for demand quantification, definition of the market requirements and choice of the are of business in which to compete

- Implementation of an effective sales network to establish an extensive presence on the market and effect a deep penetration of select segments

- Implementation of an effective net of after-sale support to assist customers 24 hours per day and worldwide

Table 2.14 is an elaboration and application to the aeronautical industry on the well known model of PORTER relative to the decomposition of the activities generating value, to their collection inside the main functional areas of a firm and to the identification of those activities that, beyond generating value for the firm, also determine a competitive advantage representing the critical factors for success in the business. As the table refers to the case of high-tech industry, the value generation activities of a high-technology firm have been highlighted (in the center).

Table 2.11
. Key Success Factors — Organization: Human Resources and Manufacturing

> Although human resources issues tend to be country-culture specific, successful aerospace companies have ensured that they attract and develop top quality aerospace engineers

	HIRING	TRAINING	SUPPORT	INCENTIVES
Key success Factors	# Do not lower standards # Dedicated education	# Ongoing commitment # Investment in facilities # Monitoring of results # Incentives	# Achieve appropriate balance of skills and experience in *support staff* # Provide adequate support	# Make compensation results-oriented # Ensure seniority based on merit
Issues	# Hire from abroad if necessary	# Benefits not always realisable in short term	# Promote the Government support in the educational programmes	# Appropriate level of compensation

> As the aerospace industry becomes more global, manufacturing organisation must minimise production costs through effective design and production processes and leverage of scale and low cost resources

	Appropriate scale	Process	Low Costs
WHY ?	# Achieve low production cost through experience	# Optimise use of resources and drive down costs	# Ensure competitive pricing and retain margins
HOW ?	# Modularity # Minimise customisation # Target few larger orders # Optimise number of programs	# Manufacturing personnel partecipate in earliest stages of design # Use new processes and technologies	# Choice a few number of locations for FAL *(centres of excellence)* # Experienced project management # Scale # Inventory control # Minimise fixed costs-overheads # Reduces variable costs-low wages # Sub-contracting

Source: Elaboration on Bain & Co., *World Aerospace Overview*, 1993

Table 2.12
Key Success Factors — Technology

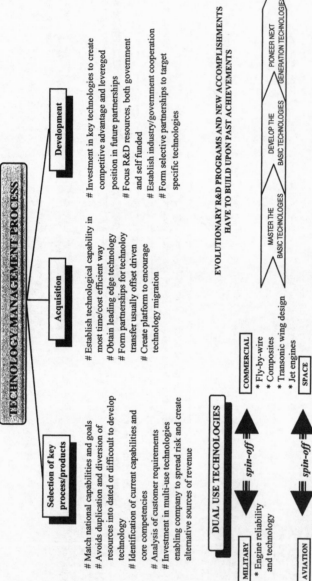

TECHNOLOGY MANAGEMENT PROCESS

Selection of key process/products

Match national capabilities and goals
Avoids duplication and diversion of resources into dated or difficult to develop technology
Identification of current capabilities and core competencies
Analysis of customer requirements
Investment in multi-use technologies enabling company to spread risk and create alternative sources of revenue

Acquisition

Establish technological capability in most time/cost efficient way
Obtain leading edge technology
Form partnerships for technology transfer usually offset driven
Create platform to encourage technology migration

Development

Investment in key technologies to create competitive advantage and levereged position in future partnerships
Focus R&D resources, both government and self funded
Establish industry/government cooperation
Form selective partnerships to target specific technologies

MASTER THE BASIC TECHNOLOGIES → DEVELOP THE BASIC TECHNOLOGIES → PIONEER NEXT GENERATION TECHNOLOGIES

EVOLUTIONARY R&D PROGRAMS AND NEW ACCOMPLISHMENTS HAVE TO BUILD UPON PAST ACHIEVEMENTS

COSTS AND ASSOCIATED RISK OF TECHNOLOGY DEVELOPMENT HAVE TO DRIVE COMPANY TOWARD COOPERATION

RISK CAN BE LIMITED BY SETTING REALISTIC TARGETS AND MEETING MARKET EXPECTATIONS

DUAL USE TECHNOLOGIES

MILITARY
* Engine reliability and technology

spin-off

COMMERCIAL
* Fly-by-wire
* Composites
* Transonic wing design
* Jet engines

AVIATION
* Digital communication
* High speed computing
* Miniaturisation

spin-off

SPACE
* Missile technology
* Propulsion systems
* Payload technologies

AEROSPACE
* Electronics
* Artificial intelligence
* Communication & information technology

spin-off

OTHER INDUSTRIES
* Materials
* Aerodynamic design
* Production technology

Source: Elaboration on Bain & Co., *World Aerospace Overview,* 1993

Table 2.13
Key Success Factors — Sales, Marketing and Product Support

Investment in Marketing, sales and customers support ensures credibility in the market place

Focus on appropriate market (s)	Establish presence in the market	Meet customers requirements
# High cost of sale for capital goods requires focussed use of resources	# Build a strong and diffuse customer base	# Acquire awareness of customer needs (market driven decision)
# Invest in quality market research	# Establish regional offices	# Build close contact with potential customers over long timeframe
# Identify realistic targets about:	# Use of communications media	- product customisation
- market size	# Develop long-term and continuative relationships with customers	- customer involvement in design process
- niche opportunities		# Deliver more than just the product
- competition degree		- financing/leasing
- internal capabilities		- offsets
# Achieve an efficient marketing organisation size, to exploit scale cost savings		- training

Aerospace companies must be aware of the different customer requirements at all stages of the marketing process and be prepared to service those requirements

	INFORMATION	DEAL	DELIVERY	SUPPORT
Requirements	# Product specifications	# Competitive pricing	# Short lead times	# Technical representatives
	# Product customisation	# Finance/leasing	# Options	# Training for pilot/engineers
	# In-service maintenance record	# Trade-off	# Punctual deliveries	# Spares
		# Offsets		# Upgrades
		# Counter trade		# Technical records and maintenance schedule
Implications	# Responsive organisation to customer requests	# Close relationships with III parties (banks, political institutions, leasing and financial companies)	# Ensure fixed production costs are minimised given variations in demand	# Worldwide, 24h support service
	# Management information systems			- tactical spares
				- stores
				- technical assistance
				# Investment in training facilities

Source: Elaboration on Bain & Co., *World Aerospace Overview*, 1993

Table 2.14
Main Activities of the Value Chain and Critical Factors for Success in the Aeronautical Industry

BROAD COMPANY FUNCTIONS	MAIN ACTIVITIES OF THE VALUE CHAIN ("HIGH TECH" SECTORS)	CRITICAL FACTORS FOR SUCCESS IN THE AERONAUTICAL INDUSTRY
	SUPPORT ACTIVITIES	
STRATEGIC MANAGEMENT AND ORGANISATION	• Choice of most favourable competitive arena for the company to exploit specific capabilities	--
	• Definition of a strategy to assure company stability and long terms development	tab. 2.11
	• Creation of an organisational structure according to company strategic objectives	tab. 2.10
	• Human resources selection, training, management, motivation	"
	• Capability to interact with the political and governmental levels	--
	• Search and finding of financial sources to feed company development	--
	• Evaluation of alliances changes (and reasons) in the relevant industrial sector	
PRODUCT/PROCESS TECHNOLOGY DEVELOPMENT	• New products and development capabilities in the cross technologies	tab. 2.12
	• Extraordinary level of embodied technology in the product/process areas	"
	• Singling out of technological paths with high development potentiality	"
	• Integration among marketing, R&D and production functions for technology push and demand pull innovations	
	• Use of dual technologies	
	• Manage the access to technologies not available inside the company	"
	• Develop and protect exclusive product/process technologies	"
	PRIMARY ACTIVITIES	
OPERATIONS AND LOGISTICS	• Capability of taking full advantage of scale and learning economies	tab. 2.11
	• Costs control	"
	- flexibility and productive efficiency	"
	- externalisation of activities when opportune (make/buy ratio optimization)	
	• Process standardisation	--
	• Punctual deliveries	tab. 2.13
	• Control and ensure quality standards to productive process	tab. 2.11
	• Meet technical and quality customers specifications and requirements	"
MARKETING, SALES AND PRODUCT SUPPORT	• Worldwide commercial network; before and after sale support	tab. 2.13
	• Acquire reputation and referenced image	"
	• Exploit volume economies in marketing, sale, before and after sale support	"
	• Promote products	--
	• Utilise all financial instruments that may help selling (leasing, financing, offsets,....)	tab. 2.13
	• Analyse and create product distribution channels	--

Source: Elaboration on M. Porter. *Competitive advantage.* NY: The Free Press, 1985

In addition, in the column to the right the activities' constituent CFS in the specific case of the aeronautical industry, taken from Tables 2.10 through 2.13 are shown.

Analysis of the charts allows the following observations:

a. In the aeronautical industry, the CFS can be found in all of the main functional company areas, proof of the coexistence of needs. In other sectors, these needs are easily classifiable in order of importance or in order of how they relate to specific company functions. This peculiarity derives both from the complexity of the production process and from the commercialization of the aircraft. It is also important that the successful strategies adopted, and therefore, successful management in the aeronautical industry, is not confined to a limited number of competencies and functions[19] (as will become clear in the following section, where the strategic options will be analyzed).

b. In the area of support activities associated with strategic management and with organization, little significance seems to be attached to the ability of the top management to promote partnership, although this has become more a strategy than an option. This characteristic is to be put in a context relative to the strategic, technological, and economic importance attached by governments to the sector and to the limited number of present actors in the business. The possible strategic options are then conditioned and limited by geopolitical factors such as affiliation to specific geographical areas or multinational organizations, and government policies in the areas of employment investment, international relations, and industrial and technological development.

c. All of the major support activities relative to the development of technology of product/process specific to high-tech firms can be found in the aeronautical industry. The only exception is the possession of exclusive capabilities (protected by patents), often present in other high-technology sectors (as for example the chemical and pharmaceutical industries). If some particular applications in the field of defense are excluded, aeronautical technologies do not constitute an insurmountable barrier to entry, as evidenced by the presence in the business of nations that are not among the most industrialized countries. Difficult to acquire, on the other hand, are other elements such as the necessary experience to develop and translate the technical knowledge for design capability, production, and above all integration. [VALDANI 1986]

d. In the area of major activities related to production and logistics, the only element not found in the aeronautical industry is the capability of standardization of production to obtain cost economies, which are very important in other high-tech industries such as the production of electronic components. Efforts to standardize processes are defeated by the complexity of aeronautical products, uncertainties in the rate and volume of production, the willingness and need to externalize part of the production that limit the ability to make high fixed investments in machinery with high automation and standardization.

e. In the area of the major functions of marketing and product support, a unique activity that assumes a relatively small importance is that associated with the distribution of the product and with promotional activities. In both cases, the traditional modes of distribution (such as the creation of nets of dealers or sales agents) and promotion (such as advertising) are replaced by activities based primarily on direct, structured and continuous connections between manufacturers and customers.

2.4.4   The Main Strategic Alternatives

A correlation between modalities of the acquisition of a competitive advantage (identification and pursuit of a competitive basic strategy) and of the objectives pursued by a firm exists.

The competitive generic strategies constitute the intermediary between the main objectives of the firm and the operating options. These last are translated, in turn, into concrete plans of action through market variables (the marketing mix management).

Figure 2.22 illustrates the complex and sequential processes that result from a firm's strategic objectives to the concrete modalities of realization. We see how many strategic objectives pursuable through basic competitive strategies, and consequent operating options, may be achieved through alliances (that, according to the objectives, will be structural of program or simply commercial), with the advantage of also lowering the level of economic, technological, and market risk for the firm.

By virtue of its commonality, the policy of accords can be regarded as a strategic option rather than a serviceable tool for favoring the realization of any of the basic strategies, that is cost leadership, differentiation or focusing. Figure 2.20 allows some preliminary observations:

- Aeronautical firms pursue the strategy of focusing, or niche marketing, only in the entry phase of business. The only way to enter an area occupied by firms of consolidated experience is to concentrate technological, production, and market efforts on a single segment of business that is currently poorly protected (according to the approach suggested by the theory of marketing warfare). Nevertheless, once a competitive, defensible position is acquired, development of the business imposes the need to widen the production range to enjoy production and commercial economies of scale and to take advantage of the product-family concept (that is the pattern Airbus has followed in developing its product policy).

- In the competitive reality of the aeronautical sector, successful firms are those that have pursued the strategy of *differentiation* and *containment of costs*. A good example is given by Airbus which progressively enlarged its offer and changed its structure from consortium to a real autonomous company in order to control costs; a negative example is that of the MDD strategy failure based on cost leadership only.

According to some modern authors, the strategy pursued must be unique at least in the long run, because each of the possible basic strategies requires a certain organizational structure and management type. Each compromise in a strategy dilutes the capability to obtain a competitive advantage.

Figure 2.22
Taxonomy of Strategic Guidelines

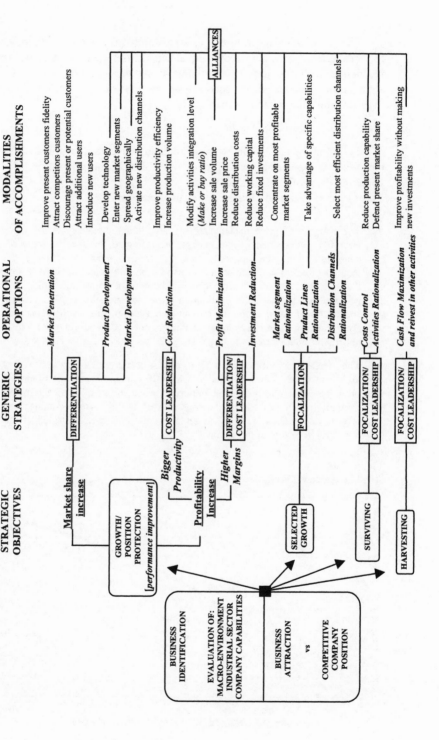

The aeronautical sector provides an example of how the technological effort for production of new, more advanced (differentiated) models must be reconciled with the need to minimize costs through tools such as flexible automation computerized organization of the design cycle, alliances, to overcome this apparent incompatibility.

2.4.4.1   Cost Leadership

This strategy has the objective of reducing costs to a level below that of the competition, operating on different variables. Controlling costs results in widening the profit margins of a firm.

This aspect is extremely important for two reasons:

- The margins of price maneuverability are limited because the sales price of an aircraft is determined by the market, according to the specific logic of a sector characterized by an apparent lack of price competition (Figure 2.23). The manufacturers in competition try to avoid a price war and adopt very similar price lists for products of the same class (although not completely alike), moving the competition to other sales negotiation areas. The possible diminution of industrial costs is transformed, therefore, into an increase of profits for the firms that obtain it (and/or additional services to the customers at no cost) but does not translate into a general diminution of the sales price.

- The increase of profit margins by means of cost controls thus improves the firms' ability to raise money internally, which is crucial for the development of new programs. This ability is most important when the sources of external financing, primarily public, are not only being reduced, but are also becoming the object of serious international scrutiny in an effort to limit their distorted effects on the competitive system of the sector.

Figure 2.23
Airplane Price vs. Weight

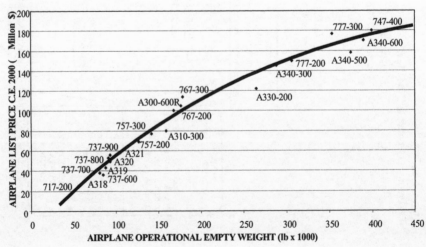

Therefore, it is possible to affirm that control of costs, more than a real competitive advantage, is imperative in any company strategy. Today, an aeronautical manufacturer tries to control the costs of development and production of a new product essentially through higher competitive pressure and a transfer of responsibility to the intermediate level of the production pyramid, also resulting in a modification and a shortening of the traditional supply chain.

Lead time is a factor with a very similar effect to that of cost reduction; product development and engineering time reduction are also similar.

The reduction of cycle time allows firms to achieve two main objectives:

• Improvement in efficiency and productivity, resulting in lower costs and allowing a competitive product price.

• Improved sales.

Together with optimization of materials management techniques, primes tend to oblige the suppler to act as a warehouse and also tend to extend the just-in-time approach from the internal to the external flows improving their working capital management and decreasing the need for funds.

The reduction of cycle times of the prime manufacturers brings additional pressure on suppliers, down to the lowest levels of the value chain. From a commercial point of view, the shortening of lead time and the improvement of on-time delivery rates are assuming an increasing importance because the possibility of losing sales due to inability to satisfy the customer's temporal needs has increased for the following reasons:

• Individual orders are always more substantial because of the concentration of the airline industry.

• Airlines are varying their offers, enlarging the scope of their missions, through the coverage of even niches of traffic, (as the case of fractional ownership programs) for which aircraft are required to be optimized to the purpose and to be available at the precise moment at which the demand occurs.

2.4.4.2   Differentiation

2.4.4.2.1.   Innovation as an Element of Differentiation

In the aeronautical sector, the technological level/degree of product innovation probably constitute the main tool for the acquisition of a stable competitive advantage and for the realization of a differentiation strategy with respect to competitors' aircraft, through continuous improvement of the product.

Although in the past technology has always held a central role, the weight of the technological variable has nevertheless changed over time. Repeated oil crises (1973 and 1979) and deregulation (1978) changed the use of technology as a main differentiation factor, rendering the economic viability of technological innovation the main condition for the introduction of new products.

Any performance improvements must demonstrate clear economic advantages for the aircraft. The necessity of satisfying the needs of economic viability has become prevalent, especially in recent years, because the cumulative effect of several factors (the energy crises, the liberalization imposed by President Carter in the United States, and the globalization of the market) have altered the structural characteristic of the airline industry, bringing about a strong increase in the intensity of competition, and therefore making less money available to the airlines.

The economic filter has forced aeronautical manufacturers to produce ever more efficient aircraft, pushing the technological lever. Most innovations reduce fuel consumption, make safer and more productive airplanes (increasing payload or autonomy), lower operating costs (in maintenance costs and through an increase in reliability), and satisfy the ever-more-stringent environmental regulations. In addition, only in sporadic cases does an innovation represent a real revolution or technology breakthrough). Rather, these innovations come about as the fruit of a process of gradual diffusion that brings about improvements often not visible but continuous and, in many cases, applicable to many fields (aerodynamics, propulsion, materials, avionics, and so on).

This aspect of technological innovation derives, on one hand, from the extreme complexity of the aeronautical product and the associated, increasing financial risks of new program development. On the other hand, this slow rate of innovation is due to a certain reluctance by the airlines to replace aircraft that have demonstrated a strong reliability with others that, although better in theory, have yet to win the confidence of users. Moreover, it should be taken into account that the acquisition of a new aircraft (particularly one with sophisticated, innovative content) means an initial effort to retrain the flight personnel and maintenance technicians. Thus, buyers will realize increased profits only after years of operation of an innovative new type of aircraft.

2.4.4.2.2   Innovation and Individual Firms

Research (and/or new product development) that an aeronautical firm is willing to make and exploit is based on the future returns that it can expect from the investment. Meanwhile, the firm must decide how much research it can achieve on its own and how much it must obtain through government funds and/or support from public agencies and bodies devoted to aeronautical research.

For in-house research, the firm then must choose between an independent strategy or a sharing of efforts with other manufacturers, as advantages and disadvantages are associated with both. For example, among the disadvantages of a joint- development of a certain technology, there is a dependence on a an ally of today that tomorrow could become a competitor. There is a loss of exclusive control of a technology that could be critical to the goals of a competitive durable advantage, and there are considerations relative to the time to market. This time to market generally is longer than that associate with research carried out by a firm on its own (provided the financial resources are internally available), but it is shorter in comparison with the time that generally would be needed to find the necessary financial resources elsewhere. Additionally, inside the firm some general principles must be in force. For instance, management must agree that technological development is a means and not a goal. Therefore, a technology has value only as a support of the firm's strategic objectives, and therefore it must blend harmoniously into the whole process of long-term company planning (Figure 2.24). Then, a change of the objectives of the strategic company plan can bring reevaluation of the importance of developing a certain technology.

Following WEISSHUHN when a technology moves from the sphere of science toward practical application to products or processes, its value and its possible limits become more appreciable. The above mentioned advantages are largely balanced by a progressive need to apply this technology to products/processes to satisfy the customer's requirements and by the firm commitments (that are progressively tighter) about "times to market" and performances of the future products. In estimating the value of the application of a technology, at a given point of time, the previously borne costs do not have any relevance. Only the costs/benefits ratio from the moment that this evaluation is made must be considered. The development of a technology certainly is an investment, but its value cannot be measured simply in terms of the resources used for its development or by its possible purchase cost. Instead, its value is found in future savings and/or performance improvement, whose application to the product increases future profit estimates [WEISSHUHN 1996].

2.4.4.2.3   Phases of Technological Development

The firm is not the only producer of technology, but rather, it is part of a universe of different entities where scientific and technical knowledge is obtained and transmitted. The distinctive aspect of the firm involvement resides in the fact that it participates at the same time in two different risks: technical risks and market risks. It must have success in selecting technologies that have real potential, not only for being developed, but also for being approved by the market. Therefore a process of monitoring, evaluation, and acquisition of technology has been created that, although varying in each individual firm, exhibits common characteristics, probably dictated by the necessity of reducing such risks.

It is then possible to define some phases during this process in which different subjects assume large or small relevance. Like every classification that tries to simplify a complex and articulate realty, the following is arbitrary to a certain extent. Nevertheless, according to WEISSHUHN from a logical and temporal point of view, it seems that some different stages can be distinguished:

A.   Observation of emergent technologies.

B. Development of the technology.

C. Concrete application of the technology to products/processes of interest.

D. Market acceptance and development of the innovative product/process.

Phase A is the observation of possible technological options. The firm monitors the development of technologies in the areas of specific interest without yet knowing which of them and when any of them might be adopted.

This phase is not expensive, because the real activity does not happen (generally) internally or with the contribution of the firm. This observation and research activity is usually done by universities and public laboratories (basic research) or by private research centers and national or international programs.

In Phase B, the firm selects some specific technologies of interest and engages in initial technology development. The firm must establish a strategy by which it will adopt and develop these technologies (through its own means, as a joint activity, through acquisition, etc.). Then it must identify the following:

• The precise application of the technology (in case of successful development).

• The magnitude of the expected benefits.

• A time schedule of activities for the development of the technology, with milestones and deadlines.

• An estimate of the resources needed to reach the first deadlines.

After succeeding in developing the technology (or after having acquired it, in some cases), the firm goes into Phase C. In this phase, the firm must begin concrete application to the product (the exploitation of technology). This phase is naturally the most expensive, and, above all, *it ties the firm to that peculiar technology,* which will determine success or failure in the face of the competition's different choices [WEISSHUHN 1996].

Proceeding further in the development of the product, there is a point at which the choice becomes irreversible. With respect to defining that point, the United States and Europe have different approaches to the development of innovative products. In most cases, in order to reduce the costs and the risks of this phase, U.S. companies, before exploiting a technology in new products, prefer to validate the technological concepts and their ability to meet specification requirements, via a demonstration phase. This demonstration permits a company to be more confident about the innovations and the related costs, and to minimize possible delays or changes in design choices.

Phase D refers to the commercialization of the innovative product, whose uniqueness also may make it difficult for the customer to accept something so new. The firm must therefore protect itself with the acquisition of a considerable number of orders before the definitive launch of the product. However, it will find difficulties in enticing initial customers, just because the proposed solution is so innovative.

Figure 2.24
Typical Long Terms Planning Process Development (Timing and Documentation)

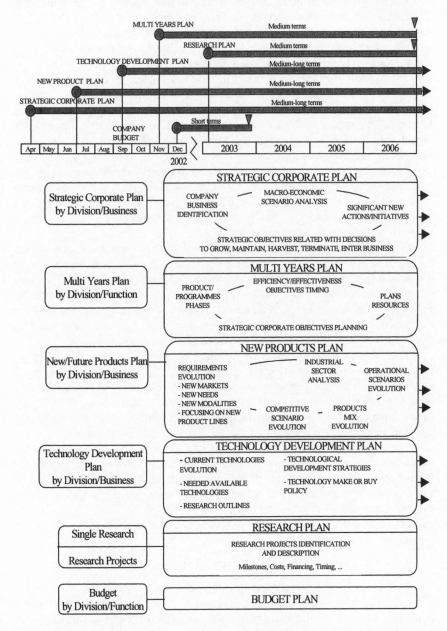

2.4.4.2.4   Denomination and Classification of Technological Innovations

The most general definition of technological knowledge may be "the translation of known scientific principles into practical applications." Articulating the concept of technological knowledge distinguishes between specialized and systemic innovations, once considered the main technological areas that converge in the creation of a product.

Specialized innovations occur in one or more technological areas. Beginning with a technological guidepost (that in the aeronautical case is defined as the "founder" aircraft), this type of innovation brings improvements to a certain basic project that remains unaffected, for a certain period, in its main aspects. (In the aeronautical case, this would eventually give way to improved versions or to derivative aircraft.)

Systemic innovations, instead, are related to aspects of systemic integration and innovative interpretation of different technological areas, sometimes stemming from advances in adjacent fields that converge in the realization of a new product (a founder). This was the case with Boeing's Sonic Cruiser program, before it was halted at the end of 2002.

Going from one guidepost to another (that in the aeronautical case means from one aircraft founder to another), requires only a different interpretation of the available technologies. It does not necessarily mean the use of the most advanced technologies but rather, a different mix, also in connection with the possibly changed market conditions. Therefore, different founders may be developed even with the same technological content, because the content is defined in relation with specialized, not systemic, innovation.

This does not mean that, in general, aeronautical firms don't try to incorporate as many technological innovations as possible when launching a new founder, with due consideration of cost and convenience. Neither does it mean that in a derivative, the innovation is totally specialized. It only means that in the latter case the specialized innovation is prevailing with respect to the systemic one.

The pros and cons of a high or low use of technological content in the development of a new project may be summarized as follows: The higher the technological level of the product, the more desirable it is, due to its ability to bring profits and avoid future problems with the regulatory bodies guarding against noise and environmental pollution. On the other hand, for the prime manufacturer and the operator, the risk increases due to the higher investment and longer development time.

2.4.4.2.5   Innovation and Expenses for Research and Development

The expense of research and development can be classified in different ways. In the aeronautical field, it is usual to distinguish between research common to more products or types of products (called precompetitive or research and technology—R & T—see Figure 2.25a) and research focused on one product or type of product (see Figure 2.25b). Often research and development (R & D) means all research leading to development of the product, including both the R & T and the R & D of Figures 2.25a and 2.25b. In the United States airplane's manufacturers often declare that the European civil aeronautical industry is strongly aided by its governments in development expenses, while the U.S. industries are not. And, as Figure 2.25b shows, although European civil programs have direct public financing, commercial U.S. programs do not seem to receive federal contributions toward development.

In both the military and civil fields, however, all of the firms under examination obviously receive some public contributions or take advantage of public research of the type classified as R & T (Figure 2.25a). The difference is mainly in perception, not reality, and depends on a different approach to the development (and application) of technology in the aeronautical field.

In reality, in the civil aeronautical field, 1992 data showed that the European aeronautical industry had received $1.2 billion versus $900 million that the U.S. civil industry had received. However, while the financing in Europe was split between direct ($800 billion) and indirect ($400 million), the entire amount in the United States ($900 million) had been given in an indirect way. If the total amount of public financing at that time is taken into account, however, considering both civil and military programs, the situation appears to have been the reverse, because the United States received $13.9 billion as opposed to the $4.9 billion received in Europe (only 35% of the U.S. amount).

The European approach distinguishes only one phase of R & T and one of R & D relative to the launch of the program and application of the technology. On the contrary, the U.S. approach, before the phase of technology development, recognizes also a phase of validation (part of R & T) that allows for the reduction of risks associated with application of the technology to a specific product, before the launch of the program. This difference is the reason why expenses of the development type, financed by the U.S. government for civil aeronautical programs, do not appear, since they are allocated to the last phase of R & T, called technology validation.

According to studies by AECMA (Table 2.15), in 1999 the research technology and development (R T & D) expenditures in the aerospace sector (aeronautics, space, and missiles) amounted to 24 billion Euro ($23.81 billion) in the United States and at 9.5 billion Euro ($9.42 billion) in Europe (40% of U.S. expenses). It is worth noting that the difference lies in U.S. public (direct) support (10 billion Euro - $9.92 billion - versus 4.5 billion Euro - $4.46 billion - in Europe), and above all in indirect support to U.S. companies dispensed via research agencies such as the National Aeronautics and Space Administration (NASA), estimated at 9 billion Euro – $8.93 billion).

The total amounts of R T & D mentioned above constitute 22% and 13% of the total revenues of the U.S. and European aerospace industries, respectively. The amount of R T & D directly funded by the companies themselves is almost the same in the United States as it is in Europe (about 5 billion Euro – $4.96 billion), corresponding to approximately 4.5% and 7%, respectively, of revenues.[20]

Figure 2.25
Governmental R&D Funding for Aeronautics, 1992 — Comparison USA/Europe

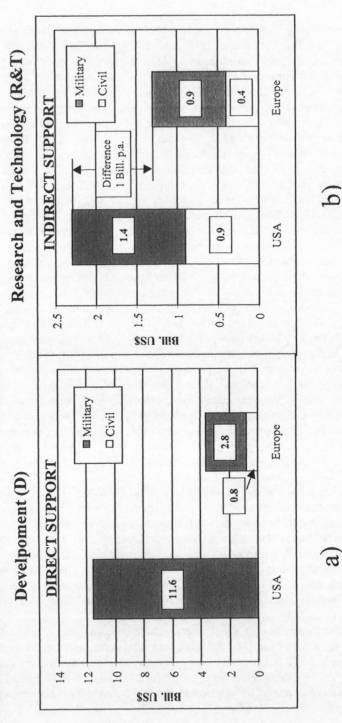

Source: Elaboration on DASA VVU/TU. *Unternehmensentwicklung-Technologie*, 1995

Table 2.15
RT&D Expenses in Aerospace (Civil and Military)

	Europe		USA	
	Bil Euro	%	Bil Euro	%
Company Funds	5	53	5	21
Gov. Funds	4.5	47	10	42
Indirect Funds	-	-	9	37
TOTAL	9.5	100	24	100

In recent years, in order to maintain the competitive strength of its aerospace industry, Europe has developed a European Research Area whose objective is to promote R & T civil activities (in aeronautics, space, and traffic control) funded by the European Union.

There seem to be no studies demonstrating that the lasting success of an aeronautical firm can be correlated with its level of R & T expenses. In a EUROMART [1988] study, however, some statistics from U.S., Japanese, and Europeans firms show a direct correlation between RT & D expenses borne by the firms (as a percent of the sales turnover) and their ranking in terms of sales turnover (but not of profit that is not indicated and would be the right parameter as a measure of the success).

Therefore, although R & T is certainly necessary for the development of new products, the investment itself is not sufficient to assure the successful management of any commercial or industrial enterprise.

2.4.4.2.6   Primary Technology Areas and Future Trends

Figure 2.26 shows a map of possible areas of application of technological innovations and furnishes a list of some crucial innovations for the competitiveness of future products and processes. The main fields are aerodynamics, structures, materials, propulsion systems, airborne systems, manufacturing technologies, and design technologies.

In the field of aerodynamic design, the enormous potential offered by today's powerful systems of calculus will be exploited. This will allow representation of the complex laws of fluid dynamics (Navier-Stokes equations) and their applications in aeronautics in a way closer to the physical reality. The objectives concern the struggle against aerodynamic drag and, more generally, the improvement of the aerodynamic performance of the lifting surfaces and the airframe, through the adoption and diffusion of innovations such as supercritical and laminar flow airfoils.

Figure 2.27, on the other hand, shows the evolution of one of the fields in which progress has been more rapid and the impact on the aircraft more significant: onboard electronics (avionics).

Figure 2.26
The Most Promising Areas of Technological Innovation in the Aeronautical Industry

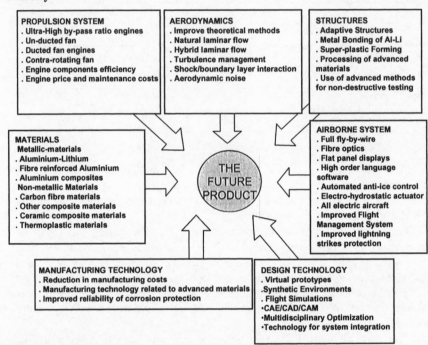

Source: Elaboration on Euromart Study Report, Loughton (UK), 1988

Figure 2.27
Avionic Systems Evolution

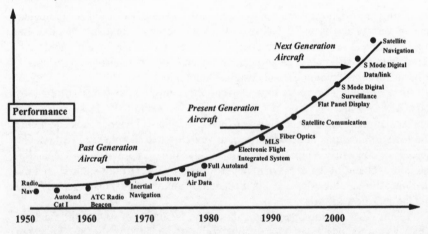

Source: Elaboration on J. E. Steiner, *How Decisions Are Made*, Seattle: 1992

CHARACTERISTICS OF THE CIVIL AERONAUTICAL INDUSTRY

All of the new programs of civil aircraft, in each of the product segments, anticipate an extensive application of the onboard electronic systems, in particular in the area of commands communications, guide and navigation apparatuses, and power plant control.

The technological breakthrough occurred in practice at the beginning of the 1980s, when some new Airbus (A-300) and Boeing (B-757 and 767) aircraft presented, for the first time, digital cockpits instead of electromechanical equipment. Digital instruments are a feature of today's aircraft.

All new airplanes, and those less sophisticated belonging to the low layer of market, have a minimum endowment of avionics and the ability to improve it through other LRUs (line replaceable units) according to the single airline needs and wants.

This differentiation will lead to a rapid diffusion of the systems now used only on the best aircraft and to the successive introduction of systems still more sophisticated.

An example of an apparatus that will quickly spread through the civil sector is the system of electric transmission of commands (fly by wire) that for the moment is used only on the most innovative aircraft, such as the A-320 (and the other members of the A320 family), the A330/340 and the B-777, since the advantages that it offers are considerable:

- It reduces the number of mechanical components, weight, and maintenance costs.

- It simplifies autopilot system interfaces and optimizes control functions.

- It allows for more common aircraft and simulators.

- It features total system redundancy.

- It protects against control runaway.

- It maximizes built-in test equipment (BITE) facility.

Equally rapid will be the diffusion of other innovative systems like the flat panel with liquid crystals (also introduced for the first time in the civil field with the B-777), the selective transponder, and the GPS system for navigation and landing.

In the field of propulsion, continuous progress has been achieved to the point that one can say that the technological discontinuity among aircraft has been rendered possible only by the availability of much more efficient propulsion systems. Their contribution has been decisive in increasing the overall efficiency of the new type of airplane, compared with the existing one. The move from the propeller power plant to jet propulsion has been followed by the turbofan, without whose introduction development of the wide-bodies would have been almost impossible. The availability of a proper propulsion apparatus now seems one of the most critical obstacles to realization of the second-generation supersonic.

There are two major areas of effort where the most significant progress has been made. The first is the lowering of fuel consumption. Figure 2.28 shows that in the first 25 years, a 38% decrease in the consumption of jet fuel was achieved, with a continuing tendency toward adoption of always greater fans capable of increasing the bypass ratio of the engines. Lowered fuel consumption also lowers polluting emissions of gas residuals, particularly CO_2. The second area where great progress has been made is control of the environmental impact of the power plant, especially in the sphere of noise pollution (Figure 2.29), responding to the pressing appeals of today's ecologists.

Another field in which technological progress has been relevant is that of composite[21] materials. Today there is a deeper knowledge of the materials' physical characteristics. Second, there has been a continuous reduction in their production and maintenance costs.

These composite materials offer outstanding advantages, not only in terms of weight reduction (allowing for consumption containment or an increase in useful load), but also in improvement of the structural characteristics of the aircraft (the composites, unlike metals, are immune to corrosion and the fatigue phenomenon). These improvements allow the reduction of overall production costs and airline maintenance costs.

Currently the percentage of composite materials in the aggregate structural weight of an aircraft is estimated to be approximately 15% (Figure 2.30), with the Airbus products occupying the top positions, attesting to the importance of technology as a differentiation factor for it. It is possible to predict a significant increase in the use of composite materials in the future, up to values that will constitute the major portion of the weight of the aircraft[22].

Figure 2.28
Reduction of Fuel Consumption and CO_2 Emission by Engine Technology

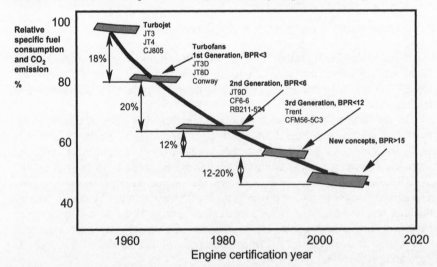

Source: Elaboration on AECMA, *Aircraft and the Environment: An European View*, 1993

Figure 2.29
Progress of Aircraft Noise Control

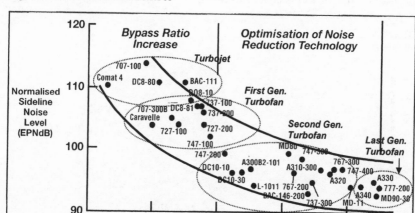

Source: Elaboration on Nouvelle Revue de Aeronautique et Astronautique, n.2 March-April, 1998

Boeing, also contributing to this continually innovative trend, notably increased its use of composites in the most recent aircraft family, the B-777, entered into service in May 1995 (Figure 2.30). The program[23] anticipated a more diffuse employment of advanced materials, given the high aggregate content of innovation of the aircraft and its head-to-head fight with direct competitors such as the very advanced Airbus (A-330/340).

This increasing use of composite materials extends even into the products in the lower market layers, demonstrating that in these segments differentiation of products through the technological variables is becoming one of the strategic levers. In the ATR aircraft, composite materials represent 16% and 23% of the total weight of models ATR-42 and ATR-72, respectively.

2.4.4.3 The Alliances.

Figure 2.31 demonstrates that, in a period of 10 years (1970–80), there have been eight international collaborations for civil and military aircraft, whereas in the 1990s (even if only those programs that had arrived at the development and production phase are considered), there were at least 19 (including risk-sharing partnerships).

The subsequent programs (both civil and military) originate in the context of ample international collaborations, the only frame in which the firms can insure the coverage of development costs of such huge entity.

Initially, the alliances were a necessary choice if a firm wanted to successfully enter the business area. Progressively, the significant advantages of alliances have induced the same market leaders to pursue international collaborations.

Figure 2.30
Composite Content in Commercial Aircraft

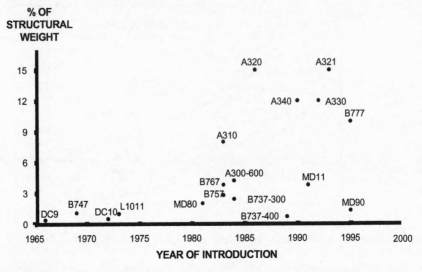

Figure 2.31
International Partnerships in the Aerospace Industry

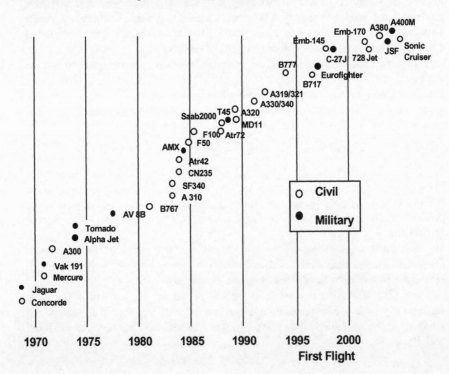

2.4.4.3.1   Advantages of Alliances

From economic, industrial, and competitive standpoints, international collaborations allow rapid advances.

2.4.4.3.1.1   Sharing of risk and program costs

According to VICARI, apart from dividing the financial burdens among the partners, a reduction of program costs can be achieved in the following ways:

- *Exploitation of international differences in labor cost.* A significant example is the subassembly contracts between the major firms and companies in less developed countries such as China, Indonesia, Brazil, Korea, and Taiwan.

- *Exploitation of government subsidies.* Boeing, for example, achieved significant economies in production of the B-767 due to contributions from Aeritalia (now Alenia)[24] and from the consortium of Japanese firms that participated in the program. Such contributions, in fact, covered not only part of the costs associated with production but also part of the R & D costs, which under other conditions would have been borne by Boeing alone. The same concept would apply to the more recent tentative alliances between well-known western companies (Airbus and Boeing) and Chinese firms (or consortia of Chinese firms, such as AVIC, Aviation Industries of China) for the development of a regional jet.

- *Exploitation of the income deriving from transfer of technologies.* In the case of the B-767, the Japanese firms gave approximately $150 million to Boeing in the 1970s for the transfer of technology, while Aeritalia paid almost $50 million of technological disproportion between the two firms that would have caused flow of technology in one directon only, according to Boeing.

- *Economies of learning and of volume.* The ability to produce a higher number of aircraft, compared with an autonomous program (deriving from a wider market and from reduction in the number of programs in direct competition) allows a firm to descend the learning curve, progressively reducing production costs, and to spread the costs of launching the project (including marketing and product support) over a greater number of aircraft.[VICARI 1991]

2.4.4.3.1.2   Pooling of resources

Resource pooling should derive from the use of already existing capabilities and exploitation of the distinctive technological competencies of the individual partners. The basis for cooperation lies in the different capabilities that each can bring to the initiative, and in the mutual access rendered possible by the accord. All members of the accord improve their own specific capabilities and benefit from the complementary abilities.[VICARI 1991]

2.4.4.3.1.3   Widening of the accessible market

By means of a collaborative accord, the partners can exploit the pooling of their respective markets and product lines, achieving the commercial synergy that allows a high level of control of the business and defense against other competitors. The collaborative accord also provides access to foreign markets, which are subject to the influence of government policies related to the strategic relevance of the sector. International cooperation overcomes the national policies that limit the globalization of the markets (for example ruling on the use of industrial compensations). [VICARI 1991]

Such a practice (offset) is common in the case of an investment in goods and services acquired by a firm of an importing country. It consists of transferring a percentage of the importing company's investment value by the foreign firm to some firm of the importing country. This may be in the form of a license to produce the acquired goods (direct offset), or in the form of buying other goods, services, or proprietary technologies (indirect offset).

Some countries have ruled specifically on this practice, such as the special laws passed by Holland and Australia. These laws establish a fixed percentage of work that must be done by a domestic firm with regard to imported goods or services.

2.4.4.3.1.4   Limiting the competition

As has been emphasized previously, one of the relevant characteristics of the aeronautical sector is the demand cycles, subject to periodic decelerations or falls. International collaborations reduce the number of competing projects and thus decrease the intensity of competition during market downswings. [VICARI 1991]

2.4.4.3.2   Obstacles to the Formation of Agreements

Despite the many advantages illustrated in the preceding sections, the politics of cooperation present difficulties. The first difficulty is optimizing the organizational structure of the corporate entity that is produced from the accord.

PORTER recognizes four different types of international strategies (see Table 2.16). They range from one extreme (multidomestic strategy, with a maximum geographical decentralization and a minimum coordination of activities) to the other (global-geocentric strategy, characterized by a high concentration of coordinated activities). The basis of a strategy of collaborative accords as an effective mode of competing on an international level is decentralizing activities to exploit the distinctive capabilities of each individual firm, overcoming the unique national natures of the different partners, and widening the market to a world scale. On one hand, it is advantageous to decentralize to conduct a geographical distribution of activities. On the other, it is more advantageous to coordinate the activities of the partners [PORTER 1986]. The degree of required coordination (and related efforts) depends directly upon the number of partners and on the decentralized activities and their content in technological and industrial terms.

The civil aeronautical industry is located in the two upper quadrants[25]. It is evident that with any type of geographical spreading of activities, a high level of coordination is necessary to exploit the homogeneity of the demand.

With respect to decentralization, on the other hand, two possible options exist:

- The firms that concentrate most of their activities in one country only, using it as a base for a global market of customers and suppliers, assure a tighter coordination throughout their activities that must be near customers or suppliers. Then the individual firms concentrate most of their R & D, production, and flight testing in a specific industrial site, in which they also assemble the parts (that constitute a reduced quota in terms of technological content and labor) made abroad. In this way, only the commercialization and product support activities are located near the customer.

- On the other hand, some international partnerships decentralize their R & D and production activities. Only the final integration of the product and (generally) the flight testing occur in a single geographical industrial area (that belongs to the leader), while each partner assumes responsibility for the design, development, engineering, and production of those parts in which it specializes.

Table 2.16 applies PORTER's [1986] model to the aeronautical sector, furnishing a representation of the positioning of the world's leading firms with respect to the two main types of accords. The consortia occupy upper left quadrant of the matrix. All of the activities of the flow of value generation are characterized by high decentralization, as the reason for subdivision of the work is to exploit the specializations of the partners.

This decentralization is evident in the examples of Airbus and ATR consortia. In the first example, BAES, DASA, and Aerospatiale (these last two are partners in EADS) are responsible, in all programs, for the design and production of the wings, airframe, and cockpit, respectively. This leads to a wider international collaboration and coordination of activities on a worldwide scale, particularly evident in the last Airbus project, the A-380 program. In this program, the European manufacturer decided to offer about 40% of the airframe subassemblies to external risk-sharing partners such as Saab, GKN Westland Aerospace, Stork Aerospace, Alenia Aeronautica.

In the second example, Alenia makes the equipped airframe and Aerospatiale (EADS) the wings and cockpits of all ATR aircraft made by the consortium. Bombardier is also situated in this area. With the acquisition of De Havilland, Lear, and Short Brothers Ltd. (an Irish firm now referred to as the "Shorts" division of Bombardier) and control of Canadair, the Canadian firm created an industrially diversified (business airplanes, commuter aircraft, regional jet, amphibians) and geographically distributed (Canada, Ireland, United States) company.

Before the crisis of the 1990s, Fokker had applied a decentralized configuration because, despite its limited dimensions, it had to compete on a world scale with the great firms of the sector. The latest programs, the production of the F-100 and the F-70, are the result of a wide international collaboration with DASA, Shorts, IPTN, and Grumman.

Table 2.16
Different International Strategies Pursued by the Civil Manufacturers in Civil Aeronautics (Regional and Commercial Sectors)

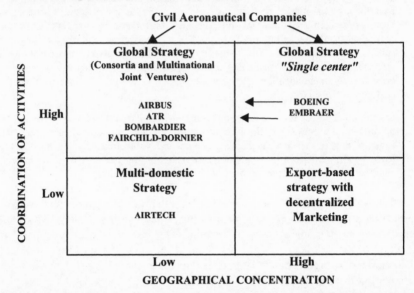

Civil Aeronautical Companies

	Global Strategy (Consortia and Multinational Joint Ventures)	Global Strategy *"Single center"*
High	AIRBUS ATR BOMBARDIER FAIRCHILD-DORNIER	← BOEING ← EMBRAER
Low	**Multi-domestic Strategy** AIRTECH	**Export-based strategy with decentralized Marketing**

COORDINATION OF ACTIVITIES

Low   High
GEOGRAPHICAL CONCENTRATION

Source: Elaboration on M. Porter, *Competition in Global Industry*. Boston: Harvard Business School Press, 1986

The Brazilian Embraer is an important example of a firm that is changing its own international strategy, moving from a highly concentrated activity to a widely diversified one. The program for the production of the EMB-145, a regional jet with 50 seats, is an example of geographical decentralization and strategic locating of specific activities.

Apart from Embraer, 13 risk-sharing partners (Honeywell, APIC, Hamilton Std., BFGoodrich, Crane Hydro-Aire, ABG-Semca, EROS-SA, Allison, Parker Hannifin, Gamesa, CD Interiors, Sonaca and Enaer) participate in this program. Each of them contributed to the costs of development of the airplane equal to the amount necessary to develop the systems for which they are responsible (such as avionics, APU (Auxiliary Power Unit), power plant, air conditioning, pressurization, braking system), covering approximately $100 million of the $300 million necessary to launch the program.

Boeing, traditionally reluctant to decentralize its activities, is currently accelerating the process of decentralization to the point that the most recent programs have seen a much wider international participation. This approach has become a valuable strategic option for Boeing, that, by means of agreements with the Japanese for the development and realization of the B-767 and then the B-777, has assured access to the Far East market, taking from the competitor, Airbus, a potential partner with outstanding financial, industrial, and technological capabilities. In the middle of 2001, the most important Japanese aeronautical industries refused a proposal from Airbus to participate as a risk-sharing partner for up to 10% of the A-380 program, allowing Airbus only the role of a pure subcontractor. The Japanese industries preferred to maintain solid relationships with Boeing, in hopes of participating in Boeing's other program, the Sonic Cruiser.

Another particularly significant factor that makes agreements difficult concerns the objectives of the potential partners. These objectives are almost never completely concordant since, more and more often, the firms that are allied in some programs are competing in others.

A necessary condition for the success of these agreements is that the contractors must appraise, in advance, the compatibility of participants' strategies. They must also devise a method by which to guarantee a balanced distribution of the benefits and possible disadvantages of the accord.

The most important conditions for success of alliances may be summarized as follows:

- From an operating (or objective) viewpoint, there are the real reciprocal interest and actual recognition of mutual advantages, sharing of strategic objectives, high priority to the alliances, similarities in project management, competence and complementary capabilities.

- From a motivational (or subjective) viewpoint, there are unity of intents, reciprocal confidence and collaborative behavior, partner broadmindedness, perseverance in reaching and keeping the agreement, compatible value hierarchies [L'IMPRESA 1992]

Among activities in which an individual firm does not fully profit from collaboration is that of investments in R & D, because of likely duplications in activities due to the willingness of the partners to develop in any case important technologies (for their own competitive advantage), that according to the division of roles set forth in the contest of the alliance should be developed by the other partner only. In some cases, the achievable advantages of an accord are not great enough to balance the complications of the collaboration. Experience, however, demonstrates that in the majority of cases, complications come more from incorrect structuring of the cooperation. [VICARI 1991]

2.4.4.3.3   Choice of a Partner: A Regional Transport Example

The regional transport business represents a significant example of a sector in which the formation of international alliances has become the prevailing practice. The specific reasons for this competitive evolution are the following:

- The industrial and commercial capabilities of the firms engaged in the sector exceed the demand, requiring a production consolidation that is translated into a reduction in the number of competitors and streamlining of their product lines.

- The financial risks have become high. The increasing development costs of regional aircraft (now more sophisticated than in the past) and their unit prices, because of the intensity of competition, are such as to barely allow coverage of program costs, making it difficult for an individual firm to survive in the business (to raise internally the financial resources necessary to develop the business).

- The scarcity of financial resources for manufacturers forces the firms to preserve the economic viability of their programs and to maintain reasonable production rates that may be incompatible with the actual market situation.

2.4.4.3.3.1   The ideal partner

Prior to the identification of a partner, there must be an evaluation of the structural characteristics of the sector. After that analysis, a firm should follow the ideal model represented in Table 2.17:

I.   Identify companies characterized by highly complementary products/markets and strong competitive positions inside attractive business segments.

II.   Check the availability of potential partners to a policy of alliance, then identify (with equal care) the best candidate for the alliance.

Assume that in the regional transport sector in the early 1990s, there was a search for partnership among the main aircraft manufacturers. Figures 2.32, 2.33, and 2.34 represent the logical steps and activities of analysis relative to the first point (I) noted above and illustrated in Table 2.17. Figure 2.32 contains a matrix that highlights the situation at that time in the regional transport sector, using ATR (one of the market leaders) as an example. The first factor for analysis of potential partners is created by product overlap; that is, the possible similarity or duplication (in technological terms) of the aircraft of different firms. The second factor is the market overlap, in terms of served markets and homogeneity of the capabilities necessary to operate in them because of the type of customers.

Alliances with firms owning products with a high degree of overlap are oriented to minimize the competitive mutual pressure, to maximize control of the common market, and to manage the elements of the marketing mix. Nevertheless, such accords create problems surmountable only with great difficulty (with respect to the antitrust authorities) and inspire strong reactions from the other competitors. The search for a solid structural alliance that allows the preservation of a dominant position in the business must imply a certain degree of product market complementarity, since a major result is the wider range of products offered without short-term investment of financial resources for new product development. So it is clear that if a potential partner is present in the market with complementary products of its own, it is easier to achieve mutually advantageous accords.

Having rejected, then, those firms characterized by a significant overlap of product/market with its own line, the company seeking a partner must choose a firm through evaluation of prospects' competitive positions on the basis of strategically relevant factors: that is, their operation in highly attractive market segments (according to significant indicators).

Table 2.17
A Possible Approach to the Potential Partners Identification

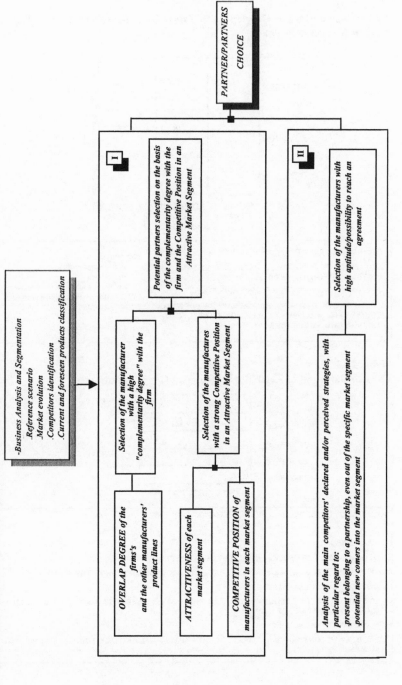

Figure 2.32
ATR Product/Market Overlap with Other Manufacturers in the 20-130 Seat Aircraft Market Segment

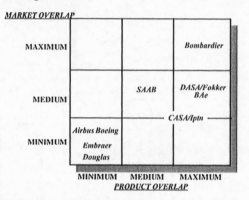

FACTORS CONTRIBUTING TO MARKET OVERLAP	*With reference to:*
- COMPETITION REFERRED TO MARKET SEGMENTS, CUSTOMER TIPOLOGY, USE DESTINATION, ETC.	. aircraft in production
FACTORS CONTRIBUTING TO PRODUCT OVERLAP	. aircraft in development
	. aircraft in study close to be launched
- COMPETITION WITH SIMILAR AIRCRAFT REFERRED TO ENGINE TYPE, SPEED PERFORMANCE, PRESSURIZATION, TECHNOLOGICAL CONTENT, ETC.	. aircraft in study with high probability to be launched

Figure 2.33
The Attractiveness of Each Market Segment (1993 Conditions)

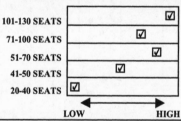

FACTORS CONTRIBUTING TO EACH SINGLE MARKET SEGMENT ATTRACTIVENESS

• FUTURE SIZE

• GLOBAL SIZE OF THE FIRMS COMPETING IN TO THE SEGMENT

• SPECIFIC SIZE *(in the aerospace production)* OF THE FIRMS COMPETING IN TO THE SEGMENT

• DEGREE OF CONCENTRATION

• OVERALL NUMBER OF PROGRAMS IN PRODUCTION, DEVELOPMENT, CLOSE TO BE LAUNCHED, WITH HIGH PROBABILITY TO BE LAUNCHED

• MATURITY OF THE PRODUCTS

• PRESENCE IN CONTIGUOUS SEGMENTS OF THE FIRMS COMPETING INTO THE SEGMENT WITH OTHER MEMBERS OF A FAMILY

Figure 2.34
The Forecasted Competitive Position of Manufacturers in Each Market Segment —
1993 Conditions

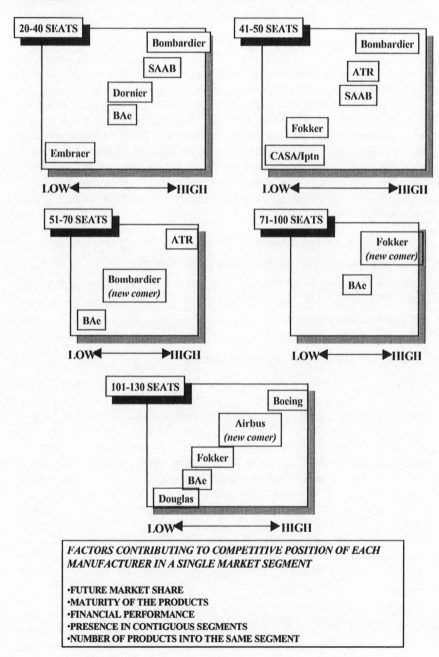

FACTORS CONTRIBUTING TO COMPETITIVE POSITION OF EACH
MANUFACTURER IN A SINGLE MARKET SEGMENT

•FUTURE MARKET SHARE
•MATURITY OF THE PRODUCTS
•FINANCIAL PERFORMANCE
•PRESENCE IN CONTIGUOUS SEGMENTS
•NUMBER OF PRODUCTS INTO THE SAME SEGMENT

Figures 2.33 and 2.34 refer to the attractiveness of the regional transport segment and to the competitive position of the firms operating there. The evaluation of the attractiveness of the business segments considers not only the rate of growth of the market, but other elements that measure the intensity of competition present there.

It is evident that a market of significant proportions and with high potential (in which, nevertheless, a great number of firms operate, with important dimensions and capabilities) could be less attractive with respect to another segment of limited size in which the intensity of competition is lower.

Similarly, the competitive position of the firms is not measured simply by their market share, but also by other factors that highlight their strengths and weaknesses in terms of their financial performance and the breadth and potential of their product range. Selecting several possible partners on the basis of these criteria, the firm can then pass to the phase of checking the real availability of the possible ally, trying to understand its strategic motivations (point II above and in Table 2.17). Some specific elements of the strategic and industrial spheres need to be better understood:

- The convergence of long-term strategic objectives.

- The expanding customer base and its geographical coverage.

- The possible reaction of competitors excluded from the alliance and of the antimonopolistic bodies.

- The decreasing competition.

- The access to financial resources necessary for the development of new products.

- The industrial coordination between the partners.

The alliance between ATR and British Aerospace, with the creation of the new company named AIR (Air International Regional), testifies that the main conditions previously indicated in point I (the potential partner's complementary and strong competitive position in attractive market segments) are very important, but that also point II elements must be considered with the same care. The ideal partner for ATR seemed to be Saab (with whom the consortium made a long negotiation without positive conclusion) and BAES In the end, British Aerospace became ATR's partner by virtue of a wider evaluation than that of only product/market. Rather, the convergence of interests and strategic paths of the three partners (Alenia, Aerospatiale, and BAES) from a long-term point of view became more important. As will be later illustrated, this factor became the most critical one, when the change in the competitive scenario (Fokker bankruptcy) made it diverging the long-term interests and objectives of the partners.

2.5   COMPETITION ANALYSIS

The product policy in its substance depends especially on the belonging to one of the strategic groups in which it is possible to diversify the offer, as mentioned above. All this clearly comes out of a historical analysis of the market leaders behavior, meaning those companies coming from the airframe sub-sector and having the responsibility of the whole program management.

2.5.1   Main Characteristics of the Competitive System

The aeronautical industry is an oligopoly. In the last 20 years, the number of prime firms present on the market has been severely contained. There were only a few primes, if one takes into account only those that had a strong control of the market in terms of percent of the total sales turnover. As a confirmation, it can be noted that in 1994, Boeing, leader of the commercial jet sector, had close to a 55% market share; Boeing and the other two leading firms (Airbus and McDonnell Douglas) held a total market share of nearly 90%, with Fokker and British Aerospace dividing the remaining percentage.

From 1996 to 1997, the concentration was additionally increased with the acquisition of McDonnell Douglas by Boeing, the exit of Fokker from the market, and the progressive loss of market shares by British Aerospace, consequent to the British firm's decision not to invest further in the segment.

In 2000, the commercial aircraft (those with more than 100 seats) sector was substantially a duopoly. Boeing had a 54% market share in terms of units ordered (57% in terms of value), while Airbus held the remaining 46% (43% in terms of value). In the regional segment, the Canadian firm Bombardier (35.8% in terms of orders, 39.6% in terms of value) and the Brazilian Embraer (49.5% of orders, 43.4% of value) had control of the sector, with the other competitors (ATR, AVRO-RJ – Regional Jet, Fairchild-Dornier) far behind.

The characteristics of the aircraft made by competing firms determine one specific type of oligopoly, the diversified oligopoly. Each manufacturer offers models that, although having a high degree of homogeneity with those of the competition (in the sense that they carry out substantially the same use, are destined for the same groups of users—airlines—and are produced with the same basic technologies of design and product/process), are different in terms of technological content and thus in terms of performance and operating costs. [ABELL 1986]

The price of aircraft is another important differentiation that is used as a competitive lever. However, the price battle occurs in a latent manner, making it to appear that the aeronautical sector is characterized by no competition on price.

In reality, the manufacturers are well aware of the disastrous consequences that would result from an open price war. Such an open battle would jeopardize the stability and profitability (already limited) of the sector. Given the strong direct and indirect involvement of governments in the industrial and commercial activities of aeronautical firms, any important change (reduction) in the price of aircraft by an individual firm would be perceived by others as a clear sign of unacceptable government support. This perception would cause the controlling bodies and authorities to intervene, and it would result in serious retaliatory behaviors from other firms (see the price war between Bombardier and Embraer in the years 1990s). It is evident that these consequences would undermine the profitability of the whole sector. Therefore, the aeronautical industries apply other market strategies that, although not appearing to be price strategies, in substance are equivalent.

These alternate strategies may include particularly advantageous sale conditions, less attractive than price reductions but similar in effect to a reduction of cost of the offer. They may consist of conspicuous sales financing, customization of the aircraft almost without charge, advantageous offers on spare parts and maintenance, and/or free training of the crews.

2.5.2   Competitive Strategies as a Function of Strategic Groupings of Affiliation

All of the firms operating in the aeronautical civil sector pursue a strategy of production diversification to compensate for the high fixed costs and to saturate to the greatest possible extent their own production capacities, particularly in the face of cyclical demand. The practicality of this strategy is nevertheless conditioned by the technological level of the firm is able to express, and by the risk that it is ready to accept.

Let's consider first the firms in the turboprop aircraft sector, characterized by a lower level of technological complexity and financial risk (represented on the left side of AT3 in Figure 2.13).

Here, the small manufacturers entered the commercial arena and were initially oriented to a high segmentation in terms of product strategies, corresponding to a limited width of the range of offer in the specific sector, to focusing in niches of products. The competitive intensity tied to the proliferation of directly competing programs and to the decline of demand induced firms in this market segment to seek to acquire the financial and technological capabilities necessary to differentiate their offer.

The recent demand for regional aircraft (shown in the upper right area of AT3 and the lower left area of AT2 of Figure 2.13) has allowed some of those firms with enough financial and technological capabilities to exploit the commercial success of programs developed in the area of the commuter and widen range of product. The regional jet manufacturers occupy the RS2 area of Figure 2.14, which corresponds to a width of intermediary range with respect to that of the manufacturers of exclusively turboprop aircraft and to that of the market leaders. This area of market includes aircraft of various sizes (50 to 100 seats), with both turboprop and turbofan propulsion.

During the early 1990s, several events had significant impact on this market segment: some significant firms' exits from the business area—Fokker, Saab, BAES in the regional turboprop segment, the AI(R) (Aero International Regional) termination and the arrival of some regional jet manufacturers (Bombardier, Embraer, and Fairchild-Dornier). A later paragraph explores these events and the consequent evolution of the competitive scenario.

Also, the primes of the commercial market (belonging to the RS1 area of Figure 2.14) have found a segment of natural diversification in regional transport, since that line of products includes airplanes that may be used for operations on short routes. This approach represents a threat for firms working in the segment with smaller airplanes, since it could reduce potential profit margins and increase the intensity of competition (for instance, aircraft such as Boeing's B-737-600 and B-717-200 of Boeing and the Airbus A-318, the smallest member of the A-320 family, shown in the upper right of area AT2 of Figure 2.13).

This situation exposes the regional segment to a doubly competitive pressure. First, there is the pressure from firms of the upper layer (RS1) that would not be stopped by the entry barriers to area RS2, since they already enjoy the technological and financial resources necessary to compete with success in this specific segment of business. The second competitive pressure comes from the most competitive firms of the lower layer of market (RS3) that wish to be involved in more complex programs. In such conditions, the regional segment, although ample in terms of both unity and value, presents outstanding risks tied to a high intensity of competition.

The high technological and financial entry barriers to area RS1 of Figure 2.14 make clear the reasons for the high concentration of primes in this specific production segment (the duopoly). These firms present a considerable width of range when compared to that of the others belonging to the two preceding groupings, but even they do not cover the totality of the market segments.

The whole strategy of each of the two firms present there is in fact aimed toward better product diversification. This diversification is accomplished through an ampler coverage of the market segments and a technological differentiation of products inside the same segments.

2.5.3   Behavior and Performance of Market Leaders

2.5.3.1   Firms Operating in the High Segments of the Offer

From the end of World War II until the 1980s, the American aeronautical industry enjoyed a practical monopoly in the field of commercial aviation, taking advantage of a particular historical situation. After the war, until the 1970s, the principal U.S. manufacturers (Boeing, Lockheed, and MDD) traditionally participated in the business through their own production, completely autonomous and integrated, and favored by the size of the internal market, by the technological and financial fallout of the enormous military market, and by their own production, managerial, and economic forces. These conditions allowed the advantage of significant reduction of cost (through the exploitation of scale and learning economies) and the obtaining of a position of cost leadership. Beyond that, a technological and financial dominance was achieved which, up to a few years ago, was unassailable.

On the opposite side, the European postwar aeronautical manufacturers were experiencing a shortage of resources and were divided. They designed their airplanes for national markets smaller than that of the United States. The assistance offered to their customers was not comparable to that offered by Boeing, Lockheed, or Douglas. The help given to military production was not of the same size as that of United States, and the national policies of orientation and support to the civil aeronautical field were not as effective as those in the United States. A change has come with the birth of the Airbus consortium; however, that success was achieved only after many years of enormous effort and huge investments.

Airbus achieved its purpose through the technological excellence of its products and the globalization of its market approach, tools that required considerable time and cost. But despite its successes in recent years, the Airbus efforts to penetrate the U.S. market are still very intense, because the U.S. domestic competition still holds a position of dominance in this geographical area where the largest world market of commercial aircraft is concentrated today. Perhaps the final major effect of this exceptional global competition in the sector has been the merging of MDD into Boeing. It must be emphasized that the U.S. industry consolidation, with the creation of the colossal Lockheed Martin corporation in the defense sector, surely had a significant influence.

Before proceeding to an analysis of the strategies of the market leaders, it is interesting to characterize the firms by means of some significant data.

Table 2.18 shows, for the year 2000, the aerospace and defense and commercial aircraft sales turnover and employees of the two main world's manufacturers. For Airbus, reference is made to its shareholders activities, EADS and BAE SYSTEMS respectively owning 80% and 20% of Airbus.

Such data allow the following observations:

- In terms of turnover, a Boeing's supremacy still exists, with its sales turnover (in the commercial sector) about 80% more than that of Airbus. Today, this is mainly due to:

  a.   The difference in number of deliveries (489 Boeing deliveries versus 311 Airbus deliveries in 2000).

  b.   The higher average unit value for the Boeing airplanes; and

  c.   The after-sale support, considering that the two manufacturers' fleets in service worldwide are quite different: about 81% for Boeing, 17% for Airbus, and 2% for Lockheed in 2000.

- The relative importance of the commercial aircraft business is quite the same for EADS and for Boeing: about 61% of total sales, a figure that reflects the significant concentration of the two companies' activities and therefore the dependence of their total results on this business area. BAE SYSTEMS is mainly focused instead on the military sector (combat aircraft and defense electronics), pursuing the commercial business as an opportunity with good profit margins.

Table 2.18
Year 2000 Aerospace & Defense and Commercial Aircraft Sales Turnover and Employees

	AIRBUS			BOEING
	EADS	BAE Systems	Total	
Total Aerospace and Defense sales (A)	$ 22.36 Bil	$ 18.43 Bil	-	$ 51.40 Bil
Commercial Aircraft sales (B)	$ 13.72 Bil	$ 3.43 Bil	$ 17.15 Bil	$ 31.17 Bil
% (B)/(A)	61%	18.6%	-	60.6%
Employees in commercial a/c business	33900	8700*	45600**	91000

* - Estimated by the author; ** - includes 3000 additional employees belonging to Airbus H/Q structure.

The difference between sales turnover for Boeing and Airbus is less evident if one compares their commercial aircraft orders values: 57% (about $34 billion) for Boeing and 43% (about $26 billion) for Airbus. The expected trend is toward a roughly 50-50 sharing of the commercial market.

2.5.3.1.1   Perceived Strategies

Analysis of the product/market matrix of the commercial jet leaders of the sector provides an understanding of the competitive strategies of the two main firms, Boeing and Airbus, and their possible long-term competitive positioning. (MDD[26] was a third competitor until 1996, when the company merged with Boeing.)

2.5.3.1.1.1   Boeing strategy

Boeing pursues a product/market strategy aimed at coverage of most segments of offer, within which it also practices an outstanding differentiation of products (see Figure 2.35). The B-747played an important role. This aircraft, by virtue of its exceptional size and performance, has enjoyed a virtual monopoly until today, reflected in a highly profitable price (about $180 million in 1999), considering that the non recurring costs were paid long ago. In the recent past, other wide-bodied aircraft, notably the MD-11, A-340, and B-777 (the nearest in terms of general characteristics to the B-747) have been operated to satisfy the demand for intercontinental connections with a lower traffic density. For this reason, they have eroded only a small quota of the 747 market.

Figure 2.35
Present Products and Future Development of Boeing Portfolio

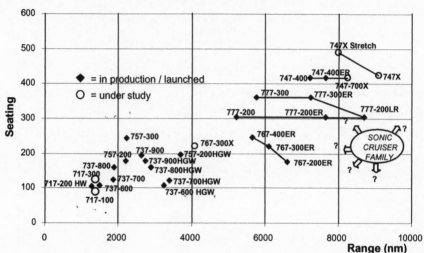

Production of the B-747 was launched in 1966, following an order for 25 units by PanAm. The effort that Boeing invested in developing the aircraft was so huge that a failure of the program would (and almost did) result in the company's bankruptcy. The history of the jumbo jet is, instead, that of an extraordinary commercial success.

After 25 years of service, the aircraft picked up its 1,285th sale in September 2001, constituting not only a relevant element in the sales turnover of Boeing, but also one of the greatest earnings of any U.S. export.

According to some industry analysts, the profit Boeing has made on B-747 has allowed huge discounts on its smaller aircraft. The privileged condition of monopoly in the B-747 segment ended with the Airbus decision in December 2000 to launch the very large A-380.

For some time before that formal Airbus decision, Boeing had been searching for a suitable product strategy to pursue the long-range aircraft segment. At the beginning (during 1996 and 1997), it seemed that the company would launch a derivative version of the B-747 with major changes (new wing, engines, fuselage) to fight a head-to-head battle with Airbus in the 400-plus seats segment. This initiative was characterized by some concerns. Notwithstanding that the product was a derivative, it would have required significant development costs ($7–$8 billion). In 1997, Boeing decided to abandon this project, announcing that, according to its market forecast, there would not be sufficient market to justify the initiative from an economic and financial point of view.

Consequently, Boeing decided to undertake a completely new product strategy based on these concepts:

- In the short to medium term, it would exploit its airplanes' capabilities and continuously add improvements to its existing products.

- In the long term, it would introduce of a new aircraft family better able to meet customers' requirements of flying faster and more comfortably.

So, in the short to medium term, Boeing's business strategy is based on exploitation of its current product portfolio, from the single-aisle segment (B-717, B-737, and B-757) to the twin-aisle (B-767 and B-777) and the very large (the B-747) segments. According to this product strategy, Boeing has recently launched (or is planning to launch) improvement programs or stretching / shortening / extended-range versions of existing products.

- The new B-737 family (B-600/-700/-800/-900 members) is characterized by a series of innovations (modified wing and tail, digital avionics, new engines, and redrawn nacelles) that have significantly improved performance in terms of speed, seating, autonomy, and operating costs.

- Extended-range and (maybe) the last, moderate stretched versions of the B-747 (presently in the study phase) will soon confront the A-380, competitively leveraging a low enough price to continue to meet the airlines' interest.

- Derivative versions of the B-757 (-200HGW – High Gross Weight - and -300) and the B-767 (-300X and -400ER – Extended Range) to fully exploit the growth potential of these programs.

- New additional versions of the B-777 render this a family of aircraft as complete as possible in terms of range, seating, and meeting the customers' needs for the long-range segment.

As far as its long-term strategy is concerned, Boeing, after having undertaken secret studies, unveiled its project of a faster, longer-range airplane family called the Sonic Cruiser, in early 2001. The Sonic Cruiser meant almost a revolution in the way that the air transportation system is conceived. In fact, until now the main goal for the airlines has been to achieve higher and higher efficiency, essentially by increasing average seating capacity; that is what Airbus is doing with the A-380.

Now, after focused market surveys, Boeing appeared confident that airlines (and their passengers) would tolerate an operating cost increase (and higher ticket prices) to achieve product differentiation and a faster transportation system. Boeing believed that in the next few years, the market would be ready to accept a new aircraft that, flying at speeds of Mach 0.95–0.98 over extended ranges (9,000 NM), would allow passengers paying a premium fare to fly directly to their destinations, wherever they want to go, avoiding congested hubs and time-wasting intermediate stops. The Sonic Cruiser would therefore be initially targeted to first-class and business passengers, who are more sensitive to time-saving advantages.

Such an aircraft, combining transonic cruise speed, longer range, and the comfort of flying at higher altitudes, had the potential to open a new era in commercial aviation, giving impetus to a trend (already evident on some long routes) toward progressive reductions in hub-to-hub connections replaced by point-to-point connections. The time saved could be significant, reducing long-distance flights from 14–15 hours to 11–12 hours. The result would be a fragmentation of the air transportation system characterized by a larger number of medium-sized aircraft, while the very large aircraft (the B-747 and A-380) would be operated essentially through the highly congested airports on high-density traffic routes and/or for mass transport.

The Sonic Cruiser project, that should have opened for service around 2008[27], was based on the development of a family of aircraft with seating capacities of 200 to 300 seats, incorporating a number of product innovations in different areas:

- Canard configuration.

- Innovative wing shape (double delta wing with strakes).

- Engine noise reduction at takeoff.

- Minimized fuel consumption at transonic speeds (formation of weak shock waves).

- Extensive use of composite materials.

These product innovations had already been partially or completely tested or proven, one by one, in other planes such as combat aircraft or business aircraft. In particular, some of these innovations would have been derived from the activities undertaken by Boeing in the JSF program. The real challenge of the Sonic Cruiser project was the contemporary adoption of many individual innovations for the first time on a commercial aircraft; that is, the systemic application of these technologies to obtain one combined product that is innovative from the operational point of view.

Boeing had declared that it intended to develop a product economically attractive for airlines compared to the present aircraft. Boeing operated on two assumptions in pursuing this objective:

- The higher cruise speed would provide a productivity increase that, on some routes, could generate an extra connection per day, improving the economics of operating the aircraft significantly.

- The improvements made in development and production processes and techniques both in the civil (B-777 and B-737 next-generation) and military fields (JSF and UCAV – Unmanned Combat Air Vehicle) would allow the design and production of the aircraft at a significantly less cost than in the past[28]. Altogether such improvements could be so great as to provide direct operating costs comparable with those of other aircraft. Thus, there would be no need to charge premium fares for Sonic Cruiser travelers already paying first class or business class tickets (This point is, without any doubt, the main issue.).

But at the end of 2002 it has been announced by Boeing that the Sonic Cruiser will not be built. The reason is, not a single airline has expressed a clear preference for the time saved by flying faster over the higher airplane price and fuel consumption. Therefore Boeing is backing away from the program on the ground of the customer preference. Instead, Boeing is ready to offer a more conventional airplane that will cost less and will have lower operating costs.

The project was being developed in parallel to the Sonic Cruiser as an alternative solution should the last one prove to be unrealistic. It would have the same size (200-300 seats) and would incorporate all results of studies and researches made for the Sonic Cruiser. But it will fly at Mach 0.8-0.9 (as today airplanes) and would burn 20% less fuel than conventional aircraft; therefore it is called the *Super Efficient Airplane* and it is designed to be cheaper, not faster than the present airplanes. The decision to stop the Sonic Cruiser is important because it confirms that aeronautics progress are made in small steps through significant innovations, but seldom through an important breakthrough.

2.5.3.1.1.2   Airbus strategy

Airbus was created in 1970 as Groupement d'Interet Economique (GIE). Technological variables played an important role in its entry into the market and in its subsequent differentiation. Apart from the innovations introduced in the avionics systems, the Airbus A-300-B1 (with 250 seats, short to medium range) offered technological advances in flight control system equipment and the use of advanced materials. Therefore, Airbus was the first wide-bodied twin-engine aircraft, able to offer fuel-saving and maintenance advantages over its competitor aircraft with three or four jet engines. In this sense, Airbus initiated a philosophy—that would have been followed only some years after by Boeing (with the B-767)—that found wide application; in fact, in the following years the power plants demonstrated greater reliability, and therefore the application of the twin-engine aircraft concept spreaded up, like in the case of the A-330 and the B-777.

The significant amount of experience acquired by the aircraft manufacturers and the new-generation engines have made it possible to extend the flights of twin-engine airplanes, originally very limited for safety and economic reasons. This research established the rules concerning maximum flight time for twin-engine planes (rules known as ETOPS—Extended Range Operations with Two-Engine Aircraft). The Federal Aviation Administration (FAA) is now evaluating a proposal to extend the ETOPS operation from 180 to 207 minutes).

The consortium's efforts of increasing its capabilities to become a global player were huge. Moreover, it was successful in its aggressive commercial policy, initially toward those nations (such as the North African and Middle East countries) characterized by consolidated political and economic connections with the nations' owners of the consortium.

Only afterward, following its first commercial successes, did Airbus progressively widen its range of products to almost total coverage of the market (Figure 2.36),   adding aircraft whose strength lies in their technological leadership (Figure 2.37) and that are positioned to directly compete with those made by the U.S. manufacturers. In addition, the expansion of the types offered allows a continuous increase of the market share (for the past at the expenses of MDD's competitive position) and enables the European consortium to compete with Boeing's economies of scale, both in production and commercial arenas.

To achieve coverage as complete as possible in its product range, Airbus progressively launched the following initiatives, in only a short time:

- The A-318 (a shortened version of the A-319) in the 100-seat segment; this program was launched after the failure of the European and Asian collaboration on the AE-31X project[29].

- The A-340-500/-600 aircraft in the long-range segment to face the competition of the B-777 extended-range versions.

- The A-380 family in the very large segment, completing the Airbus product portfolio.

This last (the A-380 initiative) will be one of the biggest factors affecting the jetliner battle in the future. Airbus waited a long time before launching the A-380 family because of the tremendous impact the success or the defeat of such a program (whose development costs have been estimated to be about $11 billion at the time of launch) would have on the future of the European aeronautical commercial industry. In particular, a critical factor for achieving success was the timing.

Figure 2.36
Present Products and Future Development of Airbus Portfolio

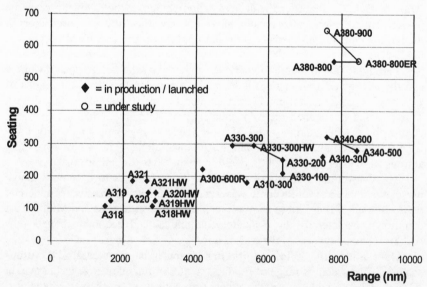

Figure 2.37
Airbus Industries Technological "Firsts"

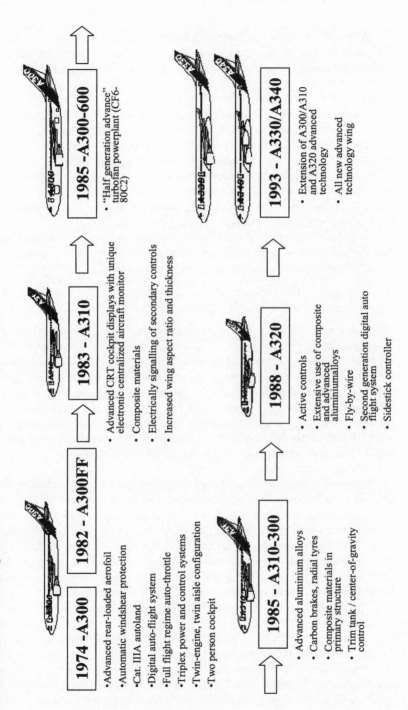

Source: Elaboration on AIRBUS. *Presentation to the Commission of the European Union - DG XII.* Toulouse: May 1997.

A mistake in the timing decision would strongly and negatively affect the European manufacturer, because the first years of the program are particularly crucial. Therefore, in addition to the achieved backlog (50 units at the moment of the go-ahead), the manufacturer had to be confident in a strong market demand in the years when the airplane will be ready for delivery (2006) and the following years, in order to assure the necessary continuity in production rate.

Moreover, it must be noted that, due to the huge amounts of money and resources needed, this program was an alternative to other possible business opportunities. That means that during the A-380 development phase, Airbus will not be able to proceed in other initiatives such as the A-300/310 replacement or the extension of the A-330/340 family, or even demanding research studies in the field of supersonic flight, should the hypothetical extension of Sonic Cruiser toward supersonic application prove to be right.

In order to lower the financial risk, Airbus has tried to enlist a number of risk-sharing partners to invest in the A-380 program, with the goal of allocating up to 40% of the total activities (recurring and nonrecurring).

2.5.3.1.2   The Competition between Europe and the United States for the Supersonic Commercial Aircraft

In the past 40 years, the main aeronautical companies have been highly interested in the possibility of developing passenger transportation in a supersonic airplane, for several reasons. From a physicist's point of view, it is possible to define a Mach range where supersonic transportation could be explored[30]. Total airplane efficiency (aerodynamic efficiency by propulsive efficiency by structural efficiency) shows a sharp decrease when exceeding about Mach 0.9 (the exact figure depends on the shape of the airplane) due to the fall of aerodynamic efficiency. But total efficiency increases at about Mach 1.2 due to the improvement of propulsive efficiency with speed. At this speed conventional materials can still be used.

Supersonic flight requires the development of front-end technologies in a number of areas: aerodynamics, materials, engine, systems, structures, and so on; therefore, the main players have been strongly interested in being involved in this sector (even though sometimes with a low-profile involvement) in order to control the competitors' technological evolution. Third, developing and producing a supersonic airplane is a question of national pride and technological progress; consequently, the major industrialized countries have supported the industry's efforts in the supersonic aircraft sector, in recent years.

The competition for the supersonic commercial transport aircraft dates back to the beginning of the '60s, when the Europeans and the U.S. companies, on the two sides of the Atlantic, separately began their activities in this sector. In Europe, under the pressure of political and technological factors, four British and French firms—airframers British Aircraft and Sud Aviation, and engine makers Bristol Siddeley and Snecma—started a collaboration at the end of 1962[31] to develop and build together the Concorde supersonic airliner.

At about the same time, the U.S. government announced the launch of its competing program called SST (SuperSonic Transport). After bids were taken, the program was finally awarded in 1966 to Boeing (other proposals came from Lockheed and North American).

The European and U.S. programs had very different characteristics:

- The Concorde: Seating about 100 passengers, Mach 2.2 cruise speed, aluminum fuselage.

- The Boeing project: Seating about 200 passengers, Mach 2.7 cruise speed, titanium fuselage, and a wing with a variable sweep.

The delays in developing the required technologies, the difficulties in obtaining the necessary funding, and public concern over environmental impact (ozone depletion and sonic booms) brought the U.S. supersonic project to a halt in 1971. After that, the airlines cancelled their options (a total of 122 aircraft).

On the other side of the Atlantic, the Anglo-French industrial collaboration succeeded in flying the first Concorde prototype in 1969 and delivering the first operational aircraft in 1974[32]; notwithstanding this, the program was not a commercial success, recording only 14 units sold to British Airways (then BOAC – British Overseas Airways Corporation) and Air France.

The scarce commercial success recorded by the Concorde proved that the available technology level was not yet sufficient to develop a supersonic transport aircraft really competitive with the subsonic transport jets and capable of compliance with the increasingly stringent environmental regulations. Consequently, during the '70s and the '80s, the research activities in this sector continued in a very low-profile fashion[33].

Boeing, McDonnell Douglas, Aerospatiale, British Aerospace, and DASA decided in 1990 to exchange the information from their still-separate efforts in the supersonic sector, by creating the Supersonic Commercial Transport (SCT) group, enlarged in 1991 to include three associated partners: Alenia, the Japanese Aircraft Development Corporation or JADC(composed of Fuji, Mitsubishi, and Kawasaki), and the Russian Tupolev[34].

The objective of this group was to study certification, environmental, commercial, and economic issues and to explore whether a global consortium could eventually develop and build the second generation supersonic airplane. The aircraft under study had a seating capacity of about 250 to 300 passengers and a maximum cruise speed of approximately Mach 2.0 to 2.4; the cost to develop and build a full-scale supersonic transport jet was estimated (in 1998) at more than $10 billion.

The activities of the industrial group proceeded slowly due to the lack of long-term common objectives; in fact, preliminary studies showed that the economical viability of such an aircraft was still too marginal, the airlines' acceptance of it would be very limited, and the technological risks were too high. At the beginning of 1999, the international group formally concluded its activities because of the slow technological progress the partners had made in trying to overcome stringent noise and emission regulations as well as building a supersonic airplane that passengers could afford.

In the United States, paralleling the efforts of the SCT Group, Boeing and engine makers General Electric and Pratt & Whitney had received $1.8 billion in funding over 10 years from NASA specially created High Speed Research program (HSR), to examine all critical aerodynamic, propulsion, and other technological areas, with the aim of launching a supersonic transport jet by 2010. In 1999, after 10 years of activities had proven that the technology and economics were not yet feasible for a 300-seat aircraft capable of cruising at Mach 2.4, the target date was changed to 2020, and the HSR program subsequently collapsed. But thanks to several studies performed under the HSR program in areas such as innovative configurations, new light materials, hybrid laminar flow control, and propulsion, Boeing has been able to develop the overall technological concept on which the Sonic Cruiser program is based.

In building the Sonic Cruiser, Boeing will be halfway to developing a supersonic aircraft; in fact, it is evident that the Boeing airplane could evolve into a true supersonic airliner (probably with a cruising speed of Mach 1.4 to 1.6) by 2015, when new technologies (especially in the propulsion area) will be ready[35].

The next step in the supersonic competition [36] will likely be the response of the European industry (which, during the '70s, won the battle for the supersonic airliner with the Concorde) to this very complex and forward-looking strategy conceived by Boeing. The move from the Europeans should be a project capable of introducing a new standard in the supersonic sector in order to beat the Sonic Cruiser family competition: a new-generation supersonic airliner cruising at least at Mach 2.0 to 2.4, or a transatmospheric plane cruising at hypersonic speeds.

2.5.3.1.3   The Boeing-MDD Merger and the Antitrust Authorities

On February 18, 1997, the European Commission received notice from Boeing of its intention to acquire MDD. On March 19, 1997, the commission began proceedings to verify whether the move would comply with Council Regulation of European Economic Community (EEC) n. 4064/89 of December 21, 1989, concerning mergers impacting the European economic area.

The European Commission decided to intervene for several reasons:

1.   The operation constituted a concentration within the meaning of Article 3 of the merger regulation.

2.   The acquisition had a European community dimension, as each of the two involved companies had a turnover in Europe in excess of 250 million ECU, around $250 millions.

3.   It had great significance in the E.E.A. (European Economic Area) and in the world market because it changed the competitive scenario.

In order to reach its final conclusion (which was in favor of the merger, with some conditional remedies accepted by Boeing), the European Commission (EC) made a wise and profound analysis of the consequences that such a merger would have on the commercial aeronautical sector, from many points of view. That evaluation [O.J.E.C. 1997] provides most information of this chapter, with all due integration and comments.

2.5.3.1.3.1   The competitive arena

According to the EC, the competitive situation in the commercial aircraft business could be expressed (Table 2.19)as a function of the following factors.

• Product segmentation in terms of different seating capacity:

Boeing	Narrow-body	B-737-200/-300/-400/-500/-600/-700/-800
	Wide-body	B-767-200/-300
		B-777-200/-300
		B-747-400
MDC	Narrow-body	MD-80/-90
	Wide-body	MD-11
Airbus	Narrow-body	A-319/A-320/A-321
	Wide-body	A-300
		A-310
		A-330-200/-300
		A340-200/-300

• Market shares in terms of value of backlog orders.

• Market presence in terms of the fleets in service (a measure of how deeply a manufacturer is involved with customers who are potential users of its future products).

Table 2.19
Manufacturers Market Shares and Presence (as of Dec. 1996)

	Orders backlog (Value %)	Fleet in service (units %)
Boeing	64 %	60 %
MDC	6 %	24 %
Airbus	30 %	14 %
Others (Lockheed)	-	2 %
Total	100 %	100 %

Source: Elaboration on O.J.E.C. 1997

The overall worldwide assessment leads to the conclusion that after a significant improvement in the late 1980s and early 1990s, Airbus maintained its position in large commercial aircraft on the same level. Boeing increased its market share during the 1990s to more than 60%, while there was a continuous decrease in the market share of MDD, particularly in the wide-body market. The combined market share of Boeing and MDD from 1989 was more or less stable at around 70%. [O.J.E.C. 1997]

2.5.3.1.3.2   Boeing's strategic positioning improvement in the market

As already noted, the objective of the EC investigation was to find if the proposed Boeing/MDD merger would significantly reduce the competition already existing in the large commercial airplane sector, particularly because of the creation of a quasi-monopolistic competitive situation in the market, or at least the achievement of a long-lasting dominant position by one of the contenders. [O.J.E.C. 1997]

The EC focused its investigation on the possible further improvement of Boeing's market positioning based on two different types of advantages:

- Short-term factors related to previous MDD markets and the acquisition strength in the commercial transport airplane business.

- Long-term factors focused on transversal or dual usage of technology and/or indirect offset deals from the military to the civil sector Tables 2.20 and 2.21 summarize the conclusions of the EC investigations.

Although fighter aircraft technology is not wholly transferable because of the more compact packaging of systems, the same technology can be transferred, to a large extent, to the commercial sector. Almost 100% of the technology developed for fighter airplanes related to navigation aids, cockpit displays, subsystem technology, avionic software processes, and advanced structures is transferable for commercial airplanes application; much less (around 50%) is transferable in the area of flight control techniques and general avionics. [O.J.E.C. 1997]

2.5.3.1.3.3   Conclusions of the European communities commission

In order to remove EC concerns brought to the attention of Boeing during the debate (see Tables 2.20 and 2.21), the U.S. company proposed some remedies, undertaking to adopt a series of structural and behavioral measures. Boeing made several promises:

1.   To keep MDD as a separate legal entity for a period of 10 years (the purpose was to give EC a window into the way the commercial business was conducted, giving evidence that Boeing would not further discount the already low-priced MDD commercial airplanes).

2.   To provide the same level of customer support service for MDD as for Boeing airplanes.

3. Not to use the existing fleet of MDD commercial airplanes to force customers to buy new Boeing products.

4. Not to use the existing exclusivity rights with American, Delta, and Continental Airlines and not to sign new ones until August 1, 2007.

5. To make available, under license, to the other airplane manufacturers any government funded patent.

6. To exchange with other airplanes' manufacturers that accept to do so any blocking patent and related know-how.

7. To give the EC full knowledge of R & D non classified projects for 10 years.

8. Not to exert subtle or improper influence on the suppliers against competitors. [O.J.E.C. 1997]

Table 2.20
Short Term Factors

SHORT TERM FACTORS	E.C. CONCLUSIONS
New market shares and strategic positioning evaluation	Boeing (64%) + MDD (6%) market shares = 70% The traditional dominant position of Boeing will be strengthened. Furthermore Boeing will strengthen its position in the 100-120 seat sector, with the Douglas MD-95 achieving a monopolistic situation.
Fleet in service	Boeing (60%) and MDD (24%) shares = 84% Boeing would increase its long-term relationships with customers and its position in customer support, and would significantly broaden its customer base.
Financial resources	Boeing (22.7 B$) + MDD (13.8 B$) = 36.5 B$ in revenues ('96)* This would significantly increase Boeing's ability to cope with the economic cycles because about 50% of total revenues are achieved in the defense and space sectors that appear to be more stable.

Source: Elaboration on O.J.E.C., 1997

Note: * - Airbus turnover ($8.9 billion in 1996) is related obviously to the commercial airplane only, while a total turnover of Boeing and MDD are more diversified and include activities in both the military and civil fields. On the other hand, if reference is made to the total turnover of the four Airbus partners ($31.4 billion in 1996) in order to compare it with the relevant figures of Boeing and MDD ($36.5 billion), still a mistake can be made. In fact, among the activities included in the $31.4 billion turnover of the four European companies, only those related to the commercial airplane business are coordinated within Airbus, while the others are made independently. On the contrary Boeing and MDD activities in the commercial, military, space fields are strictly coordinated today inside each company. What remains to be made after the merger is by far a shorter path than the process the European aerospace companies must undertake for restructuring and consolidating the industry.

Table 2.21
Long Term Factors

LONG TERM FACTORS	E.C. CONCLUSIONS
Exclusivity agreements*	The potential effect of these exclusive deals would be to block over 60% of the worldwide market (based on those airlines' existing fleets in service as a proportion of the worldwide fleet, see tab. 2.19)
Presence in the military and civil fields	The Boeing/MDD company would have a better chance of becoming the final prime contractor for the development of JSF program (at that time in competition with Lockheed), given the combination of their technological resources.
Offsets and bundling deals	Combining Boeing's dominant position in commercial aircraft with MDD's strong position in fighter aircraft, the company would be able to use them to provide offsets to dominate international fighter aircraft competition.
Access to publicly funded R&T and R&D and dual use of such technology	Boeing will reach a much greater access to R&D funded by DoD or public bodies in the defense and space sectors, and such technologies will be used for commercial application. On the contrary, the level of expenditures for R&D in Europe are much lower and the related activities are fragmented and not coordinated.
Increase of contractual power toward the suppliers	The addition of MDD's buying power (toward third party suppliers, especially in the military sector) to Boeing's already strong position in commercial aircraft would increase suppliers' overall reliance on Boeing and might put them in a position where they could not resist giving Boeing's activities a priority over Airbus'. Boeing would be able to exert pressures on suppliers to discourage them from working with its only competitor Airbus, or to induce them to favor Boeing over Airbus.

Source: Elaboration on O.J.E.C, 1997

Note: * - On 21 November 1996, on 20 March 1997 and on 10 June 1997 Boeing announced long term exclusive agreements with major the airlines: American, Delta and Continental respectively. The merger between Boeing and MDC was made public in December 1996, but rumors on the subject circulated several months before this date within the aeronautical industry community. It is clear that such agreements were favored by the consideration, made by the airlines, that such a big company, resulting from the merger, would be able to solve, alone, all current and future needs.

According to the EC, the agreement by Boeing was sufficient to overcome EC concerns about the strengthening of Boeing's dominant position in the commercial airplane sector.

Therefore, in a commission decision on July 30, 1997, the operation was declared compatible with the European rules and regulations, provided that Boeing would fully comply with the commitments made.

This EC decision admittedly was strongly influenced by two considerations:

• The difficulty of finding a buyer for MDD other than Boeing.

• The relevance of the proposed concentration for the U.S. government that was in favor of the U.S. aerospace industry restructuring.

In addition (and no less important), Europe did not want to face a commercial war with the United States, with the attendant unpredictable consequences. Moreover, the European aerospace industry was preparing to face its own period of consolidation and rationalization of activities, which would require similar investigations from the U.S. antitrust authorities.

2.5.3.1.4   Airbus and Boeing Long-Term Competitive Positioning

Since the Boeing/MDD merger, the commercial aircraft industry has been characterized by a duopoly in which the market shares of the two contenders have reached a 50-50 situation. In 2001, Airbus and Boeing shares in terms of ordered units were 53% and 47% (46% and 54% in 2000) respectively, while the cumulative backlog was about 54% (1575 units) and 46% (1357 units) respectively (50% and 50% in 2000).

In 2001, Airbus delivered 325 units (311 units in 2000), Boeing delivered 527 units (489 units in 2000), but for both companies the production rate is expected to decrease, particularly for Boeing, and to stabilize around lower values as a consequence of September 11 event. Airbus is scheduled to deliver approximately 300 aircraft starting from 2002, whereas Boeing's rate is expected to decrease to 380 units in 2002 and between 275 and 300 in 2003. Thus, the trend toward an equal split of the market appears confirmed.

A new decisive challenge is arising between the two manufacturers: their different visions of the long-range segment evolution. Airbus forecasts the need for many large-capacity aircraft (to be satisfied with the A-380 family), while Boeing envisions a trend toward network fragmentation (and consequently the foreseen development of the Sonic Cruiser or, today, the alternative *Super Efficient Airplane* of the same size). This situation could mean a head-to-head battle between the two manufacturers, because the failure of one of the two programs will seriously damage the competitive positioning of that firm. In order to understand the possible competitive scenarios as a consequence of the offer and demand evolutions, the possible Airbus and Boeing long-term positions may be summarized as follows:

• Airbus cannot change its strategy (the launch of the A-380), and it is so busy that it cannot afford to launch any new programs (other than the planned A-400M, a military transport airplane).

- Boeing will choose to launch a traditional midsize aircraft family to substitute for the B-757/767 families, lowering its overall risk (when compared with the previous Sonic Cruiser solution) but also reducing its possible advantage over Airbus. These new products would incorporate anyhow the technological improvements made available from the research activities developed for the Sonic Cruiser project.

The long-range market trend will finally determine who will lead the competition in the coming years. A significant increase in network fragmentation will give a considerable advantage to Boeing, while Airbus, with the A-380 program devoting most of its resources to the very-large-capacity segment, will face serious difficulties.

In the opposite scenario, if the airlines show a significant preference for very large airplanes, Airbus (thanks to its A-380 family) will be in a leadership position, while Boeing will have to defend itself with some marketing maneuvers (for example, on prices). In the end, however, Boeing will be progressively excluded from the lucrative large-capacity segment.

In addition to this unprecedented head-to-head competition, Airbus and Boeing are actively engaged in trying to make their industrial and management structures more efficient. At the beginning of 2001, EADS and BAE SYSTEMS agreed to transform the Airbus consortium into a stand-alone firm. Bringing all of Airbus's activities and assets into a single company would have the following effects:

- It would generate savings of at least 350 million Euros (around $350 million) per year beginning in 2004, by reducing overlap and cutting structural costs.

- It would make it easier for Airbus to raise money in capital markets for development costs of the A-380 program.

- It would streamline the management chain and speed up the decision-making process.

- It would minimize the risks of opportunist behavior of the different partners.

- It would integrate resources, facilities, and centers of excellence favoring the growth of specialized capabilities and the efficiency of manufacturing.

Besides improving of its internal structure, Airbus is trying to attain a more global dimension in its partnerships and its supplier base. In addition it has recently included within its scope the military transport business. It should also be noted that Boeing has chosen not to follow the path of structural alliances, preferring to maintain full control of its programs despite the huge amount of resources necessary to develop and produce an aircraft. As far as the risk-sharing suppliers are concerned, Boeing has focused on giving preference to the Japanese industries. The following are elements of this strategic choice.

- Japan represents an industrial power comparable to about half that of the European Community. The Gross Domestic Product (GDP) of 2000 was $4.7 thousand billion, or about 68% of the $7.0 thousand billion of the whole European Union.

- In the '70s and '80s, the Japanese aeronautical industries enjoyed strong government support (through the MITI – Ministry of International Trade and Industry) that placed strategic importance on the aerospace industry, similar to what happened in the automobile and electronic industries.

- The industrial infrastructure and technological assets of Japan, as a system, are much better than those of many European nations.

- Southeast Asia, on which Japan has and will have a strong influence, presents the greatest anticipated rate of growth in air transport (7% to 8% annual growth, against 5% to 6% worldwide increase and the 4% growth of most mature European and North American markets).

The main data related to the activities of the three Japanese industrial groups are presented in Table 2.22. Besides the Aerospace sector, the three companies are involved in the transport sector manufacturing parts and components for trains, ships and automobiles. MHI and KHI are further involved in the Environment and Energy Sector and in the Industrial Automation.

MHI is the major national group for industrial activities and for turnover ($24,600 million in 2001) and it is also the most important Japanese company in the aeronautical sector ($4,200 million in 2001), while the KHI is the company in which the aerospace activities are more significant in percentage terms (20%) compared with the total turnover.

If the sector of aeronautical engines, dominated in Japan by Ishikawajima, is not considered, MHI, KHI and FHI represent with Shin Meiwa and with Japan Aircraft Manufacturing almost the totality of the Japanese aeronautical industry[37].

2.5.3.2 The Regional Transport Business.

As already pointed out, the definition of regional transport is not simple because it cannot be referred to by any characteristics unique to the network (type of engine, aircraft size, or type of customers). This is illustrated in Figure 2.38, that identifies and segments the regional transport business with a multidimensional approach.

Nevertheless, with the limitations of each definition, it is common to define "regional" as the traffic developed by airlines belonging in Europe to the ERA (European Regional Airline Association) and in the United States to the RAA (Regional Airline Association); this traffic is carried out for the most part with "short range" aircraft with 20-70 seats; and for the residual part with aircraft with 71-100 seats. The only temporary exception is constituted of slightly bigger aircraft of greater size (101 to 130 seats, shortened versions of already existing aircraft) operated by the major airlines.

Table 2.22
Major Japanese Aeronautical Companies

	Business Areas	Specific Activities	Aeronautical Activities	Specific Programs
Mitsubishi Heavy Industry	Aerospace and Defense Energy and Environment Automation and Industrial Systems Transportation Total Sales: 24.6 B$ (2001) Employees: 37800	Aeronautics, Space and Defense Steel Structures, Energy Machinery & Plants Plants Engineering & Machinery Auto, Machinery and Components Shipbuilding, Rollig Stock	**4.2 B$ (17% of Total sales 2001)** Fixed wing a/c: airframe, engine, maintenance, repair, modifications Rotating wing a/c: airframe, engine	*Subcontractor*: B737/747/757, A330/340, P3C, MH-53 (H) *Program participant*: B767/777, A319/320, CRJ-700/900 *Co-prime*: S-92 (H), V2500 (E), PW4000 (E) *Prime*: F-2, T-2, F-1, MH2000 (H). MG5 (E) *Licensee*: F-15J, SH-60J (H), UH-6J (H), HSS-2B (H)
Kawasaki Heavy Industry	Aerospace and Defense Energy and Environment Automation and Industrial Systems Transportation Total Sales: 8.6 B$ (2001) Employees: 29000	Aeronautics, Space and Defense Steel Structures, Energy Machinery & Plants Plants Engineering & Machinery Auto, Machinery and Components Shipbuilding, Rollig Stock	**1.7 B$ (20% of Total sales 2001)** Fixed wing a/c: airframe, engine, maintenance, repair, modifications Rotating wing a/c: airframe, engine	*Subcontractor*: B737/747/757, A321 *Program participant*: B767/777 *Prime*: T-4, OH-1 (H) *Licensee*: P-3C, CH-47 (H), MD-500 (H) *International*: V2500 (E)
Fuji Heavy Industry	Aerospace Transportation Total Sales:10.6 B$ (2001) Employees: 26500	Aeronautics and Space Auto, Machinery and Components, Rolling Stock	**0.52 B$ (5% of Total sales 2001)** Fixed wing a/c: airframe Rotating wing a/c: airframe, engine	*Subcontractor*: B747/757 *Program participant*: B767/777 *Prime*: T-7 *Licensee*: UH-1H (H), AH-1S (H)

(H) Helicopters (E) Engine

Figure 2.38
The Regional Transport Business Identification through the Multi-Dimensional Approach

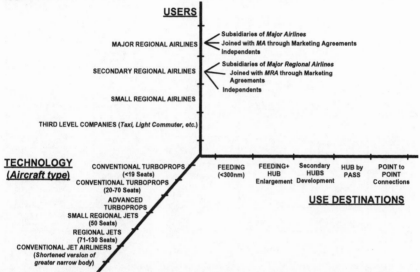

If one should think only in terms of relative size of the business, the regional turboprop or turbofan aircraft market could not arouse any particular interest with respect to commercial jets (Figure 2.39 and 2.40).

In these figures the market evolution in terms of delivered units is shown for the past and for projected future[38] (elaboration on Boeing and Airbus forecast), since it represents (and will represent) only a small part of the entire sales turnover of the civil aeronautical industry. For the period from 1998 to 2017, the regional jet segment (aircraft with between 20 and 120 seats) is worth $128 billion, which is about 10% of the total aircraft delivery value ($1,151 billion). This is essentially due to the significant differences among the sales prices of the aircraft belonging to the two market layers, even though the regional traffic growth rates are higher than those of the major airlines.

In reality, the regional aircraft business is an extremely interesting industrial sector, not only because it represents a sector relatively young in the landscape of the aeronautical industry, but above all because it is continually evolving. Some firms have chosen the regional aircraft segment for their entry into the civil aeronautical production business, due to the relative design and constructive simplicity of the aircraft (as in the case of IPTN of Indonesia or Embraer of Brazil).

Finally, although the U.S. firms have dominated the upper layer of the offer until recently (when their position was circumvented by the Airbus consortium), in the regional aircraft and commuter production segment, the European industry has played a leading role, with ATR, Saab, BAES, DASA, Fokker, Dornier, and CASA occupying the market's top positions until only a few years ago.

Figure 2.39
Overall Aircraft Market Evolution of Deliveries

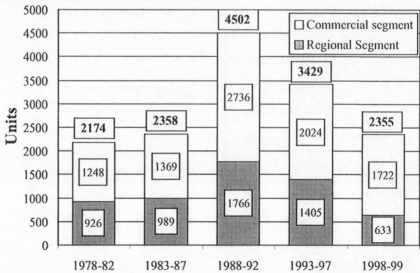

Source: Elaboration on: Airbus. *Global Market Forecast 2000-2019;* Boeing Commercial Airplane Group. *Current Market Outlook 2000*

Figure 2.40
Overall Aircraft Market Forecasted Evolution

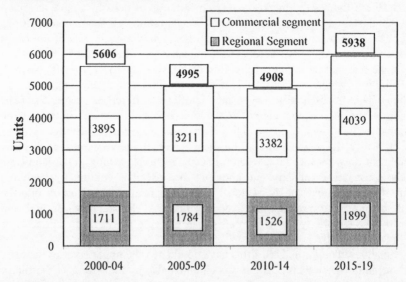

Source: Elaboration on: Airbus. *Global Market Forecast 2000-2019;* Boeing Commercial Airplane Group. *Current Market Outlook 2000*

In recent years, with the advent of regional jets, the competitive situation has significantly changed, and the European industry has lost its leadership position, while other manufacturers (Canada's Bombardier and the Brazilian Embraer) have assumed a leading role.

2.5.3.2.1 The Birth and the Boom of Regional Transport in the United States and Europe

The birth and rapid expansion of the regional transport sector followed the U.S. deregulation in 1978, when U.S. airlines proliferated due to the liberalization of fares. It should be noted that in only 3 years (from 1978 to 1981), the number of such airlines increased from 36 to 248. This phenomenon favored the development of a great quantity of new connections and the gradual transition of an increasing number of connections from the larger companies to the smaller airlines, characterized by fleets and organizational structures necessary to make the short flights, with low traffic density, profitable. These smaller airlines, in the meantime, acquired the type of aircraft that were suitable to these kinds of connections. This transition resulted in the hub and spoke system, based on a polarization of the larger airlines' traffic at a few main airports or hubs (centers of gathering and sorting of a large number of flights).

Figure 2.41, referring to the world market, shows the effect of some relevant events on the level of concentration of the air transport offer, especially the effect of deregulation in the United States. The phase following the airlines' proliferation consisted of consolidation of the offer, due to purely competitive reasons. This occurred first in the United States and later in Europe. Between 1981 and 1985, the U.S. companies were reduced from 248 to 130.

The trend toward concentration of the offer was mitigated by the liberalization that occurred in Europe concurrently with the U.S. consolidation. The successive consolidation of the offer in Europe confirms the trend toward global concentration of the world offer.

The aircraft initially used to satisfy the demand for regional transport were those already available. They were characterized by a series of common elements such as robustness, a certain design simplicity, poor performance (speeds less than 250 knots), and a capacity, in many cases, inferior to the 20 seats. Planes such as the Beech B-99, the Metro, the Nomad N-22 and N-24, EMB-110, F-27, the DHC-4, DHC-6 and DHC-7, the BAe-748, and the Shorts 330 and 360 initiated the regional transport era.

Later, the airlines sharpened their demand, requiring aircraft specifically designed for regional traffic. Figure 2.42 shows the course of regional aircraft orders in the 19- to 70-seat market.

In the years immediately following the Deregulation Act of 1978, the newly designed aircraft that achieved the best positions in the course of the 1980s in the different segments of market under examination were the Saab-340, the EMB-120, the DHC-8-100 and -200, the Jetstream 31, and ATR-42-100 and -200.

Figure 2.41
Top 20 Airlines' Share of World RPMs

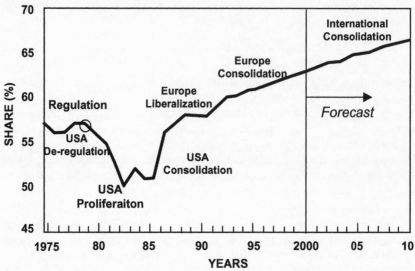

Figure 2.42
Historical Deliveries and Forecast in the 19-70 Seats Segment in Regional Aircraft Business

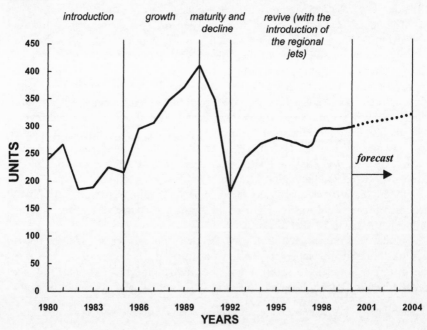

The U.S. introduction of the new hub and spoke organization of connections gave a decisive impulse to the development of the regional transport and favored also the development of dedicated airplanes of size, performance, and comfort levels decidedly better than those of their precursors. In effect, the second half of the '80s saw the entry onto the market of some new manufacturers and of many new products like the DHC-8-300, the F-50 and the CN-235, or the ATR-72 and the BAES ATP, the first group in the 40- to 50- and the second in the 60- to 70-seat segments..

The entry of new actors and the better market requirements definition increased the competitive intensity among aircraft manufacturers During the '80s the average size of U.S. airplanes had more than doubled (12 seats in 1979, 22 in 1989, and 30 in 1999) and the average length of travel legs had dramatically increased (160 NM in 1989, 200 NM in 1996, 210 NM in 1999).

In Europe the evolution of the network was more gradual, characterized by the coexistence of the direct and the hub and spokes connection systems. This coexistence came about due to two different factors:

- A higher geographical denseness of centers of a certain relevance, located in different countries (this legitimates the survival of a large number of direct connections and their coexistence with the hub system).

- A higher congestion at airports compared with that in the United States, which especially penalizes the low-density traffic (regional transport and general aviation).

In Europe, the development of regional traffic in the 1980s also increased the average size of the aircraft and the average distances of the connections. The average size has increased from 20 seats in 1978 to 50 in 1994, then to 67 in 1999; the average length of legs has grown from 200 NM in 1989 to 240 NM in 1996 and 290 NM in 1999. In the early '90s, a rapid decline of demand took place because the Gulf War and the economic world recession decelerated the market brusquely (Figure 2.42).

The main players then began to introduce onto the market updated versions or derivatives of their own aircraft (the ATR-42-500, the AVRO (BAES) RJ-70, the Fokker F-70) in order to feed the demand without the high financial exposure. This trend would continue in subsequent years when innovative products (speedy turboprops and small jets), were introduced into the market, because the demand (the regional airline industry) consolidated to the point that new, strong investments (acquisitions) could be born. Such strategies were the basis for exploiting the revitalization of the market (Fig 2.42). At the same time, in the segment, the life cycle of the turboprop products terminated. In 1997, the sales of regional jets had actually become higher than those of turboprops (Figure 2.43).

2.5.3.2.2   The Anticipated Evolution and Its Impact on Characteristics of the Required Aircraft

The regional transport maintained an importance in feeding the hub system.

Figure 2.43
Regional Aircraft Order Split — Jet vs. Turboprop — 20-70 Seats

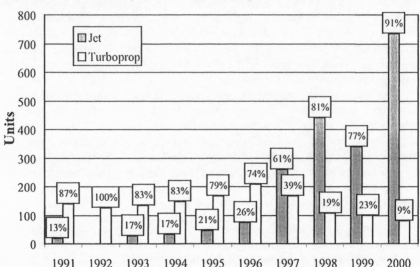

A critical factor for success in the strong competition that was created among megacarriers is represented by the efficiency of the system of feeding large flows of traffic through the regional transports. At the same time, the relationships between the major and the regional airlines became continually tighter and more consolidated, especially in the United States. In 1993, 41 of the 50 greater regional airlines managed 93% of the regional traffic in the United States, and each had some link with the megacarriers. Fourteen were fully owned by major airlines. Today, 10 of the 120 national/regional airlines manage more than the half of the total traffic (53.1%).

The process of rearrangement of the network is essentially linked to several factors:

- Congestion of the airport areas located near the hubs.

- Economic growth of some geographical areas.

- The consolidation and remodeling of the airline industries induced by the last phase of U.S. deregulation.

- Liberalization of the air transport in Europe.

The impact on the two greatest bases of users (United States and Europe) will be different and will probably bring about a different and more stable situation (consolidation), which has already been defined (Figure 2.44) in its development:

- Widening of the area of influence of the hubs.

- Bypass of the hubs.

- Development of secondary hubs.

The widening of the network that exists on a hub can be obtained only with speedier aircraft, given that all the arrivals of feeder flights must occur at the same time. This is due to the fact that passengers coming from different cities have to be in condition to catch a given flight that connects that hub with another one. With such aircraft, some small cities could be connected to a hub that otherwise would not be accessible for linkage.

The hub bypass refers to traffic directed between two small cities inserted into the system of two greater hubs. These bypass connections may be operated by major airlines and their regional affiliated directing the traffic through the hubs. Alternatively, they could be operated by independent regional operators with a direct flight.

The regional airlines that operate from point to point must choose the best aircraft for optimizing their offer in terms of size and flight frequency. The size and frequency are offered according to the density of traffic and of the range, by large-size turboprops (such as the ATR-72) and, more frequently, by 50- to 70-seat regional jets (such as the Canadair CRJ) or speedy turboprops (such as the Saab-2000, which is no longer in production).

The development of Secondary Hubs is relative to the traffic internal to a main hub. As shown in Figure 2.44, a passenger desiring to fly from point 1 to point 3 has no choice but to take a one-stop flight, as there is no point to point connection. This flight could go through the primary hub or through a secondary hub. The passenger may not care which hub the flight goes through, but for the system to avoid congestion, it is much better for such flights to be routed through secondary hubs.

There are several implications of the demand for regional transport aircraft in United States. A small and declining part of regional aircraft will still be turboprops. In fact, the structure of the dominant regional traffic today in the United States needs the low operating costs of these airplanes and will not require, even in the future, particularly high-speed airplanes, as the average length of the spokes has increased slowly, from about 150 NM to about 200 NM (1988–1997). Nevertheless, there will be more cases in which the jet will replace the turboprop in markets predominantly served by the turboprop today. Such cases are relative primarily to the emergent reasons highlighted previously.

In Europe, the hub and spoke system and the point-to-point connections should remain. The integration of markets induced by liberalization of the air transport sector will face a geopolitical division opposing development of the hub connection system. Therefore, the regional jet could have an ampler and speedy application because the point-to-point connections will represent a greater part of the total.

Figure 2.44
The Evolution of the Regional Operators Network

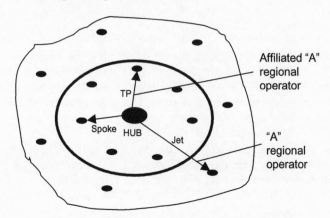

ENLARGEMENT OF A NETWORK AROUND A GIVEN "MAIN HUB"

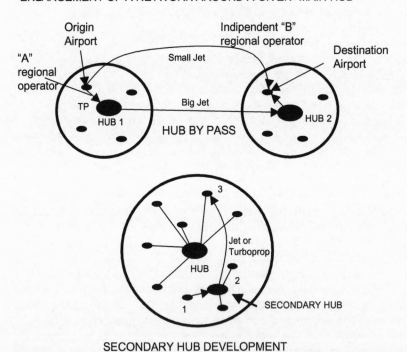

SECONDARY HUB DEVELOPMENT

Additionally, the average size of regional aircraft in Europe is roughly double that of United States, and this could favor the substitution of jets, which generally have more seats than turboprops for economic reasons. Besides, it should be noted that in the United States (but not only there), passengers tend to dislike turboprop airplanes because a number of accidents have involved such aircraft and have been strongly emphasized by the media.

Therefore, on a worldwide basis, some conclusion may be drawn about market aspects and emerging factors. Small regional jets (40–70 seats) will continue to be substituted for turboprops (although not completely). In the 71–130 seat range) the jets will dominate completely, as always. At the same time, the users have required the conventional turboprops of medium-large size (40–70 seats) to improve their performance (speed) and the level of internal comfort, which has erased the distinction among conventional and advanced (fast) turboprops.

The forecast of regional aircraft delivery by segments shown in Figure 2.43 reflects the above considerations and the strong market preference toward jet propulsion.

2.5.3.2.3   Competition in the Regional Sector and the Regional Jet Battle

Figure 2.45 highlights the firms and products of the regional transport business in production or study/development phases in 2001 by the year of their entry into service. For an analysis of the offer, it may be useful to divide the business into two layers, at the fairly clear demarcation line of about 70 seats. One of the main reasons that it is common to divide the business of regional aircraft into two layers is that in the United States, the regionals affiliated with major carriers (that constitute the majority) are limited by "scope clauses" on the type of equipment that they can operate. The scope clauses are part of the agreements between pilot unions and airlines. As a consequence, the affiliate regional airlines may not operate aircraft of more than a certain seating capacity (typically 70), and/or with a maximum takeoff weight (generally 75,000 lbs). These requirements, internal to the airlines, are evolving, and probably the recent availability of modern jet aircraft from 70–100 seats will allow the airlines to overcome them. Another (less important) reason is that the maximum size of turboprop airplanes has traditionally been 70 seats.

1. The first layer contains aircraft with 20 to 70 seats. The aircraft are mainly turboprops (conventional or fast), recently introduced regional jets (the CRJ-100/200/700 of Canadair-Bombardier, the ERJ-135/140/145 of Embraer, the Fairchild-Dornier 328 Jet), and the old British Aerospace BAES AVRO RJ-70. In this segment, the offer appears quite complete, and there are no airplanes under development and/or study.

2. The second layer includes 71 to 120-seat aircraft. The products of this market segment are characterized by turbofan propulsion (with the exception of the DHC-8-400, which has only 72 seats) and are aimed primarily at those short-range connections not transferred from the major airlines to their regional affiliates. This

situation is confirmed by the presence of Airbus and Boeing products in the high segments of the offer with shortened versions of some of their narrow-bodied aircraft to satisfy this market demand.

It is important to note that, in the competitive presence of just a few years ago, there were many other turboprop airplanes in production that have been recently phased out. This situation caused a problem of production over-capacity, which contributed to raising the level of competition to an abnormal extent, especially during the advent of the regional jet.

It may be very interesting to analyze the regional jet battle that is still being fought by the main players, and its impact on the future of regional airplanes manufacturers.

After the U.S. deregulation in 1978, many major airlines, before being forced to create (or acquire) regional affiliates, tried to manage the short-range, less dense traffic by themselves. This created a need (only for this use) for smaller aircraft very similar to those used in their fleets and resulted in the development of shortened versions of the commercial aviation aircraft (5- or 6-abreast).

Then aircraft such as the B-737-500, the A-319 (derived from the A-320), and the MD-87 appeared. These derivative models competed side by side with the Fokker and BAES products traditionally present in this segment (F-70/F-100 and BAe-146 families). At the end of the '80s, there was still no true regional jet aircraft with a suitable size and capacity to satisfy the emerging needs of regional airlines.

The first and main event that changed the picture for the regional aircraft sector was Bombardier's decision to stretch its Challenger, which, although an aircraft conceived for private use (business flights), had a wide fuselage (similar to a 4-abreast) and therefore could become a regional jet. The concerned competitors were at that time the manufacturers of turboprop airplanes: Fokker, producing the F-50 (a 50-seat turboprop derived from the F-27); British Aerospace, which made the Jetstream and the ATP (derived from the old 748 and, like the F-27, refurbished in the areas of avionics and engines); Saab, with the S-340 and the fast turboprop Saab-S-2000, and the Alenia/Aerospatiale/ATR consortium that made ATR-42 and ATR-72 turboprop airplanes, with about 50 and 70 seats respectively.

Although the first two had only rejuvenated their products (whose introduction into the market happened in the '60s) and were in the declining phase of their life cycle, Saab and ATR had relatively new products. ATR in particular made large investments and was selling its products well as the segment leader, followed by Bombardier (which, in buying De Havilland, acquired the DHC-8, a 50-seat turboprop airplane). In addition, in Europe, DASA acquired Dornier, which made the Do-228, a 19-seat turboprop, and the Do-328, an advanced 32-seat turboprop.

Figure 2.45
Regional Aircraft — In Production or Study/Development in 2001

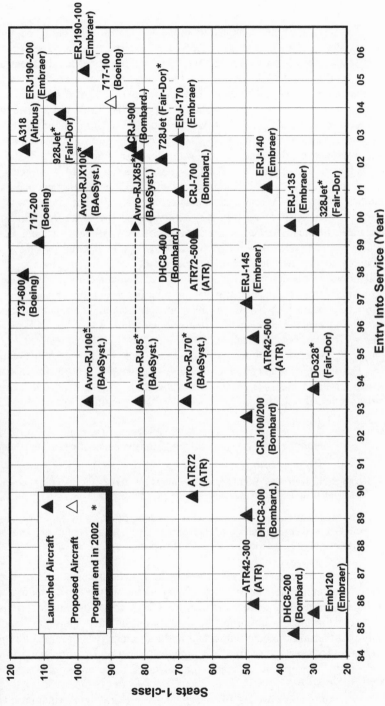

The interest of the European manufacturers in the regional jet segment was real in that period, to the point that each manufacturer had its own project. Alenia and Aerospatiale, for example, were talking about the 100-seat airplane early in 1988, although the engine type was not that clear (fast turboprop, propfan, and jet were all studied). In the same period, CASA began to carry out studies in the 100-seat segment. During the 1990s, these three manufacturers (Alenia, Aerospatiale, and CASA) tried to find a common program without success. Almost at the same time, DASA was trying to improve its presence in that segment of the market and was therefore studying a project for the development of a jet family in the 75-100-seat bracket (the MPC project).

A team was created composed of ATR, Dornier, and people from the mother companies Alenia, Aerospatiale, and DASA. The output was a very preliminary project of an airplane family called the DAA-92/122. From the technical, financial, and commercial points of view, all necessary conditions for success were present, but progress was slow due to internal problems such as disagreements   over leadership of the project and the locations of the final assembly line, the company headquarters, and the main commercial offices.

Afterwards DASA, that was trying to be present in most business segments (from turboprops with Dornier to the main commercial jet airplane with its share in Airbus) decided to enter the regional jet segment, buying 51% of Fokker shares. This last one was making the F-70 and the F-100 and was one of the two players in the market (the second being BAES with the 146 or AVRO family).

For a few years the situation remained unchanged. Except for Bombardier, which owned a business jet transformable into a regional jet due to its large cross section, the challenges for newcomers to the segment were:

a.   To develop a completely new jet with reasonable investment, so the sales price could be affordable for the small airlines, generally financially weak in that market.

b.   At the same time, to offer airplanes showing real technological improvements when compared with the Bombardier products (in terms of operating costs and/or performance), to justify the choice of the new product; and

c.   To offer airplanes that could also be competitive with the turboprop in a product/market segment where characteristics such as speed and comfort were not a high priority, as the routes were generally short, (flights of about one hour).

Other manufacturers tried to follow the Bombardier example of bypassing these problems. Not having jet airplanes to stretch, they modified their turboprops, initially transforming them into fast turboprops, and later, into jets.

Transforming a turboprop into a jet is not an easy operation because the only part that may remain untouched is the fuselage, which must be reinforced anyway. The rest must be redesigned. In particular, the wing must be redesigned, because it is made for lower speeds, unless a "slow" jet is acceptable.

Generally, the absence of sweep makes the existing wing unsuitable at typical jet speeds. Embraer entered the market with the EMB-145 and EMB-135 (50 and 35 seats, respectively), derived by taking the EMB-120 fuselage and producing a completely new wing.

In the meantime, ATR was trying again to enter the regional jet segment, joining the efforts of Italy (Alenia), France (Aerospatiale), and the United Kingdom (BAES). BAES was already present in the market with the BAe-146 family—4 engines, 80–100 seats, high wings. The number of engines and the high wings made these airplanes undesirable, therefore leading to a foreseen near exit from the market. For this reason, ATR's willingness to develop a new product was well timed with BAES's need to replace the 146 family, thus making the alliance possible.

The agreement was signed, and in January 1996, Aero International Regional, or AI(R), was born, operating with the aim of jointly commercializing existing aircraft, integrating sales structures and support, and creating an integrated study group for the joint development of new products, at that time identified as a 4-abreast, 55–70 seat family, to expand later into the 90–100 seat segment.

An unforeseen situation in 1996 upset the European manufacturers' plans. Fokker, even sustained by DASA (which was supposed to progressively increase its share from 51% to 82.2%), did not succeed in overcoming its growing financial problems. It went bankrupt in March 1996.

It is important to note how this event influenced the whole regional aircraft industry and the strategy already decided upon by the manufacturers previously mentioned. The exit from the market of the Fokker products (the F-100 jets, the F-70 and the derivative F-130 in its development phase) relaunched the BAe-146 regional jet family (until then considered merely niche) due to the total absence of competitors of the same class (around 100 seats). This naturally diminished BAES' interest in investing in products to replace its own, as the BAe-146 jets were now the only ones in their market and much easier to sell, with profits much greater than in the past. So, after useless attempts to impose a precise time to launch a common product by the ATR component of AI(R), this joint venture was dissolved in July 1998.

The picture of the sector was complete with the partial exit of BAES (with the phasing out of the ATP and the Jetstream product) and Saab (which invested a lot in the fast turboprop Saab-2000) from the turboprop segment. In June 1996 another situation occurred in the regional aircraft industry, apparently without importance, but that would have later significant implications. Fairchild Aerospace and DASA concluded an agreement for the acquisition by the American company of the 80% of the Dornier, constituting in this way a new joint venture in the regional segment: the Fairchild-Dornier (with 20% still held by DASA).

Among the declared objectives of the new company was the launch of a new family of regional jet airplanes (5-abreast) in the 70- to 90-seat segment. This objective captured the attention of ATR and CASA, which were planning something similar. The resulting negotiations were difficult and long for several reasons:

- ATR wanted leadership of the project, but between its partners there were differing opinions and interests.

- Fairchild-Dornier agreed to leave to ATR the sales of the airplanes (integrated with its salespeople) but requested as a concession to have the technical leadership of the project, this way bumping against Aerospatiale.

- CASA wanted (at least) the final assembly. This was difficult to obtain because the sales offices were in Toulouse, and tradition dictated that these two activities were strongly correlated with one another. CASA's desire was also against Alenia's interests (Alenia wanted the final assembly in Italy, in order to balance inside ATR the location of the headquarters in Toulouse). The conclusion was a break in the alliance, with the exit of ATR and a reduction of CASA's role from full partner to risk-sharing partner (with responsibility for the wing). Fairchild-Dornier went on alone toward the new 728 Jet, a 70-seat airplane, to be complemented later with additional members of that family (90 and maybe 50 seats).

The ATR consortium was present in all negotiations, but never in a positive final decision. The reasons for that could have been many and were sometimes unforeseeable, as in the case of AI(R), for example. But the slow decision making, typical of a consortium structure, likely influenced its ability to reach positive conclusions. It is worth noting that in those years, the Aerospatiale-Lagardere group merger posed inside Aerospatiale a leadership problem, creating an impasse with regard to major decisions. The paradox was that Aerospatiale was a towed partner, both inside ATR and in the wider temporary alliances.

The first entrants, thanks to good market acceptance of the regional jet airplanes, have positioned themselves very well in the market, even being able to launch other models later. Therefore, turboprop manufacturers unwilling or unable to follow the innovative technological trend in motorization (such as ATR), have been marginalized, despite the vast potential customer base constituted by the replacement of its own turboprop airplanes already on the market. This has been one of the reasons why the consortium concept is disappearing in the aeronautical industry; recently also Airbus has been changed from GIE (Groupement d'Interet Economique) to SAS (Société par Actions Simplifiée).

An interesting parallel is that, relating to the modalities used by players in the regional aircraft market in pursuing the supremacy; to achieve this goal the firms proceeded in the search of distinctive competitive advantages, essentially through these means:

1. The alliances.

2. Aggregation by acquisition.

3. Internal growth.

A specific example of the first approach is the ATR consortium created by Alenia (then Aeritalia) and Aerospatiale for producing turboprop airplanes, and also the alliance between the ATR consortium and the BAES that was the first attempt toward the rationalization of the sector, although the program in the end proved unsuccessful. The second approach was followed instead by Bombardier[39], the industrial group whose aeronautical presence stems from the merger of several important firms such as Canadair, De Havilland, Short Brothers Ltd., and Lear. The third strategy was followed by Embraer, the Brazilian manufacturer that—thanks to its low engineering and manufacturing costs, and its technological knowledge and strong government support—was able to develop alone a new family of jet aircraft.

An additional example of this strategy was given by Fairchild Dornier after the break of the negotiations with ATR (and CASA). However, the attempt to go alone with the development of the 70 seats Do-728 jet airplane proved to be unsuccessful[40].

In terms of market penetration, Figure 2.43 clearly shows the impact of the jet's triumph over the turboprop in the 20- to 100-seat segment dominated by turboprops until the mid-1990s. In this period, an unfortunate event exacerbated the falling turboprop market share and aided the fast penetration of regional jets. In October 1994, an American Eagle ATR-72 crashed in Indiana (United States) due to an irregular ice accumulation on its wings from freezing drizzle. This was an accident, and the European manufacturer was completely absolved of any liability after accurate FAA and NTSB (National Transportation Safety Board) investigations. But the accident generated a negative image of turboprop products for passengers, especially in the U.S. market, where the fatal crash had a significant impact on the media. Consequently, the introduction of the regional jets received a boost.

The preference showed by the airlines toward regional jets had a negative impact on turboprop orders, which fell to a modest 9% share of the total market in 2000, down from 79% in 1991. It must be emphasized, however, that in absolute terms, the turboprop orders reduction has not been so dramatic, falling from about 139 units in 1991 to 81 units ordered in 2000. That means the introduction of regional jets has had mainly an effect of stimulating the demand, with the possibility for airlines to transfer connections from major to regional affiliates, to extend the range of the hub systems, and to create new point-to-point connections. They have only partially substituted turboprop aircraft, that will likely still be used in their typical role in the next years (feeding the hub systems), especially in the shorter routes.

The evolution of the major manufacturers' order during the last 20 years (in the 20- to 100-seat category) is reported in Figure 2.46:

• The significant increase recorded by Bombardier during the last decade that, thanks to the success of the CRJ family (more than 1,000 orders), reached about 1,600 total orders in the 20- to 100-seat category (in 2000, the Canadian firm achieved a share of 35.8% in terms of orders (310 units) and 39.6% in terms of value).

- The impressive increase recorded by Embraer after the launch of the ERJ-145 family (1997) and the successive ERJ-170 family (more than 1,000 firm orders in just 4 years), making possible the Brazilian company's leadership of the segment with 49.5% of orders (429 units to reach 54% share of the regional market in 2000) and 43.4% in terms of value.

- Fairchild-Dornier's growing market position, due to the introduction of the 328JET. In 2000, Fairchild-Dornier recorded about 10% of orders—89 units—and about 12% in terms of value; but in 2002 the company went out of the business, as already noticed.

- ATR's progressive loss of market share, with the Alenia-Aerospatiale consortium being the only competitor of Bombardier in the turboprop segment (in the 3-year period from 1998 to 2000, ATR collected an average of nearly 25 orders per year, equal to about 4% of the entire regional market—2.8% of orders in 2000, or 24 units).

- After the phasing out of its turboprop airplanes (ATP and Jetstream) BAE SYSTEMS was present in the market in the 20- to 100-seat segment with the AVRO-RJ family, that after nearly 20 years had recorded about 400 orders (only 15 units ordered in 2000, or 1.7% of the total market). But just after the September 11 events BAES stopped the production of the AVRO family.

Figure 2.46
Regional Aircraft Cumulative Orders — 20-100 Seats Category

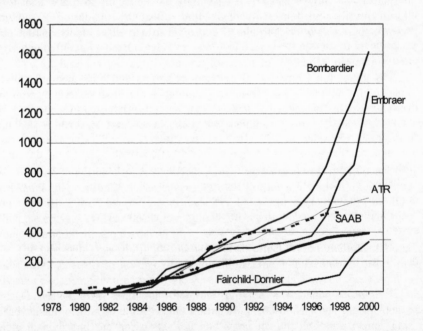

The evolution of the market is reducing the outstanding differences existing up to only few years ago among the business of regional aircraft and that of commercial jets. Certainly the width of the business, in terms of absolute size and value of the market, and the financial efforts necessary to compete with success, are still significantly different despite the increase in development costs of the regional jet, but the firms' competitive strategies and the structural characteristics of the two sectors are increasingly similar.

The autonomous and vertically integrated development of '70s and '80s is being replaced by a wider network of firms that bring their own technological, production, and commercial competencies.

These changes are affecting the total number of firms able to successfully compete in the business and, as has already occurred in the commercial jet sector, are reducing the primes in this specific sector to a few significant companies.

NOTES

1. The general downward trend in military spending is predicted to end as a consequence of the terrorist attacks on September 11, 2001, and the subsequent U.S. military campaign in Afghanistan. As U.S. defense spending, which now accounts for 36% of all military spending in the world, increases to face the new commitments (attack campaigns against rogue regimes, conflict prevention, defense diplomacy activities, and so on), this trend will likely result in a similar increase in defense budgets in other western countries. The rapid collapse of the Taliban under U.S. military power has emphasized the trend toward a growing U.S. military predominance; consequently, there will also be a general increase in defense spending in nonwestern countries to try to fill the gap between their own and U.S. military capabilities.

2. The Northrop Grumman merger with Lockheed Martin was halted in 1998.

3. The Vietnam War, for example, caused general concern and antimilitary sentiment. The new pacifist orientation blocked funding for completion of the B-70 bombardier, giving the green light to U.S. ambitions to create the first civil supersonic (using vital information from the Valkyrie strategic program).

4. Such customizations are less significant than they may appear, if it is taken into account that each airplane is generally designed to use power plants of the major engine manufacturers (such as Pratt &Whitney, General Electric, Rolls Royce) or consortia (IAE, CFM). The engine manufacturers design the power plants so that an engine model can be adapted to different airplanes in the same category with only slight changes. The airplane is also conceived with several possible interior arrangements in order to comply with specific operators' needs. Also, in the equipment field (particularly avionics), the prime airplane manufacturers often give customers the option of choosing between different brands and cockpit layouts to provide compatibility with features common to planes in the airline's existing fleet.

5. The events of September 11, 2001, have significantly affected the airline industry. In the first 14 days after the attacks, the U.S. airlines announced over 100,000 redundancies, and the U.S. Government suddenly reacted creating on September 22, 2001 the Air Transportation Stabilization Board with the purpose of issuing up to $10 billion in Federal credit instruments (e.g. loan guarantees) to compensate air carriers for losses incurred as a result of the attacks and to help them avoiding bankrupt. The consequent

slowdown in air travel, combined with a downturn in the economy, have very negatively impacted airline profitability. Notwithstanding the measures taken by the U.S. airlines to cut their costs they have lost about $6.2 billion in a year after the September 11 and the recovery appears quite slow. Many airlines (Fine Air, Midway, National Airlines, US Airways, Vanguard Airlines) have been forced to sought Chapter 11 bankruptcy protection and many others are close to it. In particular quite critical appears the situation of United Airlines, the second U.S. major airline, that on December 2002 failed to avoid the Chapter 11 filing negotiating with the pilot Unions to cut its annual labor cost of $1.5 billion and to obtain a government loan guarantee of $1.8 billion.. The negative effects of the attacks extended also to Europe, though less severely than in the U.S.; Sabena and Swissair suffered a tremendous crisis that led to the collapse of the two airlines: the former went to bankrupt in November 2001 and part of its routes and assets were taken by a smaller airline, DAT Plus, based in Brussels, whereas the latter — after having operated from October 2001 through a state aid package – at the end of March 2002 ceased to fly and its assets were partially taken over by its subsidiary Crossair that now flies under the new name "Swiss".

6. After September 11, 2001, the average passenger growth rate predictions for the next 20 years should be lowered; according to the Boeing's Current Market Outlook, the passenger traffic growth will average about 4.9% less than what was estimated before the attacks, with a negative peak in 2002–2003. In particular, for 2001 as a whole, world airline traffic fell to minus 4%, and the first half of 2002 remains at negative growth levels. World airline losses in 2001 far surpassed the losses incurred during the Gulf War of the early 1990s.

7. The main leasing companies today are: ILFC (International Lease Finance Group), GECAS (GE Capital Aviation Services), AMR Eagle Inc., GATX, Boullioun Aviation Services, Boeing Business Jets, Singapore Aircraft Leasing, Pemrocke Capital Aircraft in decreasing importance in terms of orders in the last 10 years, 1991–2000). The power of leasing companies is constantly increasing, considering that in the first half of 2000 total jet orders (commercial and regional jets) from leasing companies accounted for 263 units of the 948 aircraft orders, representing 30% of total jet sales.

8. The predominant source of emissions is engine exhaust. Fuel combustion produces gases such as carbon dioxide (CO_2), various nitrogen oxides (NO_x), carbon monoxide (CO), unburned hydrocarbons (HC), and sulfur dioxide (SO_2). Each aircraft type produces a specific emission profile during the landing/takeoff cycle; the emission data for each aircraft type is published by the FAA and other bodies.

9. Most of the work in the environmental field is undertaken through the ICAO Council's Committee on Aviation Environmental Protection (CAEP) which consists of "members" and "observers" from participating nations, as well as intergovernmental and nongovernmental organizations representing aviation industry and environmental interests.

10. Today, international and national regulations impose maximum noise exposure in three standardized recording locations: the first measuring point during the approach (at 2 km from the beginning of runway), and two other measuring points at takeoff (at 6.5 km after the beginning of runway and at 450 m on the sideline where the noise emitted is highest. The current noise regulations impose different values of the EPNdB (Effective Perceived Noise scale) as a function of takeoff weight and number of engines.

11. Aircraft certified before 1969 (B-707, DC-8), and not compliant with the noise standards introduced in that year, are classified as Stage 1; aircraft compliant with Chapter 2 and 3 are classified respectively as Stage 2 and Stage 3 aircraft.

12. In the last 10 years, the EC/ECAC (European Commission/European Civil

Aviation Conference), the FAA, and the ICAO have adopted several resolutions to progressively reduce the Stage 2 fleets still in operation. With the Airport Noise and Capacity Act of 1990, the U.S. Congress prohibited the operation of Stage 2 aircraft at U.S. airports after December 31, 1999.

13. The Kyoto Protocol will enter into effect after it has been ratified by at least 55 parties to the Convention Climate Change, including the industrialized countries that represent at least 55% of total 1990 CO_2 emissions.

14. Foo   = Rated maximum thrust (kN) at ISA SLS

     poo   = Engine pressure ratio at rated maximum thrust

     Dp   = Total mass (g) of pollutants emitted during the LTO
               (Landing–Takeoff cycle)

     Smoke   = Measured using the SAE filter paper technique

     OPR   = Overall Pressure Ratio

15. In absolute terms, even though specific fuel consumption per 100 RPK has been cut by 21% since 1991, emissions of CO_2 and NO_x in 1999 increased (in tandem with fuel consumption) by 11.8%, due to traffic growth.

16. Emission permits could be sold by industrial sector and/or companies that have been able to decrease their CO_2 emissions below the targeted level.

17. . In Europe, the engine makers, together with two universities and three research centers, are collaborating under the Fifth Framework Program in some research projects to develop advanced, efficient, environmentally friendly aircraft engines (EEFAE) as required to meet Kyoto Protocol targets; the aim is to validate technologies for two different market sectors, wide-body and narrow-body, for entry into service in 2007–2008 and to meet some economic and technical requirements.

18. In November 2001, BAE SYSTEMS announced that, due to changes in the aerospace market following the September 11th attacks on the United States, it had decided to stop its regional manufacturing programs, the decision would lead to an exceptional charge of £250 millions in the current year (2001) balance sheet. CEO John Weston added that "profit expectations for Airbus have been reduced significantly for next year and the outlook for regional aircraft has deteriorated sharply." [BAE SYSTEMS 2001]

19. In general, the uniformity of the competing strategy actually focuses the companies' efforts on the optimization of only a few areas of activity. That is, the companies pursuing a competitive advantage in terms of cost leadership concentrate their efforts mainly on the production process and industrial activities (logistics, factory layout optimization, production organization, process standardization, and so on). The companies implementing a differentiation strategy instead emphasize the product and, more generally, its technological content. Therefore, for them, R & D and marketing activities become critical: R & D for product design different from that of competitors, and marketing to create and support a known image on the market (in other words, to make their differences known to customers). A firm may also concentrate activity and attention on only one particular customer group, becoming a niche player. In this case, in order to be the best in that limited business segment, a firm must specialize to differentiate itself from other players from an organizational, production, and commercial point of view.

20. In the context of such a dispute about governmental subsidies in 1992 the European Economic Community and the U.S. Government reached an agreement concerning the application of the GATT (General Agreement on Tariffs and Trade) agreement on the trade of large civil aircraft. The agreement limits the government direct support on the development of airplanes larger than 100 seats. Main aspects concern:

- The amount of the money that can be lent to the manufacturer by its government. It should not exceed 33% of total development costs and should be returned with interests.

- The reasonable expectation that the program's breakeven is reached within 17 years from launch.

- The royalties to repay the money to the government are based on the same forecast of airplane deliveries submitted by the manufacturer in order to obtain the loan.

The agreement also limits the indirect benefits to the development of an airplane larger than 100 seats resulting from government funded research and development in the aeronautical area, made available to a manufacturer.

21. Composite material is defined as follows:

- It must be man-made.

- It must be a combination of at least two chemically distinct materials.

- It must have characteristics not achievable by any individual component.

22. The last Airbus product, the A-380, will have the wing center section made of carbon composite, the first such use in commercial aviation. The tail surfaces, rear pressure bulkhead, floor beams, and wing leading edge will be in thermoplastic. In addition, the A-380 will use GLARE (GLAss fiber REinforced aluminum—a material made of alternating aluminum and fiberglass layers bonded together) material for most of the upper fuselage panels.

23. The use of composite materials in the B-777 brings outstanding advantages in terms of weight saving, number of components, and production time. According to initial expectations, the new Boeing project, the *Super Efficient Airplane*, will also make an extensive and unprecedented use of composite materials also the airplane's primary structure. Boeing, in pursuing this initiative, will take advantage of some technologies and techniques developed for the JSF program, particularly those related to structures and materials.

24. Actually the Aeritalia participation to the 767 program is generally considered as one of the best examples of how the U.S. aerospace industry is able to take advantage of conflicts within Europe (more than an example of risk and cost sharing).

The time was 1971-72, and noise reduction had become a consideration. A large force of Italian engineers was then working in Seattle on the project. It was a learning experience, for which the teacher, Boeing, was paid – and paid very well – by Italy's state-owned aircraft company, Aeritalia. In 1971, Boeing was undergoing its crisis, and the Italian money helped keep some of its design teams intact. While negotiating with Boeing on the new airplane, Aeritalia had been strongly encouraged by the French and Germans to join the Airbus program; they, too, wanted access to Italian resources, and to Aeritalia's manufacturing capability, as well.
The Italians, after a serious debate within the government and industry, elected to join Boeing in what was supposed to be an equal partnership. Each company was to have a half-share in the new airplane. But the arrangement collapsed because Boeing, as T. Wilson puts it, "decided not to build its half." Although the agreement was one from which either party was allow to withdraw, the Italians felt badly used. "They got very sore," Wilson adds.
Whatever Boeing's motives may have been, the results of the Italian affair speak for themselves. Aeritalia was discouraged from joining the Airbus program but never did acquire Boeing as a partner in a new airplane. Given Boeing's attitude toward partnerships, it does seem unlikely that the arrangement with Aeritalia was ever destined to go very far.

What the Italian eventually got was a contract from Boeing to make the trailing edge of the wing and some tail sections of the 767, which amounted to less than 10 percent of the work on the airplane. [NEWHOUSE 1988: p.197-198]

It is also difficult to conclude that the responsibility of such a situation was (is) fully ascribed to Italy. In fact the question seems a little more complicated. The Italian Aerospace Industry seems perpetually undecided between Europe and USA. From the one side Italy may have asked for a role in Europe that was somehow higher than its capabilities would qualify; from the other hand the potential European partners myopia prevented the Italian companies to reach acceptable agreements; therefore, strategic factors were ignored or underestimated that in turn prevented a stable association of Italy to other European partners. That may be the reason why even successive attempts to enter Airbus have been unsuccessful; the envisaged EMAC (European Military Aircraft Company between EADS and Alenia Aeronautica) JV was never created; the entry of Alenia into Astrium failed.

25. The CN-235, which has been made by the Airtech joint venture (between CASA and IPTN), actually is an airplane created for dual use (civil and military transport) with sales almost exclusively in the military field.

26. Before its merger with Boeing in 1996, MDD's situation appeared very critical, with a strong disproportion between military and civil production, particularly in the late 1980s. The Long Beach firm had focused its own efforts on military products on which its future was strongly dependent (such as the C-17 or F-18) at a time when it should have made a significant effort to compete in the civil aircraft field, renewing and/or supporting its own products line.

Also, from the market coverage point of view, McDonnell Douglas had an unfavorable position compared to that of Boeing and Airbus. The firm operated in only two market segments: the narrow-body short-medium range (offering a family of aircraft: the MD-95, MD-90-30, and M-90-50) and the wide-body long-range (the MD-11). This niche strategy was based on an extremely competitive price policy allowed by the development of derivative aircraft. These products constituted an example of the application of new technologies to models whose design went back to the 1960s (the DC-9 and DC-10). Taking advantage of the economies of learning and the lower costs of derivative airplanes, MDD had been in the position of producing cheap aircraft, making it convenient for the airlines to acquire them even though their technical performance was not particularly good.

In the absence of an investment in the commercial aircraft business, MDD's management knew that the company could not hold out very long against the two leaders, because

- the technological gap between MDD and its competitors' products had become progressively wider, and

- the company could not offer a complete product line in most market segments.

In order to be competitive, MDD should have pursued the development of new models that would renew and/or complete the product line, bringing it to the level of its main competitors. However, the company appeared unable to face the technological and financial challenges brought on by its own new projects like MD-12 or MD-XX. In the end, after having failed in its search for partners that would cooperate in launching the MD-12 and also having been excluded from competition in the JSF program (that anticipated a decline in military sector activities), the more suitable solution appeared to be the merger with Boeing. For products in which an overlap existed, the MDD models (MD-90 and MD-11) were maintained in production for a short period, because the development costs had already been spent.

In the overlap of the B-737-600 and the MD-95-30 (renamed the B-717-200), the situation was quite different. Although the two models were close in seating capacity, the first is a 6-abreast, more advanced technologically, whereas the second is a less expensive 5-abreast that gave Boeing a 100-seat aircraft to complete toward the lower end of the range of products. Therefore, it has been maintained in production.

27. The events of September 11 and the consequent traffic downturn would have caused a delay of at least two years in the airplane's entry into service.

28. According to some preliminary estimates, the development cost of such a project would be around $9 billion.

29. In the reality the launch of the A318 program might be considered as the cause of the failure of the Euroasiatic collaboration, rather than the consequence of its failure. In fact Airbus, in the frame of a strategy of commercial penetration of the Asiatic market, had created a joint company with Alenia, always interested in the regional sector, that owned 38% of it. Such company in turn had created a JV with AVIC (China) and Singapore Technology with the majority of the shares owned by the Asiatic partners (AVIC 46%, Singapore Tech. 15%, Airbus + Alenia 39%). The purpose of this last company was to develop a "100 seats" airplane that from the one hand would complete the Airbus product line and from the other hand would satisfy the pride of the Asiatic partners (particularly the Chinese) to develop in house a regional jet. In fact, the constraint imposed by China was to have the final assembly line in that country, while the development would have been made jointly. Airbus accepted that conditions for the two reasons mentioned above: the need to have a new smaller aircraft to compete with B737 family of Boeing and MD-90/95 family of Douglas; the willingness to be present in a future huge market presently under development. In fact, internal studies concluded that the A319 was the smallest possible member of the A320 family because additional shortening on the airplane would have caused major penalizations. But further surveys made to some airlines which already operated the A320 and its derivatives changed drastically the preliminary and theoretical conclusions because such operators privileged the commonality even at the expenses of possible operational limitations of the new airplane. Therefore Airbus launched the program for this shortened brother of the A319, called A318, with about 110 seats. Of course at this point the launch of a new family of airplanes in the same market segment (although with 5 abreast, while the A318 was a 6 abreast) was not realistic anymore and Airbus stopped the joint program. China and Alenia were not happy at all with the evolution and conclusion of the joint initiative. Airbus insisted with its rights to protect its own strategic interest but promised compensations.

30. The commercial and economical feasibility of supersonic passenger transportation depend upon the practical possibility of achieving operating costs comparable with those of subsonic transportation (even with a premium fare in consideration of the savings in travel time). In practice, the main influencing factors are:

- the capital costs needed to develop the critical technologies to obtain the require performance (especially in terms of aerodynamic, propulsive, and structural efficiency);

- The elasticity of demand with respect to fares—that is, knowing the percentage of passengers available to pay a premium fare for the shorter travel time of supersonic jets (this value permits calculation of prospected sales and therefore the number of units to put into the business plan); and

- The achievable productivity gains [productivity = number of seats (miles/block time)] to balance the higher fuel consumption and maintenance costs of the supersonic aircraft.

In addition, the limitations imposed by aircraft noise and emissions regulations must be taken into account, because they can negatively affect supersonic aircraft operations.

31. The industrial cooperation was supported by an intergovernmental agreement between the two countries to fund the Concorde project.

32. The opening of service to the U.S. began on May 24, 1976, with simultaneous flights to Washington from London and Paris.

33. Several research programs were conducted during that period. In the United States, there were the SCR (Supersonic Cruise Research), NASA's HCST (High Speed Civil Transport), and the Battelle Center program; in France, the ATSF (Avion de Transport Supersonique Futur); in the United Kingdom, the AST (Advanced Supersonic Transport) and other activities in Japan and in the Soviet Union.

34. During the '70s, Tupolev had developed the Tu-144, an unsuccessful supersonic airliner created in response to the Concorde; the Tu-144, upgraded and refurbished as the Tu-144LL airborne laboratory, was used to provide data for the HSCT program.

35. In the meantime, supersonic research in the United States is continuing with the DARPA (Defense Advanced Research Projects Agency) Quiet Supersonic Platform (QSP) program, begun in 2001. Under the first phase of QSP, Lockheed Martin, Northrop Grumman, and Boeing are developing preliminary designs for new supersonic aircraft; also, engine manufacturers are working to design an affordable and efficient supersonic cruise engine that will meet current and future environmental rules.

36. With research in progress on a new supersonic airliner, some manufacturers are showing an increasing interest in a supersonic business jet. In 2001, Gulfstream (with an internal project called Quiet Supersonic Jet) and Boeing (in studies with Sukhoi) are working separately in this field

37. Following the failure of the first autonomous projects, the Japanese companies decide to adopt a development politics in the aerospace sector based on the international collaboration: the main three Japanese aeronautical companies, the Mitsubishi Heavy Industries (MHI), the Kawasaki Heavy Industries (KHI) and the Fuji Heavy Industries (FHI) participated with different shares to Boeing (B747, B757, B767) and Douglas (DC-10, MD-80, MD-11) programs and produced on license some fixed wing (F-104J, F-15J) and rotary wing (SH-60J, KV-107IIA, CH-47J, AH-1S. 204-B2) for U.S. military aircraft. The first collaboration agreement among the three Heavies (MHI, KHI, FHI) is dated 1978 when, through the "Civil Transport Development" consortium, they developed and jointly produced parts of the B767 airframe (15% of participation in the program). In December 1982 with an initiative of MITI (Ministry of International Trade and Industry) the three Japanese companies constituted the Japan Aircraft Development Corp. (JADC), to which later Shin Meiwa, Japan Aircraft Manufacturing, Japan Airlines, All Nippon Airways and other minority companies joined. Aims of the JADC constitution are: to promote the development of new commercial aircraft through research, studies. etc.; to coordinate the design and manufacturing capabilities of the Japanese companies in the sector of the civil aeronautical transport. The Alliance with Boeing was consolidated in the spring of 1991 with the JADC participation to twin-jet B777 program. The U.S. company assigned to JADC a risk sharing partnership corresponding to 20.8% of the aircraft, for the development and production of main fuselage and wing spar parts. After the crisis that hit the civil aeronautical industry during the period 1992-1995 (and the contemporary reduction of the Defense budgets worldwide, included Japan) the aeronautical business was not considered anymore a top

priority of the high-technology industry. The involved Japanese companies preferred to focus on the role of partners of primes (Boeing, Airbus, Bombardier) and to maintain their competitiveness in strategic businesses such as industrial machinery and automobiles.

38. According to preliminary estimates, after the events of September 11, 2001, the delivery forecast for the next 20 years should be lowered, on average, by about 5%.

39. Bombardier pursued a policy of acquisitions of aeronautical firms in the business and regional aviation segments, with the intent to develop a competitive advantage for the complete industrial group based on exploitation of all existing and possible interrelations among the two areas of business. Among the aircraft for business aviation and those for regional transport, technological similarities exist in both the products and production processes that favor sharing of technological development, acquisition of production factors, and manufacture of the components. Development of the CRJ-100, a 50-seat regional jet derived from the CL-601 business jet (and later the development of the 70-seat CRJ-700 and the 90-seat CRJ-900, belonging to the same family) represents the clear application of this strategy that has enabled the achievement of highly competitive production costs levels, together with technologically advanced solutions.

In addition, it is important to note that this synergy has been pursued from the start of business jet planning and the regional jet is derived from that effort, not vice versa. This is the key factor that has allowed the firms to charge most nonrecurring program costs to the development of an airplane belonging to a business segment (the business jet), where the demand is much less price-sensitive than in the regional transport sector. This makes it possible to set a sales price for the business jet that lets the manufacturer recover from its investments via a reasonable profit margin. Thus, only the costs of derivation need to be charged to subsequent versions (the regional jet).

Bombardier's strategy has been developed along two different paths. The 1989 acquisition of the Irish Short Brothers firm was undertaken in order to pursue the goal of production costs reduction, through a program of investments in process technologies lasted 4 years and cost about $400 million. Shorts, which built the SD-330/360 turboprop, is not longer an integrator of complete aircraft, but it has become the center of excellence for composite parts production and also, to a certain extent, for the airframe barrels production, mainly due to manpower costs that are among the lowest in Europe. Additionally, it is the supplier for different Boeing programs and made wings for the Fokker 70 and Fokker 100 airplanes.

In its second strategy path, Bombardier has prepared development programs for the activities of three other firms it acquired (Canadair in 1986, Learjet in 1990, and De Havilland in 1992), taking into account the different specialties of the three firms and sharing product and process technologies. Bombardier has not eliminated the three brands, but has encouraged their differentiation through the identification of each firm with a precise product segment: De Havilland makes commuters, Learjet makes business jets of small to medium size and price, while Canadair is identified with business jets of medium to high size and price and with the regional jet segment.

40. In effect, the insolvency in 2002 found Fairchild Dornier at almost half of the 728 development, just after the roll-out. At first glance, the unfortunate end of Fairchild Dornier in the regional jet segment, seems to give reason both to those saying that the development of a new family of regional aircraft was too expensive and risky to be carried on by a medium size company, as well as to those looking for wider alliances to venture upon the enterprise (the reference is particularly to ATR). A closer analysis of what happened in Fairchild Dornier leads to more articulated considerations which trace back causes of the failure mainly to management mistakes. It has been recalled many

times that by the concept of "marketing warfare" a new entry in a business must concentrate its efforts only on a product/segment and only after settlement it can and must enlarge the range of the products offered. Fairchild Dornier didn't follow this rule and, with the development of aircraft like the 328 Jet and the 428 Jet, dispersed its financial and managerial resources, thus inflating the budgets and losing credibility towards the shareholders and banks that had to finance the enterprise. In addition, some relevant 328 Jet sales had been blocked by the authorities of the countries of the customer airlines. Furthermore, one must consider that the cost of labor to the company was particularly high because the human resources had been recruited in any and every location hiring thousands of engineers in just a few years.

3

PRODUCT DEFINITION, EVALUATION AND COMPARISON

The design and development of a commercial airplane must be carried out with the reasonable prospect of being a successful venture from a financial point of view. Making a product that can meet favorable prospects of selling requires some activities to be carried out that are essential for the decision making process leading to an airplane program go-ahead. First of all it is necessary to perform continuously *desk* analysis whose objective is to provide the management with forecasts about airplane demand. The market demand and forecast is an attempt to quantify the number of aircraft the market will demand by class of seats, range and technology. After this initial research, if an attractive market/product segment has been identified one can decide to begin a *field analysis* by selecting a number of airlines to be interviewed (the customers of the aeronautical product).

The aim of the survey market phase is to have information that is qualitative about the product to be launched and quantitative about the consistency of the potential market concerning the class of airplanes under consideration. Information about the potential market must be in agreement with those resulting from the market demand and forecast; any discrepancies between the airplanes deliveries foreseen by the two methods must be indagated until eliminated.

In addition to those coming out from the survey, other requirements both technical and economical, are derived by comparing the product to be launched (still in prefeasibility configuration) with the competition. Other requirements from necessary compliance with airworthiness regulations.

Starting from mission and other requirements coming out from the activities seen above (airlines survey, competitive analysis and certification requirements), and after an explanation of airplane design phases classification, a method to preliminarily size a new airplane is presented and applied: at the end of this process typical weights, engines thrust and wing area of the new airplane are determined.

The impact of certification procedures and regulations on design of new airplanes is also analyzed.

3.1   MARKET REQUIREMENTS AND ANALYSIS

In this part of the chapter the set of the activities and analyses that must be carried out by an aeronautical firms will be illustrated:

1. If there is such a potential demand to justify the launch of a new (or derivative) airplane.

2. In case of positive answer to the point 1, what general characteristics the airplane must have (in terms of seating, range, and other main requirements) to meet the users needs (for example the airlines) in order that the new product can be a successful venture from the commercial point of view.

3.1.1   Market Demand and Forecast

In order to define the market demand, the following specifications are required:

*   The class of products (rather than a single product) to be marketed.
*   The type of customers and their geographical area.
*   The time period.

With these points in mind, it is possible to define the market demand as the total volume (measured in units or values) of a specific class of products that may be bought by a specific class of customers (in a specific geographical area) during a defined period of time. If the period of time refers to a future time interval, then the market demand is called the market forecast

3.1.1.1   Market Potential

The estimated market may be calculated at different levels of depth and segmentation and may assume a certain level of marketing effort. Increasing the assumed level of marketing effort increases the size of the market forecast, up to a limit over which market value does not show significant changes. This limit value is called the market potential.

3.1.1.2   Purpose of the Forecast

The market forecast is obtained by aircraft (or engine and other equipment) manufacturers as an aggregate air travel demand forecast, and subsequently is translated into an airplane delivery forecast. The standard format for measuring world air travel demand is revenue passenger miles (RPMs), or passengers carried multiplied by miles flown.

3.1.1.3 Time Scale

Generally, the level of uncertainty increases with time, so the long-term forecast may have to be bounded by a best likely level and a worst likely level, on either side of the most probable level of demand. The possible time scales for a forecast tend to be grouped somewhat arbitrarily into three:

- *Short term* (1 month to 18 months) - generally used for budgeting.
- *Medium term* (18 months to 5 years) - used for commercial planning.
- *Long term* (5 to 15 years) - used for strategic corporate planning.

3.1.1.4 The Forecasting Process

Development of a forecast within the segment of interest can be outlined by the following steps:

1. Define the market forecast horizon.
2. Identify the relevant variables.
3. Quantify the variables.
4. Select a realistic trial time period.
5. Fit variables into a mathematical form.
6. Project the variables.
7. Make the forecast.

In Figure 3.1, the forecasting methodology is shown as a sequence of logical steps. Each box requires an accurate study; relevant variables must be selected for use, and the analyst must judge the time period of their influence. The study evolves through the following phases (Figure 3.1):

1. Assumption of an economic forecast.
2. Study of the historical economic and traffic relationships (formulation of the model when a multiregression analysis approach is selected).
3. Total passenger traffic forecast, in revenue passenger miles.
4. Capacity requirements forecast, in available seat miles (ASM), based on study of the historical load factor data and trends to forecast an average passenger load factor.
5. Open lift growth calculation, as capacity requirements (ASM) less current fleet and existing orders capacity.
6. Open lift total calculation, as open lift growth plus forecasted retirement capacity.
7. New aircraft deliveries forecast, as open lift total divided by average ASM/Airplane (aircraft productivity).

Figure 3.1
Forecasting Methodology

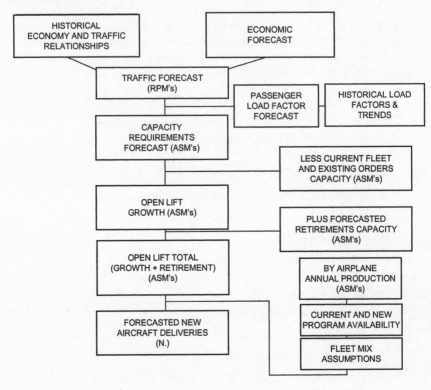

3.1.1.5 *Economic Forecast*

The value of air traffic demand is heavily influenced by economic trends; when the per capita income of a geographical area increases, more people travel, and vice versa. A numerical measurement of the economic trend of a geographical area is given by percentage change in gross national product (GNP) during a defined time interval. An estimate for future GNP may represent a good starting point for obtaining market forecasts of future air travel demand.

Once examined and processed, historical data about economic trends and the annual traffic changes make it possible to develop a method to relate, by means of a mathematical formulation, the air travel demand and economic trends (change in GNP). If an economic forecast has been carried out (or taken from a specialized publication or office) for a time period, the forecaster is ready to calculate traffic forecast for the same time period.

3.1.1.6   Traffic Forecast

The next step in the forecasting methodology (Figure 3.1) is forecasting the long-term air traffic growth, expressed as annual traffic percentage change, in order to obtain data to understand future air traffic capacity requirements. Two primary methods used to forecast long-term traffic growth are:

1. Methods based on trend projection, by which the problem is to determine a curve of future air traffic demand that can be well fitted to a given series of historical traffic data; and

2. Methods based on econometric models, by which air traffic change is related in mathematical form to governing factors such as economic growth and air traffic fares.

3.1.1.7   Forecasting by Trend Projection

Plotting on a diagram the historical traffic data on the vertical axis (as the dependent variable) and time (in years) on the horizontal axis (as the independent variable), a smooth curve that seems to come close to all points can be drawn. This curve represents a preliminary indication of annual variation of traffic data. By extending this trend for the years to come, a projection can be obtained for future air traffic data.

This kind of forecasting method works well when the growth rate of the dependent variable tends to be stable (in absolute or in percentage terms). It does not take into account traffic variation at a rate very different from the historical trend (due, for example, to a fast change in an economic variable). The problem in forecasting by trend projection is determining which curve is the most representative to best fit the data. The technique most frequently used to assess this best fit is known as the method of least squares[1].

3.1.1.8   Forecasting by Econometric Modeling

A more reliable method than the ones based simply upon a *trend projection* must take into account the way in which the governing factors, such as economic, social and operational conditions, may affect traffic development [ICAO 1985]. Such techniques are usually referred to as econometric modeling. They are based upon developing mathematical relationships that express the functionality between the dependent variable (air traffic data, as absolute value or annual percentage change) and some independent variables whose variations govern the phenomenology. Historical data are used to find the mathematical relationship. Once such a relationship is determined, it is necessary to obtain a long-term forecast for these independent variables. These types of forecasts are usually published by specialized publications.

The traffic and economic history are part of the econometric methods that follow a process whose main problem is selecting the right variables to be taken into account, which must be of enough significant importance for the development of air traffic (the dependent variable) demand. One variable often taken into account in econometric models is the cost of using air traffic service (such as the average air traffic yield per passenger-km), due to its great influence on the growth of air traffic demand. In more sophisticated models, there may be (independent) variables reflecting the influence of the quality of air service, the accessibility to airport facilities, the competitive situation with respect to other transport services, and so on. The list of possible independent variables to be used in econometric models is shown in Table 3.1.

A distinction can be made between directional and nondirectional traffic forecasts. Directional traffic forecasts refer to traffic on some specific routes (such as city-pairs traffic) or in some specific regions (such as North Atlantic traffic). In these cases, the development of air traffic demand is affected by the conditions (economic, competitive, social, and so on) in two geographical areas (such as cities, regions, states, countries, or continents).

Nondirectional traffic forecasting is concerned with the overall traffic volume generated in a certain region, independent of the destination of the traffic (such as total U.S. domestic traffic). Obviously, this type of traffic forecast is simpler than directional forecasting because its results depend only on the value of the relevant variables of the given area.

Once the most suitable variables to explain traffic growth trends are determined, the mathematical model of air traffic variation with the independent variables must be assessed. Formulation of the mathematical model uses a linear multiple regression between logarithmic values[2] of a combination of independent variables.

As an example, the results of an estimation process may be illustrated taking the model used by MDD [1984b] to forecast Europe to Middle East air traffic.

Table 3.1
Examples of Independent Variables in Econometric Air Traffic Forecasts

Type of Influence on Traffic	Variables
Size & spending ability of market	Population, Gross National Product or Gross Domestic Product, National Income, Disposable personal income, Personal consumption expenditure, Discretionary income, Total personal expenditures on travel and recreation.
Other market characteristics	Index for leisure available, Index for propensity to air travel, Index for ethnic, Linguistic & economic ties between cities or areas.
Cost of using air transport services	Published air transport tariffs, Average normal fare or rate per pass-km, Airline yield per pass-km, Fare plus value of time spent in transit, Average total journey expenses.
Transport time	Travel time or average speed airport to airport, Total transit time including airport transportation and waiting
Competition	Cost per hour saved compared with alternative transport service, Any ratio between cost, accessibility finance, speed or reliability for air service compared with alternative service.

Source: Elaboration on ICAO. *Manual on Air Traffic Forecasting*. 1985.

In this example of directional traffic forecasting, several models are tested, one trend model and three econometric models, in which scheduled historical revenue passenger-km (RPK) along these routes (Europe to Middle East) is related to some historical explanatory variables, such as gross domestic product (GDP), yield, and personal consumption expenditure (PCE).

The results of this test are the following:

1. Simple time trend model: growth in RPK is related to the time and provides a good correlation factor ($R^2 = 0.89$).

2. Weighted average GDP: RPK growth is related to GDP, and the resulting equation provides a low correlation factor ($R^2 = 0.85$).

3. Weighted average GDP and yield: RPK growth is related to a combination of these two independent variables, and the correlation factor improves ($R^2 = 0.87$), but is still lower than that of the simple time trend model.

4. Weighted average PCE and yield: in relating RPK growth to these two variables, the accuracy of the econometric model significantly increases, and the correlation factor is slightly less than 1 ($R^2 = 0.99$).

The final econometric model has the following equation form:

$$\ln (RPK) = 6.03 + 2.20 \ln (WRPCE) - 0.47 \ln (RYLD)$$

The coefficients in the equation are equivalent to the elasticity of traffic (RPK) with respect to the changes in the variables. The regression results in elasticity very similar to those expected. Air travel is most influenced by general economic conditions, as evidenced by the elastic relationship (+ 2.20) of traffic with respect to personal consumer expenditure.

Also significant in explaining the market trend is a yield with a negative - 0.47 elasticity. Both coefficients of elasticity are expected in accordance with classic economic demand theory. In fact, the model indicates that where personal consumer expenditure (PCE) rises, traffic (RPM) increases, and when airline yield (real fares) rises, demand falls. It should be noted that PCE is also a measure of availability of money to be spent on traveling by air. On the other hand, as yield rises, the cost of air travel increases for passengers. They may decide not to travel or may choose of another way of transportation. Yield data are then used as surrogates for changes in air travel costs. [McDonnell Douglas 1984b]

If we compare the results obtained by means of the time trend model and the final econometric forecasting model with historical data, the econometric model curve fits historical data better than does the simple time trend model (Figure 3.2). Although in the model other variables have been selected, Figure 3.3 (world RPM versus world economic growth) shows that the relationship between world RPM and world GDP, as well, is strong.

After the choice of an econometric model it is necessary to determine the new independent variables in the model itself, with which to derive the traffic forecast. As an example, using a forecasting model where RPM is related to GDP and airline passenger yield, long-term forecasts of aggregate air travel demand depend upon the ability of the forecaster to correctly anticipate world economic growth and the future pattern of yield. Long-term world economic growth forecasting is not an easy task, but several sources of such information are generally available. Figure 3.4 shows the world historical and forecast GDP and GDP average annual growth rate (average value is about 3.7%).

More difficult is forecasting a proper assessment of future yield. With the actual trend toward deregulated major airline markets, yield forecasting is much more problematic. Intense competition, reduction of direct operating costs, and greater efficiencies in airline operations and passenger handling will cause a declining trend in passenger yield, at a rate estimated at 1.9% (Figure 3.5).

However, an outstanding feature of econometric forecasting, and often a strong reason for using this technique, is that it offers the possibility of studying the sensitivity of air traffic development to changes in the pattern of the underlying factors.

3.1.1.9   Capacity Requirements Forecast

The logical next step, after obtaining the RPM forecast, is the transformation of the traffic data in capacity requirements (ASM) on the basis of the average load factor forecast. The following definitions apply:

RPM	revenue passenger miles
LF	load factor
ASM	available seat miles
S	average seat capacity
RAM	revenue airplane miles
pax	average number of passengers

Therefore, there is also a relationship between RPM, LF, and ASM growth:

Annual RPM growth = load factor growth x ASM growth
Annual ASM growth = average seating capacity growth x RAM growth

There is an increasing airline requirement to use aircraft more efficiently with a higher load factor; but to increase load factors (reducing the number of aircraft required), passengers will have to accept lower service levels due to fuller, less frequent flights. Analysis of historical data shows that an increase of system average load factor may result in a turn-away rate (demand not accommodated). Improved off-peak pricing and other current yield management techniques may decrease the turn-away rate. Therefore, forecasters agree that load factor levels will continue to increase but are bounded by a theoretical ceiling. Today, the average load factor for commercial aviation is about 72%; a slight increase is foreseen in the future.

Figure 3.2
Europe to Middle East Example — Econometric Model vs. Time Trend

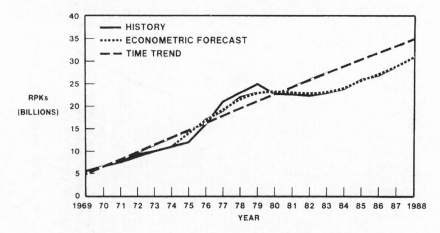

Source: McDonnell Douglas. *Economic Research*. Long Beach, CA: 1984b, p.15

Figure 3.3
World RPMs vs. World Economic Growth

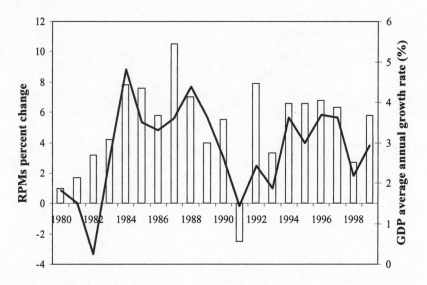

Figure 3.4
World Economic Growth

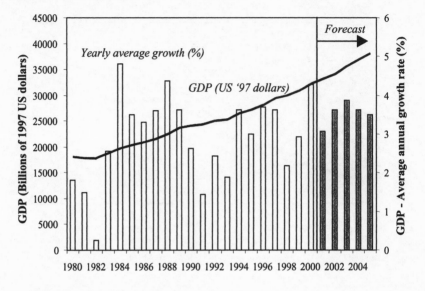

Figure 3.5
World Airline Yields

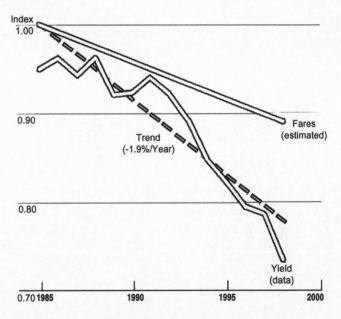

Source: Boeing Commercial Airplane Group. *Current Market Outlook 2000*, p.25

3.1.1.10 Open Lift Growth and Open Lift Total (Growth Plus Retirement)

To obtain the open lift growth, it is necessary to know the world fleet consistencies and the existing orders capacity. Then the knowledge of forecasted retirements capacity allows the characterization of the open lift total trend (Figure 3.6). Open lift growth is calculated from the total demand for airplanes (that is, capacity requirements forecast in ASMs) less current fleet (point A in Figure 3.6) plus announced orders evaluated in ASMs (point C in Figure 3.6). Therefore, once the on-hand and on-order equipment is known, it is possible to forecast the open ASM requirements.

The airplanes on hand and on order will be retired sometime in the future. Assuming that the beginning amount (point B in Figure 3.6) and the yearly amount of the retirement are known or can be estimated, it is possible to calculate the open lift for replacement. Open lift growth plus capacity available because of the forecasted retirements gives the open lift total.

The retirement assumption is concerned only with the commercial life of an airplane, which is generally less than its service life. Typical assumptions for average retirement age are, for example:

- Old technology jets (e.g., B727-100, DC-9-10, BAC 111, Caravelle): 20 years.
- Derivatives (e.g., B727-200, B737-200, DC9-30/50): 24 to 25 years.
- New technology derivatives and wide-bodies: 27 to 30 years.

The average age at which airplanes have been voluntarily removed from commercial service has slowly risen in the last few decades, moving from a retirement age of about 10 years in the early '70s to an average fleet age of about 25 years at the end of the '90s.

Figure 3.6
World Open-Lift Requirements

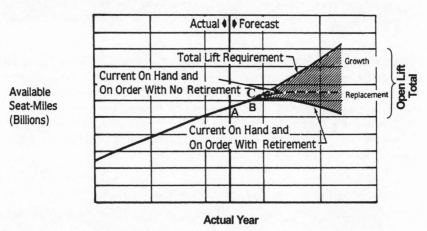

Actual Year

Principally, airlines replace aircraft when operating/maintenance costs outweigh replacement costs. It has been noted that operators are looking to use their older aircraft on shorter ranges. Often airplanes approaching retirement are sold to secondary or charter airlines that use them with lower productivity levels. Both aircraft utilization on shorter ranges and sales to other airlines reduce fleet productivity (ASMs/year available for each aircraft), as they represent a partial fleet retirement. Retirement assumptions can significantly affect production forecasts.

3.1.1.11 Product Forecast

The forecasted open lift total, evaluated in ASMs, represents the total demand in capacity requirements. The demand can be satisfied both by the ASMs available from aircraft that are in production and by those available from new programs. An accurate evaluation of respective shares would be an excellent result from a marketing effort. To obtain the total number of aircraft required by airplane size category, the forecaster must follow the steps shown in Figure 3.7:

1. Calculate the forecasted average aircraft productivity on the basis of the fleet mix assumptions and the actual and historical average productivity per aircraft type expressed in miles flown per year and per airplane. (This value is around 1.20 million in the year 2000, and it will increase to 1.25 million for 2010).

2. Determine the total number of seats required from the forecasted open lift total (ASMs) divided by the average aircraft productivity.

3. Predict the average airplane size (that is expected to grow at a rate of about 2 seats per year).

4. Calculate the new airplanes per year to be delivered from the total number of seats required divided by the forecasted average airplane size.

5. The value of the total number of aircraft to be delivered, so obtained, must now be segmented into the usual categories on the basis of actual and forecasted percentage fleet distribution (unit share per seat category).

A common way of showing the final forecast is shown in Figure 3.7 (units delivered by airplane size category). An alternative and more accurate way to reach this result is to make a separate forecast from the very beginning for each airplane segment category. For the purpose of the forecast, the relevant elements of segmentation are generally size, range, and the number of aisles (one or two).

Another way of forecasting commercial aircraft to be delivered is to split them into narrow bodies and wide bodies categories.

3.1.2   Airline Survey and Operator's Requirements

To evaluate the potential in developing a new family of aircraft, the company's top management may decide, after completion of the first marketing and technical reports, that an operator survey should be carried out before proceeding with the subsequent program phases.

The main areas of investigation in an operator survey are generally identified as:

1. A better evaluation of the market potential and market trends:
    a. Airline behavior with regard to evolution of the network.
    b. Fleet development.
    c. Aircraft needs.
    d. Competitiveness/prices.
2. A better evaluation of the airline requirements and the competitiveness of the proposed configurations:
    a. Cross-section definition.
    b. General aircraft configuration.
    c. Performance level.
    d. Size requirements.

Figure 3.7
Process to Calculate Deliveries Forecast per Year by Airplane Size Category Starting from Required (Open Lift) ASMs

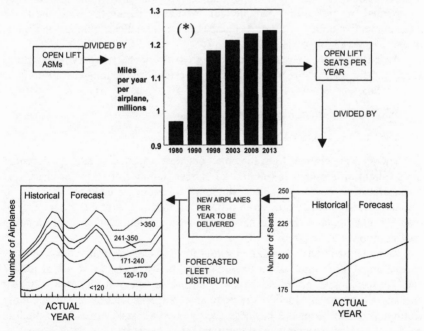

(*) *Source*: Boeing Commercial Airplane Group. *Current Market Outlook 1994*, p. 23

A presentation brochure and a questionnaire are prepared within the project team with the participation of the sales engineering organization. As an example, the following paragraphs will outline the results from a survey regarding a hypothetical regional jet in the 90- to 120-seat bracket.

The output of the survey described was based upon a sample of airlines from North America, Europe, and the Far East during the '90s. Among those airlines, 65% were previously selected on the basis of following criteria:

- Major airlines (two thirds of the 65% of the airlines surveyed):

    - The airline selected was an important 100-seater operator and had a significant backlog in the 100-seat category or,

    - The airline selected wasn't a 100-seat category operator but had a significant order for 150-seaters.

- Regional airlines (one third of the 65% of the airlines surveyed):

    - The airline selected had already chosen a 100-seat aircraft or was a large and representative operator in its category.

The remaining 35% of the airlines were selected by the sales organization based on its own criteria.

The airlines chosen were grouped into three broad geographical areas: 32% in North America, 45% in Europe, and 23% in the rest of the world. They represented a meaningful sample for whatever parameter was used for measurement: number of aircraft, number of seats in fleet, number of flights, flown seats, available seats/km.

As an example, in number of seats in their fleets, the surveyed airlines accounted for 40% of the world's total seats offered in the range of 30- to 200-seat airplanes.

3.1.2.1   Technical Requirements

3.1.2.1.1   Seating Capacity

The answers coming from the operators were adjusted to take into account the different airline layouts (number of classes, number of seats per class, seat pitch, and seats abreast). (This preliminary operation is essential in order to compare the answers coming from different airlines.) Therefore, the number of seats for a particular airline was factored to an equivalent seating in an economy configuration at 32 in pitch.

In the United States, a standard layout for first class is made with four seats abreast and a 38 in pitch and a fixed partition between classes. Thus, at least 7 and 10 seats must be added to most airline layouts for 90- and 120-seat airplanes, respectively to find the equivalent airplane seating in all economy configuration. In Europe, a business class at five abreast with a 34 in pitch is generally offered without a fixed partition between classes, so the difference in seats (with the economy layout) is due to pitch only and it is smaller.

Both configurations are offered in the rest of the world. Results are shown in Figure 3.8. A compilation of the answers given by the airlines, normalized into a one-class layout at a 32 in pitch, has the following seating capacities:

- Between 85 and 100 seats.
- Between 125 and 130 seats.

Slight differences can be appreciated among the geographical areas.

3.1.2.1.2 Range Capability

In order to better evaluate the requirement, two different but complementary approaches have been used and will be illustrated in the following paragraphs. Future needs in range capability have been evaluated based on today's airline networks served by equipment not too different from the proposed airplane. The results of this study have been compared with airline answers, and some conclusions have been drawn.

3.1.2.1.3 Airline Network Analysis

Figure 3.9 represents the cumulative distribution of range for each geographic area, considering all world airlines, corrected with airline rules that take into account airways' distance allowances. The range is adjusted with rules concerning airline reserves in each geographical area, taking into account the different layouts of airlines: number of classes, number of seats per class, seat pitch, and weight per passenger. These differences require some corrections in the range of the different areas. Data is taken from the OAG (Official Airline Guide) database. [OAG 1990]

The proposed value of 1,500 NM as the design range of the airplane under consideration seems to be adequate. It fits over 99% of the flights of surveyed airlines in Europe and the rest of the world and more than 97% of the North American flights. Moreover, in the proximity of 1,500 NM, the slopes of the curves of Figure 3.9 decrease quickly (particularly the European one), and therefore a further increase of range does not yield a substantial gain in additional number of flights.

3.1.2.1.4 Comparison with Airlines' Answers

Even supported by figures, these conclusions are subjective and therefore questionable opinions on the possible projections of the airlines on the subject. Some objective parameter should therefore be considered in order to determine the minimum value of the range that makes an airplane desirable to the airlines. This parameter could be the degree of coverage that the surveyed airlines expect to assure by introducing the new airplane into their network.

Figure 3.8
Equivalent Seating

QUESTION: Specify your seating capacity requirement in the next few years for airplanes around 100 seats

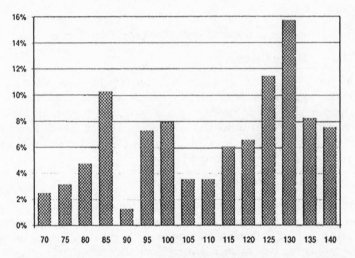

Equivalent seating in all-tourist configuration

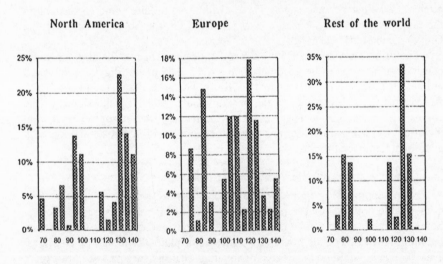

Figure 3.9
Cumulative Number of Flights vs. Range

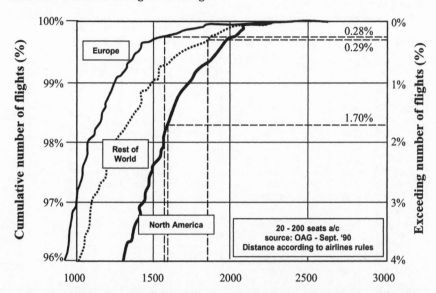

Table 3.2 shows the design range indicated by the airlines as their requirement. Values range between a minimum of 900 NM and a maximum of 2,000 NM. The number of routes and flights exceeding design range indicated values in their present networks are also reported. Airline route analysis is based on the OAG database [1990], and the network considered is the one served by aircraft having a capacity from 20 to 200 seats. Therefore, for each airline and for each airline group (by geographical area), it is possible to assess the degree of coverage of the current network that they wish to assure with the proposed aircraft.

In other words, the number (percentage) of flights exceeding the value of the range indicated by the airlines represents the degree of noncoverage accepted by the airlines when they suggest a design range covering most, but not necessarily all, of their routes.

By considering the results of the questionnaire a fair representation of the range requirement of all world airlines, it is possible to determine from the curves on Figure 3.9 the average minimum values of desired range that the proposed airplane must have in order for the degree of noncoverage to be the same as that indicated by the surveyed airlines.

Entering the curves of Figure 3.9 with the percentage values of exceeding number of flights of Table 3.2 (0.28% for Europe, 1.70% for the United States, and 0.29% for the rest of the world), the resulting minimum desired range is about 1,500 NM for the United States and Europe, and a little higher for the rest of the world.

Table 3.2
Design Range Indicated by Interviewed Airlines

AIRLINE	REGION	Design Range Indicated by Interviewed airlines	No. of flights exceeding the value indicated in the questionnaire By interviewed airlines			
			Routes No.	Routes (%)	Flight No.	Flight (%)
1	EUR		0	0	0	0
2	EUR	1300	5	2.07	21	0.72
3	EUR	1800	0	0	0	0
4	EUR	1300	0	0	0	0
5	EUR	1300	2	1.53	22	0.53
6	EUR	1300	0	0	0	0
7	EUR	1500	1	0.82	2	0.07
8	EUR	1300	0	0	0	0
9	EUR	1200	0	0	0	0
10	EUR	1500	3	1.75	12	0.33
11	EUR	1500	0	0	0	0
12	EUR	1300	0	0	0	0
13	EUR	1500	0	0	0	0
14	EUR	1200	3	5.66	10	1.09
15	EUR	1500	0	0	0	0
16	EUR	1500				
Subtotal			*14*	*1.09*	*67*	*0.28*
17	N. AME	1500	10	6.85	100	2.22
18	N. AME	1300	0	0	0	0
19	N. AME	1600	0	0	0	0
20	N. AME	1300	22	8.03	558	5.29
21	N. AME	1300	19	3.81	293	1.48
22	N. AME	1500	1	2.94	56	3.43
23	N. AME	1652	2	0.77	40	0.38
24	N. AME	1200	0	0	0	0
25	N. AME	1500	1	0.47	28	0.41
26	N. AME	1000	3	3.61	61	0.99
27	N. AME	900	0	0	0	0
28	N. AME	1500	0	0	0	0
Subtotal			*58*	*3.45*	*1136*	*1.7*
29	ROW	1500	2	3.51	28	2.03
30	ROW	1300	0	0	0	0
31	ROW	1500	0	0	0	0
32	ROW	1300	0	0	0	0
33	ROW					
34	ROW	1300	0	0	0	0
35	ROW					
36	ROW	2000	0	0	0	0
37	ROW	1000	0	0	0	0
Subtotal			*2*	*0.41*	*28*	*0.29*
TOTAL			*74*	*2.14*	*1231*	*1.23*

3.1.2.1.5   Design Point and Evaluation of the Airplane's Requirements

Since we have repetitively spoken about design range and seating requirement and we are going to analyze airfield performance, the following explanations may be needed.

3.1.2.1.5.1   Design point

Payload (seating) and range together define the design point of the airplane. The Operating Empty Weight (OEW) is highly related to the first parameter, much less to the other. Their combination is highly linked with the Maximum Take-Off Gross Weight (MTOGW) of the aircraft.

During the product life cycle there is a normal tendency to certificate the same model for higher TOGW. Likely, engine power shall be increased to avoid heavy takeoff and climb performance deterioration. Such weight increases may be "spent" to reach different objectives.

One may increase the (sum of) payload and OEW by the same amount of TOGW increase keeping constant the range parameter. Of course the airplane fuselage must be stretched to accommodate the additional seats and this will account for almost all the increase in OEW.

Alternatively one may carry onboard more fuel (almost) by the same amount of the TOGW increase, increasing the flying distance capability and keeping constant the payload of the airplane.

Of course a combination of the two changes in the airplane's characteristics is also possible. In such a way "derivatives" models may be created and put on the market occupying new segments in the market-product grid, different from that of the "founder" airplane.

Generally, the path followed is indicated in the Figure 3.10. Additional TOGW increases may be obtained afterwards.

3.1.2.1.5.2   Airfield Performance

When analyzing airplane takeoff performance against airline needs, there are always some limitations, as the airplane cannot take off with its Maximum Take Off Gross Weight (MTOGW) from all airports. This does not always translate into a payload limitation. In fact, usually when the airport of origin has a short runway, is located at high altitude and the external temperature is generally high, it may also be that the length of the leg to be flown is small, and therefore the connection can be accomplished with full payload, even if MTOGW is limited. So takeoff field length requirements should be evaluated by considering both available runway characteristics and stage lengths to be flown from that runway.

Since some connections will exceed the airplane range capability, an additional problem to be solved in the design phase is related to the evolution of the project, which will always call for increase in the design range. The answer can be either an increased gross weight version of the present project or an alternative design range.

Figure 3.10
Paths for Derivative Aircraft Models

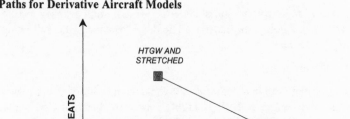

The difference is that the first solution would satisfy the extra range requirement with some performance deterioration but without changes in the airplane (except for the landing gear). The second would imply major changes to allow for the increased installed power, and margins should be built into the design phase in view of such evolution.

3.1.2.1.6   Critical Airport Field Length

Airport field lengths, given by the airlines with the associated altitudes and temperatures, have been equalized. The equivalent field length has been computed at sea level and ISA (International Standard Atmosphere) temperature (taking into account the performance variation of the airplane under study).

There is a considerable number of airports with an equivalent ISA sea-level field length just over 1,700 m (Figure 3.11). Each point of Figure 3.12 shows the maximum distance flown from the airports mentioned in the questionnaire (the airports in Figure 3.11). Distances are from the OAG database [1990], adjusted to be consistent with the range definition of the airplane under study by the manufacturer.

Figure 3.13 is similar to Figure 3.12, but in order to reach some general conclusions, all connections from North American airports (in aircraft having between 20 and 200 seats, as in Figure 3.11) are shown. In the same charts, the balanced field lengths (BFLs) needed by the airplane (as a function of range) are also drawn.

All connections situated above BFL curves are practical with proposed airplanes. It is evident that most of the city pairs can be connected, because the available field length is higher than the BFL. This situation is due to the fact that as the needed BFL increases because the range also increases, generally also the available field length of the involved airport increases. Said differently, an airport's available runway length is generally correlated with the maximum flown distance from that airport, as it is the Takeoff Gross Weight (TOGW) of the airplane (and therefore the needed BFL).

Figure 3.11
Airport Field Length

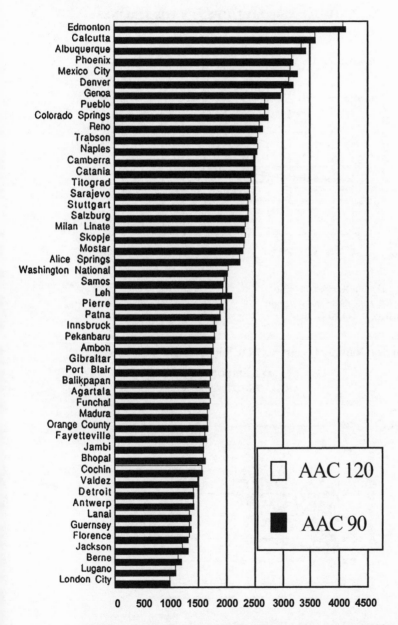

Equivalent field length (ISA - Sea Level) (m)

Figure 3.12
Airlines Runway Length* vs. Max Range (20-200 Seats Aircraft)

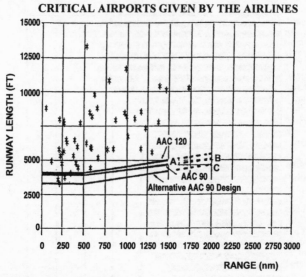

A)   Present Design Range and BFL
B)   Increased Take-Off Gross Weight
C)   Alternative AAC 90 Design

Figure 3.13
North America: Runway Length* vs. Max Range (20-200 Seats Aircraft)

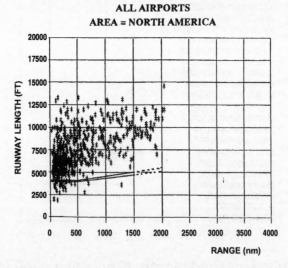

* Equivalent s.l. runway length distances modified according to standard airline rules, reserve fuel
and cabin layout

This analysis confirms that the design range is appropriate because only a few points (city pairs) fall below the BFL curves in Figures 3.12 and 3.13. Furthermore, these points refer generally to short stage lengths where airplanes of the lower end of the considered bracket (20 to 200 seats) and mostly turboprop are in service, unlike the 100-seat jets under evaluation here.

3.1.2.2   Configuration Requirements

3.1.2.2.1   Cross Section and Cabin Dimension

The analysis of cross section is usually based on survey responses, data coming from competitors' products, and airline-specific visits regarding the topics. In addition, AEA (Association of European Airlines) requirements for short- to medium-range aircraft are considered. As an example, results of such an analysis carried out for two aircraft of about 90 and 120 seats are summarized in Table 3.3.

This table shows the cross-section data of the two airplanes presented to the airlines ("current"), some suggestions obtained from the airline survey ("survey"), minimum requirements from the AEA or other sources ("minimum"), and the values assumed at the end of this analysis ("result").

Table 3.3
Cross Section Requirements

	CURRENT	SURVEY	MINIMUM	RESULT
CONTAINER CAPABALITY	NO	Not necessary	-	Not necessary
MAX CABIN HEIGHT (m)	2.06	-	1.90	2.06 is more than adequate
AISLE WIDTH (in)	20	Adequate or even ample An airline: not sufficient	19 (AEA) 17.5 (an airline) 17 Handicap. chair	20
SEAT WIDTH (in)	19	Adequate or even ample	19 (AEA)	19
SEAT ABREAST	5/6	Not interested in the 6 abreast configuration	-	5
UNDERFLOOR BAGGAGE (m³/seat)	95 pax 125pax 0.192 0.213	-	0.200	0.200
OVERHEAD BINS (m³/seat)	95 pax 125pax 0.048 0.049	-	0.057	0.057

Inside each category of airplanes (narrow and wide-body) the choice of the abreast is a strategic one.

In fact the future derivative airplanes of the family can change anything but the fuselage cross section that will last for the entire life of the airplane family.

During the product life cycle the airplane will be likely re-engined one or more times; the avionics will be updated; the area of the wing will be increased together with the fuselage stretch.

The bigger is the cross section the higher is the flexibility of the airplane to change its size. The Figure 3.14 shows that for narrow body airplanes (but the same applies for wide-bodies) for a given abreast the size is within a minimum and maximum number of seats, delimitated by economical and physical limitations.

The last is due generally to rotation problems at take-off that arise when the length becomes abnormally high. The first is due to the drug and weight penalization when the fuselage become abnormally short.

The economical and physical boundaries may be calculated theoretically using the equations of the preliminary design. On the contrary Figure 3.14 has been obtained plotting actual airplanes' seating and abreast. For each abreast there is an optimum airplane size and vice versa.

But small penalization in terms of optimum airplane performance may be well accepted (within the limits of the figure) because of the higher advantages deriving from commonality of a family member.

Figure 3.14
Capacity vs. Abreast for Passenger Airplanes

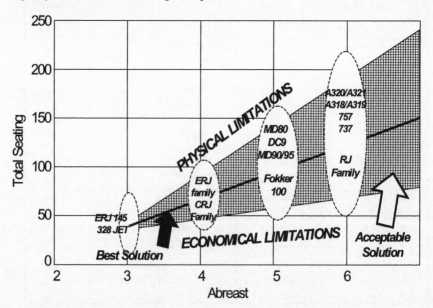

3.1.3 Additional Requirements

3.1.3.1 Cruise Speed

Cruise speed is the parameter with the most influence on block time (the time elapsed from takeoff to landing, plus taxi out and taxi in), especially at longer ranges, and therefore on operating costs. In the preliminary design phase, the cruise speed is chosen by means of a competitive analysis with respect to other aircraft of the same class. Then its final value (optimization) is implemented, considering the effect of a change in cruise speed on the overall design of the airplane and therefore on the direct operating costs through the variation of specific fuel consumption, installed thrust (power), airplane weight, and block time. Trade-offs between these variables will determine a value of cruise speed that minimizes the direct operating costs.

3.1.3.2 Initial Altitude Capability

A high initial altitude capacity is very important because it permits the choice of a higher flight altitude, enabling the aircraft to fly above overcrowded airways, thus reducing fuel consumption, block time, and operating costs. This need capability is more important under hot weather conditions when cruise thrust limitations do not permit the use of higher altitudes, thus forcing all traffic to crowd the lower altitudes.

Therefore, altitude capability is especially important to airlines flying long ranges under heavy traffic conditions. Additional altitude capacity is more meaningful to some airlines than to others. The operator flying in a cold, uncrowded environment cannot profit from increased altitude capability in the same manner as a North Atlantic operator forced to fly below the requested altitude because of its inability to fly higher, or a Middle East operator facing hot day altitude limitations.

3.1.3.3 One-Engine-Out Ceiling

The altitude capability of an airplane with a failed engine must be considered in this phase because it involves safety, apart from the economic considerations. The possibility of an engine failure must be considered when flying over mountainous terrain or long over-water routes. In these cases, the airplane may still be permitted a safe flight by flying at a lower altitude. Moreover, a higher one-engine-out ceiling (that is a greater cruise thrust at constant airplane weight) increases the number of routes that may be flown by the airplane, and therefore gives an advantage to the airplane under consideration, with respect to its competitors.

3.1.3.4 Number of Engines

With fewer engines, costs are less (including spare parts and maintenance costs). The crew workload, with two sets of controls and instruments, is less than with three. On the other hand, probably the biggest factor to consider is that all U.S. Federal Aviation Agency (FAA) performance requirements, except the landing climb gradient requirement, are based on an assumed engine failure situation. With one failed engine, the trijet retains two thirds of its total thrust, and the four-engine airplane three fourths of its total thrust. Therefore, the total installed thrust of a trijet must be higher than that of a four-engine airplane, all other things being equal.

Table 3.4 illustrates the differences in climb gradient requirements with one-engines being inoperative for airplanes having various engines' number. Note that the regulations are less stringent in requirements for airplanes with fewer engines, but this still does not completely compensate for the greater percentage of thrust loss.

3.1.3.5   Number of Restrooms and Galleys

The number of restrooms depends on the number of seats, and the minimum value is determined by the consideration of the standard comfort level adopted. The current average value is one restroom for 45 seats. Galley volume depends on number of seats and average stage length. It also depends on the split between first, business, and economy classes, and are generally higher for international/intercontinental flights. For domestic U.S. market figures, they range between 1.5 and 2.0 cu ft/pax (half or full meal service).

3.1.3.6   Cabin Pressurization

The choice of a pressurized and air-conditioned cabin gives more comfort and promotes customer satisfaction at the expense of structural weight and systems simplicity. The pressurization level comes from considerations about maximum operating altitude. Airworthiness regulations relate maximum pressure altitude inside a pressurized cabin to maximum operating altitude. Moreover, the pressurization system must be sized to assure a cabin pressure altitude rate of change of no more than 300 feet per minute (fpm) in order to respect physiological passenger limitations avoiding discomfort to them.

Table 3.4
Climb Gradient Requirements

FAR 25 CLIMB GRADIENT REQUIREMENTS WITH ONE ENGINE INOPERATIVE			
	TWO-ENGINE AIRPLANES	THREE-ENGINE AIRPLANES	FOUR-ENGINE AIRPLANES
Initial segment (FAR 25.111)	1.2%	1.5%	1.7%
Transition segment (FAR 25.121)	>0	0.3%	0.5%
Second segment (FAR 25.121)	2.4%	2.7%	3.0%
En-route (FAR 25.121)	1.2%	1.5%	1.7%
Approach (FAR 25.121)	2.1%	2.4%	2.7%

3.1.4 Economic Requirements: Direct Operating Costs

The most significant economic parameters to be considered are:

- Airplane price, which must be compatible with the financial means of potential customers, and

- Operating costs, which must allow positive economic results from the operation of the airplane and must be competitive with other available equipment.

The company generating a new airplane design must make a very careful evaluation of the resource requirements for producing the airplane. It may be constructed entirely in-house or may be partially out-sourced to subcontractors. The amortization of the new production capability investment (a nonrecurring cost) over the production life of the vehicle must be carefully analyzed for its impact on price, whether it is for tooling, for buildings, or for the engineering work of developing the design.

Of primary importance are the economics of a mission, that is the cost of delivering a passenger or a cargo, or a weapon to the objective over a given distance.

These costs are significantly influenced by the original price of the airplane and its expected life. The underlying reason for any airplane program is its ability to provide a profit to the company that designs and builds it, as well as to the buyer who uses it.

Although dramatic airplane and engine life improvements were achieved in the 1990s, the resulting increase in commercial airplane use has put added emphasis on the need for airframe, engine, and system durability. Characteristics such as airframe fatigue life and system failure rates influence airplane utilization and have become more and more the subject of initial contract negotiations.

There are two types of operating costs: direct operating costs (DOC) and indirect operating costs (IOC). Only direct operating costs are taken into account in designing airplanes, because indirect costs are related to the way planes are used, and therefore mainly to the particular operator structure.

DOC may be estimated through some methods that are all derived from the basic cost model developed by the Air Transport Association of America (ATA) at the end of the sixties. With these methods, direct operating costs are broken down into the following cost elements:

- Fuel cost.
- Crew cost (pilots and flight attendants).
- Landing and navigation fees.
- Airframe and engine maintenance cost, including both material and labor costs.
- Investment-related cost (the sum of depreciation, insurance, and interest costs).

The structures of these formulas and their dependence upon the major cost variables will be explained in detail later.

The comparison of DOC for different airplanes and for a given stage length represents a measure of the economic attractiveness of such airplanes for an operator with flights at that average stage length.

3.1.4.1   DOC Basic Concepts

The economic characteristics of a variety of airplanes can be compared by plotting the airplane's cost per mile (airplane trip cost) on the horizontal axis, and the cost per seat-mile (cost per seat) on the vertical axis. These two parameters are arithmetically related. A 100-seat airplane operating at a cost per mile of $2 will have a cost per seat-mile of $0.02 (that is, $2 divided by the number of seats). If that same airplane costs $4 per mile, its cost per seat-mile would be $0.04 (Figure 3.15).

A series of lines of constant capacity can be drawn on the chart (Figure 3.15) [MUNSON 1984]; these lines start from the origin of the axis and have an angular coefficient α related to the inverse of the number of seats (tangent α = 100/seats).

A 200-seat airplane with a $4 cost per mile would cost 2 cents per seat-mile to operate. If the 100- and 200-seat airplanes had the same cost per seat-mile, no operator would be interested in the larger airplanes, because it would be paying higher trip costs with no per seat economic benefits related to size (Figure 3.15). Only if an airline were in a frequency constrained environment, with no better alternative, would the larger airplane, with its greater costs per trip and no improvement in cost per seat-mile, appear to be of any interest [MUNSON 1984].

Figure 3.15
Airplane Direct Operating Cost: Basic Concepts

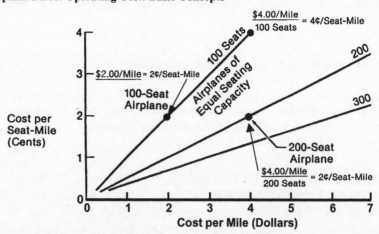

Source: Elaboration on H.C. Munson, "Fleet modernization key factors in today's environment - A manufacturer's view" - Presentation made at the Biannual Meeting of ATA/IATA Airline Financial Officers - Montreal, 1984

3.1.4.2   DOC Objectives in New Airplane Design

A rough but helpful criterion can be used in order to assess the economic viability of new airplane designs, suggesting whether or not they are worthy of further examination. This rule of thumb says that, when comparing the economic performance of two airplanes with different seating capacities, the ratio of change in cost per mile versus change in cost per seat-mile is roughly equal to 3 (Figure 3.16).

By applying this rule, it is possible to determine a relationship between the cost per mile (DOC/Mile) of two airplanes with different seating capacities (S_1 and S_2):

$$(DOC/Mile)_2 = \frac{(DOC/Mile)_1 \times (4S_2)}{(3S_1 + S_2)}$$

This relationship shows how much higher the cost per mile can be in order to reach a sufficient economy of scale with a larger airplane. As an example, considering two airplanes with $S_1 = 100$ and $S_2 = 200$ (Figure 3.16), the previous rule means that the maximum cost per mile of the larger airplane may be 60% higher than that of the smaller one (and thus the cost per seat-mile is 20% lower). If the increase of cost per mile is higher than 60%, the larger airplane will not reach a sufficient scale economy. Therefore, the line drawn on Figure 3.16 may be considered as joining airplanes of different sizes but with similar technological content.

Figure 3.16
Airplane Direct Operating Cost: A "Rule of Thumb"

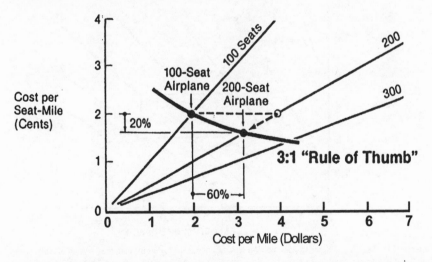

Source: H.C. Munson, "Fleet modernization key factors in today's environment - A manufacturer's view" - Presentation made at the Biannual Meeting of ATA/IATA Airline Financial Officers - Montreal, 1984, p.23

It may be interesting to look at the situation that arose in 1965, during the development phase of the B-747. When comparing its economic characteristics to the existing B-707-320B, it is easy to verify that the 3-to-1 relationship is met (Figure 3.17). Although the B-747 represented a significant improvement in technology over the B-707, because the fuel price was very low and the crew composition was similar, it was tough to obtain around the desired 3-to-1 improvement ratio.

The B-707 versus B-747 case is particularly complicated because the former is a narrow-bodied and the latter a wide-bodied airplane. This difference must be taken into account because wide-bodied planes give more room and more space for cargo per passenger, but they also burn more fuel and need more structural weight per passenger.

It must be noted that the proposed criteria should be used when comparing airplanes belonging to the same technological level and with close price/seat; in the case that the first condition is met but prices are quite apart, cash DOC (that is DOC less investments-related costs) should be considered.

The rule of thumb may be used in the design phase of a new airplane (or a new family of airplanes) by establishing a DOC objective lower than the main competitor airplanes. This consideration is shown in Figure 3.18.

Figure 3.17
Airplane Direct Operating Cost: New vs. Existing Airplanes

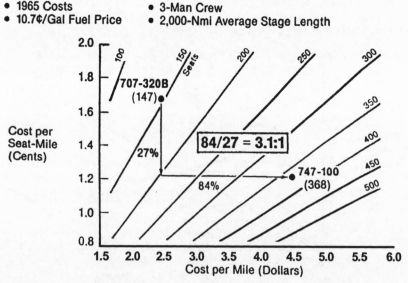

Source: H.C. Munson, "Fleet modernization key factors in today's environment - A manufacturer's view" - Presentation made at the Biannual Meeting of ATA/IATA Airline Financial Officers - Montreal, 1984, p.25

Figure 3.18
Size Effects in Airplane Economics Comparison

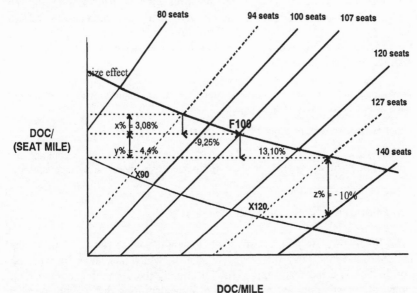

DOC/MILE

Note: - Determination of cost per seat-mile:
$DOC_{X90} = DOC_{F100}$ + change due to size (X%) + change due to technology improvements (Z%)
$DOC_{X120} = DOC_{F100}$ + change due to size (X%) + change due to technology improvements (Z%)

The DOC objective of the new family of airplanes to be developed has been put at "being better than F-100 by Z%" (in terms of cost per seat-mile), based on the manufacturer's subjective evaluation of today's state of the art as compared with the state of the art at the launch date of F-100.

In particular, it is assumed that the manufacturer wishes to develop two airplanes of 94 and 127 seats, while the F-100 can accommodate 107 seats. This means that the expected change in cost per seat-mile of the new airplanes is the sum of two different effects: the change due to the different size (that can be calculated by using the 3-to-1 ratio), and the change due to the technological improvements (amounting to Z%).

Therefore, considering the size of the two airplanes of the new family compared with the F-100's size, assuming that Z% = 10%, and applying the previous relationship (about the size effect on DOC), one concludes that the small airplane (X-90) can outperform the F-100 by only about 7% in cost per seat-mile (and still meet the requirements), whereas the larger member of the family (X-120) must be at least 14.4% lower in cost per seat-mile than the F-100.

In fact, +3.08% and -4.4% differences in cost per seat-mile between the F-100 and the new small and large aircraft, respectively, must be attributed to the size effect only.

3.1.4.3   Reaching DOC Objectives

A clear understanding of DOC composition is necessary for weighing the relative importance of single elements and their dependence on design parameters. Figure 3.19 shows the DOC breakdown for a typical airplane in the 100-seat category at an average stage length (not at design range). The DOC breakdown analysis shows that:

- Investment-related costs (depreciation, interest, and insurance—mainly depreciation) are about 34% of the total.

- Fuel expenses represent about 25% of the cost.

- Maintenance is around 20% of DOC, with airframe maintenance accounting for about 14% (airframe maintenance is more labor-intensive than engine maintenance).

- Landing fees are about 9% of DOC.

- Cockpit crew represents around 12% of the cost.

The breakdown may be useful in understanding what can be done in the design phase to reduce an airplane's DOC; that is, which parameters to work on and what the expected result might be. Of course, the above breakdown (and therefore the most important parameters to consider) may differ with the size and design range of the airplane.

Figure 3.19
100 Seater DOC Breakdown — Stage Length = 500 NM

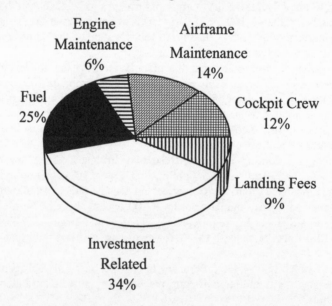

According to their nature, the cost elements can be grouped into three main cost categories:

- Price-dependent items, which are depreciation, interest, and insurance costs (investment related costs).

- Technology-related items, including fuel, engine, and airframe maintenance costs; and

- Operational items, including crew cost and landing fees.

As can be seen in Figure 3.19, direct operating costs show a very strong dependence upon purchase price (investment related costs). In particular, lowering the price by about 10% causes a reduction of DOC per trip by 3.11%. Increasing the number of flights per year (the aircraft annual utilization) may reduce the investment-related costs attributed to a single flight.

The influence of technology on operating costs is related to the reduction in block fuel, block time, and operating empty weight due to improvements in aerodynamics, propulsion, structures, materials, and systems. In particular, a reduction of block time obtained through technological advances (without increase of fuel consumption or airframe weight) results in a significant decrease of DOC. In fact, lowering the block time by 10% causes a reduction of DOC per trip by 4.80% in the case under examination.

Unfortunately, technological improvements also have an effect upon the aircraft's selling price, thus affecting development and production costs. So the new technologies aimed at reducing DOC actually increase research and development costs of the aircraft, and thus push toward an increase of its selling price. On the other hand, the greater appeal of the aircraft due to technological improvements may justify a higher selling price. In short, technological innovations introduce a trade-off between the resulting increase in R & D and production costs, and the increased buyer appeal due to reduction of direct operating costs.

3.1.5   Airworthiness Regulations

Many countries require that aircraft operating within their boundaries be certified according to established airworthiness regulations, which are intended to assure a minimum standard of safety and significantly influence the design of the airplane. The U.S. market is the biggest single potential market for any type of commercial airplane. U.S. airworthiness regulations, established by the Federal Aviation Agency, are among the most complete and detailed. In addition, the FAA regulations are recognized by many countries and are the basis of the national regulations of other countries.

From the above it follows that, in addition to market requirements, conformity to the FAA regulations is a must in designing airplanes. The following are some aspects of those regulations [FEDERAL AVIATION

186   MARKETING AND MANAGEMENT

REGULATION (FAR), PART 25] that may impact the general layout of the airplane in the conceptual phase.

3.1.5.1 Cabin Doors, Emergency Exits, Aisles, Seats Abreast

The minimum number of cabin doors and emergency exits is stated by the airworthiness regulations related to the aircraft type considered. FAR (Federal Aviation Regulations) Part. 25 sections applicable are:

- 25.783 Doors.

- 25.807 Emergency exits.

- 25.813 Emergency exist access.

- 25.815 Width of aisle.

- 25.817 Maximum number of seats abreast.

3.1.5.2 Ventilation And Pressurization

- FAR 25.831 - Ventilation.
  Each passenger and crew compartment must be ventilated, and each crew compartment must have enough fresh air (but not less than 10 cubic feet. per minute per crewmember) to enable crew members to perform their duties without undue discomfort or fatigue.

- FAR 25.841 - Pressurized cabins.
  "Pressurized cabins and compartments to be occupied must be equipped to provide a cabin pressure altitude of not more than 8,000 feet at the maximum operating altitude of the airplane under normal operating conditions.
  If certification for operation over 25,000 feet is requested, the airplane must be designed so that occupants will not be exposed to cabin pressure altitudes in excess of 15,000 feet after any probable failure condition in the pressurization system." [FAR PART 25, Sec. 25.841]

3.2 CONCEPTUAL DESIGN OF A MEDIUM-RANGE, MEDIUM-CAPACITY AIRPLANE

After having analyzed the requirements of the developing airplane coming from the airlines, it is possible now to begin the phase of conceptual design of the product. The aim of this part of the chapter, is to arrive at determining the approximated values of typical weights, wing area, engine thrust (or power), and a preliminary configuration of the new airplane by using both parametric and some simple physical equations. This will allow to determine the rough order of magnitude of non recurring and recurring costs as well as price and operating costs and to compare them with those of airplanes of same category.

3.2.1 Airplane Design Phases

Typical phases characterizing the design cycle of an aeronautical program are the conceptual design phase, preliminary design phase, and detail design phase.

1. *Conceptual design phase*—The main goal of the conceptual design phase is to achieve a preliminary sizing of the airplane and a gross estimate of its production and operating costs, in order to verify the technical and economical feasibility of the new project. To determine the general size and configuration of the aircraft, basic mission requirements (range, payload, cruise speed, altitude, takeoff distance) are assumed in order to conduct studies using rough estimates of aerodynamics and weights to calculate the best wing loading and thrust loading, and to define wing geometrical characteristics such as sweep, aspect ratio, thickness ratio, and root chord. [NICOLAI 1975]

2. *Preliminary design phase*—The main goal of the preliminary design phase is to define general airplane characteristics (freezing of configuration), starting from the preliminary sizing achieved in the conceptual phase and analyzing the industrial feasibility of program and the development of mechanical, structural, and aerodynamic concepts to be used in the new airplane. [NICOLAI 1975]

3. *Detail design phase*—After the airplane configuration is frozen and the decision has been made to "go-ahead"[3] with the airplane development, the detail design phase starts. The goal of this phase is to develop project details and to release drawings that will be used to create components, assemblies and subassemblies (production phase), as well as to issue detailed specifications of those parts that will be fabricated by program suppliers.

Characteristics of the three design phases, in terms of computational approximation for predicting technical and economical airplane performances, time, and costs necessary to realize the phase, are as follows:

- The conceptual phase has an approximation of 10–15%, requires weeks, and has a low cost.

- The preliminary phase has an approximation of 5–10%, requires months, and has a medium cost.

- The detail phase has an approximation of 1–3%, requires years, and has a high cost.

The design phases make up about 75% of total development costs; the remaining 25% goes for overhead, including data processing, flight testing, and prototype assembly. A quick method for the conceptual design of an airplane will now be shown and applied to the requirements of a medium-range, medium-capacity jet airplane.

3.2.2 Requirements of a Medium-Range, Medium-Capacity Airplane

As an example, assume that the results of an extensive market research call for a wide-bodied jet airplane, medium range, medium capacity, with slightly in excess of 200 seats; mainly, but not only, for the U.S. market; with some cargo capability, and operating costs better than those of its competitors.

Assume that a critical analysis of market research and existing competition has resulted in the following initial design requirements:

- Range = 3,500 NM (U.S. coast-to-coast connections require a 2,600 NM minimum range).

- Cruise speed = Mach 0.8 (from comparison with competitors).

- Initial altitude capability = 39,000 ft (to avoid overcrowded airways).

- Takeoff field length [4] < 6,000 ft and landing field length [5] < 5,000 ft (to permit operation in most U.S. airports).

- Propulsion system = twin turbofan (to assure low operating costs). New FAR regulations allow this type of aircraft to operate on long-range overwater missions, also.

- Fuselage cross section = lower lobe configuration, providing standard 7-abreast seating in tourist class (seat pitch = 34 in for U.S. market) and 5-abreast seating in first class (seat pitch = 38 in.), with two aisles (width = 19 in.), as demanded by FAR 25.817 and 25.815. The cross section will provide a container and cargo capability.

3.2.3   Weight Determinations

The first aim of the conceptual design phase is to determine the characteristics of the airplane, such as:

- Maximum takeoff weight (W_{to}).
- Operating empty weight (W_{oe}).
- Mission fuel weight (W_f).

This phase is conducted by using parametric studies and gross historical relationships between typical weight and airplane characteristics and design parameters (for example, W_f/W_{to} as a function of design range). After having determined a rough estimate of airplane weights, it is possible to start the successive phase in which, based upon simple equations and on statistical relationships, other main airplane characteristics are calculated, such as:

- Maximum required takeoff thrust (T_{to}).

- Wing area (S) and wing aspect ratio (A).

- Lift coefficients for takeoff, cruise, and landing. [ROSKAM 1986, Part. I]

The design objective is to wrap the most efficient airplane possible around the assigned payload (passengers) which must be delivered to a destination (mission) in a prescribed way (mission requirements).

To size aircraft systems and components in a preliminary way, statistics exist, based on past and in production airplanes, on relationship between gross weight, operating empty weight, payload weight, and range. Therefore, if passenger capacity and range are specified (payload/range), it is possible to establish a ballpark size and weight for the airplane. This statement is based on the industry's ability to extrapolate from a history of previous experience. If the current state of the art in airplane design and classical configurations are adopted, it is relatively easy to obtain airplane dimensions, weights, and performance accurate enough for a preliminary evaluation, as will be shown in the following sections.

The iterative process aimed at estimating a gross value of W_{to}, W_{oe}, and W_f may be divided into some simple steps. Before beginning the process, mission payload weight (W_{pl}) is calculated (passenger number being known), and an initial value of takeoff weight ($W_{to,tent}$) is chosen (trying to assume an initial likely value of W_{to}, comparing, for example, the airplane under design to an existing airplane with the same number of passengers). At this point, the process begins following the steps of Figure 3.20 in order to, according to ROSKAM:

1. Determine the mission fuel weight W_f (for example, as a function of W_{to} and design range);

2. Determine the $W_{oe,tent}$ from the simple relationship:

$$W_{oe,tent} = W_{to,tent} - W_f - W_{pl}$$

3. Calculate another value of operating empty weight, $W_{oe,new}$ from the historical relationship of empty weight versus takeoff weight;

4. Compare $W_{oe,tent}$ with $W_{oe,new}$. If the percentage difference is less than a preselected tolerance, the process may be stopped, and weight characteristics are known. Conversely, if the percentage difference is higher than tolerance, steps 1, 2, 3 and 4 must be repeated until the comparison condition is satisfied. Usually a tolerance of 1.0% is sufficient in this phase of the design process. [ROSKAM 1986, Part I]

Assuming:

> Cabin seating[6] = 211 passengers (18 first class + 193 tourist class)
> Passenger + baggage weight = 210 lb

and calculating the values of W_{pl}, $W_{to, tent}$ and W_f:

$$W_{pl} = (211 \text{ passengers}) \times (210 \text{ lb/ passengers}) = 44{,}310 \text{ lb}$$

$$W_{to, tent} = W_{pl} / 0.145 = 44{,}310 / 0.145 = 305{,}586 \text{ lb}^{[7]}$$

$$W_f = 0.262 \times W_{to, tent} = 0.262 \times 305{,}586 = 80{,}064 \text{ lb}^{[8]}$$

$W_{oe,tent}$ can be calculated using the above values of W_{pl}, $W_{to,tent}$, and W_f.

On the other hand, a value for the first iteration can be evaluated and compared by use of statistics:

TOGW = 2.036 x OEW + 23.68 x Range - 130,361

Where OEW means the Operational Empty Weight.

With the simple iterative method described above (Figure 3.20), the following values can be obtained:

$W_{to} = 278,111$ lb; $W_{oe} = 159,917$ lb

3.2.4   Airplane's Technical Characteristics

3.2.4.1   Wing Loading and Thrust Loading Determination.

This phase of the conceptual design process is aimed at the determination of the values of wing loading (W/S) and thrust loading (T/W) that will satisfy mission and certification requirements. These are the two most important parameters affecting aircraft performance.

Wing loading affects stall speed, climb rate, takeoff and landing distances, and cruise performance. Wing loading has a strong effect upon sizing the aircraft takeoff gross weight. If the wing loading is reduced, the wing is larger. That reduction may improve performance, but the additional drag and empty weight due to the larger wing will increase takeoff gross weight in performing the mission. This leverage effect will require a more-than-proportional weight increase when factors such as drag and empty weight are increased.

Thrust to weight ratio (T/W) directly affects the performance of the aircraft. An aircraft with a higher T/W will accelerate more quickly, climb more rapidly, reach a higher maximum speed, and sustain higher turn rates. On the other hand, the larger engines will consume more fuel throughout the mission, which will drive up the aircraft's takeoff gross weight to perform the design mission. T/W is not a constant. The weight of the aircraft varies during flight as fuel is burned. Also, the engine's thrust varies with altitude and velocity. Generally, T/W refers to the sea-level static (that is zero velocity) at standard day conditions.

To optimize the choice of values of T/W and W/S that satisfy both mission and certification requirements, a method will now be briefly described that permits calculating the relationship between thrust loading and wing loading during the takeoff and second segment, the cruise, and the landing and missed approach (Figure 3.21). All the points along these curves represent thrust loading and wing loading combinations that meet mission and FAR requirements for the corresponding phases of flight.

Parameters determination (C_{D0}, aspect ratio)—equation 1:

$$C_{D0} = (1.1 + 0.128 \times N_S + 0.0070 \times S + 0.0021 \times N_e \times T_e^{0.7}) / S$$

where C_{D0} is the zero lift drag coefficient, N_S is the number of cabin seats, S is the wing area, N_e is the number of engines, and T_e is the thrust per engine[9]. [CORNING 1953: Ch.2-p.36]

Figure 3.20
Sizing to Match Payload & Range Requirements

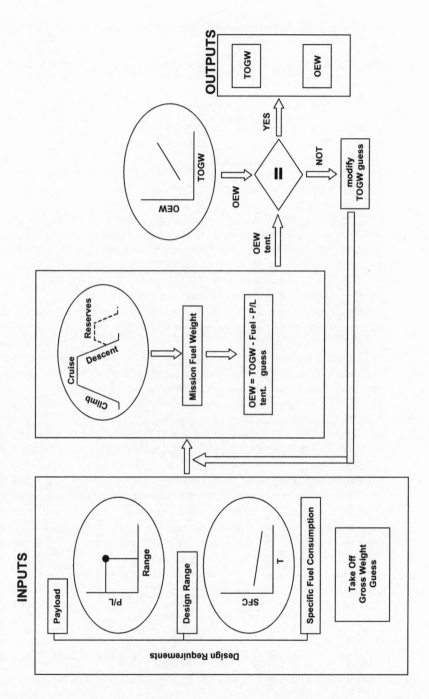

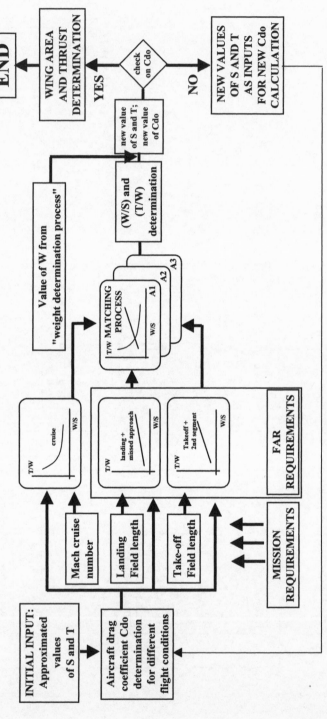

Figure 3.21
Wing Area and Engine Thrust Determination Process

Although wing area (S) and thrust (T_e) are unknown in this phase of the matching process, it is possible to calculate C_{D0} from equation 1 by using approximate values for S and T_e. Statistics reporting typical values of wing loading (W/S) and thrust loading (T/W) for commercial jet transport aircraft as a function of design range give the following results for a range of 3,500 NM;

$$(W/S)_{to} = 0.0083 \text{ x Range} + 93.722; (T/W)_{to} = -1 \text{ x } 10^{-5} \text{ x Range} + 0.3376):$$

$$(W/S)_{to} = 123 \text{ lb./sq. ft}; (T/W)_{to} = 0.30 \text{ lb./lb.}$$

and, since $W_{to} = 278,111$ lb (see previous paragraph.), then the following approximate values are obtained:

$S = 2,261$ sq ft; $T_e = 83,433 / 2 = 41,717$ lb
With $N_S = 211$, equation 1 gives:
$C_{D0} = 0.0226$

For flight conditions other than cruise, it is possible to determine C_{D0} by adding to the value obtained from equation 1 an incremental value ΔC_{D0} [ROSKAM, 1986, Part. I][10].

Statistic on aspect ratios [11] of several wide-body transport jets as a function of design range shows that:

• The newer the aircraft, the higher the aspect ratio.

• There is an appreciable increase in aspect ratio with design range.

• The average value adopted for the aspect ratio is 8.

Pairs of values of thrust loading $(T/W)_{to}$ and wing loading $(W/S)_{to}$ can now be calculated considering the requirements in different flight conditions and entering the values of C_{D0} and aspect ratio previously determined:

1. *Takeoff and second-segment requirements*[12]: Pairs of values that satisfy contemporary takeoff and second-segment requirements can be determined from the equation of motion, assuming the takeoff field length requirement (6,000 ft) (see section A of Figure 3.22; obtained $C_{D0} = 0.0376$).

2. *Cruise requirement*: Pairs of values of T/W and W/S can be obtained considering the equilibrium condition of the airplane motion in the vertical and horizontal axes during the cruise condition, with Mach cruise equal to 0.8; see section B of Figure 3.22; obtained C_{D0} x AR = 0.0226 x 8 = 0.1808. In section C of Figure 3.22, the ratio $(T/W)_{to}/(T_{to}/T_{cruise})$ is shown as a function of C_{D0} and aspect ratio; it is necessary also to calculate the ratio T_{cruise}/T_{to} for several cruise altitudes (h = 35,000–40,000 ft) to determine, during the matching process, the optimum cruise altitude for the commercial turbofan transport aircraft under evaluation[13].

3. *Landing and missed approach requirements*: As for the takeoff and second-segment requirements, landing and missed approach phases of flight path may also be treated in a unique manner because the airplane is characterized by a similar configuration during the two phases. Equations of airplane motion during the landing and missed

approach may be used to derive paired values of T/W and W/S, assuming the values of landing field requirements (5,000 ft) and design range (3,500 ft). Section D of Figure 3.22 shows the values calculated for $C_{D0} = 0.0776$ for several landing field lengths.[DRESSE 1986]

3.2.4.2   Matching Process

Pairs of values (W/S) and (T/W) at takeoff conditions have been calculated for: a) takeoff and second-segment conditions; b) cruise conditions; c) landing and missed approach conditions. Three curves can therefore be plotted and the resulting graph is shown in Figure 3.23 [DRESSE 1986].

The area situated below each curve is the locus of points where mission and certification requirements are not satisfied and therefore must be rejected. Following this process, the exercise finally determines the exact portion of the plane in which all the mission and certification requirements are met simultaneously.

Figure 3.22
Takeoff and 2nd Segment Requirements, Cruise Requirements, Landing and Missed Approach Requirements

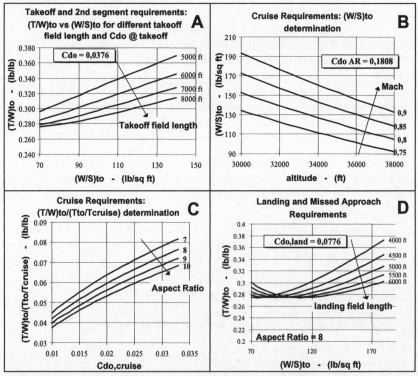

Source: Elaboration on L. Dresse., *Twin/Four Engines Jets: A Comparative Study*. ITA Documents and Reports, 1986

Figure 3.23
Matching Results for Sizing of a Turbofan Transport Aircraft: First Iteration

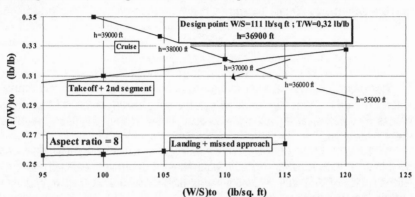

The design point (that is, the pair of values of W/S and T/W) to use for the aircraft sizing is selected in this portion of the plane, considering the combination of the lowest possible thrust loading with the highest possible wing loading. Usually this combination results in an airplane's satisfying the mission and certification requirements with the lowest operating costs [DRESSE 1986].

The cruise curve of Figure 3.23 shows a decrease in required thrust loading as wing loading increases, whereas the other two curves indicate an increase in required thrust loading as wing loading increases. The aircraft design point is selected at the intersection of the cruise curve and takeoff curve. For this example, the takeoff curve is critical for the sizing of an airplane. The landing curve, not critical in this case, may become critical at short design ranges (Range < 1,000 NM), when usually landing weight is very close to takeoff weight.

The values of thrust loading and wing loading obtained by the matching process are:

$$(W/S)_{to} = 111 \text{ lb/sq ft}; (T/W)_{to} = 0.32 \text{ lb/lb}$$

and the corresponding optimum cruise altitude (whose values are correlated with the curve of cruise requirement) is:

$$h_{opt} = 36,900 \text{ ft.}$$

Therefore values of W_{to}, S, T_{to}, C_{D0} can be calculated. The new value of C_{D0} (0.0212) must be compared with the previously calculated value of C_{D0} (0.0226); the difference is about 6%.

Adopting the new value of C_{D0} and repeating the steps previously shown (determination of pairs of values of $(T/W)_{to}$ and $(W/S)_{to}$ for takeoff, cruise, and landing requirements), the following values are obtained from the matching process:

$$(W/S)_{to} = 105.5 \text{ lb/sq ft}; (T/W)_{to} = 0.315 \text{ lb/lb}$$

$$h_{opt} = 37,300 \text{ ft.}$$

and the new values of S and T_{to} are:

$$S = 2,636 \text{ sq ft.}$$

$$T_{to} = 87,327 \text{ lb.}$$

The new value of C_{D0} obtained by means of equation 1 is 0.0205. When compared with the previous value of C_{D0} the difference is 3.5%. The matching process may be repeated until a preselected percentage difference in the values of C_{D0} is reached.

At the end of this process, a check must be made to verify whether or not the initial altitude capability (IAC) requirement is met (or exceeded) with the pair of values of T/W and W/S obtained at the intersection of the two curves. If it is not, it means that IAC is a sizing factor.

As these values have been obtained for an aspect ratio equal to 8, the matching process can be repeated for a higher value of AR (such as 8.5), and other pairs of thrust and wing loading will then define the optimum choice, with an improvement also in altitude capability for the airplane.

Nevertheless, great care should be taken when increasing the AR much above the original value, because conceptual design methods (and the one discussed here) do not generally allow for trade-off between AR and weight variation. Therefore, while the beneficial effects of AR increases are present in the above equations representing in-flight airplane behavior, the weight determination does not include the corresponding weight penalties. This consideration is due to the fact that, while the effect of AR on aerodynamics of the airplane can be explained by theoretical equations, the weight determination is based, in this phase, only on empirical and statistical correlation. The approximation in weight estimates is of the same order of magnitude as the effect of AR on airplane weight. Therefore it is not worthwhile to be introduced yet.

If still the IAC requirement is not met, it must be decided either to downgrade the requirement or to use a different pair of values for T/W and W/S. In the given example (after the AR has already been increased to a higher reasonable value), those values would be 0.345 lb/lb for T/W, and 95 lb/sq ft for W/S.

3.3   AIRPLANE GEOMETRY

After the computations we have made so far the weight, performance, and general size of the airplane are known, but definitive airplane shape is still unknown. Shape definition represents a particularly complex problem to be solved, as an airplane configured to carry a given payload could have several shapes. Moreover, shapes that yield the optimum aerodynamic performance do not necessarily yield the lightest structures, and vice versa. Therefore it is very important in this phase to conduct a thorough trade study in order to determine the best shape for the airplane.

Some aerodynamic improvements are available at the expense of increased weight, and some weight measures are achieved at the expense of aerodynamic efficiency. Total airplane efficiency (that is lift over drag) is primarily influenced by wing efficiency and fuselage size and shape.

3.3.1   Overall Airplane Configuration

The geometric shape and the geometric relationship of fuselage, wings, tail, and engine all influence aerodynamic efficiency and structural weight, which, in turn, influence operating economics. This can be stated analytically by the Range Factor equation, which ties together the effects of airplane size, geometric shape (lift and drag), engine efficiency, and weight:

$$\text{Range Factor} = RF = V/SFC \times L/D$$

where

V = velocity in knots

L = lift

D = drag

SFC = specific fuel consumption (lb fuel/lb thrust x hr)

The classic Breguet Range Equation gives:

$$\text{Range} = RF \times \ln(W_o/W_e)$$

or

$$\text{Range} = V/SFC \times L/D \times \log(W_o/W_e)$$

where:

W_o = gross weight at start of cruise

W_e = gross weight at end of cruise

$W_o - W_e$ = weight of fuel burned

From these equations, it can be seen that there are only three variables to manipulate (assuming that current jet speed is not compromised): namely, aerodynamic lift and drag, weight, and engine efficiency. These equations can be used to determine expected fuel mileage[14] and fuel burn rate[15], which are measures of airplane efficiency. The optimization of the above-mentioned variables results, therefore, in a vital aspect of conceptual design.

Range factor and fuel burn rate "goodness" do not necessarily guarantee the cheapest or the best airplane for operation, however. They say nothing of reliability, maintainability, airplane life, passenger accommodations, and other important considerations.

3.3.1.1   Fuselage Shape and Size

A commercial transport fuselage plays the important role of carrying the payload, so the aircraft general dimensions and architecture are a function of the carriable payload. Depending on payload, there are different aircraft types and fuselage layouts. Some general considerations of the aircraft type may be posed independently:

1. *Cockpit crew location.* The normal cockpit crew location is in the forward side of the fuselage, in order to provide a wide outer visibility. The airworthiness regulations require that the forward and lateral pilots' visibility must be possible within a visual view angle of 15 degrees during the landing procedure.

2. *Equipment.* The fuselage structure must also contain a lot of equipment and systems, such as

    a.   The radar system in the nose.

    b.   The forward landing gear, below the cockpit.

    c.   Electric, electronic, and mechanical systems and cables along the fuselage length.

    d.   The APU in the aft side of the fuselage.

    e.   The main landing gears, when they are not positioned under the wing (included in the engine nacelles).

    f.   The engines' pylons and nacelles, located in the aft part of the fuselage (when present in the fuselage); in this case, in this part of the fuselage there are no passengers' seats due to too-high noise levels and the absence of windows.

3.3.1.1.1   Payload Type and Fuselage Shape

The fuselage shape is a compromise between aerodynamic, structural, and production constraints. It is normally cylindrical, with a square or a circular or a double-circular lobe cross section. While the first type offers a better internal volume utilization, the other two are characteristic of a pressurized aircraft. Looking in depth at this second class we can distinguish between commercial freighter aircraft and commercial passenger transport.

3.3.1.1.1.1   Commercial freighter aircraft

In this case, the fuselage design is mainly influenced by the requirement for easy loadability. This means that:

1. The distance of the loading fuselage floor from the ground must be lower than 1.70 m.

2. The high wing solution is preferred in order to facilitate movement around the aircraft during loading and unloading operations.

3. The ideal loading room must have no obstacles on the floor and a constant cross section; and

4. The fuselage must have a lateral cargo door or an aft ramp door (which reduces the aerodynamic efficiency) or an opening nose (which creates some problems related to cockpit installation).

3.3.1.1.1.2 Commercial passenger transport

To provide a high level of passenger comfort as well as overall good flight performance, commercial passenger' transports are required to have pressurized cabins. For material stress reasons, this requirement means a circular or double lobe cross section. The optimization of the cabin's internal volume can be obtained by assigning the fuselage lower deck (under the cabin floor) to cargo and the upper deck to passenger seating. In this case, the low wing solution is the most commonly used, and the cross section height is determined by considering:

1. The width of the wing box crossing the fuselage lower deck.

2. The most common pallets' and containers' standard dimensions (for upper and lower deck height evaluation).

3. The passenger cabin height, which can never be lower than a human's standard height of 6.0 ft (for the upper deck height evaluation).

4. The average difference of 6 in to 12 in between the cabin's external and internal diameters.

3.3.1.1.2 Narrow Body and Wide Body Airplanes

The narrow-body fuselage is adopted for small or medium airplanes, while the wide-body solution (more than one aisle) is selected for larger ones. The weight versus drag trade-off associated with the one-aisle versus two-aisle fuselage alternative, depends upon the number of seats; beyond a certain number of seats, the wide-body solution is preferred. The wide-body solution also has some advantages in the areas of passengers embarking/disembarking, emergency evacuation, and carrying cargo in the belly.

3.3.1.1.3 Fuselage Sizing

As already noted for a passenger transport aircraft, the fuselage dimensions are dependent on the number of passengers N_p (shared between first, business, and tourist classes). The competitive analysis and the regulations give, at this point, the following configuration requirements:

1. The seats abreast (A) and the aisle width (W_{aisle}) and number of aisles (N_a) for each class.

2. The seat's pitch (P), related to the cabin layout choice: one class or mixed class.

3. The number of restrooms (N_t).

4. The number of cabin doors (N_d) and emergency exits (N_e).

The presence of cabin doors, emergency exits, toilets, and galleys may locally reduce the abreast seating or increase the seat pitch, which means that a certain number of rows would have to be added for a fixed number of seats. Fuselage length L_f is defined as the sum of cockpit length L', cabin length L_c, and aft-body length L'':

$$L_f = L' + L_c + L''$$

Survey requirements call for the design of a fuselage that can carry a number of seats slightly in excess of 200, in mixed class configuration. Assuming a total of 210 seats with 10% of seats in 1st class, this gives about 20 seats in the first class configuration at 5-abreast and with a 38 in Pitch seat, and about 190 seats in the tourist class configuration at 34 in Pitch seats. The solution adopted is:

- 7-abreast seating ($A = 7$).
- Two main aisles.
- Circular cross section.

In addition, assume:

- Seat width (W_{seats}) = 21 in
- Aisle width (W_{aisle}) = 19 in
- Body structure thickness (D_{body}) = 12 in

3.3.1.1.3.1 Cabin length determination

The cabin length (Lc) is the sum of L_{pax}, the part of the cabin occupied by passengers, and L_{serv}, the cabin portion occupied by services.

In order to get a correct aerodynamic shape, a gradual fuselage cross-section reduction, moving from center to forward and from center to back of the cabin, is necessary. This reduction can be obtained by reducing the abreast seating of several of the first and last rows from value A to value A'. The number of rows with a reduced abreast seating (r') with a reduced abreast seating is a fraction (X) of the total number of rows (r):

$$r' = X \, r$$

It must be considered that fraction X grows as the abreast seating A increases and the pax increases:

$$X = 0 \text{ for } A \leq 6$$

$$X = 0,2 \div 0,3 \text{ for } A > 6$$

Total number of rows (r) can be calculated by using the curves of Figure

3.24, entering the pax (in equivalent one-class configuration), the fraction of reduced abreast rows (X), the abreast seating (A), and the reduced abreast seating (A′).

Therefore, for this example assume:

$$pax = 210 \; ; A = 7; A' = 5$$

And, choosing a value of X = 0.30, the value r = 33 is obtained.

The number of rows (r′) characterized by a reduced abreast is: r′ = Xr = 0.30 x 33 = 10.

Total exact number of passengers that the airplane is able to carry in this configuration may now be calculated:

$$pax = 10 \times 5 + 23 \times 7 = 211 \; pax$$

The cabin length occupied by seats is equal to: $L_{pax} = 29 \times 34$ in/12 in + 4 x 38 in/12 in = 94.8 ft

For the current example, FAR 25.783 requests two cabin doors, located on the left fuselage side in the forward and aft part of the cabin, and in front of them, two Type I service doors (FAR 25.807) located on the right fuselage side. The related two passageways (FAR 25.813) will be at least 36 in wide. Therefore:

$$L_{serv} = (2 \times 36 \; in)/12 \; in = 6 \; ft$$

and the total cabin length L_c is:

$$L_c = L_{pax} + L_{serv} = 94.8 + 6 = 100.8 \; ft$$

Figure 3.24
Total Number of Rows Determination

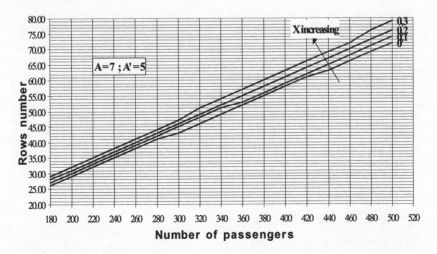

According to FAR 25.807, the seating for 211 pax requires two Type III emergency exits that can be located in correspondence to the wings (one on each side). There is no requirement for passageways, and therefore there is no impact on cabin length.

3.3.1.1.3.2   Fuselage length

Fuselage total length L_f is the sum of cabin length L_c and the cockpit and aft-body length. Usually the sum of cockpit and aft-body lengths ranges from 30% to 40% of the fuselage length L_f, so that:

$$L_c/L_f = 0.6 \div 0.7$$

Assume a ratio $L_c/L_f = 0.65$, thus obtaining:

$$L_f = L_c/(L_c/L_f) = 100.8/0.65 = 155.1 \text{ ft}$$

3.3.1.1.3.3   Body diameter

The body diameter (external fuselage diameter D_{ext}) is given by the sum of cabin internal diameter D_{int} and the body structure width D_{body}::

$$D_{ext} = D_{int} + D_{body}$$

Internal diameter is the sum of space occupied by seats and space occupied by aisles. For this example, the results are:

$$D_{int} = AW_{seats} + N_{aisle}W_{aisle} = (7 \times 21 \text{ in} + 2 \times 19 \text{ in})/12 \text{ in} = 15.4 \text{ ft}$$

and thus:

$$D_{ext} = 15.4 \text{ ft} + 12 \text{ in}/12 \text{ in} = 16.4 \text{ ft}$$

3.3.1.2   Wing Position

The vertical location of the wing on a fuselage affects the characteristics of drag, stability (dihedral effect), and operational considerations (passenger visibility, landing gear position, baggage loading and unloading). To a large extent, the choice of high, intermediate, or low wing depends on operational considerations associated with the mission of the airplane.

Because structural considerations require a wing box crossing the fuselage, in order to have the greatest internal available volume and cabin accessibility in a transport aircraft, it is best not to adopt the solution of a wing positioned in an intermediate position of the fuselage cross section (even it is known that this would produce higher aerodynamic efficiency). The adoption of a high wing solution permits:

1.   Easy ground operations.

2.   Lower loading floor.

3.   Optimum passenger outer visibility.

4. Engine location under the wing.

5. Landing gear long/heavy if wing mounted; dragging/light if fuselage mounted.

6. Stable dihedral effect.

7. High interference drag.

The adoption of a low wing solution permits:

1. Landing gear short/light on the wing; never fuselage mounted.

2. Positive aircraft floating characteristics.

3. Higher payload protection during an unsafe landing, provided to empty the wing fuel tanks before landing.

4. Unstable dihedral effect.

5. High interference drag.

3.3.2   Major Trade-Offs

The outline of configuration possibilities covers the following aspects of design choice:

- Fuselage configuration (fineness ratio, wetted area/pax, fuselage volume/pax, fuselage weight/pax).

- Wing configuration (aspect ratio, wing loading, sweep angle).

- Engine location (wing weight, yawing moment, tail weight); and

- Tail positioning and size (aerodynamic stability, vertical tail size versus engine out requirement, center of gravity and balance, and so on).

3.3.2.1   Fuselage Trade-Offs

The main parameter to be considered in fuselage design is the fineness ratio (length/diameter or l_f/d_f). The question is whether an airplane should be designed with a low value ($l_f/d_f < 3$) or with a high value of fineness ratio ($l_f/d_f > 10$).

Under certain conditions (incompressible flow, body properly streamlined), the total drag coefficient is the sum of two contributors only: the skin friction drag coefficient and the pressure drag coefficient. The first contributor increases while the second decreases, as the l_f/d_f rises. Plotting the variation of the fuselage drag coefficient and the two contributions (friction and pressure drag) with l_f/d_f, a weak minimum occurs for a fineness ratio of around 6.0. However, if considerations of "static stability"[16] are accounted for, the optimum fuselage fineness ratio from a viewpoint of drag is around 8.0. [ROSKAM 1986, Part. III]

On the other hand, when fuselage length increases, the bending moment increases. Because bending loads increase by the square of fuselage length, structural weight increases rapidly. Expressed another way, a long, slender fuselage requires more structure per unit of volume than a short, large-diameter fuselage of equal volume.

However, as fuselage diameter increases, hoop stress and floor beam length increase, which increases structural weight (but not quite so fast as the long, slender fuselage) and results in a decreased packaging efficiency (volume/passenger increase).

Fuselage utilization efficiency can be expressed in many ways, such as fuselage volume versus number of passengers, fuselage volume/passenger versus fuselage structural weight, and fuselage volume/passenger versus fuselage wetted area.

As fuselage volume/passenger increases, it is accompanied by several undesirable factors, such as larger structural weight/passenger (Figure 3.25) and larger wetted area/passenger (Figure 3.26).

Both of these items degrade range, due to greater aerodynamic drag and greater airplane structural weight. Note that, as fuselage volume/passenger increases, the associated drag and weight increase will require a larger wing (for same wing loading), which in itself increases the wetted area and weight. The effects discussed above are particularly evident when one compares wide-body versus narrow-body airplanes.

Figure 3.25
Fuselage Volume / Pax vs. Fuselage Structural Weight / Pax

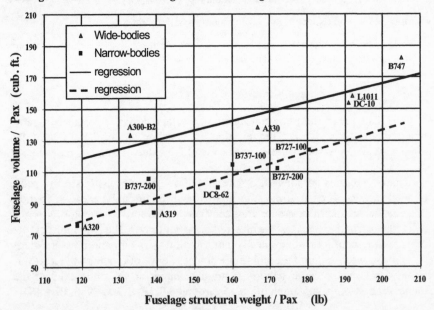

Figure 3.26
Fuselage Volume / Pax vs. Fuselage Wetted Area / Pax

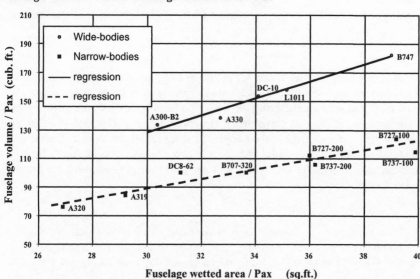

3.3.2.2   Wing Trade-Offs

The entire weight of an airplane must be supported by wing-generated lift. Wing size and configuration are a function of the total weight to be lifted (payload, fuel, structure, engines, and so on), stall speed required, cruise speed required, and its aerodynamic efficiency. Wing size and configuration are essentially governed by aspect ratio, wing loading and trailing edge sweep angle, and the airfoil section.

3.3.2.2.1   Aspect Ratio

Large aspect-ratio wings (span-to-cord ratio) give the best L/D. However, as a given area is redistributed into a very long rectangle (higher aspect ratio), the structural weight increases rapidly in order to withstand the higher bending loads, and bending loads increase by the square of the wing span. These lift-generating techniques must be traded against weight, and this introduces the square-cube rule. This rule states that the lifting ability of a wing increases by the square of the increase in wing area, and, correspondingly, the weight increases by the cube of the same area.

With regard to aspect ratio, the wing bending loads increase by the square of wing span and the structural weight increases by the cube of the span increase.

3.3.2.2.2   Wing Loading

A highly loaded wing is desirable because it decreases the required wing area which, in turn, reduces structural weight. It is desirable only to the extent that the handling characteristics of the airplane are not sacrificed. Also, the higher the wing loading, the longer the runway required for takeoff and landing (more speed is needed to get the required lift). Therefore, takeoff and landing performances worsen as wing loading increases.

3.3.2.2.3   Sweep Angle

In aerodynamic terms, increases in sweep angle increase critical Mach. This means that an airplane with a swept wing can fly at a speed approaching the speed of sound without suffering the drag problems typical of an unswept wing (a phenomenon known as wave drag). However, this higher speed is about the only positive aspect of the sweep angle, as it increases dutch roll, flutter, and structural problems. It also tends to deteriorate takeoff and landing characteristics. The more a wing is swept, the lower the generated lift for a given angle of attack.

3.3.2.3   Engine Location

Two engines of a twin-jet, and two of the three of a trijet, are usually located on the wing (B-737, DC-10, L-1011) or on the aft side fuselage (DC-9, Caravelle, B-727, BAC-111). Valid reasons exist for both locations. The wing location has the advantages of wing bending moment relief (lighter wing weight); due to the engines weight, shorter fuel lines (less hazardous, less complex); easier accessibility for improved maintenance and reduced inventory of special platforms to reach the engines; better balance with less center of gravity (CG). problems (more flexibility of loading), and the ability to install side entrance doors at the rear of the cabin. In addition, more passengers can be carried with the same length body.

The aft fuselage location is quieter for most of the cabin, producing less yawing moment with one engine inoperative (less vertical tail required) and providing a cleaner, more aerodynamically efficient wing. Also, the landing gear can be made shorter and thus lighter; baggage can be handled at reduced heights; and there is increased safety in an emergency landing.

3.3.2.4   Tail Positioning and Size

In order to define airplane configuration, a major trade-off is to choose the horizontal tail position. For passenger aircraft, the choice is limited to either the conventional or the T-tail configurations. The latter represents the only solution when the engines are rear fuselage mounted; otherwise, the engines' exhaust gas would interfere with a horizontal tail.

The horizontal tail configuration has a great effect on longitudinal stability and aircraft control. In normal flight conditions, the T-tail solution offers the advantage of a smaller area when the vertical tail presents a sweep, because it is located farther away and can therefore provide a stronger leverage. The disadvantage of this solution occurs during flight portions when the incidence angle is high and the horizontal tail and wing lie on the same plane. This condition diminishes the effectiveness of the horizontal tail because it runs down the wing-wake vortex. The size of the tail surface is a function of the inherent aerodynamic stability desired.

Vertical tail size is influenced by two factors:

1. The destabilizing moment of the fuselage volume forward of the wing; tail-mounted engines tend to increase the amount of destabilizing fuselage in the front in order to balance the airplane.

2. The destabilizing moment due to an engine-out condition; tail-mounted engines would allow a smaller vertical tail in this case.

Horizontal tail size is primarily a function of the amount of CG travel required to compensate for partial passenger loads. If a given airplane wing is augmented to increase lift, it may also be necessary to increase the horizontal tail size in order to control the pitch attitude of the airplane. Not only will wing weight and drag increase, but horizontal tail weight and drag will increase. However, the added drag associated with the larger tail is usually negligible.

3.4   CERTIFICATION   AUTHORITIES,   REQUIREMENTS,   AND PROCEDURES

3.4.1   Certification Authorities

Airworthiness regulations constitute the rules and procedures, as a whole, that a government imposes on manufacturers and airline operators in order to assure a sufficient safety level in the use of an aircraft. All critical aspects of aircraft design and flight quality, critical performance, structural strength, aeroelastic prevention, manufacturing systems, and operational procedures are covered in the rules, prescribing the precise requirements to meet. Thus, these regulations have a high impact on the design process as a whole. They are a valuable guide for airplane design, simplifying many procedures by eliminating numerous unknowns and defining the fundamental assumptions.

At the beginning of any new project, the manufacturer must decide to which set of airworthiness regulations the airplane will comply, considering that there are still some differences among different countries' rules. However, efforts to unify regulations are under way.

3.4.1.1   Regulatory Bodies

The ICAO (the International Civil Aviation Organization, founded in Chicago in 1944, brings together 144 countries) is the only international body qualified to speak for all of the nations. It is within the ICAO's responsibilities to issue standards in the field of airplane manufacturing and other matters related to safety in air transport.

Article 31 of the Chicago Convention[17] states that the airworthiness certificate, essential for every aircraft, must be issued or validated by the state in which the aircraft is registered. On March 1, 1949, the ICAO adopted the rules and the recommendations regarding aircraft navigability to draw up Annex 8 of the Chicago Convention. Annex 8 sets forth a very general basis on which to determine national airworthiness regulations.

Article 33 of the Chicago Convention states that an airworthiness certificate, issued and validated by nations in which an aircraft is registered, will be considered effective by all nations united by the Convention, provided that the operating framework by which the certificate is issued respects at least the lowest level of rules fixed by the Convention (those covered in Annex 8) [MAGDELENAT 1990]

It should be noted that Annex 8 lists rules but does not recommend procedures; rules are mandatory except when a country makes a different provision. Recommended procedures are not mandatory.

The most important airworthiness regulations are the Federal Aviation Regulations (FAR) issued by the U.S. Department of Transportation's Federal Aviation Administration and the Joint Aviation Requirements (JAR) developed by Europe's Joint Aviation Authority (JAA). All of the non-Asian countries (except Russia) have regulations that are thoroughly conform to those set by one of these two bodies. Therefore, an aircraft that complies with both FAR and JAR can obtain airworthiness certification in every country. FAA publications and processes for type certification of a new aircraft are doubtless the most important.

3.4.1.1.1   Federal Aviation Administration

The FAA answers to the U.S. Department of Transportation and also takes into consideration guidelines and concerns from the National Transportation Safety Board (NTSB).[18]

The major functions of the FAA are:

- Safety regulation—The FAA issues and enforces regulations and minimum standards relating to the manufacture, operation, and maintenance of aircraft.

- Airspace and air traffic management—The safe and efficient use of navigable airspace is a primary objective of the FAA.

- Air navigation facilities—The FAA is responsible for the construction or installation of visual and electronic aids to air navigation, and for the maintenance, operation, and quality assurance of these facilities.

- Civil aviation abroad—As mandated by legislation, the FAA promotes aviation safety and encourages civil aviation abroad.

- Commercial space transportation—The agency regulates and supports the U.S. commercial space transportation industry. It licenses commercial space launch facilities and private sector launching of space payloads on expendable launch vehicles.

- Research, engineering, and development—The FAA engages in research, engineering, and development aimed at providing the systems and procedures needed for a safe and efficient system of air navigation and air traffic control.

- Other programs—The FAA provides a system for registering aircraft and recording documents affecting title or interest in aircraft and their components. It publishes information on airways and airport services as well as on technical subjects relating to aeronautics.[FEDERAL AVIATION ADMINISTRATION 2002]

3.4.1.1.2   Joint Aviation Authority

JAA began in 1970 (as the Joint Airworthiness Authorities) with the aim of producing certification for large airplanes and engines to meet European industry needs in the field of aircraft manufacturing (particularly Airbus needs). Since 1987, this responsibility has been extended to all aircraft classes.

In 1991, the European Community took its first initiative in the field of aviation safety in harmonizing the technical legislative framework for air transport, by adopting EEC Regulation 3922/91 to bring nearer technical requirements and administrative procedures in the field of civil aviation.

Article 1 states that the regulations apply to all aspects of civil aviation safety—notably the design, manufacture, operation, and maintenance of aircraft—and to all persons and organizations involved in these tasks. It gives the force of law to the technical requirements referred to in its Annex 2. Member nations, under the supervision of the EEC, monitor compliance with the common rules. Where no common rules have been adopted, they continue to apply the national regulations in force at the time of adoption of the regulations (Article 6[2]), subject to the general obligations imposed by the treaty and in particular by Article 30.

The highest level of decision-making authority is the JAA Board, comprised of general managers of the civil aviation authorities of member countries. This body decides JAA policy and develops guidelines that are passed to the JAA Committee, which has the duty and responsibility of managing and organizing JAA structure and activities and making decisions on implementing the policies of the JAA Board. The JAA Committee is made up of the deputy general managers of civil aviation authorities of member countries.

The JAA Committee continuously addresses relevant matters that are also considered by the Joint Board, where there are permanent representatives of airplane manufactures, operators , and helicopter manufacturers and operators.

In December 1999, a modified structure to be fully implemented during 2001) was created, which will combine responsibilities of the JAA Committee and Board. Other changes foreseen are related to the various committees, which will be renamed and chaired by the organization's executive director.

3.4.1.1.3   Evolution of a Unique European Aviation Safety Authority

3.4.1.1.3.1   Disadvantages of the present JAA structure

According to both the member nations and the aviation industry, the current structure of the JAA has a number of disadvantages.

* Its decision-making procedure, which is based on unanimous votes of the JAA Board and the JAA Committee, is inefficient.

* Because of its informal status, the JAA has no delegated authority to adopt binding decisions.

* Because the JAA has neither the necessary power nor the resources required, the current system has been unable to bring about any genuine freedom of movement for aeronautical products without requiring further technical or administrative restrictions.

* The JAA has neither the legal nor the political weight needed to defend Europe's interests on the international scene, particularly against the U.S. Federal Aviation Administration (FAA).

* Ensuring high standards of aviation safety requires considerable resources, and thus it becomes very costly to maintain separate national authoritative entities in every country.

3.4.1.1.3.2   Advantages of the proposed European Aviation Safety Authority

In response to these criticisms, JAA members are considering strengthening the present cooperative system by giving JAA the formal status of an international organization. The objective of the negotiations is to establish a European organization responsible for civil aviation safety, bringing together the European Community, its member nations, and as many as possible of the European members of the ICAO. Its role will be to take all necessary measures to ensure a high level of aviation safety in Europe, facilitate the operation of the internal market, and ensure an international presence capable of promoting European standards and creating an environment that fosters European interests.

Since the last discussions in December 1999 by the Council of EU Transport Ministers, in which it was decided to continue efforts toward realization of European Aviation Safety Authority, JAA is optimistic concerning decisions to be made in the next few years.

3.4.2   Certification Requirements

3.4.2.1   FAR/JAR Areas of Interest to Aircraft Manufacturers

The areas of FAR that concern civil transport aircraft manufacturers are FAR 25 and FAR 21. FAR 25 applies to any request of type certificate for airplanes seating more than 19 passengers and constitutes the body of requirements with which an airplane under evaluation must comply. FAR 21 concerns (among other issues) the *procedural requirements for the issue of type certificates, procedural requirements for the approval of certain parts*, and *procedural requirements for the approval of organizations*. [JAR-21.1 1994]

FAR has been selected to provide the format and often the content of JAR, particularly JAR 25 and 21. Therefore, the following comments apply both to FAR and to JAR.

FAR/JAR 25 can be divided into:

a. Generalities and definitions.

b. Airplane flying requirements (minimum performance and flying standards to which an airplane must comply, and rules and regulations that define and measure the required capabilities).

c. Airplane structural issues (structural loads, mandatory security coefficients, and material composition required in aircraft).

d. Design and manufacturing standards (to ensure that airplane parts comply with security regulations during their operational life).

e. Engine installation procedures (to ensure that all power plant components and apparatuses will be manufactured and installed so that the airplane will be safe; also covered are inspections and maintenance).

f. Equipment specifications (to comply with airworthiness standards).

g. Use limitation (information concerning airplane safety that must be passed on to pilots and/or cabin crew).

FAR/JAR 21 reach their objectives through Design Organization Approval (DOA) and Production Organization Approval (POA) procedures.

3.4.2.2   Design Organization Approval

Design Organization Approval fundamentals simply establish a qualified framework in which the various activities related to demonstrating product compliance will occur. Certification that the design of a product complies with the applicable requirements is based on:

1. The certification of an organizational system by the authority.

2. The certification of the design of products by the authorities, based on compliance verification issued from that organizational system.

3.4.2.3   Production Organization Approval

Product Organization Approval for products parts and appliances is the FAR/JAR 21 subpart dealing with:

a. "Rules for the approval of a production organization and rules governing the holders of such approvals.

b. Rules for showing conformity of products, parts, and appliances with the applicable design data through the use of an Approved Production Organization." [JAR-21.131 1994]

3.4.3   Manufacturer Procedures for Certification

3.4.3.1   Type Certification Procedures

A type certificate of a new aircraft may be obtained by a manufacturer by means of a demand for a type certificate, consisting of the completion of an application form and submitting that form to the appropriate certification office.

Although the following steps for the type certification process apply specifically to the FAA procedures for new airplane certification, similar criteria must be followed when applying to any certification authority for certification that the airplane is airworthy.

3.4.3.1.1   Application for Type Certificate

An application for an aircraft type certificate must be accompanied by available preliminary basic data and a three-dimensional drawing of the aircraft. A transport aircraft must receive its certificate within five years of the date of application, or a new application is required, as type certification imposes the most recent design requirements on the airplane.

3.4.3.1.2   Type Certification Board Establishment and Meetings

A Type Certification Board, called the Type Board composed of personnel from FAA offices, was established by the FAA to coordinate the U.S. type certification program. Manufacturers may also participate in board meetings.

3.4.3.1.3   Submission of Engineering Data

All relevant technical data (drawings, specifications, test reports, and stress analysis) must be presented to the FAA for approval as part of the type certification application.

3.4.3.1.4   Ground Tests

FAR Part 25 specifies the minimum ground tests, including fatigue tests, propulsion (component and system) tests, resonance tests, static tests, and subsystem (component and installation) tests.

3.4.3.1.5   Airplane Type Inspection

FAA personnel conduct a type inspection on the first aircraft manufactured using the new design. The inspection is in of two phases:

1. Ground inspection:

    a. Conformity to type design drawings, specifications, and other FAA-approved data (this inspection begins during the manufacturing phase and continues until the aircraft is certified).

    b. Flight safety.

    c. Maintenance provisions.

    d.   Compliance with other provisions of FAR.

2.   Flight tests, which are required to show FAA personnel how the aircraft meets the airworthiness requirements (to streamline the official FAA flight test program, FAA personnel can informally participate in the precertification flight test program, at a manufacturer's request).

3.4.3.1.6   Equipment and Component Approval

There are three methods for obtaining FAA approval of equipment and components such as engines and avionics:

- *Type certification.* —The procedures are similar to those used for aircraft type certification, but they are applied to engines.

- *Technical standard orders.*— The equipment is certified by the manufacturer as exceeding or meeting all the qualifications specified in the applicable technical standard orders.

- *Approval as part of the airplane.*— The equipment or components are considered to be part of the airplane in accordance with FAR Part 25 requirements or performance requirements of the applicable technical standard orders.

All equipment manufactured with applicable military specifications is generally acceptable to the FAA.

3.4.3.1.7   Final Approval and Type Certification

The Regional Aircraft Engineering Office approves and issues the type certificate upon recommendation by the Type Certification Board. Receipt of an aircraft type certificate means that:

- The airplane design and tests have satisfied the FAA applicable airworthiness requirements. Any special condition or any provision that does not comply with FAR has been satisfied by factors providing an equivalent safety level.

- All safety standards for the category in which certification is requested have been satisfied by the aircraft.

- The holder (licensee) may obtain airworthiness certificates for production series that conform to the type design.

Any change to a type certified aircraft must have a new certification, which applies only to new or modified parts and their effect on related components or systems.

3.4.3.2   *Other Certificates Awarded*

3.4.3.2.1   Production Certificate

The FAA awards a production certificate to an applicant who qualifies in accordance with FAR Part 21, Subpart G. No manufacturer can build any airplane without prior possession of this second certificate that certifies the ability of the manufacturer to maintain the quality of all airplanes that will come out of the production line. Once this is obtained, series production may start [Magdelenat 1990].

3.4.3.2.2   Airworthiness Certificate

After the production certificate has been obtained, the manufacturer may ask for an individual airworthiness certificate for any airplane from that production line. No additional demonstrations of the airplanes' compliance with present rules and regulations is necessary, except a short production flight test. (But a plane may not be operated until this individual certificate is received.)

NOTES

1. With the least squares method, the curve is calculated so that the sum of the squares of the vertical deviations form the historical points to the curve is minimized.

2. Logarithmic values are used because the relationship between the dependent traffic variable and the independent variables is multiplicative rather than simply additive; this means that the effects of each independent variable tends to increase exponentially. A main indicator of the statistical accuracy of the multiple regression equations is used—the multiple correlation coefficient, R^2. This indicator suggests whether or not the model is highly accurate and indicates whether or not it can be used for estimating future air travel demand. The closer the correlation coefficient is to 1, the more accurate is the model.

3. The full go-ahead of an aeronautical program is subject to several constraints and conditions. Among others, from a market stand point, not less than 50 orders must be obtained, coming from at least three customers belonging to two different geopolitical areas. This corresponds (according to a rule of thumb) to obtain a total initial backlog whose value is close to the investment the manufacturer has to bear. For example, before the launch of the Airbus A380, 50 firm orders were received. Considering that the first customers will obtain a substantial discount, the traded airplane price may be assumed to be around $200 million. Therefore the value of the order is around $10 billion. The Airbus declared investment for the A380 program up to delivery to the first customer is $10.7 billion. In the regional sector to develop a family of two members the envisaged investment (by the airplane manufacturer only, excluding the investments made by the engine and avionics suppliers) should be around $1.0 billion. The traded price for a 100 seat airplane (in 2001 US$) is around $20 million. The need for about 50 airplanes orders confirms the rule that the initial order has to cover the investment.

4. Calculated at maximum takeoff weight and ISA conditions.

5. Calculated at maximum landing weight and ISA conditions.

6. Trade studies of seat pitch, galley and toilet numbers, and baggage compartment volume needs result in a cabin layout optimization of 211 passengers in the mixed class configuration, as will be shown in a later chapter.

7. For a range of 3,500 NM, statistics suggest that the ratio W_{pl}/W_{to} is equal to 0.145 ($W_{pl}/W_{to} = -1 \times 10^{-5} \times$ Range $+ 0.1796$).

8. For a range of 3,500 NM, statistics suggest that the ratio W_f/W_{to} is equal to

0.262 (the formula is $W_f/W_{to} = 0.101 + 0.0000466$ x Range)

9. The zero-lift coefficient depends both on aircraft aerodynamic characteristics (above all, wing and fuselage characteristics) and on airplane configuration (such as landing gears up or down, or flaps extension). For cruise conditions, when C_{D0} reaches the minimum value, it is possible to use an empirical relation to calculate the zero-lift drag coefficient for jet-transport aircraft.

10 For flight conditions other than cruise, it is possible to determine C_{D0} by adding to the value obtained from equation 1 an incremental value DC_{D0} [ROSKAM, 1986, Part I]:

Flight conditions	ΔC_{D0}	C_{D0}
Cruise	---	0.023
Takeoff	0.015	0.038
Landing	0.055	0.077

11. A parameter that affects aerodynamic performance in every flight condition is the aspect ratio A, whose geometrical value is given by the ratio b^2/S, where b is the wing span and S is the wing area. The main aerodynamic effect of a higher aspect ratio (at constant wing area S) is augmentation of the aerodynamic efficiency of the plane (that is, the lift to drag ratio), resulting in greater range capability and thus, for the same flown distance, lower fuel consumption and takeoff weight. But a higher aspect ratio increases the airplane's structural weight and therefore the takeoff weight optimization is needed.

12. Certification requirements (FAR 25) during the second segment of flight state that the airplane must climb with a certain climb gradient. Because the airplane configuration is similar during these two phases of the flight path and maximum lift coefficient at takeoff is related to the second segment lift coefficient through the relationship:

$$C_{L,TO} = 1.44 \, C_{L2},$$

the motion equations of the airplane can be combined to arrive at a unique determination of design parameters.

13. The equation that gives a rough relationship between T_{cruise} and T_{to} (for altitude H greater than 30,000 ft and Mach greater than 0.6) is: $T_{cruise}/T_{to} = 0.4325 - 6.416$ x 10^{-6} H.

14. Fuel mileage = miles/lb fuel = V/SFC x L/D = RF.

15. Fuel burn rate = lb fuel/hr = SFC x T; since in cruise T = D/L x W where W = mean flight weight = (Wo + We)/2, fuel burn rate = SFC x D/L x W.

16. If the fuselage length is increased for the same level of static stability, the tail sizes can be decreased, thereby reducing overall aerodynamic drag.

17. The Chicago Convention is the meeting, held in 1944, in which United States, the World War II allies and neutral countries, discussed about civil aviation creating the ICAO. From that moment onward the countries signing the convention were obliged to uphold the standards established by ICAO,

18. The NTSB is an independent, bipartisan board composed of five members appointed by the U.S. president for five-year terms, with the consent of the U.S. Senate. Its responsibilities are mainly to investigate the causes of transportation accidents and to make studies and recommendations to reduce and prevent them

4

ECONOMICS OF A COMMERCIAL
AIRPLANE PROGRAM

4.1   GENERAL CONSIDERATIONS IN PRICE SETTING

The purpose of this chapter is a general review of pricing airplanes in the commercial transport aircraft market, which represents a constant problem to the manufacturer. A manager looking for technical literature on product pricing is offered different advice from many sources that is impossible to summarize here. This chapter will therefore provide only a general approach to the pricing question and suggest certain fundamental relationships concerning pricing of a transport aircraft. Accordingly, we will be faced with the problem of reconciling economic theory with practice. Pricing theory generally assumes knowledge of the demand curve for the product under evaluation, which, per se, is extremely difficult to obtain.

A common model in economic theory is cost-based pricing. There are several ways of generating pricing models based on costs, among them the "cost plus" and the "rate of return" methods. The first requires input of the full cost of the product plus overhead costs and a markup to reach the sales price. The second is based on a target price needed to obtain a certain return on investment (ROI); in turn, the target price is based on cost-plus data and the markup is determined by the desired ROI. There are several weaknesses in both methods; I will mention just a few.

The first weakness is associated with the large impact of the allocation of general charges and fixed costs on the price of a particular product.

The second is that a markup based on percentage of costs or other internal considerations rather than opportunities brought by the market is arbitrary. A third weakness is that the manufacturer is trapped in a dilemma almost impossible to solve: Overheads (on which the price is set) must be allocated on the basis of a certain forecasted sales volume, but price level has a direct influence on sales volume.

A complete understanding of price policy for managers requires a deeper analysis than cost-plus methods or the supply and demand approach. One must therefore also take into account contributions from the fields of marketing and management to bring realism in an otherwise too theoretical approach. A specific contribution of marketing to price policy is certainly the product life cycle theory. The significance of the model is in explaining marketing objectives changes through the product life cycle and the use of price in helping to reach these marketing objectives.

In addition to being one of the four Ps (and therefore a tactical variable), price is also seen by management as a strategic tool for reaching long-term objectives. This is another departure from the economist's theory in which the firm would seek profit maximization for a quantity where marginal costs and revenues are equal. In reality, professional management of a large company may have its own interest in maximizing something other than profit. It may be preferable to increase market share and/or company total revenues and/or the workforce. Sometimes management does not even try to maximize an objective but instead seeks good results in different areas such as those previously described, although they may be conflicting.

"Price is the only element in the marketing mix that produces revenue; the other elements represent costs. Yet many companies do not handle pricing well." [KOTLER 1984: p.506] Price can be considered as having two aspects:

a. As a measure of cost: Conceptually, prices should be established independently of costs, costs being important only in determining the relative producer's profitability.

b. As a measure of value or quality: In this case, the market's (buyer's) perception of product value could be the key to pricing.

4.2   ESTIMATING PRODUCT VALUE

Product analysis pricing is based on the assumption that, in a competitive market, relative prices of competing products should be related to the physical and technical aspects of the product itself. This method is oriented toward the competitive market situation and is a useful technique for routine pricing decisions.

Price analyses are based on simple and multiple regression techniques; prices used for showing significant trends in the following pages are consistent in the same figure, but not necessarily in comparing different drawings. This refers particularly to figures 4.1 to 4.4 and to Table 4.1. This is due to the fact that the reference years (and dollar amounts) may be different. In addition, seating arrangements may be slightly modified in different figures. Therefore, ratios between prices and seating are not directly comparable outside the same figure.

4.2.1   Simple Regression Analysis

The first step may be is an analysis of certain functional relationships between price and product characteristics considered separately (simple regression analysis).

4.2.1.1   Price Versus Seats or Price Per Seat Versus Seats With Trend Lines Figure

Figures 4.1 and 4.2 compare price and price per seat of sample aircraft versus size; some typical trends can be observed. Price generally increases and price per seat generally decreases with the airplanes size (that is, with the number of seats). Prices of jet airplanes are higher than those of turboprops.

4.2.1.2   Price Versus Operational Empty Weight (OEW)

Figure 4.3 compares aircraft price versus OEW. There is a strict correlation between the two variables. Price per kilogram varies, ranging from $900 to $1,300 per kilogram for most airplanes. The reason for the difference lies in the fact that, in this figure, parameters other than OEW are not considered, while the price takes into account other significant performance of the aircraft.

Derivative airplanes may not follow trend lines: Other factors being equal, price is primarily driven by number of seats, not OEW. Therefore, airplanes stretched from a basic version have a higher price than expected from the trend (see A-321 and 737-800 in figure 4.3), because the additional OEW would allow more seats than it would permit in a basic aircraft. The contrary applies to the shortened models (A-319 and A-318). New projects are generally in the upper tier ($1,200 to $1,300 per kilogram), while older generation aircraft fall in the lower tier ($900 to $1,000 per kilogram).

Figure 4.1
Regional Aircraft List Price vs. Seats

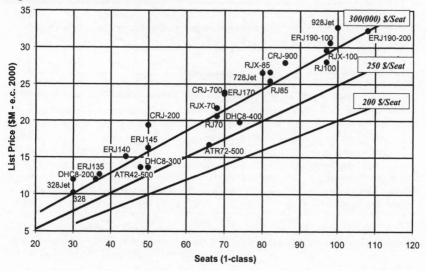

Figure 4.2
Regional Aircraft List Price per Seat vs. Seats

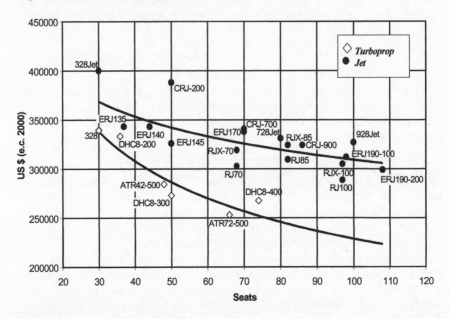

Figure 4.3
List Price vs. OEW for Narrow Body Aircraft

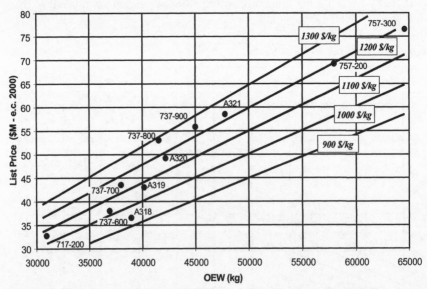

4.2.2   Multiple Correlation Analysis

The basis of this method is to combine properties and characteristics of the product that collectively generate value and therefore determine its price. The method must be applied to a specific product/market segment, including all the competing products having similar characteristics. The postulated functional relationship between price and product characteristics is:

$$P = b_1 \times X_1 + b_2 \times X_2 + \ldots \ldots + b_n \times X_n$$

where P is the product's equilibrium market price, X_i is a generic product's characteristic, and b_i is the weight characteristic X_i contributes to price building up, which value may be estimated using regression techniques. The equilibrium market price is the price that makes the product have the same overall appeal as the average of competitors, that is the same cost effectiveness from the customers stand point.

When using this method of determining the equilibrium price, the weights are estimated on the basis of market prices at a given time and may reflect the general economic conditions existing at that time. To determine the equilibrium price of a new or existing aircraft that balances the competitive situation, it is necessary to acquire the competitors' study price and technical characteristics.

The above-mentioned trends of existing aircraft prices versus different aircraft characteristics are then considered all together in a multiple regression analysis that takes into account the weighted contributions of different items. In this case, the correlation level is normally higher than that shown by the aforementioned simple regression analysis, and the unknown competitive price of the new aircraft can be better predicted.

The choice of independent variables is largely correlated with two elements: the purpose of the analysis and the type of aircraft under comparison. In considering the purpose of the analysis, it may be that, in addition to the equilibrium price determination, the aim of the work is to investigate the existence of particular links between aircraft prices and some variables (such as specific fuel consumption, range, payload capability), which should be introduced regardless of their significance. When considering the aircraft type, if comparison is being made of airplanes in the same category (such as jets only), then some variables may carry no weight because they are similar for all aircraft (for instance, OEW per seat and maximum speed). But if airplanes belonging to different classes are considered (such as commuters, wide-body, and narrow-body jets), it would be appropriate to select variables that considerably influence airplane prices with reference to the different categories and offered comfort. In this last case, for example, maximum speed (V max) and OEW per seat become significant. However, where some variables are correlated with each other, only one can be taken into account.

In the example, the variables OEW per seat and pitch times seat width are clearly correlated. In this case, only the second variable will be selected because it will produce more significant results. It is also known that seats and range are correlated not from a phisical but operational stand point; therefore, it has not be considered in this example.

Table 4.1 contains a list of regional airplanes whose technical characteristics are the independent variables of the model. In this example, the following variables have been considered relevant: number of seats, balanced field length, maximum speed, and a variable defined as the pitch times seat width (the last one takes into account passenger comfort).

To improve the significance of these parameters, it may be suitable to adopt price per seat instead of price as the dependent variable. In fact, even inside a certain market segment (such as regional aircraft), there are significant differences between airplanes belonging to the low end or the high end.

The regression analysis based on the above inputs (left side in the Table 4.1) suggests the best dependence formula between price (per seat) and technical aircraft characteristics (Table 4.2). The prices that can be derived by applying such a formula to already existing airplanes (see right side of Table 4.1) may be different from the actual aircraft market prices. The smaller the difference, the better the formula. Evaluation of the accuracy of results obtained through this methodology can be performed with a variance analysis and an errors estimate, which for this example can be found in Table 4.2.

Reasonable market prices can be determined for aircraft still in the design or development phase. This can be achieved by applying the formula based on known physical and technical characteristics.

Table 4.1
Analysis Inputs and Outputs for Regression Formula Determination

	(x1) Seats	Pitch (")	Width (")	(x2) Pitch*Width (")	(x3) BFL (m)	(x4) Max Speed (kts)	Price (MUS$)	(y) Price/Seats (US$)	(y') (US$)	EMP (MUS$)
J41	29	30	16.3	489	1525	290	7.1	244828	254450	7.38
Emb120	30	31	17.5	542.5	1420	310	8	266667	271660	8.15
Do328	30	31	18	558	1143	335	8.5	283333	292252	8.77
Saab340B	33	31	17.7	548.7	1321	282	9.4	284848	258296	8.52
Dash8-100	36	31	17.3	536.3	1050	271	9.7	269444	255260	9.19
Dash8-200	36	31	17.3	536.3	970	300	10	277778	271188	9.76
CN235-100	40	30	17.3	519	1400	248	9.9	247500	229605	9.18
Atr42-320	48	31	17.3	536.3	1130	270	11.2	233333	240730	11.56
Atr42-500	48	31	17.3	536.3	1070	300	12	250000	256646	12.32
Emb145	48	31	17.5	542.5	1520	430	14	291667	308837	14.82
Dash8-300	50	31	17.3	536.3	1230	286	12.1	242000	243956	12.20
Fokker50-100	50	32	17	544	1350	282	12.1	242000	239941	12.00
Fokker50-300	50	32	17	544	1150	282	12.5	250000	244864	12.24
Saab2000	50	32	17.7	566.4	1360	365	13.35	267000	282159	14.11
CRJ100	50	31	17.3	536.3	1600	459	17	340000	318117	15.91
ATP	64	31	16.6	514.6	1460	265	13	203125	211656	13.55
Atr72-200	66	31	17.3	536.3	1410	284	14	212121	222455	14.68
Atr72-210	66	31	17.3	536.3	1185	284	14.5	219697	227994	15.05
RJ70	70	31	19	589	1140	414	19.75	282143	293563	20.55
F70	79	32	17.4	556.8	1380	459	23	291139	296640	23.43
RJ85	83	32	19	608	1095	423	24	289157	288049	23.91
RJ100	98	32	19	608	1253	429	27.25	278061	271947	26.65
Fokker100	107	32	17.4	556.8	1301	459	30.25	282710	270398	28.93
B737-500	122	32	17	544	1900	490	31.25	256148	254036	30.99

BFL = Balanced Field length
EMP = Equilibrium Price

Table 4.2
Regression Analysis

ANALYSIS OF VARIANCE

SOURCE	DF	SUM OF SQUARES	MEAN SQUARE	F VALUE	PROB>F
MODEL	4	17945.34452	4486.33613	26.575	0.0001
ERROR	19	3207.51477	168.81657		
C TOTAL	23	21152.85929			

ROOT MSE		12.99294	R-SQUARE	0.8484
DEP MEAN		262.69580	ADJ R-SQ	0.8164
C.V.		4.94600		

PARAMETER ESTIMATES

VARIABLE	DF	PARAMETER ESTIMATE	STANDARD ERROR	T FOR H0: PARAMETER=0	PROB > !T!	STANDARDIZED ESTIMATE
INTERCEP	1	126.708339	98.43577720	1.287	0.2135	0
SEATS	1	-1.006686	0.15629043	-6.441	0.0001	-0.83099066
VMAX	1	0.481327	0.06107608	7.881	0.0001	1.25372619
SUPSEAT	1	0.112252	0.17227461	0.652	0.5225	0.09786413
BFL	1	-0.024617	0.01938253	-1.270	0.2194	-0.17020855

Price/Seat = 126.708 - 1.007 x Seats + 0.481 x Vmax + 0.112 x (Pitch x Seat Width) - 0.025 x BFL

The following conclusions can therefore be drawn from an analysis of coefficient variables in the formula:

- Price per seat is heavily influenced by airplane capacity, and it decreases as the capacity increases (size effect).

- Price per seat also decreases with any increase of balanced field length (and vice versa), because this last parameter is inversely correlated to the installed power and wing complexity (flap system, maximum lift coefficient — CL max, and so on) and therefore, in some a way, an indication of the technology level.

- Price per seat increases with maximum speed and with the above-mentioned variable (pitch times seat width) that measures the passenger comfort level. This is evident as one considers that the first variable may be considered correlated with the technological content of the airplane and that the second, in addition to measuring the airplane's appeal to passengers, is also an indirect indication of the physical dimensions of the airplane (for a given number of seats).

4.2.2.1 *Price Versus Range with Seat Trend Line Defined*

Figure 4.4 is the drawing of the correlation analysis results among three variables (list price, seats, range) in the commercial jet sector. This method of analysis is obviously not rigorous because it ignores most performance, weight, and design features. The trend of price with range, established through the graphic data noted above, is a parametric trend. In other words, for a given seat capacity, as range increases, gross weight, wing size, and engine thrust increase as required by specific point design airplanes.

Figure 4.4
Price-Range Comparison – High Density Seating (30" Pitch)

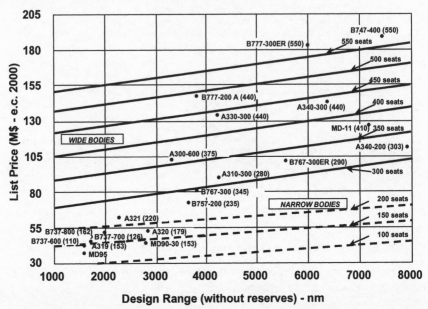

Design Range (without reserves) - nm

It should be noted that derivative airplanes (longer range) may not follow trend lines as changes to increase range are applied to the same basic structure with only gross weight increase (and some engine thrust increase to avoid excessive takeoff performance penalties). As a result, the price increase with range for derivatives appears to be about two thirds of that for the founder airplane.

For a given range, wide-body aircraft seats cost more due to the increased comfort they offer passengers and their resulting greater physical size (bigger cross-section, higher Takeoff Gross Weight (TOGW), OEW, thrust, and so on).

4.2.3   Prices and the Use of Advanced Technology

The use of new technologies cuts operating cost of the user, who will adopt the new airplane over a conventional one with a potential increase of profits. However, new technologies are not free; therefore, new and advanced airplanes generally cost more. A trade-off exists and an appreciation of future savings is mandatory for the buyer to decide whether such improvements are worth the money. In addition, such appreciation of future saving has to be translated into market value. Figure 4.5 shows schematically the perceived product value and the possible price setting.

There are several ways to add total operating cost (TOC). To facilitate understanding of this problem, TOC is split into:

- Price-related costs, which are those related to the airline's investment in the aircraft purchase (capital costs).

- Aircraft-related costs, which depend on aircraft characteristics; and

- System-related costs, which include the remaining general expenses of the airline (as a system).

Generally, system-related costs do not depend on aircraft type or age, therefore they are assumed to be equal for all aircraft under consideration; but aircraft-related costs increase as airplanes age, either through use or because of old technology. Thus price-related costs of newer aircraft can be higher than those of current or past technology and still be lower in TOC.

If operating costs are assumed as a measure of perceived product value, then the price-setting approach of newer versus older aircraft in Figure 4.5 can be followed: Being P_2 the market price of airplane 2 (the older one) the price assigned to aircraft 1 (the newer one) can exceed P_2 and reach P_1 in order for the latter to be better (or equal) than the former.

Maintenance savings are more appreciated by airlines in wealthy countries than in developing countries because of different labor costs. Fuel cost (of paramount importance after the 1973 and 1979 fuel crises) has become just one of the major items of in the TOC breakdown because of a stable, low price. Figure 4.6 shows the attractiveness of new versus current technology aircraft when fuel saving is appreciated differently due to differences in fuel price. For this purpose, operating costs are split into three cost categories: "price related," "fuel related," and "other." For simplicity's sake, it has been assumed that operational savings of newer airplanes are obtained only in the area of fuel; consequently, "other" costs have been assumed equal for different airplanes.

Figure 4.5
Cost Analysis Approach to Price Setting

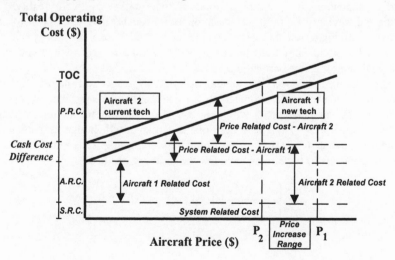

Figure 4.6
The Benefits of Advanced Technology — Fuel Related Cost Savings

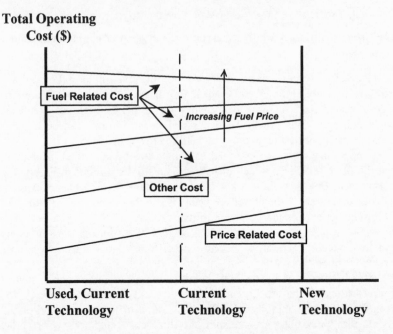

Therefore, Figure 4.6 shows a pure trade-off between investment and related benefits in terms of the monetized value of fuel saving.

Investment is represented by the difference in price-related costs. It can be seen that to overcome the investment made to assure the benefits, the fuel price has to reach a certain (high) value and therefore the return for the operator is not certain, depending on the future trend of fuel market price. In reality, the forecasted savings, in terms of cash operating costs, that are lower for an airplane with higher technological content, cannot be compared directly with its higher sales price. They must be discounted at a rate that represents the money cost (and value) for the particular operator.

Let C_0 and I_0 represent the annual cash operating cost and the price related costs, respectively, with reference to a new technology airplane. C_1 and I_1 represent the same elements with reference to a current technology airplane (with $C_0 < C_1$ and $I_0 > I_1$). The choice of the airplane with higher technological content is advantageous only if the following condition is satisfied (where n is the operating life of the airplane and DR the discount rate used):

$$\sum_{i}^{n}\left[\frac{(C_1 - C_0)_i}{(1 + DR)^i}\right] - (I_0 - I_1) = NPV > 0$$

4.3   COMMERCIAL AVIATION MARKET DEMAND

The market as a whole will not accept as many airplanes at a high price as it will at a low price. Consequently, an estimate must be made of market response as the price is varied. This may be either for the total market demand, when several manufacturers are supplying different airplanes (industry demand), or for a manufacturer supplying a particular aircraft (firm's demand).

This introduces the concept of price elasticity, that is, how responsive the market would be to a certain change in price: If the change (in percentage) of quantity is higher than the corresponding change in price, the demand curve is said to be elastic. If quantity does not change as much as the price, the demand is inelastic. When demand is inelastic, the total revenues are higher when price is increased (and vice versa when demand is elastic).

4.3.1   Characteristics of Market Competition in the Commercial Aviation Sector

For clarity's sake a few concepts on the aeronautical industry that have been introduced and covered in the previous chapters are repeated here.

The aeronautical industry was and is considered an oligopolistic sector. The number of prime contenders has been limited in the last decades; there are just two today, if only the commercial sector is considered. In the regional aircraft business, the situation is slightly different. The relatively lower entry barriers in the technological and financial fields have favored the entry of a certain number of competitors, often belonging to emerging countries that see the possibility of entry in the business of airplane manufacturers through the regional aircraft sector.

Therefore, the profitability of the business is poorer for the higher number of producers, for the lower unit value of the aircraft and for a higher sensitivity of the clients to prices. Nevertheless, a consolidation in this sector is underway that is making the regional aircraft business more similar to the commercial jet sector.

The characteristics of the airplanes produced by different players determine a special type of oligopoly referred to as "differentiated," since each manufacturer offers products that are similar to those offered by competitors (essentially the same functions and the same users) but different in some way in terms of technological content and therefore performance and operating costs. Therefore, contrary to what appears in the classical oligopolistic system[1] in the aeronautics a down-sloping curve of the demand can be found. with the associated problem of defining the optimum sales price.[2]

The presence of elements of supply differentiation in the aeronautical industry (and the existence of the down-sloping demand curve) could lead one to assume that price is one element of the competitive strategy. In reality, the situation is more complex. Sometimes this is considered to be a non-price competition sector with similar airplanes always sold for similar prices, with very limited margins of maneuverability. This is because the competition takes place around other elements. Apart from product differentiation, there are several factors that may be used to differentiate the offers made by producers and that may induce a condition of "obliged loyalty" from previous customers. This is linked to the high "switch costs" that they would bear in case of supplier change. Also evident is the importance to the customer of the producer's name in terms of confidence in on-time delivery, correspondence to project requirements, after-sale support, financing of sales, and so on.

Overall, these factors would allow the manufacturers to act upon the price as a sales leverage tool, particularly for firms with higher market share. Nevertheless, the margins around the official price remain very limited due to the competition in the sector that lets customers make their choice on the basis of elements other than price.

The main questions that require further analysis for understanding the dynamics of the sector's competitive environment are the following:

- Why is the intensity of the competition so high, although the oligopolistic system would allow collusive agreements among producers and the competition is primarily in factors other than price?

- Why is it that firms do not base their strategy on different sales prices for airplanes that are often sold for the same price per seat in the same category?

- What are the instruments and tools adopted by the aeronautical firms to maintain a high market share, acting only to a limited extent on the sales price?

In answer to the first question, the high level of competition is linked mainly to one fundamental factor: the need to acquire and maintain a significant share of the market. Although a direct correlation between market share and profitability may not be true in absolute terms, in the aeronautical industry the sales volume (and, indirectly, the market share) has a great importance due to scale and learning economies and because of R & D investments and commercial and sales semi-fixed organizations.

Concerning the second question, the explanation can be found in the disastrous consequences a price war would have on the already limited stability and profitability of the business, because of the high degree of involvement, direct or indirect, by governments in the industrial and commercial activities of their aeronautical industries. Any significant price change by a single producer would be perceived by manufactures in other countries as evidence of unacceptable public support, to be followed by a request for price controls by ad hoc bodies in response to the price change (see also note 1 in Chapter 6).

The third question relates to product differentiation through the use of advanced technology and also by means of the "augmented product." Whereas the core product may be very similar to others in the market, the final product may look and be perceived very differently by customers. This differentiation cannot be achieved on the basis of price reduction but by offering additional services at no charge and/or financial conditions particularly convenient, with the effect of a true discount and the offer of a more comprehensive package rather than only a product.

4.3.2   Determining Market Demand

In the conventional textbook approach to price problems, a company is always assumed to know what the demand for its product will be at some given price and exactly how that demand will be altered by every possible change in price. This information details the firm's down-sloping demand curve. In reality, because a product is on the market at a certain price and sold in a certain quantity, only a point of the curve is known, and the producers do not know the quantitative effect of price change upon the volume of sales.

Market research forecasts about the market share of a particular product assume implicitly that sales price will coincide with the equilibrium price (P) previously defined. The analysis generally consists of two phases:

a.   Finding the "right" sales price.
b.   Appreciating the possible sales at that price.

After assuming product characteristics and performance, the competitive scenario and the competitor's sales prices, the market research determines first the equilibrium price (P') and then the associated quantity (Q'), that is the units that the analyst determines can be sold for that price. In the (P, Q) plane, an A' point is therefore identified, for which the "a" demand curve has to fit (see Figure 4.7). However, to build that curve, one must know other points that represent other pairs of prices and related sales (all other conditions being equal). If at least one other point A" is known of the same curve (that is, for different sales prices but the same exogenous variables), it is possible to have a rough idea of the curve slope in the interval of interest (although at least three points are needed to draw a curve).

In reality it is impossible to draw the demand curve pertaining to a new product to be placed on the market because there is no historical data on prices and quantities for that product. One may think of similar products, perhaps those of competitors that are already on the market. These have a history because most likely their producers have put them on the market initially at the equilibrium price and afterward at a different price due to market contingencies, with related changes in the market share.

The analysis is particularly complex because the sales prices of airplanes under study (made homogeneous by taking into consideration differences in size and therefore the scale effect) are generally very close to their equilibrium prices. Therefore, it is difficult to judge if the historical modifications of their market share should be attributed to price changes or to a modification of the level of effort made by manufacturers in areas other than price (that have been called the exogenous variables of the problem).

Figure 4.7
The Influence of Price and Non Price-Related Factors on Sales Level

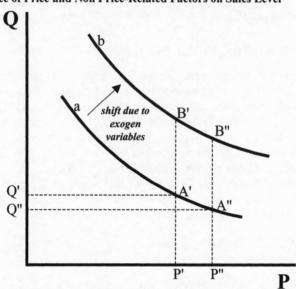

4.3.3   Industry Demand Analysis

Any price change with reference to a previous one and prices of direct competitors may determine an increase or a decrease of market share referred to as the "basic market share." As an example, we may consider a firm willing to introduce on the market a new airplane in the regional aircraft business in the size segment of around 60 to 80 seats. The basic information given by the firm's market research office is the expected open market for that particular size subsegment of the regional aircraft business. The investigation results are the following:

- The potential market in the segment is approximately 550 units as a whole, with little elasticity in the average price change. As will be demonstrated later, the same does not apply to the elasticity of the demand curve of the single model.

- The other essential information that the market research office has to provide is the product's potential market penetration (and market share). In this example, it has been evaluated to be 230 units (or 42% market share) when sold at its equilibrium price of $11.03 million.

4.3.4   Historical Analysis of Commercial Jet Airplanes Sales and Prices

A possible way to determine sales variation as function of the basic price modification is to perform a regression analysis based on historical data collection. In the present example, data have been collected and analyzed for a 14-year time period, particularly sales quantities and associated market prices for large jet planes. In order to have a more focused analysis, the sector has been segmented by taking into consideration payload (number of seats) and range. In each segment and for each year, the price per seat of each model has been compared with the average price per seat of the segment, and differences have been compared with the market shares obtained in the same year. The study results are shown in Figure 4.8.

In this figure, each point on the Y axis represents the market share obtained in a particular year by a particular aircraft model. Values on the X axis represent the difference between the model price and the average price for the segment to which the airplane belongs. The curves in the figure, obtained by interpolating the points, differ from each other by the initial relative strength of each competitor on the market, that is, the market share obtained by a certain model sold at its equilibrium price when the price per seat of the model is sold at the average price per seat of the category, and therefore the ratio is equal to 1.

The initial or basic market share derives from factors external to the product such as the manufacturer's reputation and the previous market share obtained even with airplanes of somehow different dimensions and characteristics (relative market strength). These aspects emphasize the importance of the initial market share of the single manufacturer (the historical market share) and of the particular competitive system that characterizes the sector, the differentiated oligopoly, and allows the statement:

Figure 4.8
The Influence of Price and Non Price-Related Factors on Market Share

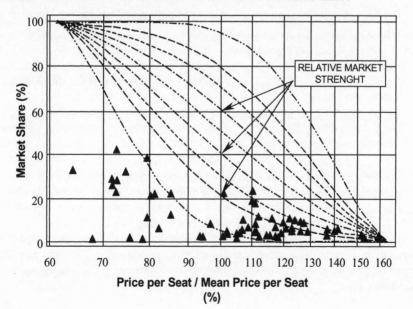

"The smaller the initial market share of a large competitor in an oligopoly, the higher will be its tendency (*ceteris paribus,* in terms of production and distribution costs) to reduce prices (if compared with big competitors with higher initial share) while its inclination to increase prices will be lower" [MOMIGLIANO 1975: p. 894](translated from the original Italian by the author).

Circumstances that may provoke such situations are found in an oligopoly with very few large competitors in which one of them—although very similar to the others in terms of technological level, production, and distribution cost—for some reason has a lower market share than the others (such as McDonnell Douglas in its last years of presence in the market). In this case, a smaller firm (among big competitors) may have a high motivation to begin a price war by reducing price and/or improving product characteristics, much more so than the other major players. Similarly, it may resist the price increase of any other major competitor. Under these circumstances, if a secret agreement does not exist for price leadership, even in the oligopolistic system aggressive initiatives may occur from these big but minor competitors that try to change the situation to improve market share.

The empirical simulation presented above seems to prove that even in the oligopoly there is room for price war due to the different slope of demand curve (of different players) that is related to the acquired market share. It has already been emphasized that such price wars in the aeronautical business are kept hidden by product differentiation and, generally speaking, by a global offer (the augmented product) that bring customers to make an evaluation on these whole packages as long as prices remain close to each other.

4.3.5   Firm Demand Curve: An Application to Turboprop Aircraft

The demand curve of a single product can now be obtained because the following information is available:

- The demand curve of the whole segment the product belongs to (550 units for the 60 to 80 seats segment).
- Competitors' market share when sales prices and initial relative market strength are known (Figure 4.8).[3]

The demand curve for the particular airplane is depicted in Figure 4.9, corresponding to the curve of 42% relative market strength in Figure 4.8. It has been transformed into absolute values of number of airplanes by multiplying the Y axis value of this curve of figure 4.8 for the total potential market, estimated to be around 550 units. It should be used the accuracy to associate 230 sales (or 42% market share), with $11.03 million (the equilibrium price of the proposed airplane) in drawing the curve; as this connection has come out from market research previous analysis; for this point, the ratio between prices has to assume the value 1.0.

Figure 4.9
New Commuter Aircraft Demand Estimate as Function of Sale Price

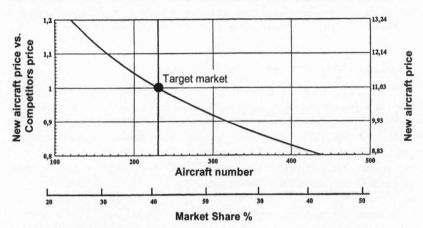

Two approximations seem evident:

• The first is the assumption that the total potential market for the segment is constant, even when the sales price of a single product changes; this would cause the average price for the whole segment to change slightly.

• The second is to consider equals a forecasted target penetration (that is to be conquered) of 42% with the relative market strength of the example of Figure 4.8 that instead represents a real market situation.

4.4   INDUSTRIAL COSTS

4.4.1   Historical Trends of Commercial Jet Aircraft Costs and Prices

Airplane prices, both commercial and military, are high and increase steadily and continuously. Essentially these higher costs derive from the escalation of development costs of all aeronautical programs (both civil and military). These in turn (in constant terms) may be attributed to two main factors. The first (common to the military sector) is the technological complexity of the aeronautical product, the many different technologies necessary to conceive, produce, and finalize it. The second is the diverging technological paths of commercial and military aviation, which is relatively new in the aeronautical industry, reducing the possibility of cost saving by the use of mature and experienced technologies from the military sector.[4]

Also, program recurring costs have been increasing in the past years (in constant dollars), although not to the same extent than non recurring costs, particularly the costs of systems acquired on the market, such as engines and avionics, because of the development costs increases of such items that must be incorporated into sales prices.

The impact of nonrecurring and recurring costs increases on airplane prices as a function of year of entry into service is shown in Figure 4.10, where two different curves are reported for standard and widebody airplanes; the curves show the trend of price per pound of airplane OEW in the last 30 years.

4.4.2   Classification of Industrial Costs

The costs a firm must bear to launch and produce a new airplane model or a derivative may be grouped in different ways. The most common is to separate costs that the manufacturer incurs only once in the life of the airplane from those that will be borne for each airplane produced, hence the split between nonrecurring and recurring activities and costs. The split in the two categories of costs allows analyzing their behavior versus two factors of paramount importance for the economy of the program:

•   The learning effect, consisting of the unit price reduction as a consequence of accumulated experience in manufacturing; costs continue to diminish because workers improve their methods, the layout of production facilities is optimized, techniques of production control and quality are refined, and so on.

•   The scale effect that determines unit cost variation when the produced quantities increase in a given time period, (that is, when the production rate increases).

4.4.2.1   Nonrecurring Costs

Nonrecurring costs (NRC) refer to all expenses that the firm or firms must bear for the conception, development, and certification of a new airplane and for the conception and realization of machinery, jigs, and tools needed for production of a specific product.

Figure 4.10
Airplane Price Trends

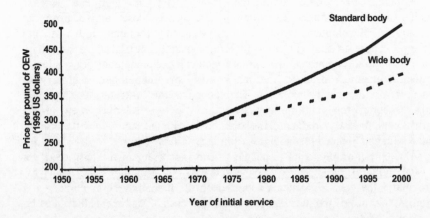

NRC elements may be grouped according to their temporal allocation before or after the final decision to launch the program ("go-ahead"), that is, in predevelopment and development costs, or they may be allocated according to their nature.

Grouping NRC elements by function would include the following categories:

1. *R & D costs,* which includes all costs borne during planning and conceptual design, preliminary design, system integration studies, wind tunnel tests, detail design, drawing, and material specifications phases. The R & D costs level depends mainly on technological complexity and on the dimensions of the airplane under development. This NRC element alone accounts for more than 50% of the NRC total.

2. *Tooling costs,* which includes all costs of production planning, design, fabrication, assembly, installation, modification, and maintenance of tools and programming and preparation of tapes for electronically controlled machines. Nonrecurring tooling costs refer to the initial set of tools and all duplicate tools produced to obtain a specific rate of production. Tooling costs increase with airplane dimensions, technological complexity, planned production rate, and (slightly) with total planned quantity. This cost element is second in magnitude among all NRC items, accounting for around 30%.

3. *Test articles costs,* which include costs incurred in producing airframes for structural tests.

4. *Preproduction costs,* which are costs of producing airplanes used for flight tests.

5. *Flight test costs,* which are costs necessary for flight testing of the preproduction airplanes to be tested.

An estimate of the relative importance (percentage) of each item in the total NRC is shown in Figure 4.11, which depicts development and predevelopment costs distribution of a jet aircraft in the 70 to 100 seats category. Note that R & D and tooling costs account for about 90% of the total, probably due to the high content of technology.

4.4.2.2   Recurring Costs

Recurring costs comprise all costs related to activities undertaken by a firm to transform raw material and semi-manufactured parts into finished products, until final delivery. These may be split into two main categories depending on their behavior with *production rate variation.* It is possible then to distinguish between fixed and variable costs.

4.4.2.2.1   Fixed Recurring Costs

These elements do not change their relative magnitude when production rate is modified; they are often called "structural costs" or "time-related costs." This group includes the general costs associated with parts production (procurement, shipment, personnel management), the overhead costs for indirect personnel and/or management, marketing, sales, and after-sale support costs.

Figure 4.11
Non Recurring Cost Distribution

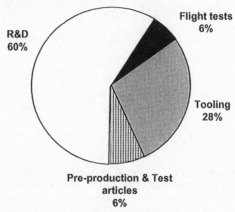

Actually, these costs are only partially "fixed," that is, within a certain interval of production rate variation. Outside it, even these elements of cost may vary. It is therefore more appropriate to describe these costs as "semi variable" and to characterize their behavior with production rate.

4.4.2.2.2   Variable Recurring Costs (Production Costs)

Some recurring costs are strictly dependent on the production rate. These are typically raw material costs, system and subsystem acquisition costs, and transformation costs. The third category, in addition to the costs of manufacturing the parts, also covers costs incurred for production engineering, tooling, quality control, and energy used in the entire manufacturing process.

Purchasing costs from vendors of systems and subsystems represent a very important element of total recurring costs. They include the costs of power plant, avionics, equipment, auxiliary power unit, and other on-board systems. These costs, of course, are not subject to the learning effect but rather depend on the relative strength between buyer and seller (although in a way that is difficult to measure) and on the total number of systems to be acquired. In Figure 4.12, the average relative values of the three major elements of variable recurring costs are shown for an airplane in the 100 seats category for a production of 300 series; material costs accounts for only 11%, while transformation and system acquisition costs are very close (44% and 45% respectively).

4.5   INDUSTRIAL COSTS AND THE MAIN STAGES OF AN AERONAUTICAL PROGRAM

Referring to the go-ahead decision, it is possible to distinguish a predevelopment (pre-go-ahead) and a development (past-go-ahead) phase. The flow of activities in both predevelopment and development phases are reported in Figure 4.13.

Figure 4.12
Percent Distribution of Mean Variable Recurring (Production) Costs for a 100 Seats Aircraft (on 300 Series Produced)

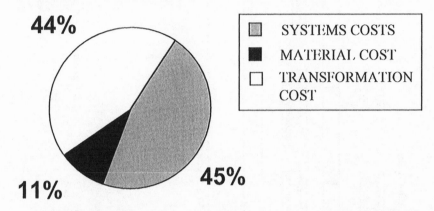

The predevelopment phase represents the whole of activities used for analyzing all conditions relating to the technical, economic, industrial, and commercial feasibility of the program and therefore for defining the general aircraft characteristics throughout the conceptual design of the airplane. The airplane development phase includes the body of activities, mainly (but not only) technical, finalized to a more precise and practical definition of what has been decided in the conception phase. It also includes further development of the project (preliminary and detailed airplane design), its industrial engineering (tool design and manufacturing), and experimental checks of the match between requirements and product capabilities (flight tests).

Particularly important is the relationship the manufacturer is able to establish with most potential customers, to get as many orders as possible and to fully understand the customers' needs. Such information will allow quantifying volumes and prices with a higher degree of confidence and therefore better evaluation of program economies, viability, and profitability. The most important milestone in the development phase is the airplane certification that may be obtained after an intensive cycle of tests. At the same time, recurring activities are initiated, particularly the pre-series units, and delivery of first airplanes to the kickoff customer will be accomplished shortly after airplane certification.

The development phase typically may include some overlap between nonrecurring and recurring activities. Figure 4.13 shows the typical profile (in percentages) of NRC as a function of time. It is not always true (as shown instead in Figure 4.13) that the nonrecurring activities (and related costs) terminate with the end of the development phase.

Figure 4.13
Typical Commercial Jet Transport Aircraft Pre-Development and Development Flow Time

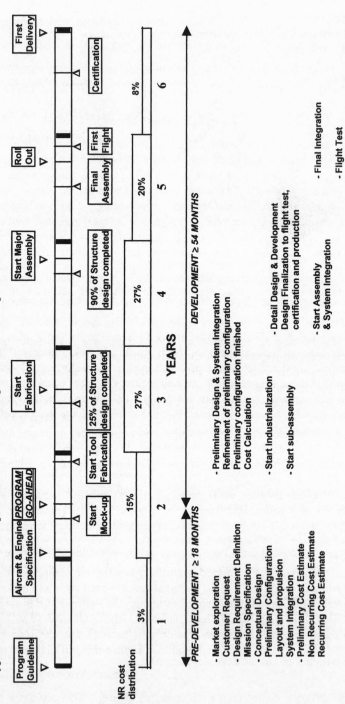

Sometimes a small but significant percentage of total NRC (5% to 15%) may be spent in the years following the first delivery because of some modification and/or product improvement that the manufacturer may decide on when the product gets close to the market.

Customer-requested modifications are not part of this example because their associated costs may be distributed among the units sold to that particular customer (and among the additional sales foreseen for that modified airplane version). Significant differences may be noted in the case of a program for the launch of a derivative version of an existing airplane. In this case, the timing of the two phases is shortened.

4.6   BEHAVIOR OF INDUSTRIAL COSTS

4.6.1   Cost Behavior as a Function of Accumulated Production

It has already pointed out the importance of the learning effect on the economics of an aeronautical program. Volumes affect essentially recurring costs unless new tools or dedicated buildings are requested for different versions of the airplane.

4.6.1.1   Nonrecurring Costs

NRC are made before production begins and therefore are based essentially on the maximum forecasted quantity to be sold in a certain number of years. The accuracy of the forecast is not critical from this point of view because the NRC sensitivity to change in quantity is very low. In fact, the most variable cost item is the tooling, but even on it the effect of change in quantity is not large, and tooling costs is only a part of total NRC (around 30%).

4.6.1.2   Recurring Costs

Costs subject to the learning effect are mainly the transformation costs, (made of manpower and energy), all part of variable recurring costs; raw and semi-finished materials are only slightly affected by savings due to the learning process. The high initial unit cost decreases with the total produced quantity. The improvement of transformation unit cost is measured just by the learning coefficient: The difference between that coefficient and 100% represents the savings in transformation unit cost when the production is doubled. The average learning coefficient for U.S. manufacturers is around 75%; for European firms, it averages about 80%.

The consequences of this difference are significant when cumulated production is considered. For a total production of 300 units, the 80% learning curve means the use of 50% more work than the amount needed if a 75% curve applies. However, the effect on total recurring costs is smaller (Figure 4.14), because transformation costs are around 44% of total recurring costs (over 300 units produced), as indicated in the "Recurring Costs" section above and in

Figure 4.12.

Total recurring costs behavior with produced quantity is shown in Figure 4.14, where two learning coefficients are considered.

4.6.2 Cost Behavior at Different Rates of Production

It is important to distinguish between planned and actual production rates. Planned production rates represent the rates that have been assumed for planning purposes. In this phase, the in-house market research department provides a forecast of the foreseen sales (generally in the hundreds) in a certain time frame (10 to 15 years). Sometime it even provides a deliveries profile that allows calculation of maximum and minimum production rates. This is, therefore, the planned range of possible variation of production rate and can be assumed for dimensioning plants and tools.

The planned production rate and actual production rate seldom coincide. In fact, they are generally quite different due to several unforeseeable factors.

4.6.2.1 Nonrecurring Costs

Because nonrecurring costs are borne by the manufacturer before airplanes are delivered, they are based on the planned production rate, not on the actual rate. But if the planned range of production rate variation is exceeded, the firm must bear additional costs for duplication of most tools in order to support the increased level of production without penalizing the efficiency of the production process. The change is not significant in terms of total NRC because tooling is only about 30% of the total (as shown in Figure 4.11).

Figure 4.14
Recurring Costs vs. Produced Quantity

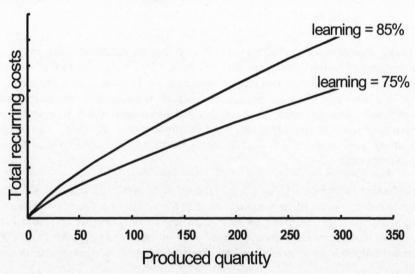

On the contrary, if a decrease in the production rate occurs, then the firm does not need any incremental investment, because it is working at lower than optimum usage of dedicated resources. However, most physical resources will be maintained because their commercial value is very low, being types of assets and machinery too specific for other uses.

4.6.2.2   Recurring Costs

Recurring costs show sensitivity to both the planned and actual production rate. Actual production rate may vary, even to a large extent, during the production phase of the program. For a given planned production rate, the unit recurring costs curve, as a function of the actual production rate, presents a minimum when the two rates coincide and the curve shows a *U* shape. The unit cost first decreases until the planned rate reaches the actual one for which plant, tools, and so on have been sized, and the use of resource allocation is maximized. Consequently, it increases because the higher than planned rate produces a lower than optimum usage of production factors. This is known in the literature as the law of decreasing marginal productivity.

By adding the overhead costs of production (that are almost fixed in a given time period) to the production costs, the total recurring costs [5] may be obtained. This is represented in Figure 4.15, where the two curves are shown for a planned production rate (5 units per month). It may be noted that the difference between the two lines narrows as the rate increases, because the importance of structural costs (as a part of the unit cost) diminishes as the quantity produced in a given span time increases.

Figure 4.15
Production and Total Mean Recurring Cost vs. Real Production Rate — Planned Rate 5 Units / Month — Constant Production Volume

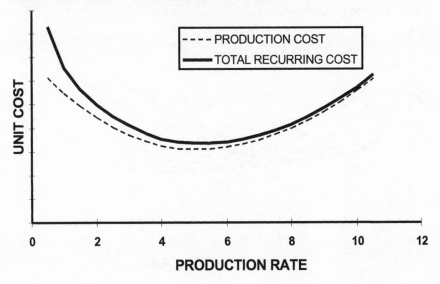

From Figure 4.15, it can be seen that the minimum on each curve is a range rather than a single value because the curvature of the line is not accentuated. This happens because with the same plant, tools, and machinery, it is possible to cover a large difference in production rate without excessive cost penalization, to the point that it is realistic to talk about a "planned range of production rate" rather than "a planned production rate." The more flexible the plant, the wider the production range rate, because the unit cost does not change too much. On the contrary, if a plant has been designed just for one particular rate without considering any future change, it may allow very low production costs, but any deviation from it will incur with a severe cost increase.

In Figure 4.16, the content of Figure 4.15 is repeated for planned production rates other than 5 units per month. The joining of the minimum of each curve of Figure 4.16 is a curve. This downsloping curve may be regarded as having the same meaning as Figure 4.15 except that modification in the physical dimensions of assets, plants, and machinery are allowed, together with possible changes in the production rates.

According to common industrial economy phraseology, this curve may be called "the production cost curve in the long-term period," while the previous one (Figure 4.15) may be called "the production cost curves in the short-term period." Curves in Figure 4.15 have been obtained without any change in the physical resources allocated for production while the production rates were changing.

The total cumulated recurring costs as a function of years of production and for different production rates is depicted in Figure 4.17, obtained by keeping constant the total volume (slightly in excess of 600 units).

Figure 4.16
Mean Total Recurring Cost vs. Real Production Rate for Different Planned Rates —
Constant Production Volume

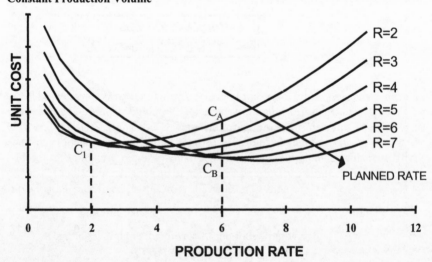

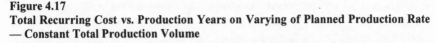

Figure 4.17
Total Recurring Cost vs. Production Years on Varying of Planned Production Rate — Constant Total Production Volume

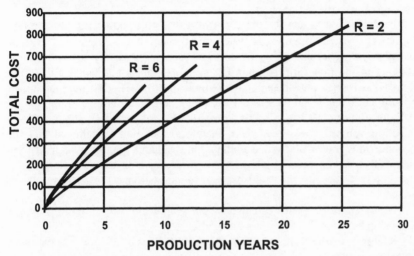

It may be noticed that the total recurring costs (for a given production) decrease while the rate increases; but for the example to be correctly illustrated, the additional tooling costs of the increasing in the production rates should also be considered. This is necessary because we are now considering an example where the planned rate has been exceeded significantly (from two to six unit per month). Both recurring costs (Figure 4.17) and tooling (a part of nonrecurring costs) change considerably.

In this case, the firm must decide between two solutions:

- *Solution A.* Continuing to produce in a situation that is far from optimal (to be preferred when it is believed that the condition will last only for a short time).

- *Solution B.* Making an additional investment in machinery and plants and specific tooling in order to increase the optimum dimension and output of the whole factory (chosen when it is understood that the situation will last for a long time).

The second solution requires additional economic effort in terms of investment and therefore fixed costs, but will result in lower average total unit cost. Solution A is associated with the average cost (C_A), which is much higher than the minimum cost (C_1) obtainable from the plant at optimum rate (R_1). Solution B is associated with the average recurring cost (C_B) relative to the long-term solution (Solution B), and it is lower than both the (C_A) and (C_1) costs, but it will require additional nonrecurring costs $(\Delta N$, Figure 4.18).

In order to further illustrate the difference between the two solutions, it may help to represent the total costs the manufacturer will have to bear in both cases as a function of the produced units from the time and the unit that the rate changes from R_1 to R_2 units per month. This has been illustrated in Figure 4.18, where the two solutions are indicated (R_2 solution A and B) together with the curves relative to the initial rate R_1.

With reference to rate R_1, the curve relative to the short-term solution (R_2, solution A) does not require additional investments, but is higher in the slope because it has higher unit recurring costs, as seen before. Conversely, the curve pertaining to the long-term solution (R_2 sol B) involves additional NRC (ΔN) but shows a lower slope than R_2 sol A (and of course R_1) because of higher production efficiency and therefore lower unit recurring costs.

From Figure 4.18 it can be observed that R_2 sol A and B curves cross at production volume V_{PAR}. It is clear, therefore, that if it is believed that the production at R_2 rate will involve a volume lower than V_{PAR}, then the short-term solution (R_2 sol A) should be adopted; otherwise, the long-term solution (R_2 sol B) is preferable because it would bring advantages from a total costs point of view.

The V_{PAR} can be easily calculated both graphically and through a simple relationship between the relevant parameters.

With reference to the terms used in Figure 4.18, it can be said that the V_{PAR} volume is given by

$$V_{PAR} = \frac{\Delta N}{(C_A - C_B)}$$

where C_A and C_B are the slopes of Solution A and Solution B curves.

Figure 4.18
Total Recurring Cost vs. Produced Units from the Decision Point: Choice between Near and Long Term Solution

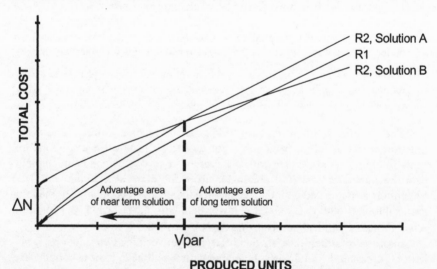

From the above value of V_{PAR} it is then possible to calculate T_{PAR} (time between the short- and long-term solutions):

$$T_{PAR} = \frac{V_{PAR}}{R_2} = \frac{\Delta N}{R_2(C_A - C_B)}$$

Therefore, if it is believed that the production at rate R_2 will last for a time $T < T_{PAR}$, then the short-term solution is the best one; otherwise, if it is forecasted that the higher rate may be required for a time longer than T_{PAR}, the long-term solution should be adopted.

4.7   DIFFERENCES IN TOTAL COSTS OF NEW AND DERIVATIVE AIRPLANES

The previously described lasting escalation of nonrecurring and recurring costs of aeronautical programs in the past 25 to 30 years has obliged firms to exploit all possible attempts to obtain derivative airplanes from existing ones to fulfill customer requirements prior to considering the launch of programs for entirely new airplanes. Derivative airplanes will incorporate all the technological advances that become available and that will make the new model state of the art.

A different approach for facing the same problem is to launch a new program with the objective, from the very beginning (that is, from the design phase), of developing of a "family" of aircraft rather than just one model.

4.7.1   Derivative Aircraft

By definition, some development costs may be saved, when a derivative airplane is considered, that have already been borne in developing the "founder" airplane. For the purpose of measuring the savings in development cost, the "commonality index" may be useful.

A commonality index of 40% between the founder and the derivative airplane means that 40% of development costs of the derivative airplane (as a stand-alone project) may be saved because the work already performed in developing the founder airplane may still be used.

The technological level of the derivative as compared to the founder airplane will determine the R & D savings. The derivative airplane, in fact, will have some improvements in the areas of power plant, aerodynamics, avionics, and systems and maybe also in the airframe structure, where additional usage of new material is a common practice. R & D costs for the derivative airplane in these areas is strictly a function of its differences from the founder. The savings in tooling costs will depend on the physical differences between the two airplanes that will determine the need for new tools and machinery.

For test articles and preproduction costs, the savings is represented by the learning effect on the common parts. For flight test costs, if the difference consists in the lengthening or shortening of the fuselage and/or re-engining with a more powerful engine belonging to the same series (and having physical dimensions close to those of the original), the new airplane may be certified as a "derivative." In that case, flight tests may be only partially repeated. (This applies to the structural tests, also.) Conversely, if changes are quite extensive as far as the general architecture of the whole airplane is concerned (new wing, new position for the engines, tail modification, and so on), flight tests must be completely repeated as if for a totally new airplane.

Unit recurring production costs of the derivative airplane are initially lower than those of a totally new airplane of the same size and general performance, because the learning effect favors the derivative. But as the total quantity produced increases, the unit recurring costs of a derivative airplane become higher than those of a new airplane. In fact, the new technologies more intensively applied to the new airplane, both in the design and production phases, generally allow manufacturing of a new airplane with less labor and material (and costs) than the derivative.

These effects may be seen in the curves of Figure 4.19, in which the total program costs are reported (NRC plus cumulative recurring costs) as a function of units produced. The curve pertaining to the new airplane total program costs (Curve A) is characterized by a significant curvature that is much less evident on Curve B for the derivative product. This is because the derivative product's learning effect is limited to the parts of the airplane not common to the founder airplane.

In addition, Figure 4.19 shows that, as a consequence of the higher unit cost of the derived product (shown by the higher slope of Curve B), there is a value of produced units, N_1, where total program costs for the two airplanes are the same. Therefore, if it were forecasted that the total number of airplanes to be produced (for that class and model) is less than N_1, it would be appropriate to launch the derivative model.

Figure 4.19
Total Industrial Costs vs. Produced Units

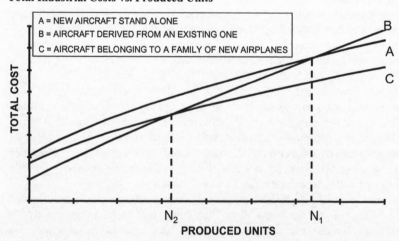

Conversely, if forecasts are for sales in excess of N_1, then it would be appropriate to make a bigger investment to produce the new airplane with lower recurring costs.[6]

Figure 4.20 shows the marginal production costs for the two airplane under study, a totally new one and a derivative (curves A and B) respectively. Marginal production costs for a totally new airplane are higher at production start (Curve A). Yet, while a certain number of units are produced, the difference from the derivative airplane (Curve B) decreases, because of the learning effect, up to a point (N'_1) that the costs of the new airplane will become lower than those of the derivative.

The decision to launch a new airplane or a derivative model does not depend on production rate, for a given volume of production. In fact, as already seen before, the production rate influences the unit cost through its effect on structural costs and indirect production costs. The percentage variation of such costs does not appear, in principle, different in the two cases.

The situation changes when a decrease in total volume of production occurs with the rate reduction. If such a reduction produces a lower than N_1 total demand for airplanes (Figure 4.19), this means that a derivative airplane has a better chance of survival than an entirely new airplane on which the forecasted demand reduction would have a more negative effect. This is more likely to happen when there is a general worsening of the world economic situation, with a drop in the demand for aircraft.

Figure 4.20
Marginal Recurring Costs vs. Produced Units

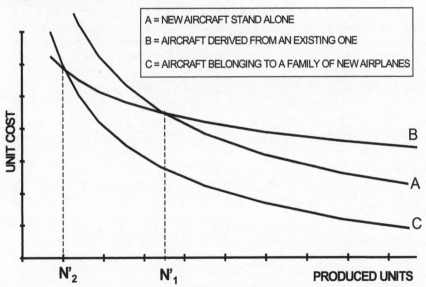

4.7.2   New Families of Aircraft

The search for economy and the pursuit of a larger market has pushed the firms to think of an aeronautical program as producing not just one but different airplanes (generally two or three); these will have different characteristics[7] and will be launched at successive dates.

The difference in this type of program from a normal program with derivatives lies in the fact that this has been planned from the beginning and the dates are relatively close and sure. This is the way to reach a high degree of commonality between family members. The common part of the development costs can therefore be shared and attributed to single airplane, according to common practice in the industry.

With regard to recurring costs, there are benefits due to the learning effect on the common parts. The commonality among models is equivalent to an increase in the total number of completely equal airplanes with the related benefits and, in the period in which more than one model is produced, there are also additional benefits related to the production rate increase.

In Figures 4.19 and 4.20, Curve C shows the advantage of the development of a family member as compared with the two solutions (Curves A and B) already discussed. The parameters considered are costs and volumes of production. It can be seen in Figure 4.19, Curve C is always lower than Curve A (that is, the nonrecurring and recurring costs of a family member are always lower than those of a new and stand alone airplane). From the N_2 value for production volume, the Curve C is also lower than Curve B because the recurring costs advantages prevail.

In the graphs, it has been assumed that the nonrecurring costs of the family member are higher than the nonrecurring costs of a derivative airplane. This may not be true, especially when the number of family members is high (more than two). In this case, it is obvious that Curves B and C would not cross for any volume of production. Therefore, total costs of the airplane belonging to a family would be always lower than those of a derivative airplane.

The unit marginal production costs (Figure 4.20) of a family member (Curve C) are slightly lower than that of a new and unique airplane (Curve A) because the learning effect favors the former. If compared with the derivative airplane (Curve B), the marginal recurring costs of the family member airplane (Curve A) are clearly lower except for the first units, where the situation may be different, depending mainly on the relative positioning of respective learning curves (that is, on the quantity and commonality of other models already produced in both cases).

In Figure 4.20, it has been arbitrarily assumed that the marginal production cost of Curve C will always be lower then those of Curve B, except for the first units. The modification induced by production rate variation on unit cost is modest, provided the total production volume is the same because of future recovery. However, if a lasting decrease of the rate produces also a total volume reduction, considering the entire life of the program, it may happen Solution B (derivative model) to be more convenient in terms of total unit cost than option C (family member). In Figure 4.19 this is true for production volume less than N_2. This result is true under the assumptions (made here) nonrecurring costs of B option being lower than option C and in the arbitrary hypothesis already mentioned the unit production cost of C being lower than those of B option.

The savings on unit recurring and nonrecurring costs that may be experienced increasingly with the number of the models launched cannot continue indefinitely. It finds a limit in some constraints on the maximum possible size variation and performance-permissible deterioration that determine the number of the members of a family. While on one hand there are the advantages of increased production volumes and consequent benefits on the economics of the program, on the other there are some compromises the designer (and the customers) of the airplane must accept in the definition phase. In other words, the dimensional and technical characteristics of the airplane belonging to a family and developed at a certain time must be obtained starting from the already existing models (although this has been planned from the beginning) and therefore can not be optimized as usual in the case of a completely new airplane.

4.8 MAIN FACTORS INFLUENCING THE ECONOMICS OF AN AERONAUTICAL PROGRAM

This section examines the effect of changes in the main variables (such as production volumes, recurring and nonrecurring costs, and rate of production) on the profitability of an aeronautical program. To measure such effects on the profitability of the investment, the usual financial indexes will be considered: NPV (net present value), IRR (internal rate of return), and BEP (break-even point).

4.8.1 Manufacturing Volumes

The increase of production volumes would produce more revenues and a higher profitability. However, to be more precise, some additional investment should also be considered (additional tooling, more sale efforts and costs). In Figure 4.21, incremental costs are neglected not just because they are relatively modest but also because the purpose of the figure is to show only one effect. Therefore, the figure shows the effect of sales volume change on cash flow results, other parameters being constant. The relevant improvement in NPV and IRR that can be achieved by increasing the production volume are clearly visible. Figure 4.21 shows that NPV goes from $638 million if 300 units are produced to $1,381 million when 500 units are made (and sold).

The break-even point is not influenced by the produced volume because its value (in units) and positioning (in years) depends on NRC and on annual operating margin (rate multiplied by revenues minus recurring costs).

Figure 4.21
Discounted Cumulated Cash Flow: Effect of Production Rate, Non Recurring and Recurring Costs, Exchange Rate, Production Volume Variations

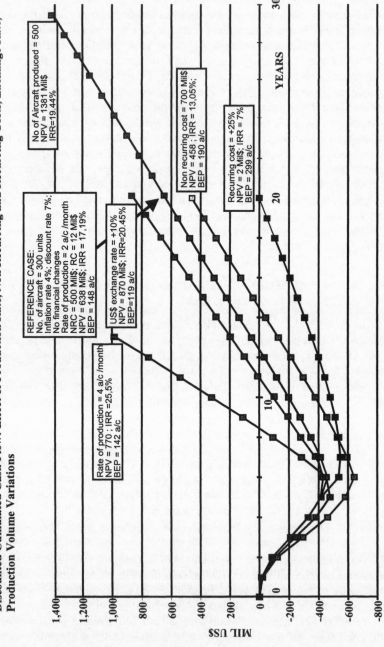

4.8.2   Manufacturing Rates

For a given total volume of production, an increase in the rate results in anticipating a positive cash flow, although at the price of a slight increase in tooling costs (not taken into account here for the reasons mentioned). The economic improvement is due to the fact that annual sales are supposed to increase with the rate. This allows anticipating the operating margin, which must offset the NRC exposure. In addition, the benefits of the learning effect are anticipated and become more significant, while the incidence of fixed or semi-variable costs on the unit cost also decrease. The effect is to reduce break-even time (and, much less, the break-even number of units) and to considerably improve the economics of the program (Figure 4.21).

Figure 4.21 shows that, in the basic example of two airplanes per month at a four-month rate curve, NPV changes from $638 million to $770 million, IRR from 17.19% to 25.5%, and BEP from 148 to 142 units. The BEP is not much affected in terms of units (but it is in terms of years), because the unit operating margin (revenues less recurring costs) does not change significantly and nonrecurring costs do not change.

4.8.3   Non Recurring Costs

A decrease in investment could have a negative impact on product quality and/or on the services offered to customers, risking the long-term technological development capability of the firm and its presence in the market. A reduction in the amount of work in progress and spare parts in the warehouses (the working capital) could result in a situation where it is difficult to satisfy the customers in the right way and time.

In order to show the sensitivity of profitability to NRC changes, Figure 4.21 indicates the cash flow curves of an aeronautical program with two different NRC assumptions of $500 (reference case) and $700 million. The economic indexes are strongly affected: NPV varies from $638 to $458 million, IRR from 17.19% to 13.05%, and BEP from 148 to 190 units.

4.8.4   Recurring Costs

A unit production cost reduction generates an increase of the enterprise profitability due to higher operating margins. The reduction may be obtained from an improvement in the production efficiency, an improvement in the procurement policy, or both. The production efficiency may be achieved through the standardization of product and process design (concurrent engineering), the mechanization of labor-intensive activities, and the application of advanced techniques for planning and controlling. Improvement in the procurement policy may be obtained applying benchmarking methods, taking full advantage of the power, and having work performed outside the firm if cheaper (a make or buy decision). Figure 4.21 shows how much the cash flow deteriorates when recurring costs are increased by 25%; NPV changes from $638 million to only

$2 million, IRR from 17.2% to 7%. BEP in the reference case was reached after 148 units produced; now, it is reached only at the end of the program (at 299 units produced).

4.8.5   Exchange Rates

Variation in exchange rates has a significant effect on the economics of an aeronautical program because of the global market. Since sales are generally made in U.S. dollars, it is interesting to show how variation of local money exchange rates with respect to the dollar may impact the profitability of the program. Figure 4.22 gives the cash flow of a non-U.S. firm's program.

A 10% increase in the value of the dollar reduces BEP from 148 to 119 units; NPV increases from $638 to $870 million, and IRR goes from 17.2% to 20.45%. Conversely, a 10% decrease in the dollar's value relative to the local currency would have the effect of moving the break-even point from 148 to 197 units and of deteriorating the other economic indexes.

4.8.6   Time Value

Time has a monetary value that may be calculated by discounting costs and revenues at a given rate t. Therefore, the effect of time-value (present value) concept application to cash flow is to diminish the cash flow during the last years of a program more than it diminishes cash flow in the first years. Since a program's last years quite often generate a positive cash flow (whereas at the beginning of the program, revenues are lower than costs), taking this effect into account will result in poorer economic indexes.

Figure 4.22 shows the discount rate effect considering cash flow discounted at 4% (instead than 7% as in the reference case); NPV and BEP improve, moving from 7% to 4% discount curves. Obviously, IRR is the same, because the program is not changed at all from an industrial point of view.

4.8.7   Interest Costs

Another important item of costs is represented by the financial burden, due to the need for the firm to borrow most or part of the money for nonrecurring costs from government sources, banks, or other financial institutions. This item assumes great significance on the total costs incurred during the program's life, so aeronautical firms need easy funding for launching a new program. These funds may be obtained with government help through direct channels (specific laws the local aeronautical industry support) or often indirectly through subsidies to military programs that will have a fallout on civil programs). But it is increasingly difficult to have new programs substantially underwritten by governments. In fact, under a 1992 GATT (General Agreement on Tariffs and Trade) agreement between the United States and the European Union, governments can fund only 33% of NRC for a new airplane larger than 100 seats.

Figure 4.22
Discounted Cumulated Cash Flow: Effect of Variation of Development Time, Discount Rate, Interest Expense

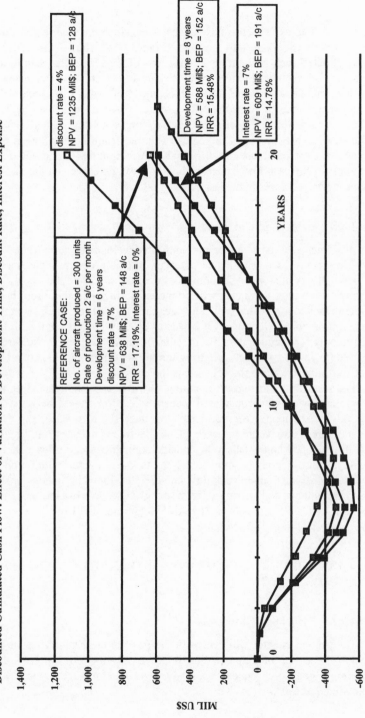

So far, interest expense has not been considered, because only industrial costs have been taken into account. Figure 4.22 shows the effect of the introduction of such costs at an interest rate of 7%. It can be seen how all the economic indexes deteriorate; the most relevant effect is the increasing of cash flow maximum exposure and BEP, which goes from 148 to 191 units.

Financial costs increase the NRC profile for some years, then they begin to decrease due to the effect of revenues deriving from airplane sales. When the cumulative cash flow becomes positive (that is, from the break-even point on) the interest on it generates now financial contribution that is additional revenues that improve the cash flow. That is why the baseline curve and the one with the interest costs get closer in the last years.

4.8.8   Development Time

Any increase in development and predevelopment time (due to many possible reasons, such as technical or organizational problems) causes a delay on the first delivery and on the economics of the program, even if costs are assumed to remain the same. Revenues will be moved further into the future because of delivery rescheduling. This will cause the cash flow of the enterprise to become worse (although not that much) because, as already mentioned, the effect of the discount rate is to reduce the present value of future cash and in the aeronautical program (as in most projects requiring initial investment), the positive cash flow is the most distant, while the negative is the nearest.

The worsening of program economics would be much higher if, in addition, the interest charges be considered, because the firm should bear the negative cash flow for a longer time and pay the interest on it. Also, the cash flow maximum exposure would increase. (This situation is not shown in Figure 4.22.) In addition, one should take into consideration that some sales could be lost forever because customers could switch to other manufacturers and products.

The negative effect on cash flow due to a development time increase from 6 to 8 years without considering interest charges and possible lost sales is shown in Figure 4.21. NPV drops from $638 to 588 million, IRR from 17.2% to 15.5%, and BEP from 148 to 152 aircraft.

4.9   IDENTIFYING   COMPANY   STRATEGY   AND   PRICING OBJECTIVES

4.9.1   Business Objectives

The present chapter will deal with the possibility of managing the price by pursuing long-term objectives. With reference to long-term internal objectives and simplifying some concepts already treated before, the objectives can be summarized as follows:

1. To achieve long-term viability of programs with improvement of market share in the relevant market segments.

2. To focus on a few market segments only in which to concentrate all efforts because of limited resources available or a particularly hostile competitive environment.

3. To decide on a progressive exit from a business segment after having obtained the maximum possible gain out of the programs, thereby extending their life as much as possible and looking for new and even marginal markets, but without the need of additional investment.

The use of price as the means of pursuing the first objective will be analyzed in the final section of this chapter. Price and the two other internal objectives of a firm will be discussed in the following 4.9.2 paragraph that focuses on links between product life cycle and the competitive strength and positioning of a firm. These topics deal with long-term objectives and global strategies typical of products' portfolio management. On a tactical basis instead, dealing specifically with price as one of the four *Ps*, it can be said that a price increase may improve the economics of the initiative because it may increase revenues. Also, the payback period may be shortened and the break-even point reached earlier. The precise effect has to be examined with reference to the demand curve slope. But a sales price increase is possible under certain circumstances only.

Price increases should be considered only when certain competitive situations exist and not in other circumstances. When it is clear that demand is declining, when there is more supply than demand, when customers are particularly price sensitive, when products are not differentiated enough, or when competition is particularly aggressive, any price increase would heavily impact sales volume, and the net effect on total revenues might be negative. The product must not only be competitive but also must appear different from the others on the market. Firms adopting a differentiation policy, even playing a role only in a few niches but with advanced products and outstanding after-sale support and services, may also adopt higher sales prices.

To increase sales prices, a firm must be a market leader. It has already pointed out that only firms with a high initial market share may increase prices of their products with only a slight penalty in terms of market penetration loss. On the contrary, if a firm is in a defensive position or if its purpose is to improve market share in order to discourage new entrances into the market segment, then a price decrease should be considered. In this situation, a decrease in price is the most common option used by firms that enjoy cost differentials due to scale or learning effect economies.

4.9.2   Price Objectives over the Product Life Cycle

This section analyzes the way a firm operating in the civil aeronautical sector develops its own strategy for satisfying the variable market demand with respect to different products' life cycle phases. We will try to apply the general product life cycle (PLC) theory, particularly with respect to how the firm defines and controls price and uses it as an element of the four Ps strategy.

4.9.2.1   Life Cycle of Product Classes, Types, and Models

The PLC concept (Figure 4.23) may be used to study the behavior of a class of products (such as jet aircraft) or a type (such as the pure jet aircraft, not considering the turbofan in it), or a model (such as the Douglas DC-9).

4.9.2.1.1   Characteristics of the Product Class Life Cycle

The presence of a main cycle followed by successive cycles is clearly visible in the aeronautical industry and is due to two main reasons:

1.   The evolution of key technologies in this field follows a particular pattern, slow but constant, that periodically brings significant innovations but rarely an important breakthrough.

2.   The sensitivity of this sector to macroenvironmental conditions. This in turn is subject to macroeconomic situations whose modification have a strong impact on air traffic demand. In fact, each of the commercial jet airplane life cycles has been due to some traumatic event in the worldwide economy (Figure 4.24) that the aeronautical industry answered, making significant improvements in existing airplanes to allow continued sales via the presence of new advanced models on the market.

Figure 4.23
The Various Life Cycles of a Product

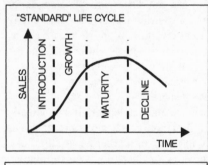
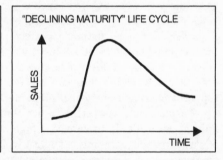
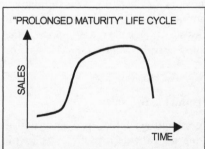
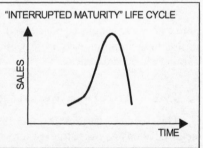

Figure 4.24
Life Cycles and Replacement of Jet Aircraft Class Product

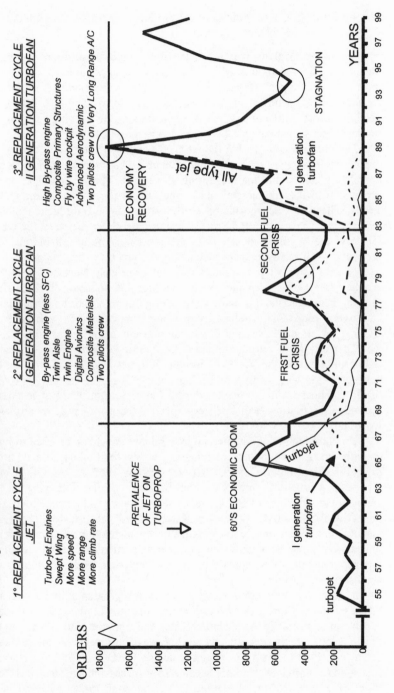

4.9.2.1.2   Characteristics of the Product Type Life Cycle and the
              Substitution Cycle

In the jet airplane market since 1950, three substitution cycles can be identified. This means that within the "class," it is possible to identify orderly three "Product types" (Figure 4.24): pure jet, first-generation turbofans, and second-generation turbofans. It is in fact possible to identify a date when the declining orders curve of a type of airplane crosses the growing curve of the new product type; such a date has been noted in Figure 4.24.

The pure jet cycle within the jet class corresponds to the victory of turbine engines technology over the existing technology based on reciprocating engines, completely out of the market during the 1960s. The first airplane to use jet propulsion in the commercial field appeared on the market at the end of the 1940s. These can be considered as the years of the introduction of the new technology. The substitution process began much later (between the end of the '50s and the begin of '60s) due to the need for a fully reliable and credible product as well as advantageous technology to present to customers.

The diffusion of jet airplanes has not been easy because of some initial accident (the Comet airplane and the problem of understanding the structural fatigue phenomena) and because they were going to substitute for airplanes that had given proof of high reliability and operating capacities such as the DC-4, DC-6, Convair airplanes, the Constellation, and many others (Some of these were derived from cargo airplanes used during World War II.). The first turboprop airplane, the Vickers Viscount 600, flew in 1948, narrowing the gap between a very innovative technology and a too-obsolete one. Jet airplanes firmly established in the market during the 1960s, in which it is possible to recognize the first cycle of civil jet airplanes, the age of pure jet airplanes that would last about 10 years.

The introduction of commercial jet airplanes should be credited to European manufacturers, since the first commercial jet was the English Comet (first order in 1947, first flight in 1949, first delivery in 1952 to the BOAC (British Overseas Airways Corporation) and because, in the following years, the aeronautical industries of Europe made several new products like the Caravelle, the Trident, the BAC 1-11, the Mercure, and the VC-10. The European manufacturers were unable to capitalize on the technological advantage reached in some critical areas of aeronautical research, particularly the jet propulsion, on the aerodynamic of swept wing, in the materials and structures, in their possession at that time.

In fact, the first commercially successful programs in the jet airplane business came from U.S. manufacturers that took advantage of the rapid expansion of air traffic in the United States and from the United States at the end of the 1950s. In these years, the B-707 was introduced on the market (first delivery in 1958 to PanAm), and subsequently the DC-8 (1959 to Delta) and the first series of airplanes that later became very successful, such as the B-727 (first flight of version 100 in 1963) and DC-9 (versions 15/20 delivered in 1965).

These airplanes made extraordinary changes in air transportation over long and short distances. In this phase, the emphasis was on airplane performance in terms of time savings and comfort when compared with piston-engine aircraft. The higher fuel consumption and, more generally, the higher operating costs were not major considerations.

The high fuel consumption of jet airplanes became significant during the first oil crisis in 1973. This crisis accelerated the first-generation pure jet decline, favoring the entrance of the turbofan jet airplanes that, because of a higher bypass ratio, burned much less fuel than the pure jets, with other performance factors close or better. Other macroeconomic events have been the true cause of modification in the air transportation and in the airplane characteristics. For several years, the economy was showing an erratic behavior that became a recession in 1974-75 after the oil crisis.

Faced with this situation, the airlines began to reduce orders of old-type airplanes and to buy the new types: The 747 orders in 1966 (first delivery in 1969) were followed by the DC-10 (first order in 1968 and first delivery in 1971) and by the L-1011 (first order in 1968, first delivery in 1972). Also, the smaller airplanes were re-engined with new turbofans or with new versions of old engines that were modified to increase the bypass ratio (for instance, the JT8D of Pratt & Whitney – P&W).

Boeing introduced the 200 series of 727s (first order in 1965, first delivery in 1967) and launched the 737 (orders for the 100 and 200 series in 1965, delivered beginning in 1967). Douglas changed the engines on the DC-8 and put on the market the 60 series with turbofan engines (orders in 1965, first delivery in 1967) and the refurbished and re-engined versions of the DC-9 (the new 30-40 series launched in 1965; the 50 series with longer fuselage launched in 1973). These airplanes, particularly the wide-bodies, are typical of the second life cycle of jet airplanes that lasted about 10 years, from the end of the 1960s through the beginning of the 1980s.

Unlike the changes that would happen later, the new engines represented the only real difference that can be addressed in order to distinguish between the first and second life cycles of jet airplanes (apart from the obvious continuous improvement in all relevant technologies). The realization of wide-body airplanes cannot be considered a breakthrough in the technologies of structures and materials, although it has motivated a greater use of composite materials in order to save weight; the reduction from three to two cockpit crew members (with the flight engineer's position discontinued) happened some years later.

A change in the macroenvironment was responsible for causing a new discontinuity in airplane sales. The second oil crisis at the end the 1970s accelerated the phasing out of the first-generation turbofan engines. The airplane manufacturers responded to the operational scenario changes by introducing more advanced airplanes, not only in terms of power plants but also in terms of the general level of the technological content of most new models. In fact, the new airplanes were characterized by a much higher content of advanced materials, digital avionics, and higher lift over drag (L/D, aerodynamic efficiency) in order to decrease the operating costs considerably while keeping the previously obtained levels of performance and comfort.

In addition, most of the new airplanes dropped the crew members from three to two, and all the new engines presented lower acoustic annoyance levels (both internal and from the community point of view) and lower pollution levels to meet more stringent noise and emission regulations. The first manufacturer to propose an airplane with most of these features was Airbus with its A-300 (first deliveries in 1974). The airplane was anticipating market requirements of differentiation from airplanes made by other manufacturers that were already present in the same market segment.

Following the Airbus move, Boeing launched the 757 and 767 (both delivered in 1982), as well as new versions of the 737 (300, 400, 500). The first flight of a 737-300 was in 1984; the airplane was powered by the very advanced CFM56 produced by SNECMA and General Electric. Meanwhile, Douglas (at this time McDonnell Douglas) was launching the 80 series of DC-9s (MD-80). But it was the first flight of the Airbus A-320 in 1987 that actually symbolized this new generation of modern aircraft that constitute the third life cycle of jet airplanes.

In addition to having all the features described above, the A-320 (and the other family members that followed) presented the innovation of having fly-by-wire flight commands. These airplanes, powered by second-generation turbofans, are also characterized by many significant innovations in several technological areas. They constitute the third life cycle of jet airplanes. The cycle may be considered as beginning in the early 1980s and being now probably in the mature or declining stage. In the early 1990s, all manufacturers experienced a sharp drop in orders caused by a recession in the world economy, but in 1995 the major manufacturers began receiving new orders once again.

In the 1980s, the sales level had been very high, due not only to world-wide favorable economic conditions but also to the fact that almost all the existing airline fleets had to be renewed with fuel-efficient, low-pollution, quieter aircraft. The first new and more severe standards of the U.S. Environmental Protection Agency go back to 1985. The decade culminated with an astonishing total of about 4,000 orders (for all manufacturers in the years 1988-90).

Airplanes such as the MD-11 (first flight in 1990), A-330/A-340 (first flights respectively in 1992 and 1991), MD-90 (first flight in 1993), and B-777 (first flight in 1994, the last introduced on the market), still belong to the third life cycle of jets by characteristics, technological level, general architecture, and so on. Yet they may be the last of this cycle, to be followed by airplanes so different that a new life cycle should be considered as beginning.

The very high capacity airplanes launched by Airbus in December 2000 are very likely the last ones belonging to the third life cycle jet airplanes.

In fact, the proposed Boeing response, the *Super Efficient Airplane*, incorporating most of the innovations developed for the abandoned Sonic Cruiser project, may define a new cycle for jet airplane type especially if the evolution in propulsion, aerodynamics, materials, and so on will bring technological improvements similar to that created by the introduction of jet propulsion to replace piston engines. New concepts in the operational aspects of flight (such as transatmospheric airplanes) or architectural aspects (such as the all wing airplanes) could also contribute to the end of the conventional jet class life cycle.

As previously shown, product types (when compared to classes) tend to present life cycles closer to the standard, that is, a unique cycle with all typical phases (introduction, growth, maturity, and decline). In addition to substantial adherence to the theoretical model, the aeronautical sector is also distinguished by having product types with very long maturity/decline phases with recycles after the main cycle. This is due to the particularly long average life of the product and to the slow and progressive evolution of the technology in the sector with the absence of frequent breakthroughs, but there are at least two additional reasons:

- The existence of derivative products is not the exception but the rule of the game. The basic model (the founder) and derivatives may even belong to different product types: According to our definition, the B-737-200, B-737-300, and B-737-700 actually are turbojets, first-generation turbofans, and second-generation turbofans respectively, although there is a significant level of commonality among the three.

- The life of the single airplane may be extended almost without limits with the right maintenance and refurbishment when needed. After having served the major airlines for 15 to 20 years, often these airplanes are replaced but continue to operate for at least another 10 to 15 years in the fleets of smaller airlines of developing countries, to which they are sold at a low price.

4.9.2.1.3   Characteristics of the Product Model Life Cycle

Product models have life cycle shorter than product types but still close to the general (PLC) theory the theoretical system (see the DC-8 and B-707 in Figure 4.25). However, the most successful models from the commercial or technical point of view (for example, the DC-8 and B-707) had a very long life cycle with many recycles via programs for re-engining and changes in avionics and systems by manufacturers to upgrade their products to the current state of the art. This practice of making derivatives out of a basic model increases the useful life of a product model considerably. However, much attention is needed to apply the life cycle concepts to these products, because derivatives are often very different from the basic model, to the point that in some cases they should be considered new models.

The life cycle of a single product may be far different from those of the type or class to which it belongs. Some of them have facilitated the transition to the next generation of aircraft. This is the case of the A-320, which advanced airplanes of its type in its effort to beat and substitute for the Boeing best-seller B-727.

Figure 4.25
Boeing B-707 and Douglas DC-8 Life Cycles

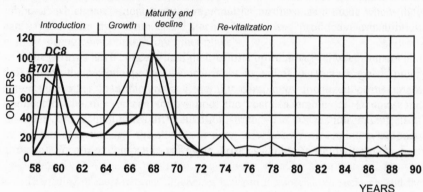

The A-320 made increased use of composite materials, digital avionics, fly by wire flight controls, and was a twin-engine airplane. In the same way, airplanes such as the B-767, B-777, and A-330, all twin-engines, have accelerated the decline of such models as the L-1011 and DC-10 (three engines) and limited the success of airplanes like the MD-11, an almost new airplane (although derived from DC-10) but still with three engines.

4.9.2.2   Product Life Cycle Stages

Sales of an airplane in the introduction phase appear discontinuous; the length of this phase may last 5 to 6 years (Figure 4.25). The introduction of a new model on the market is characterized by a high number of orders followed by erratic behavior. Most commercial aircraft have been delivered in significant quantities to their respective launch customers. This is characteristic of the aeronautical commercial sector because the costs associated with the launch of a new product are so huge that all manufacturers in the sector try in this way to reduce the financial, technological, and market risk of the project; in addition:

- They decide to go ahead with the program only with a reasonable amount of orders from a few launch airlines.

- They define the technical and physical characteristics of the airplane rigorously to meet customer needs from the very beginning, avoiding expensive modifications later.

The erratic trend typical of the introduction phase of many products is also seen in the aeronautical sector, although later if compared with the classic pattern due to one or more of the following:

- The appearance of technical or production problems that translate into a less qualitative correspondence of the product with customer requirements or expectations, and/or commercial difficulties due to competitor reaction.

- Specific weaknesses in commercialization or product support.

- Some mistake in the sales campaign or marketing strategy that should sustain the innovative aspects of the product.

- The potential inertia of customers (other than the launch customers) that may happen to be mainly followers (not leaders) and therefore afraid of new products and reluctant to abandon their present airplanes that may be obsolete but are reliable. [VALDANI 1986]

The length of the introduction phase of aeronautical products depends upon the effect of following factors that have an impact on the diffusion rapidity of new products on the market:

- The relative advantage of the new product, that is, how much better it is perceived to be than the existing product (in the aeronautical sector, the practical absence of technological breakthroughs means there is often little immediate evidence of a new product's superiority over previous products).

- The compatibility of the innovation, that is, the probability of full and rapid integration into the customer's system from a technical point of view.

- The complexity of the innovative product, that is, how difficult its use is perceived to be:

    - The possibility of testing the innovative product and evaluating the result of the experiment; first customers may experiment product introduction problems and this will be immediately known in the aeronautical community.

    - The perceived risk involved with acceptance of the new product; the lower the perceived risk, the speedier the diffusion of the product. [VALDANI 1986]

Contrary to what is the rule in other industrial sectors (where, at the beginning of a product's life cycle, the price is kept high to cover the high production and distribution costs), in the aeronautical sector, the launch price of a new airplane is relatively moderate. It is lower than the price that will be adopted in other phases of the life cycle (see Figure 4.26). The manufacturer is interested in selling as many airplanes as possible from the very beginning of the program to take advantage of the learning effect. Each airplane sold allows the next one to be sold at a significantly lower price in absolute terms. The pricing policy of aeronautical manufacturers belongs to the type known as rapid penetration (as opposed to slow penetration), because it is characterized by a huge effort to promote the airplane, with an associated moderate price.

When a manufacturer is the first to enter a business segment, there is a significant temporal advantage that may result in a temporary situation in which that manufacturer has a monopoly. The innovator soon experiences the reaction from its imitators or followers, although the advantage of being first on the market with the right product may be decisive.

Figure 4.26
Traded Sale Price Evolution with the Product Life Cycles Phases

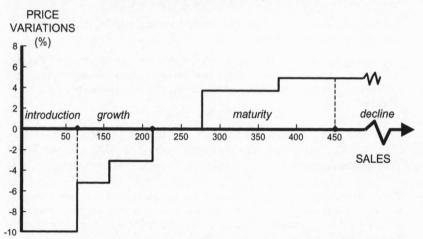

The DC-10 was put on the market in 1971. Its 1-year advantage over the Lockheed L-1011 (Tristar) may have played an important role in the victory of the DC-10 and the defeat of the Tristar. The A-330 was the first second-generation twin-engine wide-body airplane to become operational. Its temporary monopoly pushed Boeing to launch the 777 2 years later, with the need to exploit all possible ways to recover lost time in the segment already dominated by the A-330.

The innovator enjoys the advantage of being first on the market, with the real possibility of fulfilling a consistent share of the market demand. On the other hand, it has the task of partially creating the demand, thus bearing some additional costs of educating (pioneering) the customers about the product's new features. The efforts of the other manufacturers will be much easier later, with their sales to the "follower" airlines.

4.9.2.2.1   Growth

The growth phase is characterized by a quick and strong sales increase; at this time, interest in the new product reaches the follower customers that are the majority of buyers [KOTLER 1984]. In the growth phase, the aeronautical manufacturers are in a position to increase sales prices from the introduction level (in other industrial sectors, prices are stabilized at this time). The degree of such increase is related to the capacity of keeping the market share. This, in turn, is related to the soundness of the firm's commercial and competitive strategies, that in this phase are characterized by the firm's capability of improving the product, increasing the quality of existing models, and adding new versions and its success in trying to reach new market segments.

The above characteristics confirm that, in the commercial aeronautical sector, the competitive strategies within a trade expansion contest (that is, during a market demand growth period and based on product and market development) are designed to improve competitive positioning in the arena rather than to increase profits [VALDANI 1986]. (see Figure 4.26.)

4.9.2.2.2   Maturity

The maturity phase begins with "a slowdown in sales growth because the product has achieved acceptance by most of the potential buyers." [KOTLER 1984: p.355] The maturity phase may follow any of three different patterns (Figure 4.23): declining maturity, prolonged maturity, or interrupted maturity.

The aeronautical sector seems to be following the declining maturity pattern (Figure 4.25): Each growth phase ends with a peak, followed shortly by a decline in sales that lasts for a long time and is relatively slow and progressive. It is likely that this is a result of the sensitivity of the sector to external conditions that accelerate and amplify the natural cyclical pattern of the selling process. Producers respond to the demand downturn acting first of all on products that are modified deeply in their tangible (physical) and intangible (that is associated conditions to the offer) content. Results, in terms of profits, may be important particularly in this phase, because the sales price of the airplane is "full" (see Figure 4.26). However, profits may begin to decrease due to an increase in costs, particularly marketing and R & D (for the development of new versions) that are not compensated by lower production costs (because the learning effect is becoming less relevant) and because of sales slowdown.

The program cost increase is related to the desire and the need of the manufacturer to modify products in order to improve performance (autonomy, reliability, comfort, speed, and so on) and characteristics (dimensions, weights, materials, equipment) that may expand the versatility, safety, and convenience of product usage [VALDANI 1986]. Unfortunately, such improvements on their own products may be easily imitated.

In the commuter sector, almost all products have reached the maturity stage at the same time. All market leaders have then developed new versions of their best-sellers (ATR 42-500, DHC8-400 SAAB-2000, F60, J61), based on the same improvements, (that is, more speed, less noise, more autonomy, bigger dimensions), at a price per seat only slightly higher than basic models and with the use of financial aids to support sales (such as leasing, discounts on spare parts and on crew training). This approach brings some expenses, limiting margins and profits and leading to a general reduction of profitability of the whole sector.

4.9.2.2.3   Decline

Apart from the slowdown of sales, the product decline phase is characterized by other signals. Product differentiation stops after its beginning in the last part of the growth phase and explosion during the maturity stage. The producer has explored all possible differentiations of its offer, making all possible technical improvements, trying all market segments in which it was possible to sale the airplane derivatives, putting into effect all permissible promotional and pricing policies. In this phase, the trend is for the price to stabilize among the main players [KOTLER 1984; VALDANI 1986].

The decline phase (of a product type, not of a single product only) is characterized by other significant events:

- The diffusion of substitute products begin to occur.

- The traditional market share penetration of certain manufacturers may change dramatically because some of them may decide to leave the segment and stop production of the relevant models; with the decline of sales, many firms may also decide to remain only with the strongest model and stop their sales of weaker models in order to concentrate all their efforts on the "survivors".

For example, in the transition from pure jets to turbofans, many firms disappeared or downsized their activities because they did not have a product that could compete with the new models. This happened to the European manufacturers, although they had been first in the commercial jet age (with the Caravelle and the Comet). Because they were not able to make innovative products, they surrendered the field to the U.S. manufacturers. Even subsequent attempts (like the Mercure, the Trident, the VC-10, and to a lesser extent the BAC 1-11) did not achieve the predicted sales, selling much less than the products of their U.S. competitors.

4.10   SELECTING A PRICING METHOD AND SETTING THE FINAL PRICE

"Given the demand schedule, the cost function, and competitor's prices, the company is now ready to select a price. The price will be somewhere between one that is too low to produce a profit and one that is too high to produce any demand. . . . Product costs set a floor to the price." [KOTLER 1984: p.515]

4.10.1   Cost Oriented Pricing

4.10.1.1 Cost Plus Pricing.

The most elementary pricing method is to add a standard markup to the cost of the product. But any pricing method that ignores current demand and competition is not likely to result in the optimal price. A different way to approach price setting, without knowing market demand is to start from the knowledge of the maximum price customers are willing to pay for a given product. This is the equilibrium price that makes the product having the same overall appeal than competitors, that is the same cost effectiveness, which may be obtained through a regression analysis.

The maximum selling price must then be compared with the minimum affordable price, which is determined by the firm's costs level and by the margin it wishes to reach. The actual selling price in the economic evaluations will derive from this comparison. Two possibilities exist:

- *Alternative A:* The maximum sales price is *higher* than the minimum affordable by the firm.

- *Alternative B:* The maximum sales price is *lower* than the minimum affordable by the firm.

In Alternative A, therefore, the industrial costs and the margin allow setting a sales price higher than cost plus margin and lower than the maximum allowed by the market. Conversely, in Alternative B, the actual sales price must be equal to the maximum sales price coming from the regression analysis, since the sum of the firm's industrial costs plus the desired margin is already higher than the maximum sales price allowed by the market. If the industrial cost is lower than maximum sales price (from the regression), it is worthwhile to continue to produce even with a smaller than desired margin. Only when the marginal production cost is already higher than the maximum sales price is it better to quit production and sales of the product.

The cost-plus approach to the pricing problem presents the opportunity and necessity here of defining and giving examples of the airplane chain value breakdown. This has been done with reference to the regional aircraft segment.

4.10.1.2 Price And Net Yield

The pricing policy has to be examined against market conditions. To cover this subject traded prices achieved in the market place have been studied over the period from 1993 to 1995. Such prices cover details of deals known to have occurred in the market. Published catalog or sticker prices for aircraft currently on the market were subject to negotiation. Due to the market, prices actually achieved by manufacturers were lower. These prices are referred to as traded prices.

The CRJ-100 still maintained a relatively high price per seat ($372,000 sticker versus $330,000 traded price), partly through its operating cost characteristics and partly through lack of a direct competitor. AVRO RJ prices were depressed, particularly for the largest ($284,000/$237,500) products, due to the competition from Fokker and attempts to balance the higher four-engine operating costs of the AVRO RJ. Also, the advent of the B-737-600 and MD-95 had an impact, bringing down the prices of the high-end regional aircraft. For the AVRO RJ the discount requested by the market was fairly high (15% to 16%); the average value of the discounts was 11.4%.

4.10.1.2.1   Net Yield

Traded prices include certain items that will result in a lower net yield figure. Examination of the deals carried out in the years 1993 to 1995 in the regional airplane market show that these costs were around 9.1% of traded price. Certain deals that Fokker and AVRO have concluded have requested higher difference between traded price and net yield, but it is considered that these were due to particular market conditions.

The net yield in Table 4.3 has been computed using an average priced airplane as an example. Variable costs are to be considered as an average. It is acknowledged that due to conditions in some markets, these items will vary. For example, advisor (agent) fees are not customary in the United States. The resulting price/cost structure is shown in Table 4.3.

In addition, it should be remembered that, in order to enter the market, the first aircraft sold would be further discounted with reference to the traded prices, as already shown in Figure 4.26.

4.10.1.3 Break Even Analysis.

Break-even analysis can be used as a tool to provide a rough estimate to eliminate obviously unworkable prices. If we plot the average cost versus the number of aircraft sold (Figure 4.27), the break-even point is the number of aircraft for which the price equals the average cost. From then on, profits are made, since the price is greater than the average cost. The break-even point varies, of course, as the price changes.

Table 4.3
Price/Cost Structure

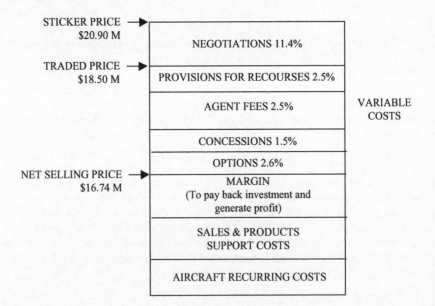

Figure 4.27
Breakeven Point

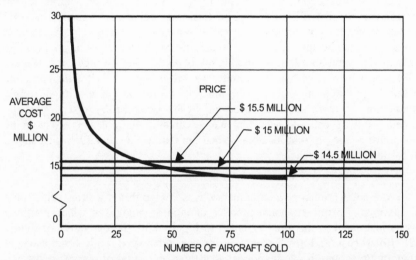

Although the graph assumes that any quantity might be sold at the assumed price, this is not true. In fact, this would be equivalent to assuming the existence of a horizontal demand curve at that price; this is a perfectly elastic demand. But in this case, there would be no pricing decision to make. Therefore, break-even analysis is only useful for eliminating obvious pricing alternatives. To find the real optimum sales price the analysis implies to know or to find the demand curve, as will be shown hereafter.

4.10.2   Demand Oriented Pricing

4.10.2.1 Mathematics of the Problem

The optimum price may be found by calculating total costs and total revenues, since all the elements are known at this point. Apart from some deviation that is necessary for a firm to follow its particular strategy, generally the optimum price is the price at which profit is maximum (or loss is minimum). Therefore, if firm demand versus price and program costs versus quantity functions are known, then such optimum price can be found directly by using mathematics.

The case is particularly simple if the above mentioned functions are (or may be approximated to) linear.

In fact, in this case, mathematics predicts that the shape of the profit equation is a parabola and this brings a lot of interesting considerations about the possible price strategy.

4.10.2.2 Total Revenues and Costs Approach

Let's consider again our example of the regional turboprop airplane: the demand curve is that of Figure 4.9. The total cost curve as a function of total produced quantities of turboprop aircraft is represented in Figure 4.28. Because both graphs may be approximated to linear, the results should be as predicted by mathematics (a parabola). It is possible to obtain the total revenue curve (Figure 4.28) simply by multiplying the X and Y values of Figure 4.9. It is then possible to build up the profit curve as a function of selling price with a simple subtraction. A more realistic result might be obtained by discounting the monetary flows (costs and revenues) at a certain discount rate. This effect on the economies of the program is already incorporated in Figure 4.29, which shows the results of this approach.

4.10.2.3 Marginal Analysis Approach

From conventional economic theory, it is known that if a firm is interested in maximizing profit, it should produce units in an amount at which marginal cost is just equal to marginal revenue. In Figure 4.30, the derivative of Figure 4.28 (total cost and total revenue) for the referenced typical aeronautical program are shown. It can be noticed that the intersection of marginal cost and marginal revenue curves occurs at the same most profitable quantity (270 units) than in Figure 4.29 relative to program profit. The selling price for this optimum quantity has to be determined by referring to this figure (or Figure 4.28), which shows what price customers are willing to pay for the optimum quantity. The marginal revenue and cost curves intersection does not give the correct optimum price.

Figure 4.28
Program Total Revenues and Costs

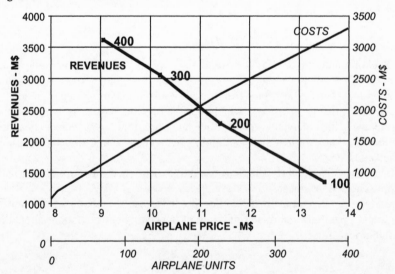

Figure 4.29
Program Profit

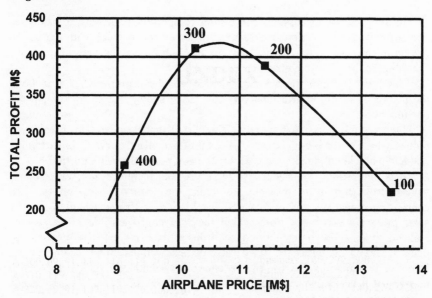

Figure 4.30
Marginal Revenue and Costs

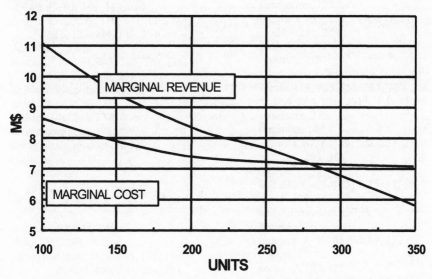

4.10.3   Setting the Final Price According to Company Strategy and Objectives

In the previous discussion concerning competitive strategies, it was noted that firms may have different objectives that they try to reach with the use of marketing mix variables, particularly price. Such objectives may also change according to the life cycle phase.

The most common alternative objectives for the firm are whether to favor the market share through a relatively low price strategy or to look for profit maximization.

Figure 4.29 shows (extrapolating the curve) that there are two break-even points (where profit is equal to zero), because the demand curve is downsloping. Inside the bracket defined by the two break-even points there is a profit.

It is interesting to consider also the sales (and therefore the market share) values; from this it is possible to obtain the trade-off between the two contrasting objectives and to quantify the dilemma a firm must often face. A sales price always exists from which the maximum possible profit can be realized, and market share continuously drops as the price increases because the demand curve is downsloping. It may also be observed that in this example there is not a maximum value for the revenue curve (although this may occur), meaning that the demand curve for the product is elastic along the price range considered.

From the above, a conclusion can be drawn with reference to firm's price strategy. It is never advisable to increase price above the value for which the maximum profit is reached; moreover, since the profit curve is relatively flat around its maximum value, it seems more advantageous to charge prices a little lower than those required to reach maximum profit.

By proceeding with a small profit penalty, it is possible to achieve an increase in market penetration. This policy is appropriate even when profit is the firm's main concern.

From the beginning of the chapter, it has been pointed out that there is no integrated theory of airplane pricing that gives satisfactory answers to most pricing problems. Rather, there are numerous approaches to the general price theory. Therefore, it would not be appropriate to rely only upon one, namely the classic economic method. The importance of price, as both a tactical and a strategic tool, leads to the necessity for a wider approach that incorporates also marketing and managerial aspects of price.

The objective of this chapter has been to give the reader an overview of theory and practice in the main aspects of airplane pricing, inside the framework of the competitive scenario that characterizes the civil aeronautical business.

NOTES

1. In the pure oligopoly, the demand curve presents a typical knee.
2. The differentiated oligopoly system typical of the aeronautical industry presents a certain degree of similarity with monopolistic competition. According to MANSFIELD

[1996] In both cases the following apply:

a. The products are similar in terms of functions offered and target market to the point that they may be substituted for each other.

b. The demand curve is down sloping.

c. The companies prefer to differentiate the products in some way rather than to compete in terms of sales prices.

In reality, apart from the above similarities, there is a substantial difference between the two systems; that difference lies in the number of players competing for the same market. The differentiated oligopoly is characterized by a limited number of competitors, as is the pure oligopoly; therefore, even if products are differentiated (in the sense specified above), the general characteristic of the oligopolistic system is maintained, that is, the strategic interdependence among the players. The monopolistic competition system (apart from the above-mentioned similarities — most important the product differentiation) is characterized by a large number of companies. Therefore, the situation is as having several partially monopolistic companies in the market from the supply side. In this case, the move of a single player (in terms of price change or product improvement) may not necessarily produce reaction from the other firms, which may ignore it because the share of business involved is relatively small.

3. The figure refers to large jet airplanes; we are assuming that the results can be extended to the contiguous category of regional airplanes.

4. In fact, the conception and realization of today's civil aircraft are oriented toward technologies that allow savings in direct operating costs (with the high bypass turbofan or propellers for high speed, composite materials, supercritical airfoils, and so on), as well as an increase in safety and reliability of aeronautical structures (airframe) with "safe life" approaches. In the military sector, the aim is to achieve ever more advanced flight conditions (iper-maneuvrability, high thrust-to-weight ratio engines, vectorial thrust nozzles, and so on) and the development of specific technologies for the safety of combat aircraft, such as low radar signals or stealth technologies.

5. For example, in a flexible manufacturing system, it is necessary to have indirect personnel for transportation, supervision, production planning, quality control, testing, and so on. If the actual rate is less than planned, these items (indirect costs of production) will have a greater influence on the unit cost of production. Some other additional costs such as maintenance of tooling not in use and of machinery halted have the same effect.

6. However, the problem is much more complex, because not only costs but also revenues should be considered. Yet, sales price and quantity are generally different for new and derivative airplanes, even very similar ones according to this comparison. The subject will be handled in more detail in the next paragraphs.

7. The main difference is generally in the number of seats but may be also lie in the range and the aircraft type (commercial, military or cargo transport).

5

AIRPLANES COMMERCIALIZATION

5.1 OFFER AND LOCATION OF SERVICES

The following analysis will show who performs the activities related to airplane commercialization and product distribution and how those activities are conducted. Then the following important topics will be addressed:

- Distinctive characteristics of the aeronautical industry.

- Modalities through which the aeronautical manufactures solve the problems related to product distribution.

Marketing channels are best used when a balance is reached among sometimes diverging objectives such as timeliness (time to market), effectiveness (percentage of success, measured as the ratio between actual and potential customers), and efficiency of the system (cost effectiveness). If the manufacturer carries out directly all or most of these activities, a risk exists that its costs (and prices) may be higher than necessary, even if a higher effectiveness is achieved. On the other hand, if most such activities are performed outside the firm, costs and prices could be reduced, but most likely some control will be lost, with possible consequences including loss of timeliness and effectiveness.

5.1.1 Customer Characteristics

When the target customers are few and account for the majority of the total orders, and each order is of paramount importance to the customer due to the significance of the investment (or for other reasons), firms prefer to use in-house structures for many activities that might otherwise be delegated outside the company.

Aeronautical products have a high unit value, and buyers need to know the product's technical characteristics and performances well for its best utilization in their own network. This need to metabolize the product is typical of high-tech sectors and may be achieved only with the assistance of highly skilled personnel employed by the manufacturer.

5.1.2   Intermediaries Characteristics

In the aviation supply chain, between the few sellers and the many buyers, there are intermediaries related mostly to support, not to the sale of the product. (Banks and other financial institutions are exceptions; these may actually help in the airplane sales.)

For example, in recent years, leasing companies have become of paramount importance in airplane selling. The value added by the leasing companies consists of making available to the airlines the huge amounts of capital necessary to acquire the aircraft.

5.2   DISTRIBUTION CHANNELS CHARACTERISTICS

"A channel alternative is described by three elements: the *types of business intermediaries*, the *number of intermediaries*, and the *terms and mutual responsibilities of each channel participant.*" [KOTLER 1984: p.553] In civil commercial aviation, the geographical dispersion of customers and their need for continuous and different levels and types of assistance makes it necessary for the manufacturers to be present worldwide with both sales offices and after-sale support facilities.

However, since a network owned by the manufacturer, in charge of all requested activities to interface with the customers, would be very expensive, some of these functions (such as maintenance, training of pilots and other crews, sales, financing) are performed with the help of other organizations (such as airlines, firms specializing in airplane maintenance, banks, and leasing companies). These organizations must be coordinated and kept updated. Some have to be supplied with spare parts. All this requires a massive effort by the manufacturers. On the other hand, the manufacturers may benefit from the image of reliability that these organizations enjoy locally, where they are well-known by the manufacturers' customers. With this setup, it is easier to solve the many different problems that customers all over the world may face.

To some extent, a certain differentiation of commercialization channels also exists in the aeronautical sector; this may be seen especially when observing certain types of markets served and products offered.

The general aviation (GA) companies instead use a network of dealers to whom they completely delegate promotion and sale of the airplanes. The dealers absorb market risks, receiving in exchange a commission that may reach 25% to 30% of airplane sales price. The reasons all GA manufacturers make this choice are essentially the following:

- The great fragmentation and geographical dispersion of demand.

- The limited unit value of the product.

- The parameters used by potential customers to make their choices, which are not generally based on economic criteria. Their selection is usually based on personal happiness about some very specific characteristics of the airplane under evaluation. Such parameters may all be better perceived, monitored, and managed locally.

The above-described distribution channels also apply to business jets. Price may range from a few million dollars to $15-$20 million. Because the after-sale support activity may be important from both a technical and economical point of view, big manufacturers such as Cessna, Gulfstream, Bombardier, and Dassault delegate sales and after-sale support of their products to authorized dealers (often with an exclusivity clause) in important local markets.

The approach to product distribution and commercialization changes drastically in the case of airplanes designed for specific purposes that are not for private or corporate use but for other operators belonging to the air transportation sector. This different approach is generally due to the following reasons:

- The aircraft has higher performance and therefore is more expensive than those used in the general or business aviation.

- The choice to acquire one airplane type instead of another depends upon precise economic parameters (such as operating costs, sales price, profit potential, and ROI) that only the manufacturer can control and support adequately for the customer (via fleet and route analysis, economic and financial analysis, and so on).

- The after-sale support is much more critical and cannot be delegated.

In the regional commuter segment, where customers are less numerous than in general aviation, but even more fragmented than in commercial aviation, firms are characterized by a significant presence in different geographical markets. They sometimes create local marketing offices that perform all administrative duties and tasks for that particular area and also marketing, sales support, sales, and after-sale support.

Embraer has local offices in the United States, Australia, and Europe that are fully responsible for promotion, sales, and after-sale assistance to the customers in these areas. ATR has local offices in Washington and Singapore, with the main purpose of coordinating after-sale support activities (in addition to providing spare parts locally), but also with the objective of keeping under control two very important commercial areas:

- The U.S. market, because of the many users of ATR products.

- The Far East market, because it is developing very fast.

Other firms adopt sales agents whose main objective is the research of sales opportunities for the manufacturers with whom they have an agency contract. They may also act as manufacturer representatives activities with the most important current or potential customers.

The sales and support activities for large commercial airplanes are more complex. Manufacturers must handle all the activities related to commercialization of the products, creating huge main offices for marketing, sales, and after-sale support, but at the same time, assuring a worldwide presence of local offices (regional sales offices, training centers, spare centers and resident customer services offices) in order for these activities to be close to their product users.

5.3   DISTRIBUTION CHANNELS FUNCTIONS

Figure 5.1 shows a typical organization for product support. This function is present in all airplane manufacturers' commercial divisions, from the largest to the smallest, although with varying degrees of complexity.

Figure 5.1
Typical Customer Support Organization

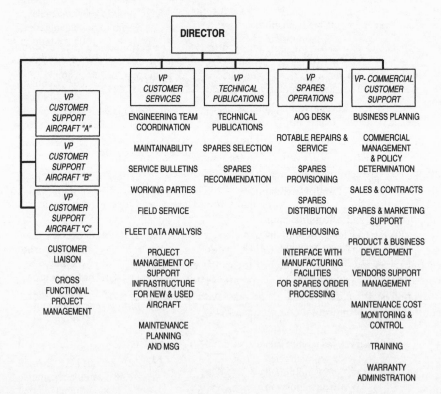

To understand the complexity of functions and activities performed by the aeronautical firms in this field, it may be useful to remember that this is a case where the augmented product concept fully applies. In fact, the airplane itself does not need a distribution channel at all. It can fly from the manufacturer's factory to the customer's site ("ferry flight" delivery).

The product sold to the customer consists not only of the physical product, but also of the services that a manufacturer provides today and agrees to provide in the future. These are the services that require creation of the distribution channel that is the subject covered by this chapter. These services may play an important role in the buyer's choice, as important as the airplane's characteristics and performance.

Therefore, in the civil aeronautical field, the distribution channel means something other than making the product available to the customer. The distribution channel represents the way to carry out all after-sale support activities that the manufacturer must provide or wishes to provide to the buyers.[1]

5.4   PRESENCE IN THE MARKET

5.4.1   After Sale Support

The success and competitiveness of major aeronautical manufacturers require a wide presence in different geographical markets. Representative offices, maintenance and logistics centers either owned or affiliated, technical documentation offices, and training centers are the structures that allow manufacturers to stay close to the customers to meet their actual needs and to monitor and understand future needs.

In each of the above fields, the main players in both the regional and commercial sectors (ATR, Bombardier, Embraer, BAE, Boeing, Airbus) are deeply committed to providing this type of customer support.

As pointed out earlier, operating assistance to the customer represents one of the most critical factors for the success in the commercial aviation market. The life cycle cost of an airplane may be as important as the acquisition cost (price) in the operators' decisions. After-sale services offered to the customers comprise the activities that may be critical both for the safety and the best and efficient management of the fleet. These activities are provided to the customers through the firms' commercialization channels that make the airplane fully available and useful to the customers according to the augmented product concept.

In fact, this focuses not only on the physical characteristics, but also on intangible elements such as:

- Training.

- Technical and operational assistance.

- Logistic support, meaning:
  - Spare part dispatching.
  - Maintenance services.
- Financial packages.

Personnel training (pilots, cabin crew, maintenance technicians, and so on) is of paramount importance for an airline with new equipment. Each airplane, although it may have commonality with other models of its class, generally has individual characteristics in terms of structural design, cockpit conception, and so on that translate into operational differences from the crew's standpoint. This may cause some constraints in the optimization of the whole fleet management. This is why the manufacturer must provide the customer with all the information it may need and the training of pilots and other crew personnel for the best use of the airplane [VICARI 1991]. Each year Boeing, trains thousands of its customers' pilots and maintenance crew members in its 22 FSBTI (FlightSafetyBoeing Training International) locations. Airbus also manages three training centers, where it can host about 13,000 trainees every year: one center in Toulouse, France; a second in Miami, Florida; and a third in Beijing.

Regional airplane manufacturers are compelled to offer comparable services. ATR, for instance, may take advantage of a training center in Toulouse where training activities are performed through the use of advanced systems like VACBI (Video and Audio Computer Based Instruction) and a flight simulator. A second flight simulator is located in Bangkok, while other training centers used by ATR are located in Houston and Fort Worth, Texas; Morlaix, France; Pori, Finland; and Athens, Greece.

Manufacturer technical support includes cooperation with the customer in solving problems that may arise during the actual operation of the aircraft with reference to factors such as safety, maintenance, and repair. Such activities are particularly critical in the introduction phase of a new airplane in the market, when even the best products show "teething problems." These are inconveniences not foreseen in the design phase and that do not appear during predelivery production tests. In many cases, these problems can be easily overcome with the manufacturer's help or support. In a few instances, they have seriously compromised the commercial success of the product.

In assuring technical support to the customers, manufacturers must deal with local certification and regulatory agencies. Practical use of the airplane may single out anomalies that call for modification of airplane parts or replacement of components and equipment that may not comply with safety or even dispatchability or maintainability rules. For this activity, the acquisition and storage of a large quantity of data is essential, requiring computer-aided management of the information as well as the use of specific software and hardware.

The technical documentation delivered to the airplane operator describes in detail the structural and operational airplane characteristics. Technical documentation generally falls into two categories:

- *Operational manuals:* These provide information on airplane performance, operational limitations, emergency procedures, weights, and balance. Consulting them allows operators to optimize airplane usage and to acquire data they may need to manage situations of potential risk such as one-engine-out scenarios and so on.

- *Maintenance manuals:* These identify and describe in detail all parts and units that can be replaced in the airplane (the parts catalog). They provide maintenance procedures (scheduled or not), information on the tools that may be used for repairs and the maintenance operations to be performed "on" or "off"—in the field or in the hangar (ground equipment and tools publications).

Logistic support certainly represents the most important function of after-sale supports, since its implications on the safe and efficient use of the airplane require a great deal of attention from the manufacturer. Logistic support refers to two main areas:

- The availability, management, and transport of spare parts and other support material.

- Activities to maintain and repair airplanes.

Although different, the two areas are clearly linked, since maintenance is only possible after spare parts are made available. The related problems and skills are quite different, however.

5.4.2 The Aviation Industry Supply Chain

The aviation supply chain is shown in the Figure 5.2, where the relationships between several kinds of actors (original equipment manufacturers or OEMs, components and parts manufacturers, nonproprietary systems manufacturers, structural parts manufacturers, aircraft manufacturers, distributors, maintenance and repair stations, and airlines) are schematized. The supply chain "is controlled to a large extent by OEMs, as they are the ultimate type certificate holders and responsible for design" [AVIATIONX INC. 2000: p.7].

Today, the aeronautics industry supply chain has the following characteristics:

1. *High fragmentation:* The aviation industry is a global business with players geographically dispersed and operating hundreds of aircraft types. "Today, more than 5,000 buyers, including 1,500 airlines, negotiate with more than 13,000 suppliers around the world" [AVIATIONX INC. 2000: p.7]. Table 5.1 illustrates the fragmentation of the supply chain by showing estimated members of several groups of players in the aviation industry (both buyers and sellers).

2. *A large manual processing component:* "Despite the need for speed, the activities of sourcing, bidding, ordering, and tracking parts in the aviation business is still largely

a manual process" [AVIATIONX INC. 2000: p.8].

3. *Rigid pricing:* "An aircraft part's price rarely reflects its true value; this being an environment where the access of sellers to buyers (and the contrary as well) is still very limited, the forces of supply and demand cannot work completely, and in the absence of robust competition the prices remain artificially high. It has been estimated that today's airlines pay aftermarket costs that are at least four times greater than the cost of the airplane" [AVIATIONX INC. 2000: p.9].

4. *Too much inventory:* "Given the difficulties in the current supply chain, airlines and suppliers had to compensate by building up excessive inventories. . . An estimated $15 to $20 billion of parts inventory is on standby today, much of it difficult to source; experts predict that in a more efficient streamlined system, that number could easily be reduced by one third" [AVIATIONX INC. 2000: p.9].

5.4.3   Characteristics of the Spare Parts Business

In the context of spare parts delivery, in addition to the purely technical aspects (which are more critical in the maintenance and repair business), organizational, administrative, accounting, and commercial capabilities become quite important due to the following considerations:

*   Product complexity of both small regional aircraft and big jets for commercial aviation.

*   Aircraft management mostly by large organizations (airlines), with significant financial interests associated with their activities.

A spare parts offer to the airlines may be made directly by a manufacturer or by specialized firms that buy parts from the manufacturer or OEM. The airlines have no interest in maintaining huge stocks of spare parts in their warehouses. Spare parts logistics are left to the aircraft manufacturers' maintenance facilities, to specialized maintenance firms, and to possible intermediaries between manufacturers, OEMs, and maintenance specialized firms (Figure 5.2).

From the aircraft manufacturer's standpoint, behind spare parts supply there is a complex procedure consisting of various aspects which may, nevertheless, be grouped into three different areas:

*   Managerial/administrative functions related to inventory techniques, order execution (transportation, consignment, possible temporary storage), and relationships with suppliers.

*   Technical functions related to analysis of in-service technical problems and identification of problem-solving actions.

*   Commercial functions related to pricing of repairs or spare parts consignment and financing (at times, particularly expensive spare parts may be financed through ad hoc plans provided by the manufacturer).

Figure 5.2
Scheme of the Aviation's Supply Chain

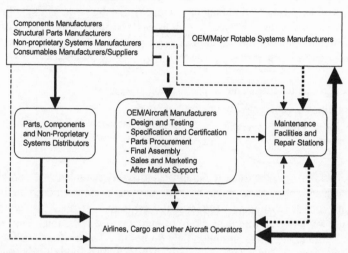

Source: AviationX Inc. *A New Kind of Hub: How B2B E-Marketplace Will Revolutionize the Aviation Industry*, p.7 - Copyright held by AviationX

Table 5.1
Who's Who in Aviation's Fragmented Supply Chain

BUYERS			
Aircraft Operators	*Maintenance Facilities*	*Repair and Overhaul Facilities*	
About 1500 commercial passenger airlines, charter airlines, and cargo airlines globally	1600 facilities worldwide, either in-house within airlines or third-party providers of scheduled and un-scheduled maintenance	2000 in-house within airlines, OEM or maintenance facilities or third parties performing repair and overhaul on rotable parts and components, as well as manufacturing of structural parts and components	
SELLERS			
Aircraft Manufacturers	*OEM-System Suppliers*	*Components and Parts Suppliers*	*Distributors*
Today a rather small group of major players thanks to restructuring and consolidation: Airbus, ATR, Boeing, Bombardier, Embraer and Fairchild/Dornier	A group of 35-40 highly specialized companies that designs, manufactures, sells and supports a number of proprietary systems such as engines, avionics and landing gear	More than 12000 manufacturers located in up to 20 different countries, these suppliers produce a large number of parts and components that are non-proprietary and of smaller dollar value	About 1200 distributors link components and parts makers with aircraft operators by outsourcing inventory management, order processing, forecasting and direct electronic communications for mostly non-proprietary low-dollar items

Source: AviationX Inc. *A New Kind of Hub: How B2B E-Marketplace Will Revolutionize the Aviation Industry*, p.8 - Copyright held by AviationX

Presently, these activities are going through a computer-managed standardization process, particularly through the Electronic Data Interchange technique (EDI). Also, communication elapsed time between the supplier and the buyer of spare parts is reduced considerably due to the elimination of most pre-repair negotiations or the dispatch of spare parts. New information exchange procedures define a common language for the following processes:

- Spare parts definitions and quick identification of required items.
- Administrative management of orders.
- Pricing policy and quotations.
- Billing.

Requests for spare parts for equipment that is grounded are particularly urgent, because the repairs must be provided in a matter of hours by the appropriate unit to avoid substantial major economic losses. (In Figure 5.3, AOG stands for "aircraft on the ground.") There are also other interventions that are called "critical" because, although they do not imply aircraft grounding, they nevertheless must be executed in a matter of days. Less urgent are "routine" interventions for which the timing is on the order of weeks (see Figure 5.3).

5.4.4   Airplane Maintenance

Maintenance activities may be divided into two main categories: scheduled maintenance and emergency maintenance.

5.4.4.1   Scheduled Maintenance

This category includes maintenance based on design characteristics and operational performance of the airplane and related to the rules and regulations of national certification authorities. Scheduled operations may also be divided into two types:

1. Periodical maintenance, whose purpose is to verify the airplane conditions and its possible need of repair or parts substitution (through routine interventions that may be made mostly in the field).

2. Refurbishing, where the airplane structure is partially disassembled to substitute the critical items, bringing the structure to "zero-hour condition" (this nonroutine intervention may be performed only in suitable facilities specialized for this purpose).

With reference to terms and modalities imposed by certification authorities, A, B, and C checks may be considered as ordinary activities, while D checks fall under heavy maintenance intervention[2] [AVMARK 1983].

The same work can be carried out in more checks, each of lesser duration and intensity. This fragmentation of operations will result in greater efficiency.

Figure 5.3
Industry Average Service Level (% of Orders Shipped within the Specified Timeframes — Regional Aircraft, 1995)

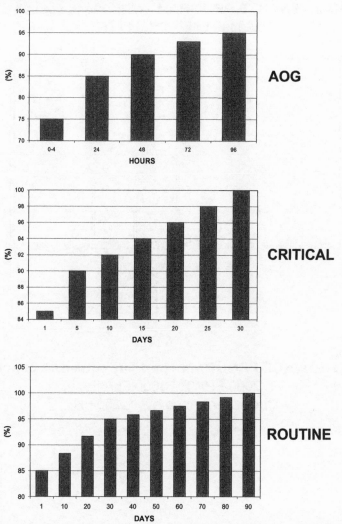

The possibility of applying such alternative methods of maintenance and inspection derives from the manufacturer's and operator's ability to store, exchange, and handle a great quantity of data related to the airplane's operational life, but also to the nowadays increased reliability of its components. In other words, the possibilities of foreseeing and describing problems that can arise with the aircraft and its main components performance during its operational life have increased substantially and therefore maintenance may be done using a guided approach rather than a totally preventive one (Figure 5.4).

Figure 5.4
The Move from the Traditional to Parceled Maintenance

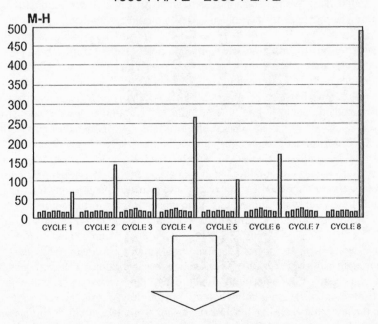

MAINTENANCE PROGRAM - MPD block concept
1500 FH/YE - 2500 FL/YE

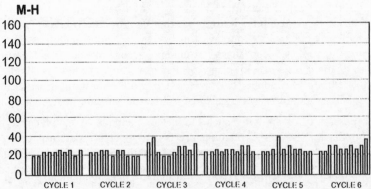

MAINTENANCE PROGRAM - partailly equalized concept
2000 FH/YE - 3000 FL/YE
Check performed every 250 FH

5.4.4.2 Emergency Maintenance

The second type of maintenance activity is that deriving from emergency situations that may suddenly occur during the aircraft's operational life (failures, small accidents, malfunctioning) and are more directly linked to spare parts delivery.

Maintenance interventions concern the whole airplane; for an airplane like the A-320, engines maintenance accounts for about 45% and airframe maintenance for 55% of the total. The breakdown of the last one is as follows: structure (36%), avionics (8%), landing gears (27%), interiors (24%), and flight controls (5%).

Many "full service" firms provide inspection and maintenance not only for the airframe but also for the entire airplane. Engines and avionics maintenance (as in the case of airframe) may be provided directly by the producer of such major equipment and systems. Sometimes these system manufacturers outsource this work to big airlines and specialized firms [AVMARK 1983].

Generally speaking, maintenance intervention in aeronautics may be performed by different aeronautical organizations:

- *Airframers* generally perform maintenance interventions strictly on their own aircraft models.

- *Airlines* perform in-house maintenance of their own airplanes and may extend the activity, when profitable, to other airlines' aircraft. A small airline may not have enough technical or financial resources for its own maintenance department. Major airlines may also split the work between them, each specializing in a different maintenance intervention to assure complete service with minimum investment.

- *Independent operators* are generally firms specialized in routine and nonroutine maintenance. Often, these firms are own huge spare stocks and therefore act as vendors to airlines, providing them with parts needed for routine, nonroutine, and critical maintenance. [AVMARK 1983]

Whether the maintenance operations are performed by the airline itself or are delegated to a specialized firm, the manufacturer is requested to provide the technical support to transfer these activities to such organizations. The airplane and the engine producers must also provide the technical literature needed for maintenance interventions, essentially providing information about what, how, and when maintenance is to be performed on the airplane.

The relevance and complexity of logistical support is proved by the magnitude of dedicated structures and efforts made by the manufacturers to assure such support. In its locations in Seattle (Washington) and Atlanta (Georgia), Boeing has dedicated facilities for spare parts storage readily available for delivery to customers. The company manages a computerized worldwide network that gives real-time inventory of spare parts orders and consignments to all customers. In addition to its Seattle and Atlanta facilities, Boeing operates seven regional distribution centers around the world.[3]

The main Airbus logistics base is located in Hamburg, Germany, with subsidiaries in Singapore, Washington (D.C.), Frankfurt, and Beijing. They provide around-the-clock spare parts delivery and stock over 220,000 parts. The ATR Consortium has three warehouses for spare parts inventory. The main base is in Toulouse and the other two are in Washington, D.C., and Singapore, where other activities are also performed for customers.

5.4.5   The Internet's Impact on the Aviation Industry: First Applications and Expected Benefits

The Internet has revolutionized communication and many aspects of business operation in the aeronautical industry as in many other fields. Even though Web-based business applications are still new, the first applications of business to business (B2B) e-commerce have permitted an understanding of its positive impact and possible savings on the purchasing process of enterprises. It increases efficiency (better service and lower cost of transactions), reduces prices (by making it easier for a larger number of suppliers to bid on business, with the increased competition pushing prices down), and guarantees a greater transparency of the market (faster and more efficient scouting).

The benefits B2B e-commerce can provide an enterprise are different sector by sector, depending upon the characteristics of the internal procurement process (such as purchase volume, number of items and average price per item, geographical dispersion of the suppliers), and upon the strategic importance of having an integrated network of activities between the enterprise, its suppliers, and its customers.

Several types of electronic tools (portals or Web sites) are available for the companies to exploit such potential benefits:

- *E-procurement:* Online tools developed to increase the efficiency of the procurement process, making it possible for a buyer to buy raw materials or other materials, parts, or components from a specific producer through a transaction conducted electronically, introducing savings of costs and time in process management.

- *E-marketplace:* Online tools in which demand and offer virtually meet one each other; in these portals, a number of suppliers make their product catalogs available online so buyers can compare prices, performance, and other characteristics in order to select the best suppliers for their purposes.

- *E-extended supply chain:* Online tools created to increase the integration between an enterprise and its strategic suppliers,[4] with a number of advantages both on the side of the management process (leaner, less costly, and faster) and on the side of the joint planning of the entire manufacturing process (better saturation of plants, less incidence of stocks, and so on).

The commercial aviation industry is particularly suited for exploiting the benefits of the B2B revolution because the aviation supply chain (from OEMs to prime manufacturers and to airlines) is complicated and in need of untangling (see Figure 5.2 and Table 5.1). A modern aircraft contains more than 3 million parts that require significant effort to research, certify, procure, and stock them.

The shift to e-commerce will provide benefits streamlining the entire supply chain, creating a less dispersed environment in which buyers and sellers will share information and data, substituting automation for manual processes and giving rise to more dynamic pricing. Large inventories will not be necessary, reducing the airlines' and suppliers' working capital and consequently improving their balance sheets.[5]

A number of initiatives are proliferating in the areas of e-procurement, e-marketplace, and e-extended supply chain in the aviation world. Particularly numerous are the examples of e-marketplace in the fields of aerospace maintenance repair and operations and aerospace and defense manufacturing. For instance, Exostar[6] (www.exostar.com), a portal jointly developed by Boeing, BAE SYSTEMS, Lockheed-Martin, Raytheon and Rolls Royce, is a typical example of a buyer-oriented portal that links many suppliers to a few (five) buyers. Another recent initiative is Aerochain, the joint ATR and Embraer e-marketplace venture (the first dedicated to regional airlines support). The two regional manufacturers have invested $21 million in Aerochain to link airlines, suppliers, and OEMs via the Internet and widen the range of support services, including spare parts inventory and forecasting, technical publications and maintenance planning. Steel24-7 (www.steel24-7.com) is a seller-oriented portal that connects a few suppliers to a virtual community of many buyers belonging to several industrial sectors (such as aeronautics, space, automotive, and shipbuilding) to facilitate procurement of steel as a raw material.

According to experts, a rapid growth of e-commerce is expected in the aviation industry. Online transactions comprise just a fraction of the industry's purchases today (in 2000, only 3% of a total market value of $188 billion), but in some analysts predict that such a number will jump from 3% to 35% in the next four years. However, such a forecast appears to be optimistic.

In fact, while the diffusion of e-commerce is expected to be very rapid in the lower end of the market (expendables and consumables parts characterized by low value per item), use of the Internet for procurement of the more strategic and high-value items such as engines, landing gear, flight data computers, avionic systems will be limited, because the relationships and mutual reliance between manufacturers, aircraft operators, and suppliers are critical factors for the conduct of business in these areas.

5.5   LEASING COMPANIES' INTERMEDIATION

In the last few years, a significant number of sales have occurred through the intermediation of leasing companies. This is because the investments needed for the acquisition of new equipment is so huge that most airlines cannot finance their purchases only with the traditional and primary source of finance (banks). Difficulties mount in situations when airlines are from the one hand obliged to renew the fleet, but from the other hand they had to bear recently recession and air traffic decline. In order to understand the problem, it should be noted that in the early 1990s, the airlines made yearly investments in new equipment acquisition on the order of $30 billion, but economic performances were very poor [AVMARK AVIATION ECONOMIST 1991]. In this type of situation, the gap between available and needed financial resources tends to become wider, creating a need for the services provided by leasing companies. In fact, in such circumstances the willingness of banks to lend money to the airlines is drastically reduced because the risk involved in the deal is too high.

The alternative provided by leasing companies typically follows this scenario:

1. The lessor acquires the airplanes and gives them to the lessee under a financial or operating lease.

2. The lessor takes advantage of discounts it may be able to obtain from the manufacturer due to the sizable orders it has placed for a model and also due to the better financial conditions it may obtain from banks.

It is considered less dangerous to lend money to a lessor than to an airline, for the acquisition of airplanes. This is due to the fact that leasing companies are considered less vulnerable to market condition changes (especially local conditions), since they can move airplanes from one geographical area to another area where economic conditions are better. They are also more able to manage the complex risks associated with airplanes ownership. Leasing companies can differentiate investments in different sectors, thus balancing risks; furthermore, they invest part of their profits in bonds, shares, and so on, as do most financial institutions, diluting the risk associated with their activities in the civil aeronautical field.

Estimates deem that airlines cannot afford more than 40% of funding new equipment acquisition. Since 1985 (when the use of leasing companies began to spread through civil commercial aviation), more than 20% of sources of airplane financing has come from leasing companies [AVMARK AVIATION ECONOMIST 1991].

Leases fall into two classic categories, the financial and the operating lease. The financial lease, in simple terms, is a lease in which the rental payments (installments) and any sum payable by the lessee on termination of the lease will be sufficient to pay off the lessor's investment in the aircraft and give the lessor a return on its investment. Since the lessee is effectively taking the residual risk on the value of the aircraft, it is normal for the lessee to get the benefit of any residual value in the aircraft at the end of the lease. This benefit may be obtained in a number of different ways, such as the grant of a fixed price option.

The operating lease is one where the residual risk in the aircraft at the end of the lease remains with the lessor, because the rentals payable under the lease (lower than in the previous case) are not sufficient to return to the lessor its full investment in the aircraft. Accordingly, the lessor must rely on re-leasing the aircraft or selling it in order to recoup its investment.

The difference between the sum of the installments and the price of the airplane constitutes the profit of the leasing company. When the operating leasing is "dry" it means that is limited to the airplane; when it is "wet" also crews and maintenance are given with the airplane; in this case the leasing company manages an intermediary activity between that of financial investor and that of the airline.

The presence of lessor in between seller and buyer seems to bring some added value to the selling process because it takes part of the ownership risk away from the operators and at the same time some risk of unsold production away from the manufacturers.

The advantage is that the operator (generally an airline) may operate with much more flexibility; if for any reason its requirement will change in the future the airline may always return airplanes without any additional burden, that is paying only for the time it has needed and used the airplane.

This is particularly the case when an airline is waiting for the delivery of an airplane already ordered and in the mean time it may rent the same type (or the closest existing in the market) from a leasing company. In fact the elapsed time between order and delivery may be as long as one, two or even three years when the ordered airplane is a "best seller" and/or in case there is an upturn in traffic demand.

In addition some fiscal advantages are generally related with the renting an airplane depending on the particular law of the airline home country.

Or the airline may wish not to make worse its balance sheet with the burden of an outright purchase.

The importance of these new subjects in the business has grown to such an extent that manufacturers have been pushed to become shareholders of some major leasing companies in order to influence their purchasing. Some manufacturers have even constituted their own fully controlled leasing companies (Special Purpose Company, SPC) in order to support their entrepreneurial activity.

Because the leasing companies place airplanes orders even before having a customer and because anyway the leasing period (on which basis the airplane is purchased) is shorter than the aircraft useful life, this procedure may become incorrect. In fact this way to operate may became dangerous for the manufacturer that in reality is financing its own production line when the airplane is only partially sold.

On the contrary generally speaking an airplane on the final assembly line is already destined to a given customer that makes invoices according to the work accomplished on its airplane; therefore the manufacturer's risk is practically not existent even in the case the customer should cancel the order.

The experience shows, in fact, that when the manufacturer is involved in the leasing its profit margin are smaller than those obtained with a cash sale [7]. The company accepts this solution when compared with worse alternatives such as production rate drastic reduction or even program halt.

Some observers fear that leasing intermediation may introduce extra price in a system that is very price-sensitive; others believe that the offer created by leasing companies is of advantage for the airlines because it may be even in competition with that one of the airplanes' manufacturer; but there would be also an advantage for the manufacturer because demand become wider.

NOTES

1. In the broader sense of making goods available to the customers, it may be worth considering some problems related mainly to the delivery rate due to their impact on production costs. In fact, a precise definition of production rate is particularly critical in the civil aeronautical sector. Airlines with a scheduled fleet modernization, which is generally associated to a change in the offered capacity, rely on precise delivery times. This aspect may even be more important in the case of best-selling airplanes, when a significant order by a single customer may take several months (or even years) of production to be satisfied. (The manufacturer usually reserves a few windows on the production line for other customers.) Medium- or small-sized airlines have to organize appropriate retirement schedules to comply with new airplane availability. From the producer's standpoint, the production rate becomes a critical variable of capacity saturation or production costs. This is particularly true when there is a downturn in demand and airlines cancel orders and options. In some cases, they even stop flying a certain number of airplanes and store them in dry desert areas, especially when grounding can last a considerable period of time. In the desert areas of the United States, as a result of market saturation, one can find not only old but also new airplanes that airlines cannot use or leasing companies cannot rent out.

2. Referring to the narrow-body airplane, scheduled maintenance is made with following modalities:

A-Check occurs about every 150 flight hours and is a primary inspection of the airframe, avionics, engines and accessories to determine the general conditions of the aircraft; the aircraft may be on the ground for 8 hours and requires about 60 manhours of work.
B-Check occurs about every 700 flight hours and is an intermediate inspection; it includes selected operational checks, fluid servicing and some lubrication tasks. It will include an A-Check; the aircraft is on the ground for about 8 hours and requires approximately 200 manhours of work.
C-Check occurs about every 3.000 flight hours and is a detailed inspection of the airframe, engines and accessories; some access panels will be removed and the areas inspected; heavy lubrication will be undertaken on this inspection; generally this check includes a portion of the corrosion prevention programme; service bulletin requirements and aircraft appearance work will be done. It will include an A-Check and a B-Check; the aircraft will be on the ground for about 72 hours and will utilise around 3.000 manhours of work.
D-Check, or heavy maintenance check, occurs about every 20.000 flight hours; it is a major overhaul, which returns the aircraft to its original condition (or *zero-rated condition*) to the extent possible. It comprises a thorough examination of the entire aircraft; the interior is completely removed along with many components; what cannot be removed is inspected and refurbished in place; when the term half-life is used, it generally means half-way between D-Check; the aircraft is on the ground for about 30 days and will require around 20.000 manhours of maintenance. [INTERAVIA AEROSPACE REVIEW 1991: p 43].

3. In 1996, the Boeing Commercial Airplane Group and UPS (United Parcel Service) launched Boeing Direct, a convenient and economical alternative delivery service for aircraft spare parts. With this method, spare parts reach any customer in the

United States within a few hours and customers in most international regions within two days, maximum.

4. The need of a close integration between the prime manufacturer and its strategic suppliers in the aeronautical industry has been treated in Chapter 2.

5. It is also important to mention some problems connected with the e-commerce revolution that in some cases may represent a serious obstacle to diffusion.

The first problem is the security of the electronic link: The industrial data exchanged, the access to the corporation's information system, the value of the transaction—all must be protected against unauthorized users. Another problem is the necessity of having guarantees from suppliers selected via the Web, because often such a firm is located very far away and is not known directly; its products' quality, its financial solidity, and its commercial capabilities are unknown.

In order to solve these problems and make development of electronic transactions and business relations easier and more reliable, a number of specialized companies now offer services such as the protection of information or guarantees about a specific firm with which a manufacturer wants to establish a relationship.

6. Exostar expects to activate more than 10,000 supplier-participants by the end of 2001; in the next two years (2002-2003) Exostar plans to connect more than 250 procurement systems currently used by the five founding partners in 20 countries, and more are expected to follow.

7. Generally additional costs and risk associated with the lease are the following:

• Fund allocation for the guarantee the manufacturer has to give to the SPC for the case of client nsolvency. in fact the SPC, that is the owner of the airplane, leases it to the airline under a leasing agreement; the airline pays leasing fees to the SPC; the SPC pays the bank that has given the money to it to acquire the airplane from the manufacturer. But, in order to lend the money, the financial institution (generally a bank) asks for guarantee from the manufacturer when the airline has not the financial strength to make directly the deal. The reserve has to be in the order of 10% of the value of the loan transaction.

• Provision for re-marketing and refurbishing of the airplane in case it is returned in advance by the lessee; such costs are about 2.5% of the airplane price.

• Costs associated with the buy-back of the used airplanes currently operated by the customer and due to:
    - Possible overestimation of the used airplanes value;
    - Possible underestimation of the cost for refurbishing the used airplanes.
    Although difficult to estimate such cost may be evaluated around 10% of the new airplane price.

Therefore the total amount of the extra-costs related with a lease (rather than a cash sale) of the airplane is in excess of 20% of its price. Considering that in general the price of an airplane for lease is around 10% higher than a price for cash (because in this last case there are no concessions) the net risk of each lease is slightly higher than 10% of the airplane price.

6

SELLING AIRPLANES

6.1 INTRODUCTION: THE SELLING (AND BUYING) PROCESS

An aeronautical manufacturer must know both its own market characteristics and its customers' market or air travelers, in order to forecast future needs that will ultimately be the real source of airplane requirements. High-tech, modern theories of marketing management [FIOCCA, SNEHOTA, CADY and DE VIO 1995] apply fully to the aeronautical field. What differentiates a high-tech product is not primarily the content of advanced technologies, but rather the experience that is necessary for a customer to thoroughly understand how to use it.

Therefore, the crucial element needed to gain a competitive advantage is the manufacturer's capability of helping the customers "digest" the product. This is a complicated task, because it has many potential applications for the customer that cannot be easily understood and fully exploited without a full support from the manufacturer It is therefore in the interest of the producer to assure that the clients' needs are met by product characteristics.

The sales cycle within the aeronautical industry is particularly complex, because the purchasing process is long and complicated. The buyer reaches a decision only after an analysis of a range of possible alternatives. Once a decision is reached, the airline commits to using a specific type of equipment for many years.

Since some requirements are common to a larger customer base while others are unique to each client, promotional activity can be split into two main types:

- Generalized methods of communication/promotion.

- Personalized approaches generally directed toward the support of a specific sales campaign.

As discussed in previous chapters, one of the general characteristics of the aeronautical business, like other investment-goods markets, is a small customer base. As a consequence, the manufacturers must directly and carefully manage relations with these few clients (ranging from dozens to hundreds, at most). For this reason, the second approach is clearly the most appropriate for aeronautical sales, while the first is more typical of consumer-goods markets.

Although generalized communication may be necessary, this approach is not based on mass communication, because advertising is rarely used by commercial airplane manufacturers and only in very specific instances. The most common generalized communication strategies include workshops, aeronautical exhibitions, and aircraft promotional tours.

The most important air shows are at Farnborough (London), Le Bourget (Paris). Other exhibitions that have a significant importance at regional level are Singapore, signifying the growing importance of the Asian market, the ILA show (Berlin), the FIDAE (Chile), the LIMA (Langkawi, Malaysia) and the Indian air show (Bangalore, India). New products are featured flying or in static display according to the program status and the manufacturer's preference. However, these exhibitions have lost much of their main purpose as a meeting place between vendors and purchasers. The ease of modern communication technology has extended opportunities for exchanging sales information.

Promotional tours also aim to bring the product to the customer, if it is determined that such an effort is cost effective. This may occur when there is a clear need for the equipment but the customer is hesitant to decide. Displaying the airplane and flying the decision-makers may speed the decision process in a manufacturer's favor.

The personalized approach supports a specific sales effort to a particular customer and is usually based on a personal relationship between the manufacturer's sales representatives and those individuals in charge of planning (first) and purchasing (later) for the customer. In reality, the entire selling and purchasing structures of the interested players are involved. The highest level of the sales management team will participate throughout the effort, and especially near the negotiation conclusion.

During the lengthy efforts to persuade the customer of the superiority of the proposal, there is a central function carried out by a special department within the commercial organization. The responsibility of this office is to conduct targeted studies and produce brochures specific to the client. Since this is generally an airline, this activity is called "airline analysis"; or, considering the prevalent technical content of this analysis, "sales engineering"; or, due to the primary sales objective, "sales support".

The airline analysis examines existing and new aircraft types, their mission capabilities, and their cost characteristics to identify possible candidate aircraft for each airline mission. The process can be divided into the following steps:

- Airline market analysis and traffic forecast.

- Equipment analysis: performance, route, and airport analysis.
- Operational analysis and fleet planning.
- Economic evaluation: cost and revenue analysis.
- Financial analysis.

Figure 6.1 shows how the input and output of different phases of the airline analysis are linked together. Clearly, a complete analysis covering all these featured aspects is not always necessary. It will depend on the real needs of the promotional campaign under way. The final aim is to derive the best solution among possible fleet alternatives to generate sufficient cash in future operations and to provide the airline a fair return on investment, assuring both to operator and manufacturer of the continuation of business profitability.

Airplane sales generally involves two main aspects: the content of the purchase agreement and the financing of the aircraft purchase. Looking at some of the most important commercial airplane sales may facilitate an understanding as to which have been the main factors in airlines' decisions to buy certain airplanes rather than others, and thus providing some ideas about the relevant factors of the winning offers.

6.2 MARKET ANALYSIS

Airline market analysis objective is to forecast the traffic in the area where the specific airline operates. Obviously, airlines must know thoroughly the traffic behavior in the market segments they serve, because in each of these segments, the air travel grows at a different rate.

Therefore, some basic traffic definitions are needed here. First, it is useful to make a distinction between passenger travel and cargo movement. These two groups include the following segments:

1. Passenger travel:
   a. Domestic.
   b. International.
   c. Discount fare.
   d. Full fare.
   e. First Class.
   f. Coach.
   g. Scheduled.
   h. Charter.
   i. Business.
   j. Leisure.

2. Cargo movement:
   a. Domestic.
   b. International.
   c. Within freighter aircraft.
   d. Within passenger aircraft.

Figure 6.1
Airline Analysis

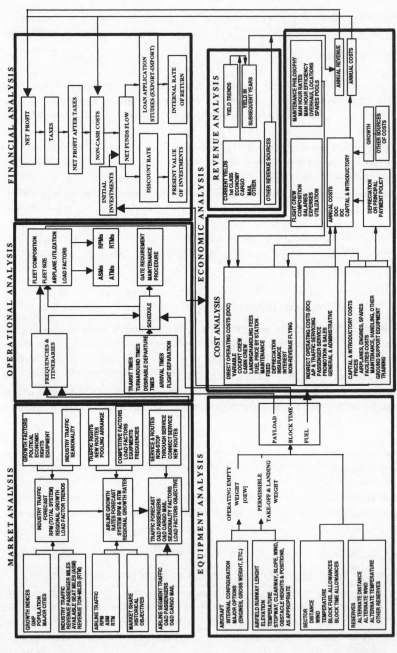

Source: Elaboration on Boeing Commercial Airplane Company. *Boeing Computer Capability in the Airline Analysis Process.* Seattle: 1977a

Air passenger traffic is measured in terms of revenue passenger miles (RPMs) or revenue passenger kilometers (RPKs), where RPMs equal the number of revenue passengers carried on a stage multiplied by the stage distance.

Air cargo movements are measured in terms of revenue ton miles (RTMs) or RTKs, which represent tons of revenue cargo multiplied by the miles (or kilometers) the cargo is flown.

An airline needs a detailed traffic forecast in order to develop fleet requirements and scheduling, determine financial requirements related to fleet procurement, provide a basis for evaluating staffing and facilities requirements, and develop marketing strategy.

The airline's traffic forecast needs inputs from two sources:

a. A macroforecast related to the entire system: industry, region, and airline subsystem.

b. A microanalysis of the airline's competitive environment: city pair flights, competition and new services.

The main steps of the market analysis are the industry traffic forecast, the airline (growth) forecast, and the origin & destination (O & D) passenger forecast.

Figure 6.1 shows the step-by-step market analysis methodology.

6.2.1   Industry Traffic Forecast

Air traffic forecasting has been discussed in chapter 3. Most of the information there also applies in this case. The only difference is that the present analysis has a more limited scope.

Aircraft manufacturers are interested in a thorough understanding of the worldwide long-term needs of the particular type of airplane under study. The airline is generally concerned with a long-term geographically limited forecast. Therefore, topics already analyzed in previous chapters will be summarized here only to give continuity to the subject, trying at same time to reflect the airline particular point of view.

6.2.1.1   Gross National Product, Population, and Fare Levels

In order to identify the forces that play roles in shaping traffic growth, it is necessary to analyze the market environment and the specific geographical area in which a carrier operates.

There are two kinds of forces influencing traffic growth:

1. Socioeconomic influences (income measures):

    a. Gross national product (GNP).
    b. Disposable income.
    c. Buying power index.

1.   Demographic influences (population and culture):

     a.   Growth.

     b.   Age distribution.

     c.   Propensity to travel.

     d.   Common interests.

The first for importance of these forces is gross national product growth.

Population growth is the second fundamental force that affects traffic growth. Combining the growths of GNP and population leads the forecast of per capita GNP. This is really the underlying factor in determining both business and nonbusiness air transportation requirements. The next fundamental parameter that needs to be considered is the cost of transportation to the user. This is the fare expressed in cents per revenue passenger-mile, which relates directly to the user.

Figure 6.2 shows an example of GNP growth versus traffic growth, depending on the level of fares. The magnitude of the shift from one line to the other depends on the passenger type. Passenger market can be segmented into two broad groups: business travelers and personal pleasure travelers, who may be further defined as vacation travelers and travelers visiting relatives and friends. Business travelers are almost insensitive to fare levels or changes, but travelers in the second group are very responsive to any variation in travel cost.

Figure 6.3 shows the typical correlation between air passenger revenue and GNP for a given market area. The average number of trips per year made by a passenger in a given market area will increase according to the related GNP per capita increases. Growth rate will slow down after a while, and, according to market life cycle theory, saturation will occur.

Figure 6.2
Traffic Growth as Function of GNP Growth

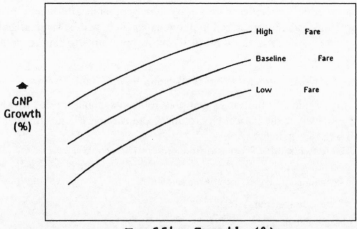

Figure 6.3
Air Passenger Revenue Relative to GNP

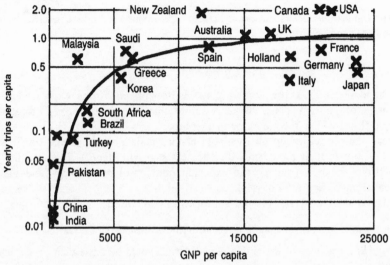

Source: IMF. In L.R. Jenkinson, P. Simpkin and D. Rhodes. *Civil Jet Aircraft Design* London: Arnold Publishers, 1999.

6.2.1.2 Traffic Forecast

The most common method used by airlines to forecasting industry traffic growth is econometric modeling. An example of it has been given in the chapter 3 in the section related to product definition.

The input needed for the econometric model is equal or similar to the forces analyzed previously. The models are explanations of the traffic growth based on a set of relationships between the historical trends and the explanatory variables.

Some econometric models give RPM growth according to the relationship between GNP and airline yields. Regional combined GNP is generally used in econometric models as a measure of changing personal consumption expenditure (PCE) of the population involved. Airline yields reflect changes in air fares, which in turn constitute the cost of traveling by air for passengers.

6.2.2 Airline Growth Forecast

Knowing the industry traffic forecast, the planner can determine the airline growth, taking into account these factors:

- The airline traffic in terms of RPM or RPK (revenue passenger miles or revenue passenger kilometers), ASM or ASK (available passenger miles or available passenger kilometers), and RTM or RTK (revenue tons miles or revenue tons kilometers).

- The market share, both historical and targeted.

- The new routes and other variables as load factors.

- The competitive factors such as equipment type, frequencies, prices, service levels, and promotion efforts.

6.2.2.1   Airline Traffic and Market Share

The market share is the number of RPMs flown by an airline, expressed as a percentage of the total. Thus, the analyst must share the industry traffic forecast among airlines which operate in the market area.

The planner will need all available historical data about airline traffic in order to evaluate their future growth. The next step will identify the most likely competitive situation (that is, the expected number of competitors and their relative strengths and weaknesses).

Market share analysis is important for two main reasons:

1.   It is helpful in understanding if the airline traffic growth forecast is reasonable.

2.   It gives a real idea of the airline growth, which could be misleading in absolute terms.

Regarding the first point, it should be noted that an airline traffic growth forecast, either based on projection methods or more sophisticated techniques, should be compatible with the growth foreseen by other airlines applying the same methodology. Therefore, the sum of individual airlines' growth forecasts must coincide with the forecast industry growth, and the sum of single market shares must equal 100%.

With regard to the second point, assume for this discussion that a specific airline growth forecast in a given market is 15%, which looks very good. Accordingly, a judgment about the airline management performance looks positive.

But the actual situation may be different: If the relevant market is expected to grow at a much higher 25% per year, the particular airline growing at a good 15% per year is, in effect, losing market share.

6.2.2.2   Competitive Factors

Differentiating the offer by airlines became very important after the introduction of the air traffic deregulation in 1978. The airlines had to gain their market share by offering better quality service and/or better fares. New airlines began offering different products characterized by a different costs structure and network configuration. Generally, these airlines started as niche competitors but then developed as full competitors on a broader scale.

6.2.2.3   Growth Forecast

To make the airline growth forecast, the planner must combine numerous variables, evaluating the weight of each in the airline growth, verifying that the targeted market share is compatible with competitors' objectives. To determine the airline growth, the most common method used by analysts is the growth factor method based on historical trends and statistical data, taking into account the relationships between industry growth and airline growth. The industry traffic growth is shared in order to forecast airline growth, depending on airline structure, fleet size, and fare and marketing policies (Figure 6.4).

6.2.3   Airline Traffic Forecast Split

6.2.3.1   Origin and Destination Traffic

Once airline growth has been forecast as total RPMs, it is necessary to divide and allocate it according to origin and destination traffic. Each city pair market forecast represents, at the current step, a microforecast compared with airline growth, which is now a macroforecast. True traffic origin and destination affects the airline's operating plan and route pattern.

To determine the origin and destination passenger traffic, it is first necessary to prepare a city-pair market share forecast, using historical and estimated total RPMs for all city-pair and historical O & D passengers for each pair of cities.

According to BOEING [1974], the forecast must take into account that city-pair can be divided into two categories:

1.   Mature markets with a market share that is decreasing and tending toward a stable value.

2.   Growing markets with a market share that is increasing and tending toward a stable value.

The mathematical function that best models markets of both types has the typical formula:

$$\text{Market Share} = K + H\,e^{-\alpha t}\ [\text{BOEING 1974}]$$

Forecasts derived from market share data are consistent both with the total traffic forecast and with the recent growth history of city-pair relative to the total.

The forecast market share may be converted back to the number of passengers given the total traffic forecast (macroforecast). Available data about nonstop services or multiple-stop flights must be taken into consideration in order to evaluate true O & D passengers accurately. Also, information about new routes must be considered by the analyst, because new routes can attract passengers in varying degrees. Other important factors in determining true O & D passengers include maturity of the market, seasonality, and particular fare policies.

Figure 6.4
The Airline Growth Forecast

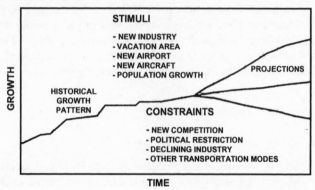

Source: Elaboration on McDonnell Douglas. *Airline Market Planning.* Long Beach, CA: MDD Paper, 1984a

6.2.3.2   Industry Traffic Seasonality.

Traffic seasonality is one of the variables that affects the forecast; peaks and valleys must be forecasted to provide correct input for the fleet planning process. An airline can effectively counter fluctuations of seasonality when these are anticipated, shifting airplanes from one market to others according to changes in the market.

6.3   EQUIPMENT ANALYSIS

The purpose of the equipment analysis is to verify the performance of a specific model aircraft (with special emphasis on payload) operating over specific customer routes, using specific customer rules. The equipment analysis follows a well-established procedure in order to give these standard outputs: allowable payload, needed block time, and fuel consumption. These in turn will be the inputs for other steps.

In determining the performance of a specific model aircraft, factors that may limit payload (such as airport field length, elevation, temperature, distance flown, and reserve fuel requirements) are considered. Likewise, the effects of route temperature, wind, and airline allowances are applied to identify how these factors affect payload capability.

6.3.1   Aircraft Configuration

The major configuration elements affecting aircraft performance (and operating costs) are engine thrust, takeoff gross weight, fuel capacity, internal configuration (seating), and OEW.

Engine thrust has a direct bearing on the takeoff gross weight (TOW) permissible from a given runway. An aircraft can be offered for sale with various engine ratings; so it is necessary to select the engine most suitable to perform the takeoff mission without overpowering the aircraft. The use of more thrust than required may cost more than necessary. Another consideration may be the selection of an engine common in the airline fleet. The takeoff gross weight and fuel capacity are selected to meet the airline mission requirement. Sometimes the maximum takeoff weight of an aircraft is deliberately understated in order to reduce cost such as cockpit crew, landing fees and handling fees [MCDONNELL DOUGLAS 1985a].

Of course, the internal configuration (seating) directly influences the operating costs per seat mile. The most important definitions to be assumed, with the concurrence of the airline, are seat pitch, mixed class or all economy, and galley number and size.

6.3.2   Aircraft Weight Definition

Figure 6.5 shows a breakdown of aircraft weights, both operating and structural limiting weights.

6.3.2.1   Manufacturer's Empty Weight

Airplane weight is determined from a basic airplane specification adjusted for optional features and seating arrangement to give the airplane empty weight; it is the weight of the structure, power plant, furnishings, systems, and other items of equipment. It is a dry weight, including only those fluids contained in closed systems.

Figure 6.5
Aircraft Weight Definition

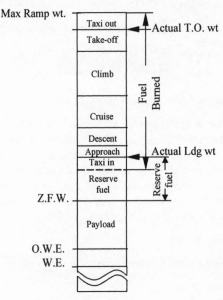

6.3.2.2   Operational Empty Weight

Operational empty weight (OEW) is obtained by adding operational items (those items required to operate the aircraft in commercial service) such as:

- Unusable fuel.
- Engine oil.
- Flight and cabin crews.
- Emergency equipment.
- Toilet fluid and chemical.
- Passenger items such as food and drink.
- Optional items required by airlines.

$$OEW = MEW + \text{Operational Items}$$

6.3.2.3   Maximum Allowable Payload

The payload consists of passenger weight plus baggage and cargo weight. The maximum allowable payload (MAP) is determined either by structural limits, subtracting the operational empty weight from the maximum zero fuel weight (MZFW):

$$MAP = MZFW - OEW$$

or by volumetric limit, adding the passenger weight to baggage weight to cargo weight, that is, residual volume times standard density, after accommodating for passenger baggage, according to which limit is lower.

6.3.2.4   Maximum Zero Fuel Weight

The maximum zero fuel weight is the maximum airplane weight permitted when there is no fuel on board.

$$MZFW = OEW + MAP$$

6.3.2.5   Minimum Reserve Fuel Quantity

The Federal Air Regulations (FAR) (and also other European or non-European government regulations) specify minimum reserve fuel quantities for U.S. and non-U.S. domestic air carriers. Sometimes airline rules used in route analysis studies result in higher total reserve fuel quantities. This is due to the addition of company requirements to permit easy compliance with regulations (FAR 121.647). Such higher quantities must be usually examined more critically if payload is sacrificed [MCDONNELL DOUGLAS 1985a].

6.3.2.6   Landing Weight

The landing weight is the lowest of the following weights:

a.   The sum of maximum zero fuel weight and reserve fuel.

b.   The certified maximum allowable weight of the airplane at touchdown determined by the structural loads on the landing gear.

c.   The allowable landing weight at the destination airport of a city-pair route.

6.3.2.7   Trip Fuel

Trip or block fuel is the amount of fuel required for the airplane to perform all segments of the mission flight profile, from start and taxi-out to taxi-in and engine shutdown.

6.3.2.8   Maximum Ramp Weight

The ramp weight is the lower of the following weights:

a.   The sum of landing weight and block fuel.

b.   The certified maximum allowable weight of the airplane when it is on the ground (determined by the structural loading on the landing gear under a specified set of conditions).

6.3.2.9   Maximum Takeoff Weight

The takeoff weight is the lowest of the following weights:

a.   The difference between the ramp weight and the taxi-out fuel.

b.   The maximum structural takeoff weight (this limitation is based on wing bending moment and structural loads on the wing).

c.   The allowable takeoff weight at the origin airport of a city-pair route.

6.3.3   Airport Analysis

To complete the equipment analysis, after determination of the airplane configuration and weights, an analysis of the airline's network airports has to be carried out. The allowable aircraft takeoff and landing weights will be determined in accordance with FAA requirements and with the airports' characteristics.

The airport data that must be supplied to carry out the analysis include:

- Runway length (including stopway and/or clearway).
- Runway elevation.
- Runway slope.
- Runway surface strength.
- Obstacles (heights and positions).
- Airport temperature and wind. [MCDONNELL DOUGLAS 1985a]

In the following airport analysis example, the most emphasis is put on takeoff rather than landing limitation. Usually takeoff performance is most critical. Landing performance calculations are illustrated here only using available runway length, not obstacles or other constraints. While this may be considered a correct assumption for initial planning purposes, actual airplane scheduling must be checked against complete landing performance.

6.3.3.1   Takeoff Weight as Determined by Runway Limitation

6.3.3.1.1   Takeoff Field Length

The takeoff field length required is the greatest of the following three distances:

1. The takeoff distance required to overcome an obstacle of 35 feet high is established for both with and without engine failure conditions at close to a speed of V_1 (see definition below). A 15% margin is applied.

2. The distance to accelerate to the same V_1 speed and then stop is also established for a dry runway surface without using thrust reversers.

The optimum (minimum) field length is when the takeoff distance required is the same as the accelerate/stop distance required. This case is often referred to as a *balanced field length*. In the above calculations, three operational speeds are significant:

1. V_1 is the most critical speed at which an engine failure is recognized. For takeoff weight calculation, engine failure occurs just before this speed is reached.

2. V_R is the rotation speed occurring when the pilot lifts the nose of the airplane.

3. V_2 is the takeoff safety speed, which is at least 120% of stall speed for jet airplanes. [MCDONNELL DOUGLAS 1985a: p.11]

A number of factors affect takeoff weight:

• As airport surface temperatures rise and/or altitude increases, engine thrust deteriorates and takeoff weight allowed decreases.

• A positive slope decreases the effective runway length, thereby decreasing the allowable takeoff weight (vice versa for a negative slope).

• A headwind increases the effective runway and a tailwind decreases it.

• Clearway and stopway both increase the effective runways.

• Any engine bleed condition reduces the thrust available from the engine for takeoff, thereby decreasing takeoff weight.

• Obstacles in the flight path may cause a reduction in allowable takeoff weight.

- Tire speed limits and brake energy limits must not be exceeded.

- Overspeed allows a higher V_1 to be used and therefore a higher takeoff weight.

- As climb gradients required get larger, weight must be reduced.

- Landing weight limits must be considered in case an emergency occurs shortly after takeoff and fuel dumping is not possible on a specific airplane. [BOEING 1977b: p.66, 68]

6.3.3.1.2   Maximum Taxi Weight

The maximum taxi weight is a structural design weight. It is the maximum weight that meets all certification requirements and is approved by the certification authorities.

6.3.3.2   Landing Weight as Determined by Runway Length

"The FAA specifies that the landing distance required for an aircraft be established from a point 50 feet above the end of the runway to the end of landing roll with use of brakes only (no thrust reversers) and then increased by a margin of 66.7%. For wet runways, the FAA requires an additional 15% unless a different margin is demonstrated by measuring stopping distances on a wet runway" [MCDONNELL DOUGLAS 1985a: p.12].

6.3.3.3   Takeoff Weight as Determined by Obstacle Limitation

"In order to insure proper terrain clearance under all conditions, the regulations specify a minimum or "net" flight path that will give the necessary assurance. Under FAR Regulations, the net flight path must clear all obstacles in the takeoff segment by at least 35 feet, where the net flight path is defined as the gross path available reduced by a gradient of climb equal to 0.8% of two-engine airplanes, 0.9% of three-engine airplanes, and 1.0% percent of four-engine airplanes." [BOEING 1977b: p.60]

6.3.3.4   Takeoff Weight as Determined by Climb Limit

The takeoff climb acceleration flight segment begins when the aircraft passes over a point at 35 feet height (Figure 6.6). In order that certain climb minimum standards be fulfilled, necessary in the event that problems arise during this phase of the flight, the regulations require some limitations, in terms of "climb limits" or "climb gradient limits". These limits are mostly defined in the flight condition of "critical" engine inoperative, as in the takeoff segment.
As regards the definition of "critical" engine, it is considered the most important engine from the point of view of the airplane controllability being it dependent generally on the engine location. Under normal conditions the actual path of the aircraft is above the gross flight path.

6.3.3.5   Airport Analysis Details

An example of airport analysis is shown on the Tables 6.1 and 6.2. It has been performed on some Philippine Airlines airports with a turboprop airliner.

Figure 6.6
Take-Off Path Definition

ENGINE RATING	*TAKE-OFF*	*TAKE-OFF*	*TAKE-OFF*	*MAX CONTINUOUS*
FLAP SETTING	*TAKE-OFF*	*TAKE-OFF*	*RETRACTED*	*RETRACTED*
LANDING GEAR	*DOWN*	*UP*	*UP*	*UP*
REQUIRED GROSS CLIMB GRADIENT	(O.E.I. JAR 25/21 (B))			
TWO ENGINES	*> 0%*	*2.4%*		*1.2%*
THREE ENGINES	*0.3%*	*2.7%*		*1.5%*
FOUR ENGINES	*0.5%*	*3%*		*1.7%*

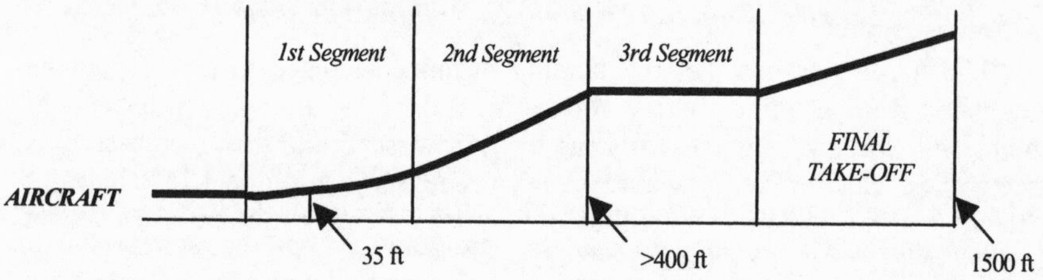

Table 6.1
Airport Analysis — Input

Airport Name	Code	Runway Elev.(m)	Runway Lenght (m)	Temp. ISA + (°C)		Obstacle Distance (m) from brake release point	Obstacle Height (m) from runway surface	Runway Slope% +=up
ALLAH VALLEY	AAV	185	1330	15	0	1750.0	24.0	-0.05
BACOLOD	BCD	6	1968	15	0			-0.25
BAGUIO	BAG	1292	1730	15	0			-0.71
BASA	BSA	10	2500	15	0			
BASCO	BSO	56	1287	15	0			-4.45
BISLIG	BPH	3	1260	15	0	1638.0	16.0	-0.03
BUTUAN	BXU	43	1300	15	0			-0.25
CALBAYOG	CYP	2	1385	15	0	2344.0	37.0	-0.17
CATARMAN	CRM	2	1060	15	0	3479.0	81.0	-0.06
CAUAYAN	CYZ	61	1400	15	0	1739.0	9.0	-0.30
CEBU	CEB	10	2513	15	0			
CAGAYAN DE ORO	CGY	182	2729	15	0	3493.0	20.0	-0.08
COTABATO	CBO	58	1930	15	0			
DAVAO	DVO	27	2600	15	0	2790.0	6.0	-0.36
DIPOLOG	DPL	4	1670	15	0	2400.0	29.0	-0.03

Table 6.2
Airport Analysis — Output

CODE	AIRPORT NAME	RUNWAY LENGHT (M)	RUNWAY ELEV. (M)	AVERAGE TEMP. °C ISA+	RUNWAY SURFACE	SLOPE %	TAKE-OFF WEIGHT (KG)	WEIGHT LIMIT.	LANDING WEIGHT (KG)	WEIGHT LIMIT.
AAV	ALLAH VALLEY	1330	185	29	15	GRAVEL	0.05	15287	HOBST.	16000	STRUCT.
BCD	BACOLOD	1968	6	30	15	GROOVED CONCRETE	0.25	16150	STRUCT.	16000	STRUCT. *
BAG	BAGUIO	1730	1292	22	15	GROOVED CONCRETE	0.71	16150	STRUCT.	16000	STRUCT.
BSA	BASA	2500	10	30	15	CONCRETE	0.0	16150	STRUCT.	16000	STRUCT.
BSO	BASCO	1287	56	30	15	GRAVEL	4.45	16150	STRUCT.	16000	STRUCT.
BPH	BISLIG	1260	3	30	15	CRUSHED CORAL	0.03	15911	HOBST.	16000	STRUCT.
BXU	BUTUAN	1300	43	30	15	GROOVED CONCRETE	0.25	16150	STRUCT.	16000	STRUCT.
CYP	CALBAYOG	1385	2	30	15	CONCRETE	0.17	16135	HOBST.	16000	STRUCT.
CRM	CATARMAN	1060	2	30	15	CONCRETE	0.06	15699	HOBST.	16000	STRUCT.
CYZ	CAUAYAN	1400	61	30	15	CONCRETE	0.3	16150	STRUCT.	16000	STRUCT.
CEB	CEBU	2513	10	30	15	CONCRETE	0.0	16150	STRUCT.	16000	STRUCT. *
CGY	CAGAYAN DE ORO	2729	182	29	15	GROOVED CONCRETE	0.08	16150	STRUCT.	16000	STRUCT. *
CBO	COTABATO	1930	58	30	15	GROOVED CONCRETE	0.4	16150	STRUCT.	16000	STRUCT. *
DVO	DAVAO	2600	27	30	15	CONCRETE	0.36	16150	STRUCT.	16000	STRUCT. *
DPL	DIPOLOG	1670	4	30	15	CONCRETE	0.03	16150	STRUCT.	16000	STRUCT.

* DOMESTIC STATION WITH REFUELING FACILITIES

The input airport data are summarized in Table 6.1, while the airport analysis printout in Table 6.2 indicates the maximum permissible takeoff and landing weights and the related limitations due to the Philippine airports' characteristics.

6.3.4   Route Analysis

The next step of equipment analysis is the calculation of aircraft en route performance (route analysis) to determine the mission payload that can be carried and the fuel burned (block fuel) on every city-pair connection of the airline's network. This procedure involves the determination of time, fuel, and distance for each flight segment of a flight profile such as that shown in Figure 6.7. Time, fuel, and distance for each segment may be obtained from the airplane's performance manual.

Performance data are generally shown for a standard day atmosphere, meaning that air temperature varies with altitude in a standard, internationally agreed-upon manner. Provisions for different conditions are made throughout the performance document where applicable.

The input data for en route performance include the following:

- Fuel and time allowances for taxi-in and taxi-out, takeoff and acceleration, approach and landing phases.

- Flight operating techniques such as climb, cruise and descent speeds, cruise pressure altitude and procedure, en route temperature and wind speed.

- Fuel reserves.

- Unit weight of passenger plus baggage.

- Route distance (including possible allowances given by airlines).

As shown in Figure 6.7 every route distance (range) can be divided, in first approximation, into three phases.

6.3.4.1   Climb Phase

Starting at 1,500 feet above the origin airport, the aircraft climbs at an assigned calibrated airspeed (CAS) until it reaches the cruise altitude or an altitude where CAS is equal to the assigned Mach number M and, in this case, from that altitude it climbs at constant M to cruise altitude.

Figure 6.8 shows typical climb profiles for a jet airplane adopting two different climb procedures. A high-speed climb results in more distance being covered for about the same climb time as a low-speed climb when climbing to the same altitude. This tends to minimize block time; a low-speed climb tends to minimize block fuel.

6.3.4.2   Cruise Phase

The example shown in Figure 6.9 is a typical chart of the way fuel consumption varies with speed for a turboprop airplane. Shown is a plot for a specific procedures and various altitudes and weights. This will give the nautical miles flown for each pound of fuel consumed; knowing the distance to be flown between climb and descent, one can then compute the amount of fuel consumed.

Figure 6.7
Typical Flight Profile

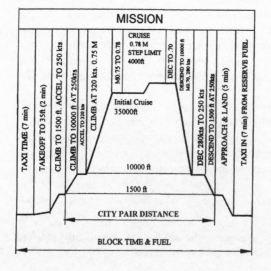
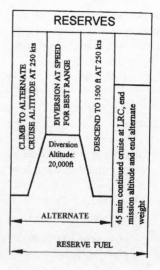

Figure 6.8
Typical Climb Profile

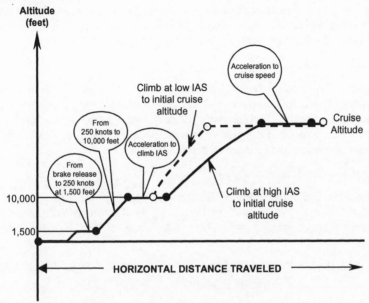

Figure 6.9
Fuel Economy with Speed

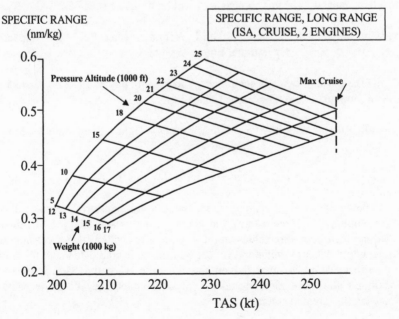

The long-range cruise procedure results in 99% of the maximum range because it provides a considerable increase in speed at the expense of 1% higher fuel consumption. Speed computation can also be made at a constant Mach number or at maximum cruise thrust. The maximum speed is reached in the latter case, and this maximum speed will vary with temperature.

6.3.4.3   Descent Phase

Figure 6.10 shows typical descent profiles for low- and high-speed procedures. Time, fuel burned, and distance traveled may be found in the performance manual as a function of initial (descent) altitude, weight, and adopted descent speed. Temperature variations usually have only a negligible effect on fuel burned and distance in descent.

6.3.4.4   Route Analysis Output

The time, fuel, and distance for each segment of the flight profile are calculated, determining the block fuel and time for the considered mission with an interactive procedure that involves calculation of the available mission payload:

Mission Payload = Mission Takeoff Weight - Loaded Fuel (Block Fuel + Reserves) – Operational Empty Weight

where the mission takeoff weight is restricted by origin and/or destination airport limitations or is equal to structural design value.

If the mission range is so long that the loaded fuel is equal to the maximum fuel tank capacity, the mission payload will be limited to

Mission Payload = Mission Takeoff Weight - Max Fuel tank capacity – Operational Empty Weight

If the mission range is such that the maximum payload can be carried, then the mission takeoff weight can be reduced to

Mission Takeoff Weight = Operational Empty Weight + Loaded Fuel + Max Payload

An example of the computer printout for this route analysis is shown in Table 6.3.

The aircraft design weights are indicated in the upper right corner; the last three columns show the takeoff and landing weights and the type of limitation affecting their operating values on the city pair connections under consideration. Main output data are shown in the center of the table, and data about missions to be performed are summarized on the left side. A comparison between the maximum allowable payload and the mission payload can be made using the values in the payload column.

Figure 6.10
Typical Descent Profile

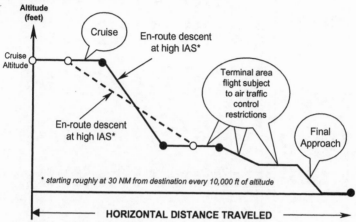

* starting roughly at 30 NM from destination every 10,000 ft of altitude

HORIZONTAL DISTANCE TRAVELED

6.3.5   Payload Range Curve

A schematic illustration of the relationship of the many weight and range limitations is shown in Figure 6.11. Basically, the payload/range chart estimates how far an airplane can carry a given payload. The maximum payload can be carried to a certain range (Condition A). Beyond that range, the aircraft becomes limited by its takeoff gross weight.

This may be either because of airport limitations (Condition B) or because the maximum gross weight is reached (Condition C). Then payload can be exchanged for fuel (keeping the same TOGW) so that the aircraft may fly a greater distance. This may be continued until the volume of the tanks does not allow more fuel.

Thereafter, additional range is only possible by reducing the average aircraft in-flight weight, which improves the specific range performance. This is accomplished by reducing payload and therefore TOGW (Condition D). Note that very large reductions in payload are required to provide small range increases when operating at distances requiring full fuel load.

Figure 6.12 shows the effects of takeoff gross weight decreases and OEW increases on the payload range chart. As noted previously, a takeoff weight reduction may be the result of airport limitations such as obstacles or high temperatures on the field, while an OEW increase may be due to the airline's own requirements about the cabin layout and special equipment installed.

Other important effects on the payload range, due to reasons other than changes in airplane weight characteristics, are shown in Figure 6.13. Headwind decreases the range capability of an airplane, whereas tailwind increases it. Additional fuel capacity provides an increase of the aircraft range, but it can be used only at low payloads, because at high payloads, takeoff weight limitation occurs.

Table 6.3
An Example Printout of Route Analysis

Aircraft type :

Refuelling Point *		(kg)
Max. Take-Off Wt.	......	16150
Max. Landing Wt.	......	16000
Max. Op. Empty Wt.	......	10203
Max. Allow. Payload Wt.	......	4598
Max. Fuel Wt.	......	4500
Max. Pass. Avail. Seats + Bag. Wt.	......	48 83

ORIG	DEST	DIST. (nm)	DIVE	DIST. (nm)	CRUISE PROC.	CRUISE ALTT. (ft)	WIND (kt)	TEMP. ISA (°C)	BLOCK FUEL (kg)	BLOCK TIME (hh:mm)	PASS. NUMB.	RESID. CARGO (kg)	LOADED FUEL (kg)	PAYLOAD (kg)	TAKE-OFF WEIGHT (kg)	LANDING WEIGHT (kg)	LIMIT.
* MNL	BAG	117	MNL	121	LRC	21000	0	15	418	0:52	48	613	1230	4598	15932	15648	MAX P/L
BAG	MNL	121	BSA	57	LRC	21000	0	15	414	0:52	48	614	812	4598	15514	15234	MAX P/L
* MNL	CYZ	156	TUG	43	LRC	23000	0	15	485	1:01	48	613	1189	4598	15890	15540	MAX P/L
CYZ	TUG	43	LAO	76	LRC	12000	0	15	269	0:32	48	614	704	4598	15406	15271	MAX P/L
* TUG	MNL	200	BSA	57	LRC	25000	0	15	555	1:11	48	613	945	4598	15647	15225	MAX P/L
* MNL	TUG	200	LAO	76	LRC	25000	0	15	556	1:11	48	613	985	4598	15686	15265	MAX P/L
* TUG	MNL	200	BSA	57	LRC	25000	0	15	555	1:11	48	613	945	4598	15647	15225	MAX P/L
MNL	LAO	224	TUG	76	LRC	25000	0	15	594	1:17	48	613	1025	4598	15726	15266	MAX P/L
* LAO	BSO	160	LAO	160	LRC	23000	0	15	494	1:02	48	613	1425	4598	16126	15766	MAX P/L
BSO	LAO	160	TUG	76	LRC	23000	0	15	489	1:02	48	614	931	4598	15633	15278	MAX P/L
* LAO	MNL	224	BSA	57	LRC	25000	0	15	594	1:17	48	613	985	4598	15686	15227	MAX P/L
* LAO	MNL	224	BSA	57	LRC	25000	0	15	600	1:17	48	418	1644	4403	16150	15683	STR T-O
MNL	LAO	224	TUG	76	LRC	25000	0	15	594	1:17	48	613	1043	4598	15745	15284	MAX P/L
* MNL	TUG	200	LAO	76	LRC	25000	0	15	556	1:11	48	613	985	4598	15686	15265	MAX P/L
* TUG	BSO	168	TUG	168	LRC	23000	0	15	507	1:04	48	609	1453	4593	16150	15777	STR T-O
BSO	TUG	168	LAO	76	LRC	24000	0	15	503	1:04	48	614	946	4598	15647	15279	MAX P/L
* TUG	MNL	200	BSA	57	LRC	25000	0	15	555	1:11	48	613	945	4598	15647	15225	MAX P/L

Fuel Reserves:
* 3% Stage Fuel
* Holding for 30 min. at 1,500 ft above alternate airport
* Fuel for flight to alternate airport (including missed approach, climb, cruise and descent)

Figure 6.11
Payload-Range

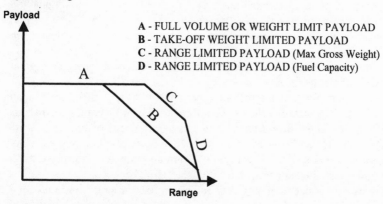

A - FULL VOLUME OR WEIGHT LIMIT PAYLOAD
B - TAKE-OFF WEIGHT LIMITED PAYLOAD
C - RANGE LIMITED PAYLOAD (Max Gross Weight)
D - RANGE LIMITED PAYLOAD (Fuel Capacity)

Figure 6.12
Effect of Weight on Payload-Range

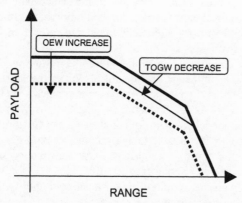

Figure 6.13
Effect of Wind and Fuel Capacity on Payload-Range Capability

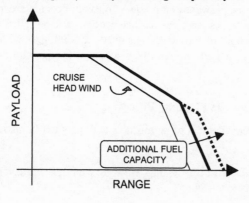

6.4   OPERATIONAL ANALYSIS

The purpose of an operational analysis is to find the bets fleet composition, to optimize flight itineraries, and frequencies by developing one or more operational plans. Therefore in our approach the "Operational Analysis" and "Fleet Planning" will have the same meaning. To achieve this objective an analyst must accurately simulate an airline's operation considering all requirements and objectives.

Links between the Operational and other phases of the Airline Analysis are shown in Figure 6.1 that also shows the different steps of Operational Analysis. Most information come from Market Analysis (Traffic) or Equipment Analysis (Aircraft); some of them (route Structure) have to be selected on purpose using internal and external sources. Fleet modification and airplane choice constitute the most important single decision the airline has to make.

The reason why fleet planning is so important is because it tries to take into account and reduce most of uncertainties in order to minimize the risk in addition to quantify the future needs and help in planning other resources. The most critical future needs for properly run airline (other than aircraft types and quantities) are: additional crews acquisition and training; facilities acquisition or modification; ground support equipment adaptation; provision for traffic rights on new route, and so on.

After fleet planning studies completion, the airline will know with a sufficient degree of confidence and details its future necessities in terms of: aircraft number, capacity, type, performance requirements, timing, and so on. This approach is also useful during final negotiations with more than one manufacturer, if the model allow for quick answers and flexibility when input is changed. In fact it may be possible to analyze and quantify economical benefits (or losses) from the basic assumptions. Any new concession of airplane manufacturers can be used to compare final offers.

A fleet plan is always required by financial institution when the operator asks for money in order to buy or lease airplanes. After establishing the requirements and objectives, and collecting the required input, the analyst may chose an analytical model as an aid in developing the required output of the operational analysis. Nowadays a model can easily become a computer program and, for large route systems, can reduce weeks of hand calculations to a few minutes. Best programs allow the analysts to dialogue with the computer through its screen and the possibility to change the assumptions and get new results in real time.

6.4.1   The Fleet Planning Process

During the management of an airline's activities two fundamental questions arise:

- How many aircraft, of what seating and type, should be operated by the airline at a certain moment in the future?

- Considering a given fleet and the routes operated by the airline, how to optimize the use of this fleet?

The answers for the first question are achieved implementing the fleet planning process, whereas to reply to the second question the schedule planning procedures must be taken into account. These answers are also dependent upon the main objective pursued by the airline: it may be an internal objective (to maximise profits or to have the best service at the lower possible cost) or instead an external objective (for instance to contribute in maintaining the international role and prestige of the country); in some cases it may be a mix of these ones.

The key element involved in the fleet planning process is the plan that reports — for the future — the route operated and for each route the related flight frequencies (the route and frequencies plan). If the route and frequencies plan foresees only small changes in terms of frequency and fleet size, the new capacity requirements can be achieved by using a method based on a simple extrapolation from current data; if the acquisition of an entirely new fleet must be taken into account, this simple method doesn't work satisfactorily. Then most airlines, in order to include all the possible relevant details, decide to develop a complete new plan extending the time frame up to 5-10 years into the future.

Another way of looking at the difference between fleet planning and aircraft scheduling is that, even when made at the microlevel (see the Micro Approach to Fleet Planning paragraph in this chapter), the aircraft number of each model in the first type of analysis is a rough estimate calculated using requested flying hours divided by aircraft planned use (and rounded to the next integer).

In aircraft scheduling, each airplane is followed in its routing by its tail code and it has to comply with the constraints that could be experienced in true oparations. For example, airplanes should be scheduled so as to end their day's flying at the origin of the next day's flight, thereby minimizing nonrevenue flights. Each itinerary should also be as close as possible to maintenance shops, engine spare-parts centers, and crew exchange locations to optimize airline resources and minimize problems in case of failure in airplane systems. The number of aircraft is simply the number of the tail codes. Sometimes the distinction between the two different approaches to fleet planning is not that clear and not necessary: The more detailed a fleet plan becomes, the closer it will be to a schedule plan.

There are several ways to proceed, involving alternative choices. It must be decided in advance if wide-body airplanes are under consideration, because they may cause special problems in the airline ground facilities at airports not yet used. Will freight have a dedicated fleet or be carried in passenger aircraft? Will the future network be close to the present one, or will airports with particular constraints be served, that have to be considered at present?

There are also general rules to be followed by the fleet planner, rules derived from past experience such as the following.

1. The transition period cannot be too long for several reasons:

a. The presence of new and older airplanes on the same route must be avoided or limited in time for crew (and other) optimization problems.

b. The evolution of the technology may bring differences between the first and last airplane delivered of the same type.

c. The capacity needed may change, and the last airplanes may be too small.

2. The transition period cannot be too short for reasons such as the following:

a. The introductory rate must be kept reasonable in order to control problems such as investment flow and training of crew and support staff.

b. The older airplanes' grounding rate should not be high in order to keep good resale value.

3. The number of different airplane types should be kept to a minimum for the purpose of economies of scale and to minimize introductory costs.

6.4.2   Two Approaches to Fleet Planning

"In analyzing traffic, the planner looks at the total [airline] market and the route-by-route breakdown." [CRANDALL 1982: p.233] In the following pages, these two approaches to solving the problems associated with fleet planning will be discussed.

Macro fleet planning is useful in obtaining global information about what kind of fleet mix would best fit a network system. The data required to perform the analysis include complete information about system traffic (RPK), load factors, and so on. *Micro fleet planning* takes into consideration a more detailed set of information and requires a deeper analysis of the airline's activity. Each approach requires a specific traffic investigation and specific differences that will be discussed here.

When micro fleet planning is the object of the study, it is necessary to construct a microforecast, built up from origin and destination markets. Since a macroforecast is performed anyway, the macroforecast and microforecast are then reconciled to ensure reasonableness.

6.4.2.1   *The Macro Approach to Fleet Planning*

When fleet planning is based on a macro approach it means that:

•   It is performed at a system or subsystem level.

•   RPK forecasts instead of O & D (origin-destination) passenger information are used.

•   The resulting fleet mix must meet macro requirements.

One of the most used techniques in the macro approach to fleet planning is top-down analysis, which will be illustrated in the following pages, together with a simple case study.

6.4.2.1.1   The Top-Down Analysis

A simple top-down analysis requires defining an airline as one or more subsystems (i.e., international, domestic, local, and so on). The airline annual totals will represent the input data:

1. Revenue passenger kilometers (RPK) and revenue ton kilometers (RTK) for the base year (the last year for which data are available).

2. Starting from the base year, all planned changes must conform to some ground rules. These ground rules may be decided by the analyst, specified by the sales representative, or designated by the airline in earlier discussions. These may include the following:

    a. Planning load factor.

    b. Subsystem traffic growth rate.

    c. Average stage length.

    d. Annual fleet utilization.

3. Aircraft on hand or on order that must be known, in terms of:

    a. Seating capacity.

    b. Productivity (average seats per airplane x block speed x annual utilization).

4. Aircraft types to fill residual (future) need (GAP) in terms of:

    a. Seating capacity.

    b. Productivity.

5. A formula for distributing residual need (GAP) between the available aircraft types.

The annual difference between the ASK forecast and the ASK offered by the current fleet minus the retirements is the capacity gap that may be filled in different ways by the acquisition of a different aircraft type.

The following case study refers to a hypothetical "Mina" Airlines and its domestic subsystem. The current "Mina" Airlines fleet for domestic services includes four new jets (150 seats) and two F-100s (100 seats). "Mina" Airlines will replace its F-100s with a certain number of new jets that it is planning to purchase because the F-100s are becoming old. At the same time, the airline must consider that the traffic is growing, and therefore a higher capacity airplane may be appropriate. We should take into consideration that the planning looks ahead 5 years.

Input needed are indicated in Table 6.4. In order to better understand the case, the main phases of the analysis are indicated below.

Phase 1. Calculate next-year RPK at the given growth rate and calculate passenger load factor (LF) using the current fleet only (see the productivity formula below for calculating ASK). In the example, the existing fleet cannot satisfy the future need for transporting the forecasted traffic, and therefore additional capacity is required. In fact, at year 1, the calculated LF ($723/1,067 = 0.68$) would be higher than the planning LF of 0.65.

Table 6.4

"Mina" Airlines: Top-Down Analysis

INPUT DATA

* Base fleet data
* Annual traffic growth
* Planning load factor less than 65%
* Route structure evolution and related information
* Aircraft data

ANNUAL OPERATING DATA		BASE FLEET	1	2	3	4	5	
Growth Rate %		0	13	13	13	10	8	INPUT
Revenue Pax Kms	RPK (MIL)	640	723	818	924	1,016	1,098	
Available Seat Kms	ASK (MIL)	1,067	1,183	1,305	1,522	1,736	1,736	INPUT
Pax Load Factor	L.F. %	60	61	63	61	58	63	INPUT
Existing 150 seats Aircraft		04	04	05	06	07	08	INPUT
Existing 100 seats Aircraft		02	01	0	0	0	0	INPUT
Additional 150 seats Aircraft		0	01	01	01	01	00	
Total Aircraft		06	06	06	07	08	08	
Average Stage Lenght	(Kms)	1,000	1,100	1,210	1,331	1,300	1,280	INPUT
Block Hours		13,800	14,400	15,000	17,500	20,000	20,000	
Departures		8,004	7,590	7,190	7,624	8,902	9,041	
Productivity (ASK/Airplane)	(MIL)	178	197	217	217	217	217	
Utilization (HRS/Airplane)		2,300	2,400	2,500	2,500	2,500	2,500	INPUT
Block Speed	(Km/H)	580	580	580	580	580	580	INPUT
Aircraft Kms (000)		8,004	8,349	8,700	10,147	11,573	11,573	
Average seats/airplane		133.3	141.7	150	150	150	150	INPUT

It has to be clear that the planning load factor shown above is a final result after a certain number of tentatives and iterations into given boundaries.
In fact some adjustement between the load factor and the number of aircraft is required in order to avoid fractionary portions of airplanes that would not make sense.

Changes in the productivity for same airplane type shown above come from variations in the utilization (and slightly from aircraft block-speed if any).
But productivity is a key element in determining the number of required airplane.
Therefore by means of airplane utilization it is possible to balance the route system and avoid the scatter in some other parameters while introducing the additional airplane.

Phase 2. Replace one old F-100 with a new and bigger airplane, the new jet (when all the F-100s will be dismissed, add only one new type of airplane).

Phase 3. Calculate the new fleet ASK (1,183 in the given example) by the productivity formula. This is based on the physical airplane's characteristics and on its use.

Phase 4. Calculate the present LF and verify that it is lower (but not much) than the planning one (0.61 versus 0.65 in the example). If the LF results are higher than planned, ground an additional old F-100. Calculate the LF again and make opportune adjustments by means of the utilization factor that may vary within reasonable minimum and maximum values.

Phase 5. Calculate block hours, aircraft kms and departures using the following relationships:

Fleet ASK = average seats p. airplane x average block speed x fleet block hours

Fleet Block Hours = number of aircraft x annual utilization (hours/airplane)

$$\text{Fleet Aircraft Kms} = \frac{\text{Available Seats Kms}}{\text{Average seats per airplane}}$$

$$\text{Fleet Departures} = \frac{\text{Fleet aircraft Kms}}{\text{Average stage length}}$$

6.4.2.2   The Micro Approach to Fleet Planning

Fleet planning for an airline at the micro level will typically include:

1. Traffic flow determination.
2. Aircraft route assignment.
3. Analyzing segment traffic loads.
4. Verifying fleet plan scheduling.
5. Evaluating alternative schedule with different equipment type.
6. Generating operating statistics.

In seeking to make the best choice of aircraft to operate a route system, . . . [the planner is] concerned with a number of main factors These will usually include some at least of the following:

1. The capacity requirement of the individual routes.

2. The minimum frequency judged necessary to adequately service the route.

3. Prohibition of the use of a particular aircraft on certain routes for technical or commercial reasons.

4. The maximum frequency at airports limited by the availability of slots.

5.   The maximum frequency on routes limited by bilateral treaty [or other reasons].

6.   The maximum capacity of individual aircraft types, and load factor limitations. . . .

7.   The availability of particular types of aircraft in the period under consideration.[TREVETT 1982: p.2]

There are basically three different types of "models" of an airline flight schedule: aircraft routing models, traffic flow models, and schedule generation models. Aircraft routing models are of the type that focus on the movement of each individual aircraft through a cyclical pattern in the schedule, starting from the assigned timetable related to the base year. Of concern here is the gate activity, the balanced movement of the fleet, and the aircraft cycle. Traffic flow models trace passengers or cargo units instead of aircraft through the schedule from their origin to their destination. In this model we are concerned with load factors, available seat miles, passenger miles, costs, and revenues. Schedule generation models attempt to create an aircraft schedule and simultaneously to accomplish what both models mentioned above have accomplished. . . . But no general solution to the "scheduling problem" has yet been found. Typical scheduling practice instead is one of progressive refinement [MATHAISEL 1972: p.1].

6.4.2.2.1   Traffic Flow General Model Description

To build an airline network that serves a number of cities a traffic flow model is used. The objective is to transform a true O & D traffic into a network characterised by two classes of services: non-stop services (direct link between the cities) and multi-stop services.

The model is conceived to maximise the number of non-stop traffic segments. It can be split into two phases (Figure 6.14); during the phase 1 the O & D demand for each city pairs is allocated step by step into traffic segments following a criterion based on the assumption that O & D demand must be higher than minimum airplane capacity times planned load factor on that route. The minimum, in turn, depends on a city-pair distance. The O & D city pairs demand that satisfies the criterion receive non-stop services (direct link), otherwise the relevant demand is considered insufficient and is assigned later in phase two. At the end of the first phase a number of non-stop traffic segments are originated.

In phase two the remaining traffic demand is processed following the criterion that each O & D traffic can be routed by a one-stop flight (that is passing through another city) provided the total one-stop distance flown is only slightly longer than a direct flight and that the obtained traffic build up is higher than a certain minimum. If only one city satisfies the above criterion than the whole traffic is channeled through that city otherwise, if more cities are found, the demand is split among those cities according to some rules that consider still the shortest distance travelled as the main driven factor.

Figure 6.14
A Traffic Flow Model

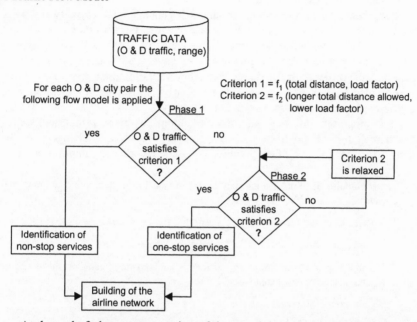

At the end of phase two a portion of the remaining O & D demand has been allocated; the rest of the O & D demand will be assigned applying the same procedure illustrated in phase two but relaxing progressively the criterion of choice (the distance flown between the cities, the number of stops and the load factor).

6.4.3   More on Fleet Planning Techniques

Apart from the macro or micro approach to fleet planning, there are some other fundamental differences in the way future airplane needs can be determined. To explain some general trade-offs between fleet planning variables, it may be useful to consider the two following possibilities:

- In one case the total capacity of two fleets is kept equal, while the size (and performance) of two airplane types under examination is different.

- In the second case, the frequencies are considered equal, while size and other characteristics, as in the case above, are different.

In the first case, the size of the smaller airplane requires more frequencies to satisfy the same capacity as the bigger one; therefore, its market share and earnings will be higher because of higher load factor due to better appeal (higher frequencies) of the provided service. Of course this also means that total operating cost will likely be higher due to more needed flights and more investment for airplane acquisition.

In the second case, the bigger airplane will generate more capacity and more earnings due to the better appeal (lower load factor), but also its operating cost will be higher, together with higher investment. In both cases, since size is different, the problem for the planner is to have a tool sensitive enough to appreciate the different traffic due to frequency variation in the first case or total capacity offer variation in the second one (apart from calculating operating cost of different size airplanes with sufficient accuracy).

It is important to note that fleet planning involves a high degree of uncertainty due to possible and unexpected events and changes in the competitive scenario. Any fleet planning is based on certain assumptions about

- The sociopolitical future, which may be significant for airplane manufacturers and operators.

- The macroeconomic forecast of the relevant geographical areas.

- The competitive future situation for airplanes and manufacturers.

- The technology forecast for future airplane characteristics related to the usage of advanced materials, new propulsion systems, and so on.

- Other forecasts on relevant matters.

All together, the above information constitutes the scenario on which the planning is based.

The analyst's experience consists of making a few appropriate alternative scenarios aggregating alternative events and excluding the combinations that are not compatible with each other, in addition to ranking results according to their credibility and probability.

6.5   ECONOMIC ANALYSIS

A huge body of literature exists on direct operating cost (DOC) and indirect operating cost (IOC) calculation methods, their evolution, and their attitude to be used for some particular aspects of the economic evaluation. Thus, cost methods developed by airlines are mainly concerned with the flexibility to modify individual parameters to simulate airline conditions to be used as a support tool in selecting between different manufacturers' proposals. On the contrary, methods developed by manufacturers may be more concerned with taking into account the technological improvements effect.

In Figure 6.1 there is a flow chart of the steps generally followed during an economic evaluation of one or more airplanes.

Before any economic comparison of airplanes can be made, it is essential that each airplane is configured following identical rules. For example, interiors should provide equal passenger comfort and service levels, since this will have a direct impact on the number of seats of an airplane. Finally, airplane and engine prices should reflect the same delivery year dollars and include comparable allowances for special features and airline furnished equipment. All this in itself is a major task for an analysis but an essential part of any economic evaluation of competing airplanes [BOEING 1985: p.2].

6.5.1 Aircraft Operating Costs

The most common way to classify airline expenses is to differentiate between direct and indirect costs. Direct costs are principally concerned with the utilization of the aircraft itself in a transportation system, and indirect costs represent all other operating costs that derive from the activity of a commercial airline.

But airplane costs classification is to some extent arbitrary. For example, sometimes landing/handling fees and navigation charges are considered indirect costs, while sometimes they are put on the DOC list.

Direct operating costs (DOC) and indirect operating costs (IOC) make up the total operating cost (TOC) of an airplane. Depending on the purpose of the analysis, airline operating expenses can be segmented into four categories:

1. Aircraft related expense.
2. Payload related expense.
3. Annual (period) expense.
4. System-related expense.

According to a slightly different approach, costs are first differentiated between fixed and variable costs, where fixed costs cover what are in effect the overhead costs and variable costs are those costs directly associated with the hours flown and the number of landings performed:

* Fixed costs (system related and aircraft related).

* Variable costs, distinguishing between time-related (system- and aircraft-related) costs, and cycle-related (system- and aircraft-related) costs.

Costs can be further divided, but it is important to note that in the end, they are all related to two elements only, the airline system and the airplane type. These two are the costs drivers.

6.5.1.1 Direct Operating Costs

Direct operating costs are those directly related to the operation of an aircraft and strictly related to the airplane type. Most important items are the following:

- Cockpit crew.

- Cabin crew.

- Fuel.

- Maintenance.

- Landing/handling fees.

- Depreciation, aircraft/spares.

- Insurance.

- Interest.

The DOC items provide a basis for measuring the productivity and cost-effectiveness of an aircraft. Each of the DOC items listed above will be discussed on the following pages.

Direct operating costs are calculated as block-to-block trip costs, usually expressed as cost per trip, cost per mile, or cost per seat-mile. Dollars per mile, cents per seat-mile, and cents per ton-mile are common expressions of direct operating costs (Figure 6.15).

Most DOC items depend on flight duration, but some are charged on a per-trip basis; therefore, although per-trip costs increase with distance flown, per-mile or per seat-mile costs decrease with stage length. Of course, after the maximum distance a given airplane can fly with maximum payload is reached, then the cost per seat-mile increases, because seat-miles decrease [MCDONNELL DOUGLAS 1985a].

6.5.1.1.1   Flight Crew Costs

The rules by which flight crews are paid are complicated and vary from operator to operator. There are, however, a number of common characteristics in the pay formulas. They are usually based on the number of block hours flown, on seniority, and on aircraft productivity as manifested by the cruise speed and the maximum takeoff gross weight of the aircraft. Therefore, the smaller the airplane (the seating), the greater the impact of crew cost on operating costs.

6.5.1.1.2   Cabin Crew Cost

Federal Air Regulations (FAR) specify the minimum number of flight attendants for U.S.-certificated air carriers as a function of the seating capacity of the aircraft, as follows: between 9 and 50 seats one attendant is required; up to 100 seats a second attendant has to be added; above 100 seats one additional flight attendant for each unit (or part of unit) of 50 passenger seats.

Additional attendants may be required based on emergency evacuation considerations or level of comfort to be offered to the passengers [MCDONNELL DOUGLAS 1985a]. The present standard is 1 cabin attendant for each 30 seats installed in the airplane.

Figure 6.15
Allocation of Direct Operating Costs

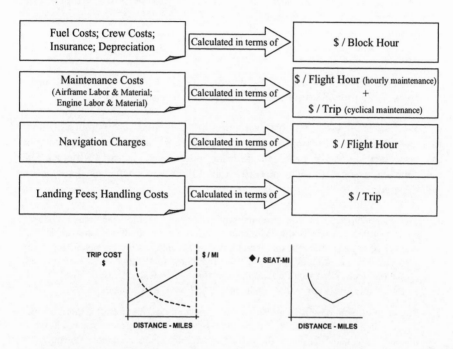

In addition to the base pay, other main elements apply both to cockpit and cabin crew cost:

- Fringe benefits that increase the cost 20% or more.

- Travel cost.

- Overnight stays away from home base.

6.5.1.1.3 Fuel Cost

Two items of information are needed in order to calculate the fuel cost:

- The amount consumed.

- The cost per gallon of the fuel.

Item 1 consists of block fuel, which is estimated for each airplane and each mission considered. The cost per gallon of fuel (historical and forecasted) is reported in Figure 6.16.

6.5.1.1.4   Airframe and Engine Maintenance Cost

Maintenance cost estimating for airline analysis purposes presents two possible cases:

a.   The case when the airplanes to be considered are already in service in that or other airlines.

b.   The case when an airplane in the developing stage has to be considered in the network of a particular airline and compared with an existing one.

While it is obvious that cost evaluation in the second case is more difficult to accomplish, the following are some considerations about the complexity of the task in general. In order to describe how many factors influence the maintenance costs of each aircraft, the following categories have been individuated:

1.   The characteristics of the aircraft type (type of engines, airframe, systems, equipment); for instance the maintenance hours rise with the engine power, the number of engines, the airframe weight, and so on. The level of maintenance hours associated with an aircraft changes with the time and total flight hours accumulated: on the one hand it increases due to the age of the aircraft, on the other hand there is an effect of learning curve that results in a reduction of maintenance hours.

2.   The level of technological innovation and complexity of the aircraft design; a state-of-art design will facilitate the systems accessability and the inspections and the total maintenance manhours per flight will decrease; the lower the number of parts the less the maintenance hours required.

3.   The characteristics of the airline operating the aircraft, such as the maintenance policies and training, utilization, labor productivity and cost, learning curves, type of routes, etc.

"Maintenance costs are broken into hourly and cyclic components. Cyclic costs may be thought of as those associated with one takeoff and one landing, such as those of the landing gear. Hourly costs represent those associated mainly with hours of use. Maintenance overhead, commonly called "burden," is usually expressed as a factor applied to direct labor cost." [MCDONNELL DOUGLAS 1985a: p.35]

6.5.1.1.5   Airplane Utilization

The cost of operations based on a fixed period of time (generally 1 year) can be grouped and called "standing costs." These include depreciation of airplanes and spare parts, insurance, and interest on borrowed capital. In addition, other cost elements can be accounted partially hourly and partially annually; therefore, it is important to know the airplane annual utilization over which fixed costs can be spread.

Figure 6.16
Fuel Price

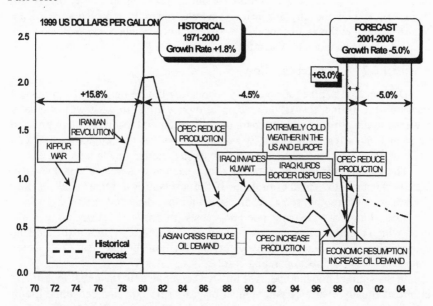

Several variables can influence the utilization reached by a certain airplane on a certain system (network):

- Operating hours per day and per week.

- Operating days per year.

- Time spent on the ground between flights.

- Average stage length.

- Airplane speed.

Some of these variables are related to each other, and formulas exist that take most of them into account. The single most important element in predicting the utilization level for an airplane to be introduced in a given network is the average distance the airplane will fly. The longer the time the airplane will spend flying, the higher the utilization will be. Intuitively, this is clear, and it is related mostly to the fact that when block time is high, the number of flights per day or per week is low (and vice versa), and therefore the time spent on ground between flights (that is lost time in terms of utilization) is low.

6.5.1.1.6   Insurance Cost

Insurance cost, as used in computation of DOC, is the cost of hull insurance associated with the airplane. Premiums are high at the introduction of a new model, but as experience and confidence build, the premiums taper off. About 0.5% to 1.0% of the airplane price is a rate generally representative of the industry average; this is an annual cost. But it may vary when international crisis occur, reaching as much as 3% to 5%.

6.5.1.1.7   Depreciation Cost

Depreciation can be viewed as an accounting device designed to produce a return on the airline, that is, an amount of money equal to what was originally invested in the airplane and the spare parts. The amount received each year is to be placed into a reserve account, so that an amount has accumulated by the end of the service life of the airplane sufficient to buy another one to take its place.

The amount that the governments allows each year is treated exactly as if it were a payment to rent the airplane. If the airplane was rented and put into passenger service, the rental charges would be deducted from the year's revenues along with all other operating costs, to arrive at an operating profit upon which corporate income taxes would be computed. So, too, if the airplane was purchased, the amount allowed for depreciation for that year is deducted from revenues as a direct operating cost.

In the straight line method used for DOC computation, the initial investment is spread equally over a certain number of years (the expected economic life of the airplane), with some residual value (usually 15 years with 10% of residual value). For tax accounting purposes and for cash flow analysis, airlines uses other methods with accelerated depreciation schedules.

6.5.1.1.8   Landing Fees

Landing fees comprise an item not included in some direct cost methods but that is nevertheless a direct operating expense and, as such, a factor that may be significant in actual and comparative aircraft cost estimates. Landing fees at most airports are based on aircraft weight. In the United States, this fee is generally lower than what is charged in other countries.

6.5.1.1.9   Interest Expense

With the increasing unit cost of transport aircraft, airlines are less able to provide from internal sources the capital necessary to support the cost of new equipment. Although interest payments will decline each year, an average annual interest cost is used when comparing aircraft, to reflect the average effect over the depreciable life of the aircraft:

$$\text{Average annual interest} = \frac{AC \,\&\, SC \times \dfrac{[(LP \times P / Y) + 1]}{[2 \times P / Y]} \times IR}{DP}$$

where

AC&SC = Aircraft & Spares Costs

LP = Loan Period

P/Y = Payment / Year

IR = Interest Rate

DP = Depreciation Period [MCDONNELL DOUGLAS 1985a]

$$\text{Interest per block hour} = \frac{\text{Average annual interest}}{\text{Annual utilization}}$$

6.5.1.1.10 Aircraft Handling

"These are the costs associated with the handling and routine servicing of the aircraft during the time it is at the gate. They include airplane towing, refueling, cabin cleaning, food and lavatory servicing, positioning of passenger bridges and ground power equipment" [BOEING 1985: p.7]. The conventional methods of estimating this cost component assume that it is a function of the gross weight of the airplane.

Thus, the equation is of the form:

$$\text{Cost per trip} = k \text{ (Maximum Takeoff Gross Weight)}$$

6.5.1.1.11 Navigation Charges

Sometimes this cost item is not included in DOC computation. Nevertheless, it is a cost incurred in flying for using navigation aids of one or more national or transnational entities created for this purpose, and therefore it should be taken into account. The navigation charges item is a function of gross weight and is related with distance flown.

6.5.1.2 Indirect Operating Costs

Indirect operating costs are those that are not directly related to the operation of an aircraft. They are reported as total system cost by the operator and they vary significantly from one airline to another. They are important to airline cost control, much less for the purpose of comparing aircraft types. In addition, manufacturers have little leverage in designing airplanes over the magnitude of IOC.

There are more than a hundred line items that could be listed as IOC, but for convenience we may group these into six categories. This list is by no means complete but does show basically what is in each IOC category.

- *Traffic servicing:* Payload handling and clerical wages; terminal rent and utilities; traffic liability insurance; customs and duties (international); supervisory and administration costs; professional fees; payroll taxes.

- *Aircraft servicing:* Expenses for scheduling and controlling flight assignments; communications.

- *Reservations and sales:* Wages of sales representatives, instructors, clerical personnel and other support staff; development of tariffs and schedules; office costs.

- *Advertising and publicity:* Wages, promotional brochures; expense accounts; direct advertising.

- *Ground property and equipment:* Direct costs of wages, supplies, payroll, taxes, and other items; depreciation of maintenance hangars and equipment, as well as terminal and equipment.

- *General and administrative:* Expenses of a general corporate nature, including wages of general management, accountants and economists; insurance and taxes other than payroll; uncollectable accounts; legal fees; memberships to IATA; professional and technical fees.

Such IOC groups are generally made of fixed and variable components that are system-, airplane-, and traffic-related. There is a lot of discretionary power in the allocation of some cost elements; therefore, methods may differ greatly one from each other. Figure 6.17 shows a tentative IOC allocation. Accordingly, IOC behavior versus stage length is shown in the lower part of Figure 6.17.

Depending on the purpose of IOC computation, other valid methods of allocation may be considered. For example, a manufacturer may wish to classify all IOC elements as airplane-related, passenger-related, and cargo-related items.

Figure 6.17
Allocation of Indirect Operating Costs

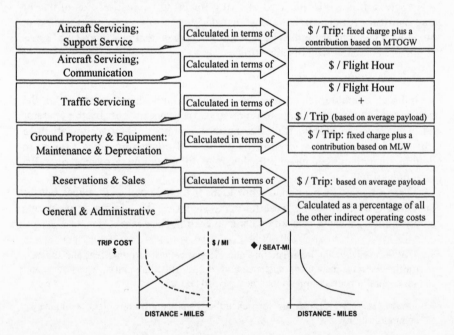

6.5.1.2.1 Airplane Related Costs

They are generally considered on a per trip basis and are attributed on the basis of the airplane size; they include the costs of all the equipment and infrastructure related to the aircraft such as maintenance tools, shops hangars, mobile power equipment, tractors, baggage carts, loading ramps, control and communication including the cost associated directly with aircraft dispatch and in-flight control.

Also a portion of general and administrative costs (overhead costs not included elsewhere) are considered and are attributed to airplanes in proportion to the amount of total operating costs less general and administrative costs.

6.5.1.2.2 Passenger Related Costs

They include costs related to passengers such as: meals, reservations and ticketing, pasengers and baggage handling (check-in, loading, unloading), insurances (for passengers and baggage), agent commissions and advertising. In addition a portion of general and administrative costs are considered (the passenger related overhead cost) and attributed as a function of on board passengers and trip distance.

6.5.1.2.3 Cargo Related Costs

This item include the cargo handling and insurance costs, reservation costs, commissions, advertising and a portion of general & administratice costs (the cargo related overhead cost) calculated as a function of the weight of cargo loaded and trip distance.

6.5.1.3 Introductory Costs

The assessment of costs associated with the introduction into service of new types of transport aircraft is a fundamental part of an analysis of the total costs of operation. The magnitude of these cost items and the length of the introductory phase grow with the degree of newness of engines, systems, and equipment.

Therefore, in a plan for acquisition of new aircraft, an airline must add some additional costs to the purchase costs. These are noted below.

6.5.1.3.1 Initial Costs

These are closely joined to the introduction of a new aircraft into an airline's fleet. They include spare parts costs, ground support equipment costs, and crew training costs (ground school, simulator training, flight training, and the out of production costs of salaries and expenses for the trainees).

6.5.1.3.2 Maintenance

Maintenance labor for a new aircraft type is generally higher during the first years of utilization than that for an aircraft already in the fleet, following the usual learning process.

6.5.1.3.3   Burden

Analysis of historical data about direct operating costs shows that general expenses related to maintenance items (burden) increase 5% to 7% with a new aircraft type introduction to the fleet.

6.5.1.3.4   Flight Crew

The introduction of a new aircraft type includes the need for new flight crew. In fact, crew utilization is a function of the number of the same aircraft type in service. Therefore, it is less than if that aircraft type was already in the fleet. The result is that, under the same condition of offered service (same aircraft utilization), a higher flight crew number will be necessary.

6.5.2   Airplane Economic Evaluation and Selection Criteria

The purpose of the present paragraph is to show how operating costs may be utilized in practice to make a preliminar choice among airplanes of different characteristics, including size.

6.5.2.1   Airline Revenues

Airline operating revenues are earned by carrying passengers and cargo. A small amount of additional revenue is generated from miscellaneous other sources. The vast majority of airline revenues, however, are from passenger travel.

6.5.2.2   DOC Comparison

Direct operating costs are often used in airplane comparison studies that require consideration of only those elements most sensitive to variations in airplane design and characteristics.

[The chart in Figure 6.18] commonly referred to as a "fan chart" presents a comparison of aircraft trip cost and seat-mile cost. The further the aircraft is to the left, the better the trip cost, and the lower the aircraft is, the better the seat-mile cost. Aircraft B is the reference aircraft and all other aircraft are shown relative to it. Ideally, the best aircraft would appear in the lower left corner, but seldom if ever would any aircraft appear there. [In Figure 6.18,] C has the lowest trip cost and a lower seat-mile cost than D or E, so D and E would probably not be selected by an airline. A has the lowest seat-mile cost. Traffic and frequency requirements along with [the information provided by] this chart would dictate the aircraft best suited economically to the airline [among A, B and C] [MCDONNELL DOUGLAS 1985a: p.45].

6.5.2.3   Total Operating Costs and Profit Potential

With revenue per passenger and total cost for a given flight, the break-even number of passengers is computed. Any number of passengers above the number required to break even gives extra revenue or profit up to a maximum determined by the number of seats that may be offered.

Figure 6.18
Direct Operating Cost Comparison — 500 NM Trip

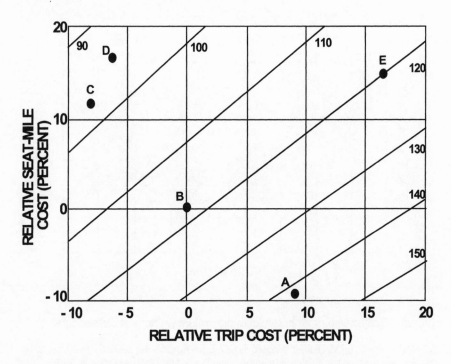

Source: McDonnell Douglas. *Sales Engineering Briefing Manual: An Outline of the Functions and Technology of Sales Engineering.* Long Beach, CA: Douglas Document, 1985a, p.45

The profit potential area is defined by the upper lines that reflect the payload range capability of the airplane and the lower line (which could be considered the break-even line in number of passengers), for the given set of operating and economic assumptions.

The graph in Figure 6.19 is repeated for the aircraft under evaluation and the results for a given range are then compared.

Another way of looking at profit potential is shown in Figure 6.20. The aircraft are those of Figure 6.18 from which, on the basis of DOC, only A, B, C have been selected.

The present comparison adds some elements in order to make a choice among the airplanes, since introduces a trade-off between potential profit and potential risk for the airline. In fact, for economies of scale the bigger the airplane, the higher the profit potential, but the number of filled seats necessary for the airline to break even is also higher.

Figure 6.19
Profit Potential — Airplane A

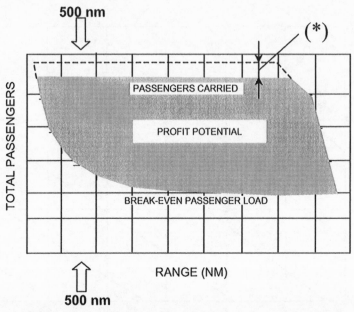

(*) - Belly cargo profit potential in equivalent number of passengers

Source: Elaboration on McDonnell Douglas. *Sales Engineering Briefing Manual: An Outline of the Functions and Technology of Sales Engineering*. Long Beach, CA: Douglas Document, 1985a

Figure 6.20
Profit Potential — 500 NM Stage Length in 1995 $

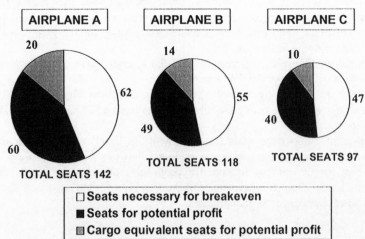

6.5.2.4   Airline System Operating Economics by Airplane Type

Applying general methods can help the airline to select from the many existing airplanes just a few of different size and characteristic.

But to make a final choice, airplane economics must be calculated, taking into account the limitations resulting from the equipment analysis and the operational analysis.

The following is an example of such an analysis, with main operating cost assumptions listed.

- Aircraft price: $6.5 million.

- Engine price: 465,000 US$.

- Spare parts: 15% of aircraft price for initial airframe spares (expendable spares, 25% plus rotable spares, 75%); 35% of total engine price and accessories spares.

- Depreciation aircraft + expendable spares: 15 years with 10% residual value.

- Depreciation GSE: 8 years without residual value.

- Depreciation rotable spares: 15 years with 50% residual value.

- Depreciation training expenses: 8 years without residual value.

- Total Investment: 2 aircraft + total spares + GSE + training.

Note that financial costs are not taken into account here. This is because cost analysis in the present case is part of a more comprehensive study that will include financial analysis (see next paragraph of this chapter) where the impact of financial charges on the economics of the project will be fully explored.

Detailed results from the computer printout (see Tables 6.5 and 6.6) show

- Direct operating costs per trip.

- Indirect operating costs (administrative, sales, ground operations expenses) per trip.

- Total operating costs, in terms of:

    - Stage cost.

    - Cost per nautical mile.

    - Cost per seat-nautical-mile.

    - Cost per year.

- Expected revenue for each stage per year.

- Profit or loss for each stage per year.

- The same values as the above for the whole network.

Table 6.5
Route and Cost Analysis for "Mina" Airlines (Partial Network)

MISS NO	FROM	TO	SECT DIST (NM)	NO: PAX	RESID. CARGO (LB)	BLOCK TIME (hh:mm)	BLOCK FUEL (LB)	FREQ/ WEEK	D.O.C./ TRIP ($)	I.O.C./ TRIP ($)	T.O.C./ TRIP ($)	T.O.C./ N.MI ($ NM)	T.O.C./ SEAT/NMI (C/ASM)	T.O.C./ YEAR ($)	TOT.REV./ YEAR ($)	PROFIT YEAR OP LOSS ($)
1	LUN	NLA	141	46	331	0:55	895	16/7	971	366	1337	9.48	20.62	1112650	1323846	211196
2	NLA	LUN	141	46	331	0:53	838	16/7	933	366	1299	9.21	20.03	1080923	1323846	242923
3	LUN KIW	KIW LUN	150 150	43 46	97 331	0:57 0:55	932 886	4/7 4/7	1004 960	383 383	1387 1343	9.25 8.95	21.50 19.46	288449 279353	346459 346459	58010 67107
4	LUN	LVI	212	46	0	1:9	1140	5/7	1204	414	1618	7.63	16.59	420619	468052	47433
5	LVI	LUN	212	45	0	1:13	1232	5/7	1345	414	1760	8.30	18.44	457477	468052	10575
6	LUN MFU	MFU LUN	237 237	39 45	88 123	1:18 1:16	1292 1298	2/7 2/7	1357 1340	230 230	1587 1569	6.70 6.62	17.17 14.71	165056 163201	103839 103839	-61217 -59362
7	LUN	CIP	263	46	159	1:24	1413	1/7	1459	335	1794	6.82	14.83	93275	75711	-17564
8	CIP	LUN	263	44	65	1:22	1378	1/7	1506	335	1841	7.00	15.91	95711	75711	-20000
9	NLA	KAA	224	45	112	1:15	1263	2/7	1311	298	1608	7.18	15.96	167282	134666	-32616
10	KAA ZKB	ZKB KAA	104 104	44 22	108 0	0:44 0:43	717 721	2/7 2/7	814 798	107 107	921 905	8.85 8.70	20.12 39.57	95739 94147	48358 48358	-47381 -45789
11	KAA	NLA	224	46	331	1:12	1204	2/7	1306	298	1604	7.16	15.57	166832	134666	-32166

O P E R A T I N G   C O S T   D A T A

Table 6.6
Total Values of the Whole Network: Year "X"

| CITY - PAIRS | : | 28 | | |
| SEGMENTS | : | 78 | | |

ESTIMATED VALUES		VALUES PER WEEK	VALUES PER YEAR	HOURLY AVERAGE	AVERAGE PER TRIP
TOTAL BLACK TIME	(HRS)	74.86	3892.91	1.00	0.96
TOTAL RANGE	(NM)	12290.00	639081.00	164.17	157.56
TOTAL FUEL	(LB)	73588.37	3826603.00	982.97	943.44
DEPRECIATION	(US $)	17251.11	897059.69	230.43	221.17
G.S.E. INVEST. DEPREC.	"	375.60	19531.00	5.02	4.82
TRAINING EXPENSES	"	383.51	19942.00	5.12	4.92
TOTAL INSURANCE	"	11448.60	595328.56	152.93	146.78
COCKPIT CREW	"	4866.12	253038.56	65.00	62.39
CABIN CREW	"	2695.09	140145.06	36.00	34.55
LANDING & NAVIG. FEES	"	4404.44	229031.44	58.83	56.47
FUEL	"	20136.45	1047097.06	268.98	258.16
MAINTENANCE	"	18438.37	959797.37	246.29	236.39
AGM. + SAL. + GR.OP. EXPEN.	"	22927.37	1192225.00	306.26	293.94
TOTAL OPERATING COSTS	"	102926.25	5352176.00	1374.85	1319.57
TOTAL REVENUES	"	99683.75	5183565.00	1331.54	1278.00
PROFIT OR DEBIT BALANCE	"	-3242.50	-168611.00	-43.31	-41.57

6.6   FINANCIAL PLANNING ANALYSIS

The final, and often most important, step in a comprehensive study of an airline's future fleet requirements is an analysis of forecasted return on its investment funds. Using the results of previous steps of analysis along with data produced by the airline, airline financial planning will measure the worth of a sales proposal using various financial tools including cash flow, return on investment, break-even and capital decision analyses (Figure 6.1). All performance requirements, routing considerations, scheduling demands, fare determinations, and other equipment selection processes are only contributions to the ultimate goal of maximizing the long term gain for current airline stockholders.

6.6.1   Income Statement

6.6.1.1   Airline Revenue and Expenses

The income statement is the main element of a financial analysis (Figure 6.21). The Revenues connected with the fleet operated by the airline are calculated on the basis of the traffic forecast and yield assumptions; in addition to this revenues other activities that prodece revenues to the airline must be considered. The Annual Operating Expenses are the total costs of the airline related to the aforementioned activities; the values are achieved through unit cost values and available data included in the detailed fleet plan. Subtracting the Annual Operating Expenses from Revenues, the Profitability is also determined after having considered also the depreciation, financial charges and taxes [MC DONNELL DOUGLAS 1985b]

6.6.1.2   Non-Operating Income

The most common items regarding non-operating income (expenses) are as follows:

- Interest expense that is interest on long and short-term debt.
- Interest income that is interest earned.
- Gain (loss) on sales of assets that is realized value less net book value.
- Dividend income.
- Foreign exchange earnings (loss).

6.6.1.3   Taxes

No estimate of profit would be complete without a provision for taxes, so a tax computation must be taken into account.

6.6.1.4   Income Statement Example

An in-depth look at the airline income statement means determination of the airline's revenue and expenses.

Figure 6.21
Income Statement

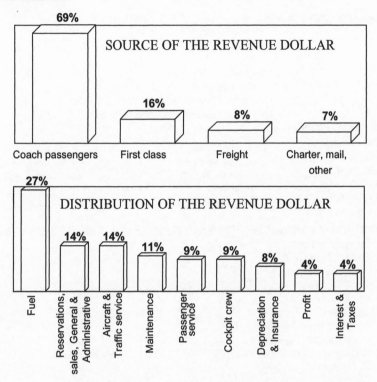

Source: Elaboration on McDonnell Douglas, *Airline Financial Planning*, Long Beach, 1985b

The airline under examination may not run some activities and related revenues and expenses (such as mail and on-board sales) or may not have a standard accounting system regarding cost items, but it should be possible to obtain an overall summary using the system given in Table 6.7. In the previous step, the economic analysis of an airline operating two airplanes on a given network was carried out (see Table 6.6). The income statement for the same airline can then be prepared (see Table 6.8).

The operator is borrowing the capital at 13% interest and repaying it with semi-annual installments. Principal payments are a constant amount per period (although they are not taken into account in this case, as the depreciation is included in the expenses). The repayment will be completed in 10 years.

6.6.2 Cash Flow Analysis

In order to evaluate different fleet mix alternatives and/or the capability of the proposed investment to generate enough cash to give an appropriate return, a cash flow analysis is the initial stage.

Table 6.7
Income Statements (Profit and Loss Account)

OPERATING REVENUES:
- Passenger traffic
- Freight   "
- Mail   "
- Charter   "
- Onboard sales
- Maintenance & Handling for other airlines
- Lease of equipment to other airlines

OPERATING EXPENSES:

Aircraft Related:
- Cockpit & Cabin Crew
- Fuel & Oil
- Aircraft Service
- Landing Fees
- Navigation Fees

Payload Related:
- Traffic Servicing
- Food & Liability
  Insurance
- Reservation & Sales

Annual Related:
- Depreciation
- Hull Insurance
- Lease/Rental

System Related:
- Advertising
  & Publicity
- General &
  Administrative

OPERATING INCOME (or Loss)= OPERATING REVENUES-OPERATING EXPENSES
(Operating Profit or Loss)
FINANCIAL CHARGES
- Interest Expenses
NET PROFIT (or Loss)   = OPERATING INCOME - INTEREST EXPENSES
(Profit before Taxes)
INCOME TAXES
- Government Tax Rates
- Investment Tax Credits
NET INCOME (or Loss)   = PROFIT BEFORE TAXES - INCOME TAXES
(Profit after Taxes)

Table 6.8
Income Statement (Profit and Loss Account) — ($ x 1,000)

Years	1	2	3	4	5	6	7	8
Operating Revenues	5,183	5,900	6,662	7,503	8,341	9,262	10,242	11,282
Operating Expenses (including Depreciation)	5,352	5,837	6,364	6,905	7,548	8,273	9,037	9,763
Operating Income	-169	63	298	598	793	989	1,205	1,519
Interest Expenses	1,955	1,755	1,554	1,354	1,153	953	932	552
Profit before Taxes	-2,124	-1,692	-1,256	-756	-360	36	273	967

Cash flow differs from the income statement because instead of considering depreciation plus interest as expenses, the true loan repayment schedule is introduced. Depreciation is the allocation of the cost of a tangible asset (the airplane) over the period in which it is expected to produce revenue. The loan repayment period is very often shorter than the useful airplane life; therefore principal payment is higher than depreciation. Thus, cash flow results look worse than profit and loss statement, but of course this is only a matter of different accounting methods and purposes.

Table 6.9 illustrates cash cost analysis results for the airline under examination.

6.6.3   Discounted Cash Flow Analysis

6.6.3.1   Discounted Cash Flow Application: Present Value Analysis

It is possible to render different financial situations directly comparable by discounting their stream of cash inflow and cash outflow to their equivalent present values.

That is, at an assumed interest (discount) rate, we can convert the whole future estimated cash stream to a financially equivalent dollar value at the beginning year of the program. For an airline that knows its own cost of capital, the reciprocal ratio is used here for discounting.

6.6.3.2   ROI Computation

In the previous paragraph, we said we can discount all future net cash streams down to year zero, using the reciprocal of the airline's cost of capital.

Table 6.9
Cash Flow Analysis

($)

	1	2	3	4	5	6	7	8
Total Revenue	5,183,585	5,900,481	6,662,058	7,503,162	8,340,986	9,262,510	10,242,038	11,282,634
Total Operating Costs	5,352,176	5,837,145	6,363,659	6,905,593	7,548,037	8,273,263	9,037,157	9,763,541
Operating Profit	-168,611	63,336	296,399	597,569	792,949	989,247	1,204,881	1,519,093
Depreciation	897,060	897,060	897,060	897,060	897,060	897,060	897,060	897,060
Cash Costs	4,455,166	4,940,085	5,466,599	6,008,533	6,650,977	7,376,203	8,140,097	8,866,481
Cash Profit	728,449	960,396	1,195,459	1,494,629	1,690,009	1,886,307	2,101,941	2,416,153
Interests	1,955,830	1,755,232	1,554,634	1,354,036	1,153,438	952,840	752,242	551,644
Principal Payment	1,591,680	1,591,680	1,591,680	1,591,680	1,591,680	1,591,680	1,591,680	1,591,680
Capital Costs	3,547,510	3,346,912	3,146,314	2,945,716	2,745,118	2,544,520	2,343,922	2,143,324
Cash Flow	-2,819,061	-2,386,516	-1,950,855	-1,451,087	-1,055,109	-658,213	-241,981	272,829
Cumulated Cash Flow		-5,205,577	-7,156,432	-8,607,519	-9,662,628	-10,320,841	-10,562,822	-10,289,993

CAPITAL COST	= PRINCIPAL PAYMENT + INTEREST
CASH COST	= OPERATING COST (or EXPENSES) - DEPRECIATION
CASH PROFIT	= OPERATING REVENUES - CASH COST
CASH FLOW	= CASH PROFIT - CAPITAL COST

Figure 6.22
Present Value Analysis and ROI Determination

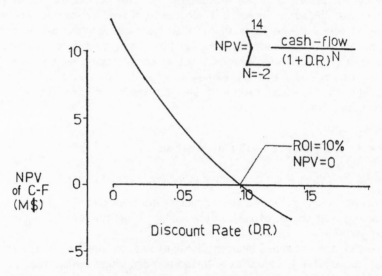

If we assume not knowing the cost of capital, we may discount by successive trials until we have equated the present value (PV) of the stream of the cash inflow, to the present value of the stream of the cash outflow (Figure 6.22).

When we have obtained that we have determined the discount factor that allows to receive back the exact time-adjusted financial amount equivalent to the original investment. The reciprocal of this single discount factor is the return on investment for the proposed fleet. The calculations of separate ROI for the proposed fleets allows for their objective comparison on the basis of pure financial advantages. The ROI can measure the investment value of various alternative mixes of existing and available competing aircraft that satisfy flight requirements throughout the system.

6.7   SALE AND FINANCING OF A COMMERCIAL AIRCRAFT PURCHASE

The concept of *augmented product* in aeronautics has been already outlined. It has been also pointed out that the perceived value for the customer is related to the product rather than to the physical aircraft characteristics. The augmented product is the last one plus tangible and intangible elements such as after sale support, training, maintenance and financial conditions. This section deals with these subjects in some details.

6.7.1   Purchase Agreement for a Commercial Aircraft

"For new aircraft, *separate prices* are provided for the airframe, engines, airline-specified equipment, and, often, for avionics. The airframe and much airline-specified equipment are the responsibility of the aircraft manufacturer; the engines and avionics are often bought separately." [GOLASZEWSKI, KLEIN 1998: p.194]. The following are some characteristics of the typical contract for a commercial aircraft purchasing.

6.7.1.1   Aircraft Definition

According to MONIKA STOOS-CAVÈ [1990], although the airplane is an industrial product and therefore has a high level of construction uniformity, in the contract it is necessary to give the exact definition of the product agreed on by seller and buyer.

6.7.1.2   Airplane Delivery

This is a main step in the relationship between the two parties, because it enacts the transfer of the ownership of the aircraft, with all related economic and legal aspects. The purchase agreement establishes the delivery date, place, and modality of acceptance of the product, a report that attests that the consigned aircraft is compliant to the definition of the contract and similarly a document that highlights any possible manufacturing or performance default is signed [STOOS-CAVÈ 1990].

6.7.1.3   Guarantees

"Agreements covering the purchase of new aircraft also include *performance* and *warranty guarantees*. Performance guarantees include fuel efficiency and payload/range relationships as well as other operating parameters (for example, maintenance man-hours per flight hour). Warranties usually cover the manufacturer's obligations for repair of the aircraft within a specified time period or number of flight hours after it has been placed in service." [GOLASZEWSKI, KLEIN 1998: p.195]

6.7.1.4   Documentation

The after-sale support service of the manufacturer must provide to the airline all necessary documentation for the correct and advantageous use of the aircraft and of the most significant systems, giving indication on the maintenance plan to follow, the modalities of intervention, and so on [STOOS-CAVÈ 1990].

6.7.1.5   Training and Spares

Aircraft operaton requires knowledge of the aircraft and practice flights that only the manufacturer can provide in an acceptable way. "*Training* and *spares* also are typically included in the offering price for new aircraft. Training of the air and ground crews and the availability of spare parts are important determinants of the ease and efficiency with which new aircraft can be integrated into an airline's fleet." [GOLASZEWSKI, KLEIN 1998: p.194]

6.7.2 Sales Financing

The changed reference framework with increased difficulties experienced by the buyers to raise the money needed for airplanes purchase has pushed airlines and manufacturers to try to jointly find a solution by looking for a third party able and available to support the financial effort related to the acquisition of an aircraft. The following sections include information about the methods of the most common financing forms.

6.7.2.1 Credit to Export

According to LAURENCE BARRON [1990], all the industrial countries have their own organizations to support the export credit; these are governmental national bodies to support collaboration between countries. The export credit has been the most used tool for financing aircraft sales abroad, first by the main manufacturers and later also by the medium and small ones.[1]

Sales financing is agreed on among four key actors: manufacturer, airline, bank and institute for the export credit (from the manufacturer's country). They interact according to the following system:

- The manufacturer delivers the aircraft to the airline receiving the agreed-on amount of money. A bank (or a pool of national or international banks) have anticipated the capital to the airline.

- The airline receives the aircraft and contracts a debt with the bank with a defined plan of extinction.

- The bank receives guarantees from the institute of the export credit that undertakes to operate in case of insolvency of the airline.

- The institute of export credit belongs to the manufacturer country and works in the sphere of the collaboration agreements that its own government stipulates with other countries.

6.7.2.2 Private Financing

This is activated by the manufacturer, operating similarly to a business broker by offering to the airline contacts with financial operators capable to realize solutions for each specific case. The small airlines are appreciative of this additional service from the manufacturer. In these circumstances, the airplane constitutes the guarantee for the coverage of the risk (*financement sur actif*) assumed by the financier and/or bank; it is a sort of mortgage credit.

The utilization of this title of guarantee imposes that the ownership of the aircraft is transferred on delivery from the manufacturer to the financier and not to the airline;, similarly, the registration of the aircraft is made in the financier's country. The financier company assumes the ownership of the aircraft only to protect its exposure, not with the aim of managing the aircraft. The manufacturer is not involved financially [BARRON 1990].

6.7.2.3   Manufacturer's Risk Assumption

In some circumstances, the manufacturer is asked to assume guarantees toward the financiers and then to support the sales financing; this happens when the financier company wants to protect itself during the time the value of the aircraft is taken to guarantee its own exposure.

For the above purpose many different guarantee formulas have been conceived; following BARRON [1990] the most significant are considered:

6.7.2.3.1   First Loss Deficiency Guarantee

If an airline is not able to make payments as agreed, it is constrained to render the aircraft to the financier, which will sell it as used. The manufacturer undertakes to indemnify the financier in case the market value results lower than the amount due by the airline.

6.7.2.3.2   Asset Value Guarantee

The logic of this formula is similar to the previous one, with the difference that the mechanism of compensation is activated under airline's choice that voluntarily gives back the aircraft not necessarily due to financial difficulties.

6.7.2.3.3   Residual Value Guarantee

The manufacturer guarantees the financier in respect to the risks that could come out only at the end of the financing as difference between actual and foreseen market value.

6.7.2.4   Leasing

Leasing is one of the tools at an airline's disposal for the acquisition of the aircraft needed to conduct its own entrepreneurial activity. With the payment of a periodic installment for the agreed period, the leasing allows the airline possession and the use of the aircraft and but not ownership of it, which remains with the leasing company in a temporary or final way. Leasing has been described in more depth in Chapter 5 (dealing with airplane distribution channels), because of the intermediation role of leasing companies.

6.8   SUCCESS FACTORS IN THE MOST IMPORTANT AIRCRAFT SALES OF THE LAST DECADES

In the following sections, some important commercial airplane sales in the last 30 years are examined to identify the main factors in the decisions to buy and thus the relevant elements characterizing the winning proposals. Most information on this matter have been obtained from LYNN [1997], some from NEWHOUSE [1988].

6.8.1   Political / Social Influence

This is the case when sales have been obtained with the direct intervention of the government of airplane or engine manufacturers supporting the transaction directly

6.8.1.1   British Airways Sale (Mid-1970s)

Although the B-757 was a Boeing product in competition with the Airbus A-320, it received the full support of the British prime minister because of its Rolls Royce engine. Other European leaders (such as French President Giscard d'Estaing and German Chancellor Schmidt) didn't support the European products in this way, allowing the U.S. product to win the deal.

6.8.1.2   Western Airlines Sale (1977)

Airbus was almost sure to sell A-300s to Western Airlines, but shortly before the deal, the French government released a Palestinian terrorist, angering the United States. As a result, Western Airlines ordered B-727s and DC-10s instead.

6.8.1.3   Middle East Countries Sale (1980)

The Airbus success in this deal was possible because the United States was unpopular in some Middle East countries due to its support of Israel, while the Airbus parent companies contributed to the French national effort (of Giscard d'Estaing) that concentrated on defending Palestinian positions. This drew favorable attention to Airbus from the airlines of Lebanon, Kuwait, and Saudi Arabia, which bought the European airplanes.

6.8.1.4   Turkish Sale (1984)

Boeing was convinced that its 767 would have won this deal, because France wasn't popular in Turkey. A few days before the airline's decision, however, an Airbus manager convinced the Turkish company that the A-310 was a German plane or even a Turkish plane, because of many Turkish workers involved in Germany in making it. Airbus made the sale.

6.8.1.5   Saudi Arabian Airlines Sale (1993)

Shortly after the Gulf War's conclusion, Saudi Arabia needed to acquire a large number of airplanes for its national airline. It seemed certain that a U.S. company's airplanes would be chosen, to thank the United States for the military help received.

President Clinton himself solicited King Faud for this purpose. From the European side, similar strong attempts were made by President Mitterand of France, Prime Minister Major of the United Kingdom, and Chancellor Kohl of Germany, all stressing the important roles their countries had played during the Middle East crisis.

In the end, the U.S. manufacturers (Boeing and Douglas) were chosen without a real struggle on the best offer, convincing Pierson (president of Airbus) to say, "When does an airline say which manufacturers it is buying from before it has even chosen the aircraft it wants? It is extraordinary."[LYNN 1997: p.8]

6.8.2   Price / Financial Conditions

The price of the offer or the particular financial conditions defined by the seller (sometimes in collaboration with the engine manufacturer) often determine the buyer's choice of one airplane over another.

6.8.2.1   U.S. Airlines Sale (Early 1970s)

In the competition for the launch campaign of the Lockheed 1011 and Douglas DC-10 and for the sale of middle- to long-range aircraft to U.S. airlines, Lockheed was able to convince TWA, Eastern and Delta to choose the L-1011 (with a Rolls Royce engine), simply by lowering the price by $1.2 million per airplane in respect to the offer made by McDonnell Douglas for its DC-10.

6.8.2.2   TransBrasil Airlines Sale (1975)

Airbus was trying to sell TransBrasil Airlines two A-300s that would have been financed in U.S. dollars, but Airbus personnel reported that the United States prevented the export of the money to Brazil, saying that it was already too heavily indebted to U.S. banks. The order finally was taken by Boeing.

6.8.2.3   Eastern Airlines Sale (1977)

In its struggle to penetrate the U.S. market for the first time, Airbus sold 23 A-300s to Eastern Airlines, winning the $778 million deal despite competition from the U.S. manufacturers. Because Eastern didn't have the money to buy airplanes and Airbus wanted to sell them, Airbus was able to arrange financing from the Bank of America, Credit Lyonnais, Dresdner Bank, Airbus itself, and General Electric (the engine provider). Furthermore, as Eastern wanted a 170-seat-class airplane and nothing bigger, Airbus proposed to pay for the airplanes as they had only 170 seats; if it had used more seats of the airplanes it would have paid an extra price.

The deal was made thanks to Airbus export financing that, according to Frank Borman, president of Eastern Airlines, was able to finance the airline for more than $100 million. [BUSINESS WEEK 1982]

6.8.2.4   PanAm Sale (1978)

In 1978, there was a sale of 12 L-1011 aircraft to PanAm to replace B-707s. The true competition in this case involved the engines of the airplanes under consideration. The competitors were Rolls Royce, Pratt & Withney, and General Electric. When Rolls Royce representatives met with PanAm they discovered that General Electric had made a proposal covering 100% of the financing (airframe and engines) over 15 years.

The British prime minister, utilizing his Export Credit Guaranty Department financed a Rolls Royce similar proposal for 15 years (5 years longer than any previous offer they had made), even if that department was used to finance English products abroad rather than U.S. products (Boeing airplanes) in the United States. This move allowed Rolls Royce to win the contract.

6.8.2.5   U.S. Airlines Sale (Late 1970s)

The airplanes under consideration were the B-767 and the new A-310. In this case, three of the "Big Four" U.S. airlines (Delta, American, and United) chose a U.S. airplane by matter of principle, while the fourth (TWA) was analyzing the financial offer made by Airbus. It was only when Boeing proposed a financial package in line with that of Airbus (Boeing and Pratt & Withney, the engine manufacturer, would finance almost half the funds needed) that TWA also chose the U.S. product.

6.8.2.6   British Caledonian Sale (Early 1980s)

After a 2-year battle with Boeing, Airbus received seven orders for A-320s with an option for 10 more from this launch customer, but it had to make two concessions. The first was to install another fuel tank, giving the A-320 a longer range; the second was to support the re-equipping cost of the older airline aircraft (to meet new noise restrictions) and to produce a financial package in which a group of banks would buy the airplanes and lease them to the airline. Finally the sale was made, with Airbus supplying the planes as well as the financing.

6.8.2.7   PanAm Sale (1984)

In 1984, trying to get rid of white-tails airplanes (unsold airplanes) lying in Toulouse, Airbus accepted an offer to sell them to PanAm (28 A-300s) through leasing procedures and at a very low price, probably below full cost.

6.8.2.8   American Airlines Sale (1985)

In 1985, Airbus sold 15 A-320s to American Airlines after a struggle with Boeing in which there was another financial innovation. American wanted the planes but did not want the debt associated with the purchase on its balance sheet. Therefore, the "walkaway lease" was introduced: The airline took the airplanes with the option to return them with notice in advance of only 30 days. This can be considered a lease rather than an acquisition, and the buyer is allowed to not show the correspondent burden on the balance sheet.

6.8.2.9   1999 – Continental Sales

Continental Airlines in 1999 took delivery of 85 new jets, among which Boeing aircraft were the bigger part. The choice of the aircraft, in addition to meeting all noise regulations and fuel efficiency, was made for the attractive financing associated with the new fleet. To notice that the airline since 1997 has been the Boeing's largest customer in the U.S. purchasing 143 new jets but financed at low interest rates.

6.8.2.10   2000 – Westjet Sales

Westjet Airline finalized the order for 24 Boeing B737-700. Ten of these aircraft were leased from GECAS with a clause for interest rate protection during the operation. The purchasing of the other aircraft was made with financial plans that, coupled with the low aircraft unit cost, allowed the airline to continue to provide low fares on the traditional routes.

6.8.2.11   2001 - Qantas Sales

In November 2001 Qantas Airways selected the Boeing B737-800 (15 aircraft) to improve its Australian operations after the collapse of Ansett Airlines and the consequent demand. The selection of B737 followed a period of competition with Airbus A320 ended with the final selection of the Boeing aircraft for its more competitive pricing conditions.

6.8.3   Manufacturer / Aircraft Performance

The following are some important sales where no external factors (that is, no factors other than from product characteristics, sales price, and quality) may be found in the rationale of the buyer's decision.

6.8.3.1   TWA Sale (1979)

Airbus and Boeing for the TWA bid (10 aircraft plus 45 options) proposed the A-310 and the B-767 respectively. After the first meeting between Airbus and TWA presidents, in which it seemed that the European company would win the bid, the difference was instead made by the Boeing delivery schedule, which Airbus could not afford at that time.

6.8.3.2   Northwest Airlines Sale (1986)

In October 1986, after the Northwest Airlines delegation visited Toulouse to see the production site, Northwest ordered 10 A-320s to be delivered in 1990-91 with an option for another 90. The Airbus planes had been sold due to their low operating cost, so their quality was the deciding factor rather than financial operations or other reasons.

6.8.3.3   Northwest Sales (1999)

Northwest Airlines announced on June 1999 the firm orders for 30 Airbus aircraft, 18 A319 and 12 A320. The airline choice was made following the big confidence and trust in the Airbus family, considered popular with their customers and crews, offering cabin comfort and commonality, providing also improved operating economics.

6.8.3.4   SAS (Scandinavian Airlines System) Sale (1999)

At the end of 1999, SAS announced its intention to replace its long-range fleet by a mixed fleet made up of A-340-300s and A-330-300s. The decision was made due to the excellence of the aircraft but above all due to the full commonality existing between the two aircraft types.

6.8.3.5   A-320 Sales (2000)

The majority of the orders for the A-320 family was in the form of repeated orders, mainly due to operator satisfaction with the product. Apart from new customers such as Frontier Airlines and Air Bosnia, most of the orders came from major leasing companies (Commercial Investment Trust - CIT Group, GE Capital Aviation Services - GECAS, International Lease Finance Corp. - ILFC, and Singapore Aircraft Leasing Enterprise - SALE), highlighting both the airplane's operational success and its remarketability potential and residual value.

6.8.3.6   Southwest Airlines (2000)

On June 2000, the Southwest Airlines announced firm orders for 94 new aircraft Boeing 737-700, continuing a tradition of collaboration with the Boeing Company. The B737 was in service with the airline in the last thirty years and was considered safe, reliable and cost effective. This is the reason why the airline is the only major operator to have an all-jet fleet of Boeing 737s.

6.8.3.7   A-380 Sales (2001)

The Airbus corporate image in the Pacific Rim has significantly grown in recent years, allowing the European company to secure launch orders from Singapore Airlines and Qantas. Airbus has also reached the advanced stage of negotiations with other airlines in the region because the Asian aviation community appreciates its technology-driven strategy.

6.8.3.8   American Airlines Sales (2001)

On may 2001 American Airlines announced the purchase of 15 Boeing 767-300ER. The choice was made by the airline to standardize its transatlantic operations to only two aircraft: 767 and 777. This process of standardization, in the opinion of the of the finance officers, could allow to obtain improvements in efficiencies for the airline.

6.8.3.9   Conclusions

Of course, there have been many more commercial airplanes sales in the last 30 years than those reported above, but these are the ones for which a clear rationale has been found that made them suitable for our purpose. This analysis reveals the existence of a competitive arena made of visible trade factors and hidden distortions due to extensive government subsidies and interventions. Visible trade factors include the following:

• Product.
• Price terms.

- Product availability.
- Product support package.

Hidden factors include:

- Subsidized sales financing such as loan guarantees/government-backed loans, low-cost leases.
- Political leverage, such as links to economic aids and links to foreign politics.

To sum up this short analysis of some major sales (those whose sales mechanism are somehow known), three conclusions can be drawn.

The first confirms the thesis of this book, that it would be wrong to look at the physical product to understand anything about the business of selling airplanes. Rather, the augmented product is the object of the sale, and this concept is very clearly understood by buyers.

The second conclusion is that, even considering this last approach, the goodness of the augmented product (the whole package constituting the deal, including financial conditions and after-sale support) explains only partially the process of selling airplanes[2].

Dealing with airplanes' selling some most important success factors are those related to political and social influence. This may be because purchases of such magnitude may be done in exchange for political favors or because (other conditions being substantially similar) the airline's management feels closer to one manufacturer than another for emotional reasons. These last are the causes of sales obtained as a matter of principle.

The final conclusion is that, in any case, the proposals are seldom far apart and often are very close to each other. Thus, matching the competitor's proposal is a condition that is necessary, although not sufficient, to winning the deal.

NOTES

1. Of course this has created often disputes between airplane manufacturers, as the recent one between Bombardier and Embraer.

Since 1996, when Embraer with the introduction of its aircraft ERJ-145 gained a substantial share in the 50-seat regional jet segment — until then dominated by the Bombardier CRJ-200 — a trade dispute began centered on the subsidies the two manufacturers were obtaining from each Government to help them in competing in the growing market of regional jets.

Specifically the allegations were the following:

- The Canadians alleged the Brazil's ProEx subsidy package an export financing program that — according to Bombardier — favored Embraer in pricing its aircraft violating the international standards. The Canadians claimed that the ProEx package, reducing the cost of financing for purchasers of Embraer regional jets by about 3.8%, permitted to the Brazilian manufacturer to achieve an advantage in terms of a more competitive price by about 15-20% with respect to the CRJ-200.

- On the other side the Brazilians alleged that Bombardier received illegal subsidies from the Canadian Government both for the development of its regional jets (CRJ-100-200 and -700) and for the export sales financing through the programs: "Export Development Corp.", "Technology Partnership Canada" and "Canada Debt Financing". Embraer evaluated the total illegal support obtained by Bombardier equal to $2.3 billion.

These allegations were submitted to the WTO, the World Trade Organization, that on March 1999 declared illegal the Brazilian ProEx package, prohibiting Embraer to use it. The WTO rejected the argument that Brazil, as a developing nation, should be granted special status and allowed to gradually phase out the ProEx subsidy program, as requested by Embraer. The WTO ruling did not apply to deals that Embraer had already closed, meaning firm aircraft orders and options could be allowed to stand at current financing conditions. But the trade war was not ended because, after the conclusion of the WTO, Embraer declared that "the company will continue to use ProEx program, as adapted, as a valid instrument for sales financing". Consequently Brazil changed its export financing program to ProEx II and, when the ProEx II was also found to be not conforming the ProEx III was introduced. According to Canadians though, the subsidy package was never substantially modified. In December 2000 another WTO panel authorized Ottawa to impose sanctions of $233.5 million a year over five to six years on Brazilian imports . This WTO ruling had a historical importance because, until then, only a handful of disputes have gone as far as trade sanctions in the history of WTO and it would be the first time that a developed country (Canada) had imposed sanctions on a developing nation (Brazil). During 2001 the trade war intensified when other four WTO rulings went in favor of Canadians with Brazil refusing to comply with. The Ottawa Government decided to fight "fire with fire" responding with an unprecedented direct export subsidy: During the negotiations for the sale of 75 aircraft (plus 75 options) to Northwest Airlines and 75 aircraft to Air Wisconsin, Bombardier achieved from its Government a low-interest loan, covering about 75% of the value of each contract, to help it in beating Embraer's competition. In January 2002 another WTO ruling stated that Ottawa had broken trade rules by offering loans to help Bombardier in winning recent orders (from Air Wisconsin, Northwest and another Spanish airline for a total value of about $4 billion) and decided that the financing of these transactions did not comply with WTO rules and therefore this subsidy had to be withdrawn without delay. At this point, after the saga had touched its apex, the two countries decided to try to solve the dispute through bilateral talks rather than through continued WTO litigations. Presently the two Governments are still negotiating in the search of a mutually satisfactory solution that will permit to settle this long-running dispute.

2. The net effect of the purchase of a high number of airplanes (for example 100) by a certain airline from a manufacturer of a different country is a movement of wealth toward that country, apart from a certain degree of compensation that the local manufacturing industry may or may not obtain. This effect is particularly visible if one compares the style (level) of life of the populations leaving near factories and headquarters of the exporting manufacturer. This is the case of Seattle (Boeing) and Tolouse (Airbus) whose increased population in the last twenty years experienced a high quality of life due also to the additional related activities generated on the territory by the "prime" success. Good examples are also Montreal (Bombardier) and Sao Paulo (Embraer). Therefore in addition to national government, also local authorities strongly support the aeronautical industry as much as they can, by means of guarantees, and or space concessions and any other help they can offer.

CONCLUSIONS

There were two main motivations for writing this book. The first, which can be called "descriptive," was my desire to describe one of the most fascinating high-tech industrial sectors (as I have spent almost 30 years working in it), particularly its evolution both in the United States and in Europe (due to the change of the political and strategic scenario), including the new market structure and companies' struggle for survival. The second, which can be called "speculative," was to attempt to answer the questions: "Are traditional interpretation methods for the companies' behaviors valid, or is aeronautics so different from other business sectors that established schemes are not applicable because the rules of the game are different for this industry? If traditional methods are appropriate, to what extent are they applicable?" These were ambitious goals, especially the second one, due to the uniqueness of the aeronautical industry as compared with other high-tech sectors.

I am not sure I have been able to give the answers to the questions posed in the preface of this book and summarized above. I will be happy if to have provoked doubts and presented enough information to encourage readers to develop their own ideas and thoughts on the issues under discussion and then to compare them with mine, which I will now summarize by following the structure of the book's two levels, concerning the strategic (Chapter 2) and the tactical (the four *Ps* discussed in Chapters 3 through 6) management of the business. The first aspect includes strategic grouping, generic basic strategies (cost leadership, differentiation, focusing), critical factors for success and the source of the competitive advantage.

Let's start with basic competitive strategies that are of course related with the way competing firms occupy the business segments.

Satisfying customers' needs and wants is perceived by an aeronautical company as the first step to acquiring a competitive advantage. This may be reached in two ways.

The first is by implementing a focalized strategy, by identifying the segment (or segments) where it is possible to pursue an important competitive advantage due to company's specific characteristics, as in the case of Bombardier and Embraer, which have identified the regional jet business as a niche where they can exploit their own commercial, technological, and productive capabilities, with no strong competition from other players.

These firms have concentrated their efforts on relatively few customers and thus giving their products the characteristics to satisfy customers' needs much better than other manufacturers. Generally companies focalized on a certain segment of the market can follow both the cost leadership (as Douglas and Embraer) and technological differentiation strategy (as Airbus introducing itself in the business through the A-300, a new, advanced twin-engine wide-body airplane). Focalized companies run typical risks such as the following:

- The fading of most relevant differences between the specialized segments and the market as a whole, with evident advantage for the non specialized firms; for example, the difference between regional and commercial airplanes tends to vanish when regional airplanes with more than 50 seats are considered. This may represent a threat for companies specialized in this segment of the business.

- The increment, above a reasonable limit, of the difference between prices of non specialized versus specialized airplanes. This has happened sometimes in the high end of the regional segment where special airplanes like AVRO RJ-100/200 (high wing, four engines) of BAE have suffered the competition coming from the smallest (generally shortened versions) commercial airplanes like A-318, B-717, B-737-600, that enjoy cost (and price) scale economy due to belonging to families of airplanes.

- A too-narrow presence that may become a weakness when new specialized airplanes are introduced. This may be the case for Bombardier when the next future families of airplanes (like ERJ-170/ERJ-190 of Embraer now under development) are introduced.

The conclusion is that focusing in aeronautics (especially in the commercial aviation) can be only a strategy for entering the business, not a strategy to compete lastingly within it.

The second way to acquiring and keeping a competitive advantage is by exploiting a wider product-market strategy (a rule in commercial aviation), but in any case identifying the right product for each market segment in which to compete; in this case, products are optimized for each market segment to fully satisfy the potential customers, as in the case of Boeing and Airbus following cost leadership and/or differentiation strategies.

It will remembered that, according to some modern authors, the strategy pursued must be unique at least in the long term because each possible basic strategy implies a different structure of the firm and a different management attitude. Each compromise in strategy would dilute the capability to obtain a competitive advantage.

According to the findings of this book, the aeronautical sector instead constitutes an example of how the technological effort for the realization of new models having characteristics always more advanced (differentiation) must be reconciled with the need to optimize the costs through tools (flexible automation, computerized organization of the cycle of the design, development, production, and commercialization, the politics of the alliances, and so on) that have allowed the overcoming of this seeming incompatibility. More generally, this does not mean that a strategy does not exist; rather, it may be (or must be) a mix of what we call the (single) basic or generic strategies.

The critical factors for success necessary in the aeronautical industry have been examined in the book. The elements that are considered essential for the development and preservation of a strong and durable presence in the aerospace industry are:

- Correct management of complex systems of human resources and of productive processes.

- Exploitation of the technology.

- Effective implementation of marketing and sales.

- Government support.

Therefore in the aeronautical industry, the critical factors for success seem to belong to all main functional areas of a company, while in other sectors they result much more concentrated in a few areas and easily classifiable in order of importance.

The peculiarity of aeronautics derives from the complexity of the realization and commercialization of an aircraft and from the fact that the strategy adopted by the firms is not generally unique.

Another characteristic of the companies acting in the aeronautical sector is represented by cyclical behavior with reference to the strategy exploited. This is probably due to the fact that the technological variable has a cyclical pattern with time and therefore influences in some way the companies' behavior.

In fact, the history and the evolution of the aeronautical industry demonstrate that the same company has periodically preferred differentiation or cost leadership strategies because of the technology changes and the use the competitors are making of it.

After World War II, the U.S. companies had fully taken advantage of the economies deriving from volume. Their usage of technology was only an indirect follow up of the research and development in the military field, not a way to differentiate their products. The only possibility for European manufacturers to break such a monopoly was to play with the technological innovation.

After a few attempts failed for technical or commercial reasons (Comet, Caravelle, Concorde), the true breakthrough of the European industry into the aeronautical business was through the A300, a twin-engine wide-body airplane for short- and medium-range trips. The airplane was introduced in the market at the right time (1974) because the oil crisis greatly increase customers' appreciation of airplanes with low fuel consumption and high efficiency.

But after a while, the spread of the winning technologies present in the A-300 (high bypass ratio, advanced avionics, onboard computers, and so on) changed the role of the technological variables that, instead of driving differentiation, began to drive homogenization.

For example, although a few years later, Lockheed with its Tristar L-1011-500 (entry in service - EIS, in 1979), Douglas with its DC-10-30ER version (EIS in 1980), and Boeing with 757 (EIS in 1982) and 767 (EIS in 1982) were able to match the Airbus move with products equally innovative therefore bringing again the battle back in the field of cost reduction and leadership, rather than in that-one of differentiation through technology innovation.

Due to the fact that the U.S. companies inevitably enjoyed scale economy, the answer from Airbus was again based on innovation, coupled to an enlargement of the offer. Airbus therefore introduced the A-320 on the market (1988), an airplane much newer than the competing older airplanes like the DC-9/MD-80 and B-727/737, whose strengths were only their low price and their presence in the fleets of most airlines. The A-320 was instead an airplane able to assure savings immediately in terms of operating costs and in the future due to high commonality with foreseen derivatives (A-321, A-319, A-318). The cyclic alternation between cost leadership and technological differentiation has continued to the present, with A-330/340s and the B-777, and could continue in the future, maybe with inverted roles between Airbus and Boeing.

I am talking about the big new projects of the two main manufacturers, that are the A-380 and the *Super Efficient Airplane*. This time, Airbus has followed a traditional way to get more efficiency, that is through size economy with an airplane even bigger than the 747. To the contrary, Boeing is studying a completely new family of airplane that is a smaller size (200-300 seats bracket). By incorporating the cutting edge of technological knowledge in the many fields of airplane design (developed for the abandoned Sonic Cruiser), this family may represent a breakthrough in the civil aeronautical sector. Differences in their choices seem so relevant that the loser this time could see its role as prime manufacturer considerably reduced.

In the end, the analysis of the aeronautical civil sector has shown that companies' behaviors and management strategies are similar to those practiced in other high-tech fields, although with differences. Some of the most significant seem to be:

- The coexistence of more than one generic strategy.
- The alternation of the basic strategies followed by the winning companies; and accordingly
- The needed skills are not concentrated on some "critical" areas but located in most functional areas of the successful company.

The player that had first followed successfully cost leadership strategy has changed its mind when:

- The introduction of new technologies has canceled the competitive advantages acquired through volume economies and learning effect.

- The coming out of new industrial players with very low manpower costs (particularly in the regional airplane business) has challenged the already acquired competitive advantage.

To the contrary, a company that had initially pursued a differentiation strategy has necessarily changed its approach and become cost concerned when:

- Due to the high R & D costs the price difference needed to keep distinctive characteristics on its own product has become too high.

- The demand for products with special characteristics was declining, for one of a number of reasons (for example, economic recession).

- The imitations produced by competitors have reduced the peculiarity of the proposed differentiated airplane.

- The spread of technologies among imitators has occurred at low cost.

I will now try to identify other differentiation factors in the aeronautical sector, considering how firms manage the controllable variables of marketing mix (the four *Ps*).

In the book, a strict correlation between technological content of the products and their performance and cost has been demonstrated. However, the conclusion has been reached that the increments in the technological content are progressively smaller than the related price increases. In other words, a small increase in airplane performance may require a huge additional investment in R & D and therefore a high increase in the airplane's final sales price. This means that the relationship between technology and airplane price in highly inelastic. Therefore, financial efforts (and risks) are strictly related to the innovation content of the (new) product.

All these considerations push the company operating in this field to a special behavior with reference to two variables in the marketing mix, *product* and *price*:

- The firms try to establish ways of collaborating with the airlines in order to arrive at a definition of airplane configuration and characteristics shared with them, to the point that launch customers (airlines) are sometimes invited to participate in the conceptual airplane design phase, when the general architecture and performance are conceived.

- The firms try to get a substantial number of orders (kickoff customers) and options in advance of giving the full go-ahead for the program and, in order to reach such an objective, they grant important discounts, sales financing, and advanced financial tools (like leasing). This is unusual in other industries, where products are sold for full price at the beginning (introductory phase) and afterward offered for a lower price.

- The firms try to incorporate progressive improvements in the "founder" model, even with the development of derivative versions, rather than putting on the market a completely new airplane model.

Through these moves, the companies try to obtain a kind of dilution and sharing of risk with their customers, the airlines. This behavior encourages customer loyalty and creates an intimacy and interdependency between buyer and seller that is unusual in other businesses.

The manufacturer's *distribution* system in aeronautics is not mainly concerned with the physical presence of the product. In fact, it can be delivered by flying the product to any location chosen by the customer.

It has also to be pointed out the relevance of the augmented product concept (the physical product plus some tangible and intangible additional elements) in trying to understand the manufacturer's needs and policy in building up its distribution network. The additional elements to be considered are those related to financial conditions associated with sales, after-sale support and spare parts delivery, training center locations and services offered, maintenance centers, and so on. A manufacturer's reputation depends on its capability of offering these services within a reasonable time period and at reasonable prices.

Promotion activities in the aeronautical industry are also special somehow. This is because the players are relatively few and know each other very well and also due to something mentioned before: Actually, the firms do not sell the product "airplane" but rather the whole of product/service that is called the augmented product.

High-tech modern theories of marketing management seem to fully apply to the aeronautical field, that is, the manufacturer's promotion actions are similar to those of a consultant rather than a seller and the relationship with the buyer is based totally on credibility, trust, and professionalism. But the peculiarity of the promotion and sale of an aeronautical product derives mainly from a different reason. It often involves a nation as a whole and its government. Often a sale goes through a group of the airframe, engine, and avionics manufacturers who lobby against another group. The "short list" of airplanes to choose from is made by the airline on an exclusively technical and economic basis, but the final decision may be made due to political considerations and/or belonging to a given geopolitical area.

The above considerations on the specialization of the marketing mix elements in the aeronautical field show how complex their handling may be; they also demonstrate that the definition of these variables as tactical is narrow. In fact, their proper management represents a real challenge for the managers of a company, but when all are manipulated successfully they may represent a strategic leverage to get definitive advantages over competitors.

BIBLIOGRAPHY

ABELL, D.F. *Business e Scelte Aziendali*. Milan: Italian edition, IPSOA, 1986.

AECMA (EUROPEAN ASSOCIATION OF AEROSPACE INDUSTRIES). *Aircraft and the Environment: A European View*. 1993.

AECMA. *Aerospace Industry Restructuring*. Irwing Report: September 1997.

AIRBUS. *Global Market Forecast 2000–2019*, 2000.

AIRBUS. *Presentation to the Commission of European Union – DG XII*. Toulouse: May 1997.

ATW's *World Airline Report* 2000.

AVIATIONX INC. *A New Kind of Hub: How B2b E-Marketplace Will Revolutionize the Aviation Industry*. www.aviationx.com, 2000.

AVMARK. *Maintenance Market Survey*. London: 1983.

AVMARK AVIATION ECONOMIST. London: 1991 Collection.

AVMARK AVIATION ECONOMIST. January–February 2001.

BACHER, T.J. *International Collaboration on Commercial Airplane Programmes*. Conference Sponsored by Society of Japanese Aerospace Companies. Tokyo: 1983.

BAE SYSTEMS. *Virtual News Room*. www.baesystems.com: November 27, 2001.

BAIN & COMPANY. *World Aerospace Overview*, 1993.

BARRON L. "Le Finencement des Achats et des Locations d'Appareils – Le Role du Constructeur". In VELLAS, P. *La Vie de l'Avion Commercial*. Paris: Editions A. Pedone, 1990.

BOEING COMMERCIAL AIRPLANE COMPANY. *User Guide SSF Program*. Seattle, WA: Internal Guide, 1974.

BOEING COMMERCIAL AIRPLANE COMPANY. *Boeing Computer Capability in the Airline Analysis Process*. Seattle, WA: 1977a.

BOEING COMMERCIAL AIRPLANE COMPANY. *Performance Analysis of Commercial Airplanes for Sales Support*. Document prepared by Boeing sales technology staff. Seattle, WA: 1977b.

BOEING COMMERCIAL AIRPLANE COMPANY. *The Economics of Civil Aircraft Industry*. Seattle, WA: 1981.

BOEING COMMERCIAL AIRPLANE COMPANY. *The Boeing method for generalized airplane operating economics*. Internal document. Seattle, WA: 1985.

BOEING COMMERCIAL AIRPLANE GROUP. *Current Market Outlook 1994*.

BOEING COMMERCIAL AIRPLANE GROUP. *Current Market Outlook 2000*.

BUSINESS WEEK, January 11, 1982. In LYNN, M. *Birds of Prey*. New York: Four Walls

Eight Windows, 1997.

CADY, J.F. "Strategie di Marketing nel Settore Informatico". In SEBASTIANI C. *High Tech Marketing.* Turin, Italy: ISEDI Petrini Editore, 1995.

CORNING, G. *Supersonic and Subsonic Airplane Design.* Ann Arbor, Michigan: Edwards Brothers Inc., 1953.

CRANDALL, R.L. "Marketing Planning". In JAMES, G.W. *Airline Economics.* Toronto, Canada: Lexington Books, 1982.

DASA VVU/TU. *Unternehmensentwicklung-Technologie,* 1995.

DAY, G.S. *Strategie di Mercato e Vantaggio Competitivo* Turin, Italy: ISEDI Petrini Editore, 1991.

DE VIO, S. *"Azione di Marketing e Potenzialità del Prodotto".* In SEBASTIANI C. *High Tech Marketing.* Turin, Italy: ISEDI Petrini Editore, 1995.

DRESSE, L. *Twin/Four-Engine Jets: A Comparative Study.* ITA Documents and Reports, 1986.

EUROPEAN COMMISSION (EC). *DG III.* Bristol Polytechnic, 1994.

EUROPEAN COMMISSION COUNCIL REGULATION. *Commission's Notice on the Distinction Between Merger-Type and Cooperative Operations.* Brussels, Belgium: 1990.

ESPOSITO, E., RAFFA, M., AND ZOLLO, G. *Tre Livelli di Impresa nello Sviluppo di un Prodotto High-Tech: Evidenze Empiriche a Supporto della Rete di Imprese e dell'Impresa Rete.* Sviluppo e Organizzazione n.114, 1989.

EUROMART STUDY REPORT. *Commercial in Confidence.* Loughton, UK: Specialized Printing Services Ltd., 1988.

FEDERAL AVIATION ADMINISTRATION (FAA). Web Site. www.faa.gov, 2002.

FEDERAL AVIATION REGULATION (FAR) PART 25. *Airworthiness Standards: Transport Category Airplane.*

FIOCCA, R. AND SNEHOTA, I. "Marketing e Alta Tecnologia". In SEBASTIANI C. *High Tech Marketing.* Turin, Italy: ISEDI Petrini Editore, 1995.

GOLASZEWSKI, R.S. AND KLEIN, F.J. "Airline and Manufacturer Issues in Marketing Large Commercial Transport Aircraft". In Handbook of Airline Marketing. Mc Graw-Hill Companies, Inc., 1998.

IL FORO. *Commissione delle Comunità Europee, October 2, 1991, Decision, ATR-De Havilland.* Milan: 1992.

IMF. In JENKINSON L.R., SIMPKIN P., RHODES D. *Civil Jet Aircraft Design.* London: Arnold Publishers, 1999.

INTERAVIA AEROSPACE REVIEW. March 1991, December 1995, December 2000.

INTERNATIONAL CIVIL AVIATION ORGANIZATION (ICAO). *Manual of Air Traffic Forecasting,* 1985.

JOINT AVIATION REQUIREMENTS (JAR) 21. *Certification Procedures for Aircraft and Related Products and Parts.* June 1994.

KOTLER, P. *Marketing Management: Analysis, Planning, and Control.* Englewood Cliffs, NJ: Prentice Hall Inc., 1984.

L'IMPRESA. *Rivista Italiana di Management.* Milano: SEME S.p.A.,1992

LEAVITT, T. "The Globalization of the Markets". *Harvard Business Review,* May-June 1983.

LYNN, M. *Birds of Prey.* New York: Four Walls Eight Windows, 1997.

MAGDELENAT, J.L. "Certificats de Navigabilité et Responsabilité du Government Emetteur – L'example Americain". In VELLAS, P. *La Vie de l'Avion Commercial.* Paris: Editions A. Pedone, 1990.

MANSFIELD, E. *Microeconomics: Theory and Applications.* New York: W.W. Norton & Co., 1996.

MATHAISEL, D.F.X. (MC DONNELL DOUGLAS). *Airline Schedule Planning and Evaluation Model.* Paper presented to Airline Group of the International Federation of Operational Research Societies. San Francisco, CA: 1972.

MCDONNELL DOUGLAS. *Airline Market Planning.* Long Beach, CA: MDD Paper, 1984a.

MCDONNELL DOUGLAS. *Economic Research.* Long Beach, CA: 1984b.

MCDONNELL DOUGLAS. *Sales Engineering Briefing Manual: An Outline of the Functions and Technology of Sales Engineering.* Long Beach, CA: 1985a.

MCDONNELL DOUGLAS. *Airline Financial Planning.* Long Beach, CA: 1985b.

MOMIGLIANO, F. *Economia Industriale e Teoria d'Impresa.* Bologna, Italy: Il Mulino, 1975

MORIARTY, R.T. AND KOSNIK, T.J. "High Tech Marketing: Concetti, Continuità e Cambiamenti". In SEBASTIANI C. *High Tech Marketing.* Turin, Italy: ISEDI Petrini Editore, 1995.

MUNSON, H.C. *Fleet Modernization Key Factors in Today's Environment: A Manufacturer's View.* Presentation at the Biannual Meeting of ATA/IATA Airline Financial Officers. Montreal, Canada: 1984.

NETELENBOS, T. MINISTRY OF TRANSPORT, PUBLIC WORKS, AND WATER MANAGEMENT, THE NETHERLANDS. "Schiphol Airport: Fostering a Junction in the Global Network Economy". In *The Economic Significance of Mainport Schipol*, Dutch Government, June 2000.

NEWHOUSE, J. *The Sporty Game.* New York: Alfred A. Knopf Inc., 1988

NICOLAI, L. M. *Fundamentals of Aircraft Design.* University of Dayton, Ohio: School of Engineering, 1975.

NOUVELLE REVUE DE AERONAUTIQUE ET ASTRONAUTIQUE, Issue n.2, March-April, 1998.

OFFICIAL AIRLINE GUIDE (OAG) 1990.

OFFICIAL JOURNAL OF THE EUROPEAN COMMUNITY (O.J.E.C.), Commission Decision of July 30th, 1997, Case no. IV/M877, Boeing/McDonnell Douglas, 97/816/EC, December 8, 1997.

PORTER, M. *Competitive Advantage.* New York: Free Press, 1985.

PORTER, M. *Competition in Global Industry.* Boston: Harvard Business School Press, 1986.

RIES, A. AND TROUT, J. *Marketing Warfare.* New York: McGraw-Hill, 1986.

ROLLS ROYCE PLC. *The Outlook* 2000.

ROSKAM, J. *Airplane Design Part I–Preliminary Sizing of Airplanes; Airplane Design Part III–Layout Design of Cockpit, Fuselage, Wing and Empennage: Cutaways and Inboard Profiles.* Ottawa, KS: Roskam Aviation and Engineering Corporation, 1986.

SEBASTIANI, C. *High Tech Marketing.* Turin, Italy: ISEDI Petrini Editore, 1995.

STEINER, J.E. *How Decisions Are Made.* Seattle, WA: Boeing, 1992.

STOOS-CAVÉ, M. "Contrat de Vente d'Avion". In VELLAS, P. *La Vie de l'Avion Commercial.* Paris: Editions A. Pedone, 1990.

TARRY, C. *Airline Economic — Results & Prospects, Part I.* IATA, 1999.

TREVETT, J. C. *Fleet Planning Models.* Lecture in Air Transport, College of Aeronautics, Cranfield, 1982

VALDANI, E. *Marketing Strategico.* Milan: ETASLIBRI, 1986.

VICARI, S. *Le Alleanze nei Settori ad Alta Tecnologia.* Milan: EGEA S.p.A., 1991.

WEISSHUHN, P. *The Value of Technology in Development Project.* D96-2004. SRI Consulting, Business Intelligence Program, June 1996.

INDEX

About the Author

DOMENICO FERRERI is Vice President of Business Development at Alenia Aeronautica S.p.A., a leading Italian firm owned by the Finmeccanica Group. An aeronautical engineer and veteran of the Italian Air Force, he has accumulated many years of experience in the aerospace industry in product development, marketing, and building strategic alliances. Mr. Ferreri can be contacted at domenicoferreri@yahoo.it.